THE GLORY OF

Southern Cooking

OTHER BOOKS BY JAMES VILLAS

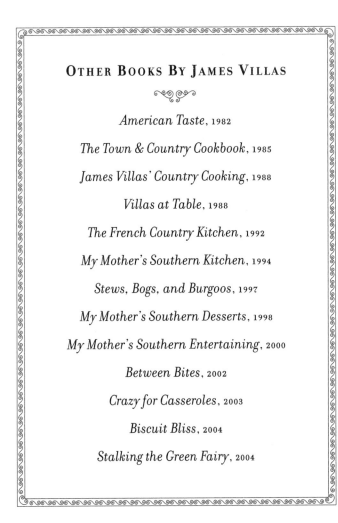

American Taste, 1982

The Town & Country Cookbook, 1985

James Villas' Country Cooking, 1988

Villas at Table, 1988

The French Country Kitchen, 1992

My Mother's Southern Kitchen, 1994

Stews, Bogs, and Burgoos, 1997

My Mother's Southern Desserts, 1998

My Mother's Southern Entertaining, 2000

Between Bites, 2002

Crazy for Casseroles, 2003

Biscuit Bliss, 2004

Stalking the Green Fairy, 2004

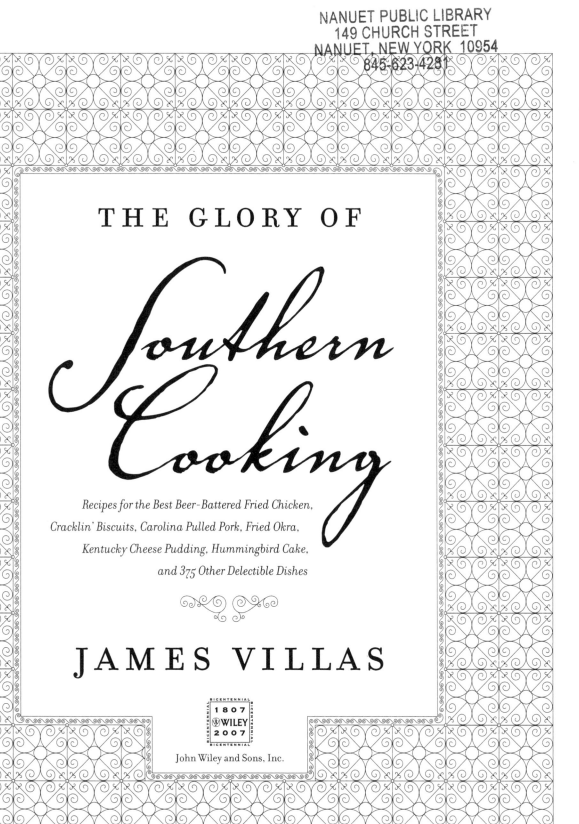

THE GLORY OF

Southern Cooking

Recipes for the Best Beer-Battered Fried Chicken,
Cracklin' Biscuits, Carolina Pulled Pork, Fried Okra,
Kentucky Cheese Pudding, Hummingbird Cake,
and 375 Other Delectible Dishes

JAMES VILLAS

BICENTENNIAL
1807
WILEY
2007
BICENTENNIAL

John Wiley and Sons, Inc.

Published by John Wiley & Sons, Inc., Hoboken, New Jersey
Published simultaneously in Canada

For general information about our other products and services, please contact our Customer Care Department within the United States at (800) 762-2974, outside the United States at (317) 572-3993 or fax (317) 572-4002.

Wiley also publishes its books in a variety of electronic formats. Some content that appears in print may not be available in electronic books. For more information about Wiley products, visit our Web site at www.wiley.com.

DESIGNED BY JOEL AVIROM AND JASON SNYDER
DESIGN ASSISTANT: MEGHAN DAY HEALEY

Library of Congress Cataloging-in-Publication Data

Villas, James.
   The glory of Southern cooking / James Villas.
      p. cm.
   Includes bibliographical references and index.
   ISBN-13 978-0-7645-7601-0 (cloth)
   ISBN-10 0-7645-7601-1 (cloth)
   1. Cookery, American--Southern style. I. Title.
   TX715.2.S68V547 2007
   641.5975--dc22

                                        2006001109

Printed in the United States of America

10 9 8 7 6 5 4 3 2 1

To

Gail Killian Kennedy

We Were Never Too Young

CONTENTS

⊷⊶

PREFACE

It's appropriate to say that the basic foundation of this cookbook can be traced back over a decade to a much more limited book I wrote on my mother's Southern kitchen. It's also only fair to reveal that this cookbook was not really my idea but that of one of my editors—a Yankee, no less. Things came to a head a couple of years back when, having devoted an entire chapter of a book of collected food essays to such topics as Southern pig, grits, okra, and Brunswick stew, I exclaimed one day, in my typically florid and shameless way, "I've come to the definite conclusion that Southern cooking is not only the one legitimate cuisine in this country but that what I've written about so far is just the tip of the iceberg." And to reinforce my stern conviction, I had to add, "As far as I'm concerned, Southern cookery is right there on the same level with French *cuisine bourgeoise* and Italian *cucina casereccia*—the sacred traditions, the incredible variety of regional dishes, the prevalence of fresh local ingredients, the distinctive cooking techniques, everything."

For a moment, my stunned editor simply glared at me as if I were indulging in more than a bit of prejudicial hyperbole or were slightly mad. Then, popping into her mouth another small pecan-cheese biscuit I'd brought to the office, she calmly asked me to talk beyond fried chicken and congealed salad and cornbread and pecan pie. Perhaps for an hour, I went on about Kentucky beer cheese, Charleston hobotee, Cajun maque choux, Pamlico muddle, Lowcountry bog, Arkansas dirty rice, Maryland crabmeat Dewey, West Virginia deviled

oxtails, New Orleans calas, and Lord knows how many other unusual dishes drawn from all over Dixie. She waited, succumbed to the temptation of still another biscuit, then, hurling a hand in the air, declared bluntly, "Okay, that's the book you need to do. The whole she-bang. Make your case. Everything you know about Southern cooking and why it's so special."

No doubt the proposition was a little daunting, but the challenge was just too compelling to turn down. Born and bred in North Carolina, I haven't actually lived in the South since finishing college, due to the demands of my profession. Ask anyone who knows me, my rebellious spirit, and my drawl, however, and they'll most likely insist that I've never really left home. My entire family still resides in the South; I return routinely to visit relatives and friends and to venerate my roots; for over two decades I roamed the major cities and small towns and back roads from Maryland to Kentucky to Louisiana in order to report on food traditions and restaurants for *Town & Country* and other magazines; and just the thought of going more than a few months without nourishing my belly and soul with genuine pork barbecue, bowls of she-crab soup and gumbo, fried okra and catfish, and baskets of hush puppies is still enough to provoke panic. At home, my kitchen is never without at least five pounds of Southern whole-hog sausage, slabs of perfectly cured and aged North Carolina or Tennessee country ham, tubs of hickory-smoked chopped barbecue, sacks of Southern flour, and carefully labeled jars of homemade fruit preserves. And when friends come to eat, there's never any question what style of food they'll be served.

Such is the sovereignty of Southern cookery to anybody (Reb and outsider alike) who has fully indulged in its many glories that comparisons with other American styles are almost ludicrous. To be sure, each section of the country can boast a few wonderful and distinctly American dishes (New England clam chowder and brown bread, New York corned beef and pastrami, Midwestern smoked sausages and honey cakes, California Cobb salad and cioppino, Pacific Northwestern planked salmon and cherry soup, Southwestern chili and barbecued beef brisket, Hawaiian roast suckling pig and baked coconut yams). But only the South, if only by the sheer number and variety of its dishes developed over the centuries, can claim to have created and codified a regional cuisine that is as readily identifiable as, indeed, those of France, Italy, and even China. The story of that evolution is long, complex, and often mysterious, and while I do delve consistently into many of its aspects throughout this book, it was never my intention to recount the entire cultural history in such intricate and brilliant detail as that provided in John Egerton's definitive study, *Southern Food,* or Damon Lee Fowler's more limited but equally impressive *Classical Southern Cooking.*

Instead, the primary goal I set for myself with this book was to canvass the food traditions of every single state in the South, try to clarify the similarities and differences among most of the best-known classic dishes, expose numerous area specialties that remain obscure and could even be on the verge of extinction, and generally document, in recipes and headnotes, the most important factors inherent in this unique style of cooking. Like most Southern food writers, I do not consider Texas to be part of the South, but rather a state (if not almost a separate country) with its own individual gastronomic format based largely on other proud traditions and influences. Consequently, there are no Texas recipes in this book, renowned and delicious though many are. Moreover, if such states as Delaware and West Virginia appear to be underrepresented, it's only because, for historical or geographical reasons, their innovations in the development of Southern cooking have been relatively minor compared with those of the Virginia Tidewater, the Carolina and Georgia Lowcountry, the river deltas of Mississippi and Louisiana, the piedmont hills of Kentucky and Tennessee, the two coasts of Florida, and other areas.

In these pages you'll certainly find a full display of what most consider to be staples of the Southern table—the fried chicken and pork barbecue, the grits and greens, the biscuits and cornbread, the cobblers and pound cakes—but there are also many recipes for neglected dishes that are so indigenous to certain areas that not even Southerners from other states are likely to recognize them: Kentucky hot browns and cheese pudding, Mississippi fried dill pickles and chicken spaghetti, Alabama thyme tongue and biscuit muffins, Louisiana Natchitoches meat pies and baked mirlitons, Tennessee frozen tomato and casserole cheese bread, South Carolina frogmore stew and awendaw, and Florida conch fritters and papaya cobbler. Such amazing diversity is the result not only of the South's vast abundance of natural food ingredients and the ability of regional cooks to transform these components into distinctive dishes, but also of centuries of multiple ethnic influences, without which Southern cookery would never have evolved as it has.

From the time the first English settlers stepped ashore with a few pigs at Jamestown, Virginia, in 1607 and were introduced to corn by the local Powhatan Indians, cooking in the South has been virtually governed by the intermingling of domestic and foreign food traditions: British, French, and even Asian all along the mid-Atlantic seaboard; Spanish, Caribbean, and Greek in Florida; Hispanic, French, and Italian along the Gulf coasts; Scotch Irish and German in Appalachia and Arkansas. While all of these ethnic forces were instrumental in the eventual development of a style of cooking unique to the South, perhaps no single incident in Southern gastronomic history was more pivotal than the day in 1619 when a Dutch captain sold fifteen African slaves to the Jamestown colonists. During the next century and a half, of course, the number of slaves would multiply over and over as plantation society blossomed and a lavish way of life like none America had ever seen flourished in Virginia and other Southern states. And it was in the kitchens of the privileged gentry that black woman slaves would learn from their masters, fashion countless dishes according to the provisions available and their instincts, and serve the elaborate meals that became the bedrock for what would become known as classic Southern cookery. It was also the black slaves who introduced vital new African foods to the colonies: okra, collard greens, yams, field peas, benne (sesame) seeds, sorghum, watermelon, and possibly even tomatoes. Today, it's hard to reconcile the golden age of Southern cooking following the American Revolution with the ignominy of slavery that made it possible. The only recompense is that, in the most intolerable of circumstances, black cooks demonstrated a creative skill and genius in the kitchen that was in great part responsible for one of the most original regional cuisines on earth.

If, after all my traveling, eating, observing, and talking with Southerners from one state to the next, I've developed any salient impression that might clash with some contemporary perceptions, it's that Southern cookery has blessedly undergone the fewest changes and suffered the least damage from certain pretentious culinary trends and reforms that have managed to stifle most regional traditions in this country almost into oblivion. That's certainly not to imply that the cooking of the South has failed to evolve in the last decades and is stodgy—not when such a venerable arbiter as *Southern Living* magazine (referred to by some natives as the "Southern Bible") is constantly modifying and updating dishes for home cooks; when professional organizations such as the Southern Foodways Alliance in Oxford, Mississippi, are striving to promote and enhance the diverse food cultures of the South; and when such brilliant Southern professional chefs as Frank Stitt in Birmingham, Alabama, Louis Osteen on Pawleys Island, South Carolina, Ben Barker in Durham, North Carolina, and, yes, Emeril Lagasse in New Orleans have been intelligently reinterpreting numerous traditional dishes without compromising their basic integrity, and creating sensible new ones that only add exciting dimension to the whole repertory. Farmers markets were routine throughout the South decades before self-proclaimed food messiahs elsewhere discovered their first organic head of lettuce, and today, greengrocers, specialty shops, and most supermarkets stock everything from exotic chile peppers, pastas, herbs, and spices to premium cooking oils and vinegars to unusual sausages and farm-raised game birds. Just in recent years, tremendous progress has been made from Virginia to Louisiana in the production of new Southern artisanal cheeses and wines; different varieties of sweet potatoes, rice, corn, and greens are forever appearing; and at least a few experts are experimenting with regional honeys, pecan truffles, and, perhaps most important of all, stone-ground grits and cornmeals.

No doubt Southerners, like all Americans, are curious about some of the innovative culinary activity occurring throughout the country (especially in upscale restaurants), but rest assured that in Dixie you're not likely to see anytime soon shrimp remoulade replaced by sushi, red rice and jambalaya by risotto, fried catfish by rare sautéed tuna belly, country-cured slab bacon by pancetta, or buttermilk biscuits by croissants and focaccia. Nor are you likely to witness much change in the sacred tradition of preparing and serving lots of good food and drink to large numbers of family, friends, and even strangers—better known as Southern hospitality. After a devastating civil war, a grim period of reconstruction, and a caustic national economic depression, when hunger and even starvation were more often the norm than the exception, Southerners learned not only to feast when food was available but to maintain a wary eye on both the present and future. The result has been a culture in which regional food traditions must be generally respected and preserved at all costs, and in which gastronomic novelty just for the sake of novelty has no place.

This is not to say that there aren't gastronomic problems in the South, engendered by various salubrious, social, and legal forces that often depress me beyond words. It's deeply disturbing, for example, to see the ritual of a hot, full Southern breakfast replaced by a bowl of Special K, to realize that a "sophisticated" city such as Atlanta can no longer boast more than a couple of restaurants serving genuine Southern food, and to note the once-proud institutions known as the Southern cafeteria and diner (always strongholds of regional cooking) are dwindling more each year in metropolitan areas. The nation's health police seem to be working overtime to re-duce the proportion of evil (and flavorful) fat in sausage, bacon, country hams, and even barbecue, and I sometimes think there's a veritable campaign to ban outright the use of lard and other tasty animal fats in deep frying and baking. (What I propose serving the fanatics behind such fatuous endeavors is chicken or hush puppies fried in olive oil.) As fashionable new products are introduced to the fickle market in some areas, left in the wake to vanish are pole beans and real butter beans, damson plums, scuppernong grapes, turtle meat, croquettes, Virginia peanuts, genuine buttermilk, and dozens of other staples once considered essential in Southern kitchens. Gradually, beaten biscuits, homemade pickles and preserves, and holiday fruitcakes are being replaced by commercial substitutes; ridiculous new laws are being passed regularly restricting the locations of open-air barbecue pits; and, of course, lurking ominously in the background, trendy, contrived, Yankeefied restaurants are serving the same homogenized New Wave dishes found all over the country. And then there are the unholy golden arches of McDonald's.

No matter. Southern cooking has withstood much worse changes, upheavals, and intrusions over the past four centuries, and it will surely overcome most current threats so long as the vast majority of the population continues to revere delicious home cooking and as long as truly serious professional chefs make further headway in revitalizing native foods and elevating multiple dishes to impressive new levels of distinction in top-notch restaurants. Naysayers augur that authentic Southern food could be in jeopardy of disappearing, like so many other regional styles, just another victim of rampant commercialism and standardization, unruly celebrity chefs out to reinvent the potato, public health prejudices and phobias, and hectic, time-consuming lifestyles. I refuse to believe any of the nonsense, as this book makes crystal clear. We Southerners are obstinate and forever rebellious mavericks who still take as much pride in our cultural heritage as in the foods that have sustained us through development and prosperity, grief and glory, defeat and recovery. For generations, our style of cooking has served not only as a focus of our lives but as a veritable symbol of survival. Despite my explicit worries and reservations, I have little reason to doubt that this tradition will prove to be as steadfast as it has always been. All Southerners voice a philosophy about the role that food plays in our culture, but nobody has summed it up better than John Egerton when he writes, "Our dishes and beverages express our faith, our good humor, our binding ties, our eternal joys and sorrows, our readiness for whatever awaits us."

"Soul food," which nourished Southern slaves and poor mountain farmers for over two centuries, is based on such staples as pork, grits, boiled greens, black-eyed peas, sweet potatoes, cornbread, and fried fish. As one historian has written, "While all soul food is Southern, not all Southern food is soul."

INTRODUCTION

Equipment

CAST-IRON COOKWARE

Southern cooking couldn't exist without cast-iron pots, skillets, and corn-stick molds, all of which stand up to high-temperature frying, distribute heat evenly for slow simmering and baking like no other cookware, and are indestructible. Cast-iron equipment can last a lifetime or longer, if maintained properly; many of the pieces in my large collection were used by my grandmother and her mother. New cast-iron must be seasoned to seal the surface. To do so, scrub the inner surface with steel-wool soap pads, rinse and dry well, spread a layer of vegetable oil or shortening over the inside, and place in a 250°F oven for 15 minutes. Pour off the oil, place back in the oven for 2 hours, then let cool to room temperature. Repeat the procedure at least once a year to maintain a smooth surface. Some say you should never wash cast-iron with soap and water—simply wipe it clean with paper towels. I've been washing my cast-iron for decades, and the surfaces remain smooth as silk, with never a trace of rust. On the other hand, I'd never put cast-iron in the dishwasher or scour it with a steel-wool pad.

CASSEROLES

So important are casseroles in the South that no kitchen is complete without at least half a dozen of different sizes, shapes, and designs. (Southern cooks still prize nothing more as a birthday, holiday, or wedding gift than a beautiful ovenproof casserole dish to display on the dinner table or buffet.) When purchasing any casserole, look for both quality and beauty, remembering that some vessels are not suitable for stove-top cooking (glazed earthenware and ovenproof glassware), others are highly durable (enameled cast-iron, heavy-gauge stainless steel, and lined copper), and others are the easiest to clean (anodized aluminum and ovenproof porcelain). Unless a shallow casserole is specified, most of the recipes in this book require a deep casserole with a lid. Generally, the most practical sizes are 1-, 2-, and 3-quart casseroles, although, since these dishes can involve so many variables, the sizes should be considered approximate. A casserole that is too large can cause the food to dry out; one that is too small risks the possibility of uneven cooking and messy spills. A good rule of thumb is to allow about 1 inch between the ingredients and the rim of the vessel. Equally valuable in the Southern kitchen for certain dips and appetizers is a nice collection of ½- to 1½-cup ovenproof ceramic or glass ramekins.

DEEP-FAT FRYER

Considering the cardinal role that deep-fat frying plays in Southern cooking, it's no wonder that kitchen, hardware, and other retail shops all over the South carry a wide variety of standard and electric deep-fat fryers. Of course, it's possible to fry foods in large cast-iron pots or skillets (often preferable for chicken or fish), but for such popular items as hush puppies, okra, shrimp and oysters, seafood fritters, and beignets, nothing is safer or more convenient than a special deep-fat fryer with a fitted wire or stainless-steel basket for easy cooking and draining. The best pots for even heat distribution are cast-iron or black steel, but what matters most is that the pot is deep enough (4 to 5 inches deep) to prevent spattering and ensure that all the ingredients will be fully immersed in the fat. Some fancy fryers come with controlled thermostats, nickel-and-chrome baskets, and built-in timers. The only problem is that most of these are unwieldy and cook only limited amounts of food at one time. Finally, with traditional equipment, make sure to buy a good deep-fat thermometer so you can monitor the temperature of the fat at all times.

MEAT GRINDER

A meat grinder is an invaluable tool for grinding sausage, meats and poultry for spreads and pastes, hard cheeses, and nuts. If you don't have one, a heavy, sharp knife can often do the job, but beware of trying to use a blender or food processor when a meat grinder is called for—the result can be mush. Beware also of cheap plastic grinders, which can crack and split from frequent use. Electric grinders are quick and efficient but prohibitively expensive, so most Southern home cooks still depend on the ever-reliable, cast-iron, hand-powered grinder that clamps to a working surface and comes with two cutting plates of different sizes. Another option is a meat-grinder attachment for your home mixer.

BISCUIT BOWL

One of my most valuable kitchen possessions is a 3-quart ceramic bowl ordered years ago from the Arm & Hammer (baking soda) company for the exclusive purpose of mixing biscuit dough. It has just the right width, depth, and flared sides for hand-mixing the ingredients, cutting in the fat evenly, and gathering the dough easily into a ball. Other

cooks I know also have special biscuit bowls (wooden, glass, unglazed earthenware), and each has his or her reasons for using the item only for biscuit making. The point is, of course, that biscuit making is serious business in the South, and the sooner you find a special large mixing bowl that proves repeatedly to produce perfect biscuits, the better. It may all be mental, but I can report that when I'm forced to make biscuits away from home without my beloved bowl, the results are never the same.

PASTRY CUTTER (OR BLENDER)

Some experienced Southern cooks can "cut" fat into the dry ingredients for biscuits and other breads and pastries using only their fingers, but even these experts agree that nothing is more useful for getting the job done fast than a sturdy, stainless-steel, oval pastry cutter. No Southerner would dream of executing this simple procedure with a food processor (especially when making biscuits), aware not only of the unnecessary inconvenience and mess but also that the mixture could be easily overprocessed.

BISCUIT CUTTERS

For Southerners, it would be inconceivable to make any style of biscuit without the appropriate small-handled, sharp, metal biscuit cutter to ensure even biscuits and promote rising by not sealing the biscuit's edges with a blunt substitute (e.g., a juice glass). Cooks normally use cutters ranging in sizes from 1½ to 3½ inches, and since all are inexpensive, there's really no excuse for trying to substitute a dull juice glass or rough tin can.

CHEESE GRINDER

Ground, grated, and shredded cheese is as indispensable to Southern cookery as chopped pecans, and when it comes to specialties such as pimento cheese, cheese biscuits, hot browns, quiches, gratins, and any number of cheese toppings for casseroles and stratas, cheese grinders work overtime from Virginia to Mississippi. To facilitate the work required in the recipes in this book, I usually call for cheese to be grated or shredded, since almost everybody has a metal or plastic box grater in their kitchen. In my own cooking, however, I grind virtually all of my cheese in a trusty hand-grinder, which I pamper as carefully as I do my knives—and you'll do the same once you acquire a good one. Not only is it much quicker than grating or shredding, but also the texture of the cheese makes for more even mixing and cooking. Most important, settle for nothing less than a sturdy, stainless-steel, relatively expensive grinder that will last for years. The cheap metal ones can bend out of shape, and I once had one that, despite careful and constant washing, deposited strange black specks in the cheese.

SCALE

Any Southern cook who does lots of baking and canning, or who makes confections and cheese dishes, knows the importance of a well-balanced scale for measuring ingredients by weight instead of volume or number. There can be no guesswork, for instance, when you're making a fruitcake, measuring the ingredients for cheese biscuits, or pickling okra or watermelon rind. Ditto when you're measuring a cup of flour, which can vary dramatically depending on the way it's placed in the cup—sifted first till light and airy, or lifted from canister to cup in near-solid spoonfuls. Expensive electronic scales (which require a battery or adapter) might be a bit more accurate and easier to read than mechanical ones, but, for the difference in price and durability, I'm quite satisfied with my well-built mechanical model, which has a 10-pound measuring capacity and has lasted more than twenty years.

CANNING EQUIPMENT

Home canning may not be as popular in other regions of the country as it was fifty years ago, but there are still plenty of Southern cooks (me included) who put up their own pickles and preserves and are never without the basic equipment required to accomplish this labor of love. For many of the canning recipes in this book, you will need an assortment of standard pots (never aluminum), wooden or stainless-steel spoons, glass measures, measuring spoons, scales, a timer, tongs, a wide-mouth funnel, glass mason jars, lids, metal ring bands, and a large kettle or roasting pan (with or without a wire jar rack) to double as a water bath for sterilizing jars. Jar sizes depend on personal tastes and needs, but, generally, fruit jellies, jams, preserves, and curds are canned in half-pint or pint jars; pickles, relishes, and marmalades in pints; and large whole fruits (such as pickled peaches) and chutneys in quarts. Serious Southern canners also pride themselves on their personalized labels (FROM THE KITCHEN OF . . .), affixed to jars intended as gifts.

CHARCOAL GRILL

As far as I'm concerned, you can take every wildly popular, hideously expensive, and ever-so-convenient gas grill and heave it into the dump. Furthermore, attend any barbecue festival in the South, and there won't be a gas grill in sight. A charcoal grill might be a bit messier to deal with and require more supervision during the cooking process, but that's a small price to pay for its versatility, for the freedom to toss wood chips onto the coals, and for the more authentic smoke flavor imparted to all grilled foods. Serious Southern cooks are perfectly content with an ordinary kettle grill, bags of charcoal and hardwood chips, and a looped electric starter, which has the coals blazing in fifteen minutes. Any grilled foods in this book are intended to be cooked on a charcoal grill or, if absolutely necessary, under an oven broiler. Of course, if you're a real fanatic about producing great barbecue and grilled foods, you'll invest in a large iron drum smoker or, better yet, dig a pit somewhere outdoors, line it with bricks or cinder blocks, and fit a grid on top. Now, that would truly be whistling Dixie!

ICE CREAM MAKER

Homemade ice cream is one of the most sacred traditions in the South, made easy today by any number of updated hand-cranked and state-of-the-art electric machines that produce from one to six quarts of luscious, fresh ice cream. Although I've been exposed repeatedly to the more sophisticated (and expensive) ice cream makers, I've yet to find one that can equal the old-fashioned, wooden-bucket White Mountain freezers that have been around for ages. The hand-cranked version still boasts the same fine workmanship and reliability for which it's always been famous, and the electric model, with its commercial-grade universal motor and stainless-steel canister, couldn't be easier to use. Remember that you must buy plenty of cracked ice and rock salt for these machines, a requirement that, in many respects, makes the hand-cranking procedure all the more fun for children and adults alike.

Ingredients

BOURBON WHISKEY

First distilled in the late eighteenth century in Bourbon County, Virginia (now part of Kentucky), bourbon must, by law, be aged at least two years in new, charred, white-oak barrels and diluted with only limestone-filtered spring water to lower the alcoholic proof. All bourbon is sour mash whiskey, but all sour mash whiskey is not legally bourbon if a single regulation is altered. (Jack Daniel's, for example, cannot use the word *bourbon* on its label since the whiskey is filtered through charcoal to heighten its distinctive flavor.) The finest bourbon is made in Kentucky and Tennessee.

COUNTRY HAM

Virtually every region of the South turns out dry-cured, aged country hams, the most famous being Smithfield hams of Virginia. Produced since colonial times and a favorite of Thomas Jefferson and Queen Victoria, Smithfield ham must be processed according to strict state regulations within the small town of Smithfield, Virginia, in order to carry the Smithfield label. Typically, the ham is dry-cured with salt, sugar, and sodium nitrate, refrigerated and salted over and over, smoked about 10 days, then aged 6 months or more. Once, Smithfields were made by individual producers from only local peanut-fed hogs for a distinctive ham texture, but today the various brands come from the town's one climate-controlled cooperative factory, Smithfield Foods, which uses Virginia and North Carolina hogs that are fed nutritionally calculated diets with supposedly equal good results. (Since the hogs are much leaner than before, some fans are beginning to question the integrity of the hams.) Smithfield hams are available in finer markets everywhere, and they are expensive.

Less accessible but often just as good or better than Smithfields are country hams cured elsewhere in Virginia, and in North Carolina, Tennessee, and Kentucky, by relatively small producers whose families have often been in the business for generations. Each has a special technique that makes the individual hams distinctive (different dry-cures, different woods for smoking, different natural age-ing procedures), and each can recommend certain styles of ham for individual palates and provide cooking direc-tions. Generally, the hams are available whole (cooked or uncooked) or in prepackaged slices. For a fully concentrat-ed flavor (often an acquired taste for non-Southerners), choose a 12- to 14-pound uncooked ham that's been aged 9 to 12 months; for a milder flavor, ask for one that has been aged 5 or 6 months. Before being cooked or sliced, all whole cured country hams should be scrubbed thoroughly with warm water and vinegar to remove any mold, then possibly soaked briefly or longer in a large roasting pan to restore moisture and remove salt (according to individual taste). Unsoaked country ham slices keep almost indefi-nitely in the freezer wrapped in freezer paper; soaked ones can be kept in the refrigerator about 2 weeks or frozen up to about 2 months without losing moisture. Any reliable butcher should be willing to slice a country ham (perhaps for a fee) not intended to be baked whole. The standard width of the slices is about ¼ inch.

Country hams can be ordered from the following producers:

Smithfield Foods, Smithfield, Virginia (800-926-8448; www.smithfieldhams.com)

Gwaltney of Smithfield, Smithfield, Virginia (800-292-2773)

S. Wallace Edwards & Sons, Surry, Virginia (800-222-4267; www.virginiatrations.com)

Wayco Ham Company, Goldsboro, North Carolina (800-962-2614)

Meacham Country Hams, Sturgis, Kentucky (800-552-3190)

G & W Hamery Country Hams, Murfreesboro, Tennessee (615-893-9712)

B & B Food Products, Inc., Cadiz, Kentucky (502-235-5294)

SAUSAGE

Bulk pork sausage is as vital to Southern cooking as cornmeal and rice, and supermarkets in every state are fully stocked with numerous local styles intended to be fried for breakfast or used in all types of cocktail appe-tizers, stuffings, casseroles, stratas, croquettes, loaves, and breads. In the old days, sausage making was always the final step in the fall hog-killing operation, and each family had its own special recipe and blend of season-ings. Today, sausage plants are located all over the South, and three of the most venerable and popular re-gional brands are George Jones (Tennessee), Neese's (North Carolina), and Odom's (Tennessee). Elsewhere, the most reliable national brand is Jimmy Dean—just the right proportions of lean meat to fat. (Note: Italian-style sausage, so popular in other areas of the country, should never be substituted for standard bulk sausage.) Sausage freezes well up to about six months, after which it begins to lose savor and taste of freezer burn.

BACON

Bacon is one of the most indispensable staples in South-ern cookery. While ordinary sliced commercial bacon is acceptable for most recipes, I much prefer buying more flavorful slab bacon and cutting my own slices in various widths. I keep all opened bacon in tightly sealed plastic bags in the refrigerator to prolong freshness, and when I find it on sale in these grossly overpriced times, I might buy a lot and store it in the freezer up to about three months. Reject any bacon with lean meat that has begun to turn grayish brown.

Streak-o'-Lean

Essential as a flavoring for numerous boiled peas, beans, greens, and other vegetables, salt-cured pork fat with streaks of lean meat (also known as "salt pork") is available in the meat department of all supermarkets. I keep a big chunk of it in the freezer at all times (the fat never freezes solid) and simply cut off pieces as needed. Streak-o'-lean is often confused with fatback, which is the unsalted cut of pork fat used to make lard and cracklin's.

Crabmeat

From Maryland's Chesapeake Bay down to the Gulf of Mexico, the delectably sweet crabmeat used to make crab cakes, crab Norfolk, crab imperial, she-crab soup, gumbos, and numerous other specialties comes from highly prized blue crabs, with the color referring to the blue-green underside of the crab's large claws. Blue crabs molt (shed their hard shells) as many as twenty times in their natural three-year life span, each time increasing their size by one-third. Before molting, a crab develops a new, inner soft shell, and there's only a twenty-four-hour period when the new shell is soft enough so that the entire body can be eaten. To produce the great delicacy known as soft-shell (or "buster") crabs, Chesapeake Bay and Gulf crabbers hold the crabs in special floating pens till they shed their hard shells, then pack them in ice for shipment.

All live blue crabs (hard-shell and soft-shell) should be refrigerated and used on the day they're purchased. Fresh crabmeat is also available pasteurized, canned, and frozen, but only the pasteurized product (usually available in 1-pound tubs at seafood markets) is acceptable unless you care to deal with mushy crabmeat. The finest and most delicate crabmeat is "lump" from the back; claw meat is actually sweeter (and less expensive) but contains much more cartilage to be picked away. Pasteurized crabmeat should be used within 3 or 4 days of opening.

The other famous Southern crab is Florida's huge stone crab, available fresh in finer seafood markets during the fall and winter and frozen the rest of the year. Since only the succulent claws of stone crabs are cracked and eaten, Florida fisherman twist them off and throw the crab back in the water, to regenerate new claws in about a year.

Southern Cheeses

Much of Southern cookery couldn't exist without cheddar cheese and, to some extent, Parmesan. Bland, processed American cheese is virtually worthless in good cooking, and I buy nothing but sharp or extra-sharp natural cheddar that's been aged from 9 to 12 months—preferably New York State, Vermont, or Canadian. Some freshly grated domestic Parmesan cheese is acceptable for certain cocktail spreads, casserole toppings, croquettes, and the like, but generally there simply is no substitute for genuine Italian Parmigiano-Reggiano (which, since it dries out quickly, should be bought in relatively small quantities, kept tightly wrapped in plastic, and stored in the refrigerator).

Southern cheese making is not an oxymoron. In fact, just in the past decade, numerous delectable artisanal cheeses have been produced on small farms from Maryland to Georgia to Louisiana. Here are some of the best Southern cheese makers, all of whom can be contacted for information on prices and on how and where to obtain their cheeses:

Bittersweet Plantation Dairy, Gonzales, Louisiana. Rich, buttery, triple-cream cow's milk cheese (800-256-2433; www.jfolse.com)

Clemson Blue, Clemson, South Carolina. Cow's milk aged blue-veined cheese (800-599-0181)

Everona Dairy, Rapidan, Virginia. Aged sheep's milk cheese (540-854-4159)

Firefly Farms, Bittinger, Maryland. Aged goat's milk blue-veined cheese (301-245-4630; www.fireflyfarms.com)

Fromagerie Belle Chèvre, Elkmont, Alabama. Creamy white goat's milk cheese (800-735-2238)

Goat Lady Dairy, Climax, North Carolina. A variety of goat's milk cheeses (336-824-2163; www.goatladydairy.com)

Meadow Creek Dairy, Galax, Virginia. Cheddar, Rosemary Jack, and other cow's milk cheeses (888-236-0622; www.meadowcreekdairy.com)

Sweet Grass Dairy, Thomasville, Georgia. Pecan goat's milk cheese (229-227-0752)

Yellow Branch Farm, Robbinsville, North Carolina. Cow's milk farmstead and pepper cheeses (828-479-6710; www.yellowbranch.com)

PECANS

The only nut native to the continental United States, pecans were being harvested by Indians in the lower Mississippi Valley long before the arrival of the first Eu-

ropean settlers. (The name itself was a Cree word meaning "hard shell.") Thomas Jefferson had pecan trees transported from Louisiana to Monticello, but it was a Louisiana slave who first successfully grafted and cultivated the first pecans trees in 1846. By the late nineteenth century, vast orchards had been planted in Louisiana, Mississippi, Alabama, and Georgia, and the trees adapted so well to Georgia's soil and climate that by the 1950s the state was the South's largest producer of pecans. Today, Georgia supplies the nation with no less than 100 million pounds of pecans annually.

The importance of pecans in Southern cookery can never be overemphasized; they appear in muffins, waffles, pancakes, dips, salads, casseroles, stuffings, toppings, and numerous breads and desserts. Consequently, serious cooks know not only to wait patiently every year for the first fall harvest of fresh nuts but also how to distinguish between such varieties of pecans as Schley (thin shelled and high in oil), Desirable (fat and meaty), Elliot (small, rounded, and buttery), and Louisiana Centennial, (silken and sweet). The differences between golden, plump, mellow fresh pecans and the dark, shriveled, often rancid packaged nuts you find in supermarkets are the same as those between fresh and canned peaches. Since fresh pecans have such a high fat content (70 percent), they quickly turn rancid unless refrigerated (up to about 9 months) or frozen (up to 2 years). In November and December, fresh shelled pecans can be ordered by the pound or case (usually considerably cheaper) from the following sources:

Sunnyland Farms, Albany, Georgia (800-999-2488; www.nutsandcandies.com)

Pearson Farm, Perry, Georgia (888-423-7374; www.pearsonfarm.com)

Atwell Pecan Company, Wrens, Georgia (800-548-6887)

Ellis Brothers Pecans, Vienna, Georgia (800-635-0616; www.werenuts.com)

Young Pecan Company, Florence, South Carolina (800-729-8004; www.youngpecanplantations.com)

Priester's Pecans, Fort Deposit, Alabama (800-277-3226; www.priester.com)

PEANUTS

Despite the attention that President Jimmy Carter brought to small, round Georgia peanuts, the majority of which are transformed into peanut butter and peanut oil, the noblest Southern peanuts (which are technically not nuts but legumes) remain the same plump, oval, delectably unctuous Virginia variety that was most likely introduced to that state and North Carolina from Africa during the slave trade. (Actually, peanuts are native to our hemisphere, but before being cultivated in the South, they were taken to Africa by South American explorers.) One of the most distinctive seasonal specialties of Georgia, Alabama, and the Carolinas are freshly harvested unshelled peanuts that are boiled in brine in huge kettles till soft, and served as a snack at outdoor summer events and sold along roadsides. People either love or hate boiled peanuts, and no doubt they are an acquired taste due to their soft texture and briny flavor.

Genuine raw, shelled, extra-large Virginia peanuts (with or without their red skins) can be ordered in different-size burlap bags from Wakefield Peanut Company, in Wakefield, Virginia (800-803-1309; www.wakefield-peanutco.com). To roast them, preheat the oven to 325°F, spread the nuts in a single layer on a baking sheet with melted butter to taste, and roast till golden brown

(about 20 to 30 minutes), turning them once or twice. Drain on paper towels and salt to taste. Raw peanuts keep in sealed containers in the refrigerator for up to 3 months and in the freezer indefinitely.

FLOUR

The South is blessed with any number of soft winter wheat flours for baked goods and other uses. All you have to do to test the superiority of Southern flour over the hard-wheat flours found in most other areas of the country is make two batches of biscuits, muffins, pancakes, or hush puppies, side by side, using the Southern flour and a competing type of flour, and observe the differences in height and fluffiness. The main reason for this is that Southern flour contains less gluten-forming proteins than most flours, making it less dense. Markets in the South are full of White Lily, Martha White, Red Band, Melrose, and other such local flours, but if you live outside the region, the only solution is to order the all-purpose flours from the two producers who ship them in 5-pound bags:

White Lily Foods (800-264-5459; www.whitelily.com)

Martha White Foods (800-663-6317; www.marthawhite.com)

Self-rising flour is simply enriched all-purpose flour to which baking powder and salt have been added. Although most of today's self-rising flours can be effectively substituted for the all-purpose flour (minus any baking soda and salt indicated in the recipe) called for in this book, many Southern cooks don't trust them since, during delays in merchandising or storing, the leavening can lose some of its potency. Always be sure to check the expiration date on bags of self-rising flour.

Cake flour, which is sometimes called for in Southern cake recipes, is a fine-textured, soft-wheat flour with a high starch content that gives cakes a lighter texture than all-purpose flour. If you don't have any, you can sift and resift all-purpose flour eight to ten times and get the same results.

BAKING POWDER AND BAKING SODA

Many Southern breads and baked goods would be inconceivable without baking powder and/or baking soda for leavening. The baking powder called for in virtually all recipes is double-acting, meaning that carbon dioxide gas is released when liquid is added, and again when the powder is exposed to oven heat. Since baking powder is perishable, be sure to check the expiration date stamped on the can and store it in a cool, dry area. To test if a baking powder still packs a punch, drop a teaspoon of it into ⅓ cup of hot water to see if it bubbles. For optimal results, I buy only small 4-ounce cans of baking powder at a time, and I replace boxes of baking soda about every six months. Remember that any acid ingredient used in baking (such as buttermilk, yogurt, and molasses) must be neutralized with a little baking soda for perfect leavening.

SORGHUM

The most important sweetener throughout the South till refined cane sugar became cheaper after World War I, sorghum (also "sorghum molasses" or "sorghum syrup") is the boiled-down juice pressed from sorghum stalks, much the same way that molasses is pressed from sugarcane. Today, sorghum is still produced in much of Appalachia ("lassie-making," in local lingo) and can be found in specialty food shops and better Southern supermarkets. It's most often used as a table syrup (delicious drizzled over biscuits, waffles, and pancakes) and to make cakes, delicate cookies, and other baked goods. One mail-order source for sorghum is Golden Kentucky Products in Livingston, Kentucky (606-453-9800).

RICE

Long-grain white rice, along with corn, remains one of the major foundations of Southern cookery. Introduced to the South Carolina Lowcountry in the late seventeenth century by a sea captain who gave some Madagascar grains to a Charleston planter, rice flourished in the swampy terrain. Before long, slave labor made possible the cultivation of some 150,000 acres of rice fields between Charleston and Georgetown, and throughout the eighteenth and early nineteenth centuries, "Carolina Gold" was responsible for one of the wealthiest and most lavish societies in American history. When slavery was abolished after the Civil War, however, the gigantic rice culture of South Carolina all but disappeared, replaced by industries in Louisiana and Arkansas, where land was better suited to machine harvesting. A minute amount of Carolina Gold is still grown by a handful of gentlemen farmers in the Lowcountry, but today nearly half the U.S. rice harvest of some half-billion bushels comes from more than four thousand farms in Arkansas, many located near the town of Stuttgart. Serious cooks and epicures go out of their way to obtain what little superior Carolina Gold is produced in South Carolina (the delicate, nutty grains have a creaminess like no other long-grain rice). It can be ordered from Charleston Favorites, at 800-538-0003; www.charlestonfavorites.com.

Also popular in many Southern kitchens are both brown rice (which includes the grain's high-fiber bran coating that accounts for its coloring) and wild rice (actually a long-grain marsh grass). White rice can be stored almost indefinitely in a cool, dark area, but since the presence of the bran means that brown rice is subject to rancidity, it should be kept no longer than about six months—even in the refrigerator. I wrap all my rice tightly in plastic for protection against bugs.

GRITS AND CORNMEAL

A staple of the Southern breakfast table, grits are basically the same as hominy. Technically, when whole kernels of corn are soaked in a solution of water and lye (or wood ash) to remove the outer hulls, the result is the softened germs (or "eyes") of the kernels, called hominy. When hominy is then dried and coarsely ground, you have grits; when dried hominy is finely ground, the end product is cornmeal. Soft (or "pearl") hominy is sold in markets as a canned vegetable. The finest and rarest grits are made from mature corn kernels that have been neither degerminated nor treated with lye but simply stone- or water-ground and bolted (sifted) to remove the husks. Most packaged regular grits found in supermarkets have been blanched and are blander than stone-ground, full-flavored grits; "quick" grits are acceptable in a pinch, but overly processed "instant" grits are virtually tasteless.

Generally, the color and texture of cornmeal used in Southern cooking is a matter of personal taste. Southerners debate endlessly the virtues of white cornmeal (sweeter, more refined, etc.) over yellow (better flavored, coarser, etc.), but most agree that any stone-ground meal is superior to that milled with steel rollers for wide commercial marketing. Personally, I try to stock many types: medium-texture stone-ground yellow for cornbread, corn sticks, fritters, and hush puppies; regular commercial fine-texture yellow for muffins and other baked goods; and both fine stone-ground and ordinary white for spoon-

breads and certain breads and puddings, and for sprinkling over baking sheets. Since stone-ground cornmeal is still not readily available in most markets, the meal I call for most in this book is what you find packaged in supermarkets, a perfectly respectable product. (Quaker is the leading brand.) If, on the other hand, you can lay hands on fresh stone-ground meal (any color or texture), so much the better.

Superior stone-ground grits must be kept refrigerated or frozen and boiled slowly for at least 1 hour to achieve optimum creaminess. To avoid bugs, all cornmeal should be tightly closed in plastic and stored in the refrigerator. Difficult to find even in the best Southern markets, stone-ground grits and cornmeal can be ordered from the following sources:

Anson Mills, Columbia, South Carolina (843-709-7399; www.ansonmills.com)

Old Mill of Guilford, Oak Ridge, North Carolina (336-643-4783; www.oldmillofguilford.com)

Morgan Mill, Brevard, North Carolina (828-862-4084)

Falls Mill, Belvidere, Tennessee (931-469-7161; www.fallsmill.com)

Nora Mill Granary, Helen, Georgia (800-927-2375; www.noramill.com)

Adams Foods & Milling, Dothan, Alabama (800-239-4233)

PEACHES

No peaches elsewhere in the country (especially in California) can compare with a South Carolina or Georgia peach—in flavor, sweetness, or texture—and while most

Americans simply grab any summer peaches when they first appear in the markets, true Southern peach fans not only know the differences between June clingstones and July freestones but can distinguish between Coronets and Lorings, Sunhighs and Blakes, and White Ladies and Georgia Belles. (Peach varieties come in by a specific date, given ideal weather conditions, and South Carolina and Georgia orchards generally keep regular customers near and far informed of what's available when.)

Southern peaches are shipped to most of the country during the summer months, and the best still have a little fuzz on their skins and are slightly soft. To choose ripe peaches, don't look for redness, which varies by type, but for background color, which should never be green. Most June peaches are clingstones, which are ideal for canning and cooking. Freestones are in season from July to early September and are best for eating out of hand, making ice cream and other raw-peach desserts, and freezing. All fresh peaches ripen very quickly at room temperature and should be eaten or used as soon as possible, or frozen in plastic freezer bags. Peaches stored in the refrigerator keep longer but lose considerable flavor. To peel peaches quickly, drop them into boiling water for 30 seconds, then in ice water, and slip off the skins.

SWEET POTATOES

Contrary to the labeling in markets, the all-American sweet potatoes grown so widely in the South are not yams, which are an altogether different species of tuber indigenous to South America, Asia, and Africa and rarely found anywhere in the United States. Rich in vitamin A, potassium, and calcium, sweet potatoes should never be bought in the summer, since a few months of storage are required for a certain enzyme to convert a "green" sweet potato's starch to sugar. Sweet potatoes are best in November and after. Although North Carolina is the country's leading producer of sweet potatoes, Louisiana is the only state that actually grades its large harvest, and epicures consider Louisiana Beauregards to be the finest, sweetest, moistest potatoes found anywhere. Other superior varieties are Garnet, Jewel, and Hernandez.

CANNED TOMATOES

Whole or crushed, canned tomatoes (often preferred to fresh in cooking) are a major component of many Southern soups, stews, and casseroles. I normally have plenty of 28- and 14½-ounce cans on hand.

ONIONS

In addition to ordinary yellow bulb onions, scallions (or green onions), fresh chives, and, when in season from May through June, Vidalia onions are needed for countless Southern dishes. When a recipe in this book calls for part of the green leaves of scallions, this means only the tender light green leaves. Vidalia onions keep about a month when stored in a well-aerated wicker basket, and considerably longer in the refrigerator. When buying genuine Vidalia onions, make sure they bear the official tag of certification by the Vidalia, Georgia, Chamber of Commerce.

PIMENTOS

A major ingredient in many Southern dips, salads, casseroles, seafood dishes, and, of course, classic pimento cheese spread, the heart-shaped pimento pepper is *not* the same as its humbler red bell cousin. The distinctive sweet peppers are available whole, sliced, or chopped in 4- and 7-ounce jars in supermarkets nationwide—though you may have to search the shelves carefully to find them. Never try to substitute roasted red bell peppers for genuine pimentos.

BUTTERMILK

Genuine buttermilk is the leftover thick liquid produced from the processing of milk or cream into butter, and its tangy flavor derives from the milk product's natural fermentation. For centuries, Southerners have prized buttermilk not only as a delicious, buttery drink but also as a key ingredient in certain styles of biscuits, cornbread, and sweet baked goods. (When combined with baking soda, buttermilk is also an age-old leavening for any number of dishes.) Today, most buttermilk is pasteurized skim milk treated with special bacteria to make it slightly sour (and, of course, safe). While this modified product is certainly acceptable in cooking, its flavor is almost bland compared with the natural buttermilk I drank as a child. Perhaps the most unusual buttermilk dish is a Cajun breakfast specialty of western Louisiana called couche-couche, a crusty cornmeal-and-buttermilk crêpe served with cane sugar or topped with a fried egg. Elsewhere in the rural South, some people love nothing more at breakfast than a bowl of buttermilk with cornbread crumbled in it. Buttermilk keeps for days and days in the refrigerator.

LARD

Rendered and clarified pork fat, lard (which, curiously, contains considerably less cholesterol than butter) produces the tenderest, flakiest biscuits and pastries of all fats, and is also ideal for flavorful deep-fat frying. Available in 1-pound packages (Armour is the most popular brand), processed, pure-white lard is usually found unrefrigerated near the meat counter in supermarkets. Most commercial lard contains preservatives and has been treated with emulsifiers to prolong its shelf life and

hold its solid state. If the package has dark or greasy spots, the lard is too old and should be rejected. Stored in the refrigerator, lard keeps at least one year.

PEANUT OIL

Often used throughout the South in place of less flavorful vegetable oil, peanut oil is not only excellent for salads but also, because of its high smoke point, prized for frying. Stored in a dark, cool area, the oil keeps indefinitely.

BACON GREASE

All serious Southern cooks keep a coffee can of leftover bacon grease (or "drippings") to flavor any number of dishes and enhance other fats used for frying. I can't imagine frying chicken, for example, without adding a tablespoon or so of bacon grease to the pan, and some cooks wouldn't dream of frying something like okra, dill pickles, or seafood fritters in anything but pure bacon grease. Since bacon grease can become slightly rancid at room temperature over time, I start a new can about every six months.

CANDIED FRUITS

These fruits boiled in sugar syrup are essential for not only fruitcakes but also other Southern cakes, puddings, and confections. Just before the winter holidays, they are widely available in all Southern and some out-of-region markets. Otherwise, look for them in specialty food shops. The fruits should be stored airtight in a cool, dry area.

CAYENNE PEPPER, RED PEPPER FLAKES, AND TABASCO

Each of these is important in the preparation of numerous dishes, and each should be replaced when the bright red color and zest begin to fade. I always keep bottles of Tabasco in the refrigerator for maximum longevity.

MOLASSES

Still used widely in the South as a table syrup and to make pies, puddings, candies, pralines, brittles, and other confections, molasses (produced from refined sugarcane juice) comes in three styles: light, dark, and blackstrap. Light, unsulphured molasses, delicious on waffles and pancakes, is the most prized; dark is best for baked dishes; and thick, bitter blackstrap (the dregs of the boiling process) is popular only as a nutritional panacea with health food fanatics and as a supplement in cattle feedlots. Light and dark molasses is available in all supermarkets and keeps almost indefinitely.

Special Cooking Techniques

FRYING

No cooking technique is more important or popular in Southern cookery than deep- and shallow-fat frying, and over the centuries Southerners have elevated the method to a veritable art. For successful frying of fish, chicken, shrimp, hush puppies, and vegetables, follow these simple ground rules:

1. For even heat distribution and retention of heat at high temperature, no cookware equals cast-iron. Next best is stainless steel or heavy-gauge aluminum.

2. Since some fats (soybean and olive oils, for example) break down at high temperature (smoke point), use only lard or vegetable shortening and such oils as corn, peanut, and safflower for deep- and shallow-fat frying. If any fat begins to smoke, discard it, start over, and regulate the temperature correctly. Frying food breaks down any fat, so never reuse a fat more than twice. Cooking fat should be strained and kept in the refrigerator before being reused.

3. Never crowd the pan or pot, and always maintain the fat at an even temperature, using a candy thermometer if necessary. If the fat's not hot enough, the food will soak it up and be greasy; it the fat's too hot, the surface of the food will burn and the interior will be soggy. When frying food in batches, be sure that the fat returns to the right temperature before repeating the procedure.

BARBECUE

Don't ask me to explain Southern barbecue. Like other Americans, Southerners barbecue everything from pork to chicken to shrimp, yet when Southerners talk seriously about "barbecue," what they're really referring to is pork and only pork. To confuse matters more, the word *barbecue* in the South is never a piece of cooking equipment, nor rapid broiling on a gas grill, nor a sauce, but, rather, a specialized cooking method whereby meat (almost always pork and never beef, as in Texas) is placed on a gridiron, mopped with an aromatic basting sauce, and cooked very slowly over charcoal and/or hardwood coals till very succulent and permeated with the rich flavor of smoke. Each region has variations on the technique, the types and cuts of meat, the hardwoods, the seasonings, and the sauce, but, in states such as Florida, Maryland, and Alabama, the concept can be distorted to accommodate foods that would never be "barbecued" in other areas and can be cooked without a grill.

Memphis, Tennessee, is known for its exceptional barbecued pork ribs crusted with a spicy dry-rub, Georgia and Alabama for pork shoulders basted with a tomatoey vinegar sauce, South Carolina for sliced pork barbecue seasoned with mustard sauce, and North Carolina (often called the "Barbecue Capital of the World") for western-style chopped barbecued shoulders and eastern-style whole hogs ("pulled pork") mopped with a peppery vinegar sauce. But Louisianians are also fiercely proud of their barbecued Gulf shrimp; Floridians love barbecued swordfish; and Arkansans rave about their barbecued duck and wild game. Southern barbecue is maddening.

The ideal setup for authentic Southern pork barbecue is an outdoor pit covered with some type of gridiron, but equally efficient are the huge steel cookers ("drums" or "smokers") used at the dozens of barbecue cook-offs held throughout the South. More practical for the purposes of this book is an ordinary charcoal kettle grill (with vents in the lid and on the bottom) large enough to barbecue not only a whole pork shoulder or loin but also plenty of chicken and duck pieces, fish steaks, a couple of rabbits, and the like. For recipes that call for soaked wood chips, hickory is most popular in the South, though some cooks prefer the milder flavor of oak. (Both can be found in most hardware stores and many mega marts.) Whether you're cooking over only charcoal briquettes or briquettes and wood chips, the briquettes should always first be allowed to burn till they're ashen (30 to 45 minutes), and when meats are intended to cook slowly for many hours (indirect cooking), the coals must be pushed around the sides of the grill and a drip pan placed in the center. For slow, indirect cooking, the grill rack should be positioned at least 6 inches from the heat;

for more rapid barbecuing, about 4 inches should suffice. Some Southern cooks baste foods with any variety of sauces from the moment they're placed on the grill; others, wary of overwhelming the foods and of flare-ups from the coals, baste only toward the end.

BISCUITS

It's no secret that Southerners relish biscuits—morning, noon, and night—more than any other bread, and have elevated the technique of making them to a veritable art. While the principles governing the preparation of beaten biscuits, drop biscuits, tea biscuits, and other distinctive styles are covered briefly in this book, special attention should be paid to perfecting traditional baking powder biscuits, since these are the ones made on a regular basis.

- ❧ Ideally, baking powder biscuits should be at least 1 inch high, with craggy tops, light golden brown outsides, and flaky and moist insides; they should be light and tender in texture and clean tasting.

- ❧ You can premix the dry ingredients, but since the first leavening action of the baking powder occurs when liquid is added (the second is when it's exposed to high heat), never add liquid till you're ready to bake.

- ❧ To prevent toughness, never handle biscuit dough any longer than it takes to just mix the ingredients, kneading it no more than a few strokes. Patting out the dough gently is preferable to rolling it.

- ❧ To avoid overly compressed biscuits, always cut them with a sturdy, sharp metal biscuit cutter, and to prevent uneven baking of the sides, cut straight down in one quick stroke.

- The best baking sheets for biscuits are heavy, sturdy metal or silicone ones with no lips except on one side. If the sheet is too thin and flimsy, the biscuits can burn on the bottom; if it has lips on all sides, the biscuits might not bake evenly. Because of the fat in the biscuit dough, there's no need to grease the baking sheet.

- Bake biscuits in the top third of the oven. For fully browned biscuits, bake them about 1 inch apart; for browned tops and soft sides, space them about ½ inch apart.

ROUX

Used as a thickener and flavoring agent in some Southern soups, stews, sauces, and especially gumbos, roux is a toasty mixture of flour and oil cooked fairly quickly till just honey colored, medium brown, or dark mahogany. The trick is not to burn a roux, so a little experimentation may be required to master the technique. Basically, a roux should be cooked in a cast-iron skillet large enough so that the oil does not fill it more than one-quarter full. The oil (preferably peanut) should be smoking hot before the flour is added. Once the oil is heated (about 5 minutes over high heat), gradually add the flour, whisking quickly and constantly with a wire whisk to avoid burning the mixture. (If black specks appear, the roux has burned and you must start over again.) A light roux will take about 1 minute, a medium, reddish brown one 2 to 3 minutes, and a dark one about 4 minutes. When the roux reaches the desired color, remove the pan from the heat, add the recipe ingredients to be thickened and flavored, and continue stirring. (If the roux seems to be darkening too fast, immediately remove it from the heat and continue whisking till you have control of it.) Never begin making a roux till you have all the cooking utensils and recipe ingredients at hand, and remember that extreme care and concentration are essential for success. When I made my first Creole gumbo (even with Paul Prudhomme's supervision), I must have destroyed a half dozen roux before perfecting the dark one I wanted.

RED-EYE GRAVY

Cured country ham with red-eye gravy is one of the South's great breakfast treats, especially when accompanied by soft-fried eggs, grits, fresh fruit, and hot biscuits to sop up part of the gravy. To fry ham slices, render a little fat cut off the edges in a cast-iron skillet over moderate heat, fry the ham in the fat 3 to 5 minutes on each side (depending on the width), and transfer to a hot platter or individual serving plates. To make the gravy, add about 3 tablespoons of water per slice of ham to the skillet, reduce till the gravy begins to thicken, scraping up bits and pieces of debris from the bottom of the pan with a spoon, and pour equal amounts of gravy over the ham slices. For a richer, stronger gravy, substitute brewed coffee for the water. (If you object to salty country ham—few Southerners do—you can soak the slices in water about an hour. But be warned: part of the delectable flavor will be lost.)

COBBLERS

One of the most legendary of Southern desserts, deep-dish fruit and berry cobblers are made different ways with different styles of filling and different crusts. Some cobblers use fruits and berries that are naturally softened with sugar before baking, the one stipulation being that they must be perfectly ripe; others involve preboiling the ingredients to produce maximum juice and flavor when the cobbler is baked. Cobbler crusts can be made with standard all-purpose flour or flour and cornmeal dough, with a tangy buttermilk biscuit dough, or with a crispy, feathery pastry dough leavened with lard. Cobblers can be made with both a bottom and top crust (to contain as much moisture and flavor as possible) or simply a top crust, either vented or woven into a lattice. Some incorporate crunchy pieces of baked pastry strips or pieces in the filling itself for nice textural contrast. No matter how you construct a hot cobbler, the main principle is that the filling should never be either soggy or dried out and the crust must be crisp enough to create good counterpoint with the soft fruits or berries—not to mention the obligatory scoop of ice cream on top.

PICKLING AND PRESERVING

For the most intricate details involved in pickling and preserving fruits, berries, and vegetables, I've found no better sources than the excellent booklets provided by the manufacturers of canning jars and processors of pectins. Although the headnotes to the preserve and pickling recipes in this book are pretty explicit about dealing with the various major ingredients and cooking techniques, I do have a few tips that can help guarantee success.

- Always use the highest-quality fresh fruits and vegetables, preferably picked just before canning.

- Never attempt to can vast quantities at a time, only amounts you can work with easily and comfortably in the kitchen.

- Measure or weigh ingredients exactly to avoid cooking distortions and the temptation to over- or under-pack the jars.

- Pack and seal the jars one at a time (allowing about ¼ inch of head space at the tops) so there is no chance of the boiling hot ingredients and liquid cooling and the jars not sealing properly when capped.

- Make sure the liquid covers the solids completely.

- Before sealing the jars, carefully wipe the edges clean with a damp cloth or wet paper towel.

- The lids will ping when a jar is sealed airtight. Another test is to press down on the lid after about 1 hour: if the jar is sealed, the lid will be very firm; if the lid can be pressed down, store the jar in the refrigerator.

- All pickles and preserves should be allowed to age a month or longer to allow the flavors to mellow.

- Never try to reuse rubber jar lids for canning.

To Sterilize and Seal Jars for Canning

Unscrew the ring bands from the canning jars, remove the lids, and wash both thoroughly with soap and hot water. Arrange the jars open ends down in a large baking pan (with or without a jar rack) and add about 2 inches of water. Bring the water to a boil and sterilize the jars for 10 minutes.

Using tongs, remove the jars from the water one at a time and pack them with the food to be canned, taking care not to touch the insides of the jars once they have been sterilized. Wipe the rims very clean with a wet cloth or moist paper towel, then use tongs to dip the sealing lids into the water used for sterilizing the jars. (Do not leave the lids long in the water, to prevent the bands from shrinking.) Fit the lids on top of the jars. Then, holding the jars with a dishcloth, screw the ring bands on tightly.

Place the filled jars in a draft-free area till the lids ping and remain down when pushed with a finger (signs that they are sealed). Any jars whose lids remain convex should be stored in the refrigerator.

A Southern Glossary

ANGEL BISCUIT: Any small, light biscuit leavened with yeast. Also called *wedding biscuit.*

BEATEN BISCUIT: A hard, crisp biscuit made by beating the biscuit dough repeatedly with a mallet or rolling pin. Also known as a *Maryland biscuit.*

BEIGNET: A small, deep-fried, doughnutlike fritter sprinkled with confectioners' sugar and traditionally served with cups of chicory coffee in New Orleans.

BENNE SEED: Sesame seed. Widely used in Carolina and Georgia Lowcountry cooking.

BIG YELLOW: A rutabaga, member of the turnip family.

BIRD'S-EYE PEPPER: A tiny chile pepper usually grown in pots in the Carolinas, Georgia, and the Gulf states.

BISQUE: A chowderlike seafood soup popular in coastal North Carolina and New Orleans.

BOBWHITE: Southern term for quail, which is also called *partridge.*

BOG: Any stew of the Carolina Lowcountry that contains wet, soggy rice (as opposed to perloo).

BURGOO: A thick stew of many meats and vegetables considered to be the state dish of Kentucky.

BUSTER CRAB: A soft-shell blue crab that has "busted" loose from its shell. Also called a *peeler.*

CAJUN COOKING: The robust country style of cookery of western Louisiana that makes heavy use of animal fats, dark roux, and spices.

CALAS: Hot, spongy Creole rice balls popular in New Orleans.

CAROLINA GOLD: Long-grain rice grown in coastal Carolina Lowcountry.

CHITLINS: Small pig intestines that are boiled, then battered and fried or added to soups and stews. Also called *chitterlings.*

CONCH: A mollusk in a large pink shell found in Florida waters and used to make fritters, chowders, and salads. Pronounced "conk."

CRAWDADDY: Louisiana slang for crawfish. Also *mudbug* and *yabby.*

CREOLE COOKING: The complex, sophisticated cooking style of New Orleans derived from French, Italian, Caribbean, and African traditions, with an emphasis on butter and cream.

CRISP: A fruit dessert topped with either a "rubbed" mixture of butter, sugar, flour, and nuts or mixed oats, butter, flour, and brown sugar. When a dry mixture is layered with fruit on top, the dessert becomes a Brown Betty. Also called a *crumble.*

CROQUETTE: A mixture of minced meat or poultry, cream, and seasonings formed into ovals, dipped in egg and breadcrumbs, and fried golden brown.

'CUE: Shortened term for *barbecue* in North Carolina.

DAMSON PLUM: A small, oval, bluish, very tart plum highly prized for preserves.

DEVILED: A cooking procedure whereby any food is made spicy with hot mustard, cayenne pepper, or Tabasco sauce.

DEWBERRY: A large variety of blackberry found mostly in Appalachia.

DIRTY RICE: Boiled long-grain rice with chicken livers and gizzards.

DIVINITY: A light, fluffy, creamy style of fudge made with sugar, corn syrup, and stiffly beaten egg whites and often enriched with nuts or coconut.

DRY-RUB: Any spiced dry mixture rubbed on meat and poultry to be barbecued.

ÉTOUFFÉE: A Louisiana Creole dish in which shellfish is "smothered" with liquid and cooked in a tightly closed vessel.

FIELD PEAS: General term for black-eyed, crowder, lady, and cowpeas.

FILÉ POWDER: Ground dried leaves of the sassafras tree used as a thickening and flavoring agent in Louisiana Creole and Cajun cookery.

GRILLADES: Creole dish of small pieces of beef or veal pounded thin and braised with tomatoes and other vegetables.

GRUNT: A cobbler steamed in a cast-iron skillet on top of the stove instead of being baked. Also *slump.*

GUINEA SQUASH: Louisiana term for eggplant.

GULLAH: A descendant of black plantation slaves on the South Carolina Sea Islands. Also, a pattern of black speech and style of cooking in that area.

HASH: In South Carolina, a thick meat gravy served over rice or grits as a main course.

HOECAKE: A flat corn griddle cake originally cooked on the metal end of a hoe over open fires by Indians and black slaves and today baked like cornbread.

HOG POT: A large pot of various pork cuts simmered slowly with cabbage and other vegetables and served at large social, religious, and political gatherings in Appalachia and the Deep South.

HOMINY: Dried yellow or white corn kernels from which the outer hull and germ have been removed. When ground, hominy becomes hominy grits or simply grits.

HOPPIN' JOHN: A dish of simmered black-eyed peas and some form of pork traditionally eaten on New Year's Day to bring good luck.

HOT BROWN: A special Kentucky open-face sandwich of bacon and tomato with a glazed creamy cheese sauce.

HUSH PUPPY: Small cornmeal and scallion dumplings that are deep-fried and served with seafood (especially fried catfish) and pork barbecue. Supposedly, the name refers to cooks during the Civil War who, to quiet hungry dogs, tossed them scraps of fried bread batter and admonished, "Hush, puppy!"

ICEBOX PIE: Any chilled pie (Key lime, black bottom, butterscotch, grasshopper) that's not subjected to a final baking.

KEY LIME: A small, yellowish, highly acidic lime indigenous to South Florida and the Keys.

LIVERMUSH: A mixture composed of 30 percent pork liver plus other pork meat and cornmeal and either fried in patties like sausage or chilled in blocks and sliced cold for sandwiches.

LOWCOUNTRY (or Low Country): The coastal region from Wilmington, North Carolina, to Savannah, Georgia. Often referred to as "Plantation Country," since this is where the great rice plantations flourished in the nineteenth century.

MALLARD: A green-headed, grain-eating species of wild duck highly prized in Southern cooking and particularly abundant in Arkansas and Louisiana.

MAQUE CHOUX: A Cajun combination of bacon, corn, okra, and other vegetables simmered together in a heavy skillet and served with grilled or roasted meats.

MOPPIN' SAUCE: A vinegar or tomato sauce "mopped" over pit-cooked barbecue.

MOUNTAIN OYSTERS: Pig's testicles that are breaded and deep-fried. Considered a delicacy in West Virginia, Tennessee, and Arkansas.

MULL AND MUDDLE: A robust seafood stew (or "mess of fish") found along North Carolina's Outer Banks.

PECTIN: A substance found naturally in many fruits that, when in perfect balance with acid and sugar, causes canned goods to gel. Also produced and packaged commercially.

PERLOO: Any meat, poultry, or vegetable stew of the Carolina Lowcountry that contains dry, fluffy rice (as opposed to a bog).

POT LIKKER: The flavorful, nutritious liquid in which greens and side meat are boiled and in which corn bread is dunked.

POLE BEAN: A broad, flat, slightly tough, very flavorful green bean with a fibrous string that requires long simmering. Also called *string bean* or *snap bean* (for the sound the bean makes when broken in pieces).

PULLED PORK: Pork pulled in shreds off a whole barbecued pig at an outdoor "pig pickin'"—most famously in North Carolina. Chopped pork barbecue is not the same as pulled pork.

PRALINE: A rich confection of white and brown sugar, butter, corn syrup, evaporated milk, and pecans found primarily in New Orleans but also popular in Florida and the Carolina Lowcountry.

PULLY BONE: A two-pronged bone cut from a fried chicken breast and pulled by two people to make a wish (granted to the person pulling the short end). Also called a *wishbone*.

RAMPS: Wild leeks that grow abundantly in the mountains of Tennessee and West Virginia.

SAD STREAK: A soft, sweet, undercooked streak of batter in a pound cake. Highly prized by many Southerners.

SALLY LUND: A rich tea cake thought to have originated in Bath, England.

SALT PORK: A salt-cured, fatty cut of pig's belly and sides used to flavor boiled beans and vegetables or rendered to make cracklin's.

SHE-CRAB: The female Atlantic blue crab used, along with its roe, to make South Carolina she-crab soup.

SIDE MEAT: Any form of fatty pork (streak-o'-lean, fatback, ham hock, bacon) used to season boiled beans, peas, and vegetables.

SKILLET BREAD: Any cornbread, biscuit, spoonbread, ash cake, hoecake, or johnnycake baked in a cast-iron skillet.

SCUPPERNONG: A thick-skinned, purple, musky grape used primarily to make a sweet wine.

SMOTHERED: A cooking technique (especially in Mississippi) whereby chicken, quail, or other birds are split, weighted in a cast-iron skillet, covered, and braised in gravy till fork-tender.

SOUL FOOD: Traditional African American fare including grits, collard greens, black-eyed peas, ham hocks, chitlins, and cornbread.

SOUR GRASS: Kentucky term for sorrel.

SNAPPIES: Green beans that are snapped in pieces for cooking.

SOUFFLÉ: Any savory dish that contains eggs and is baked in a casserole.

SOUSE: To pickle shellfish in vinegar, onions, and spices. Also, a chilled jellied hog's head cheese traditionally served at Christmas.

SOUTHERN COMFORT: A potent liqueur made from bourbon and peaches.

SPECS: Creamy-white butter beans speckled with red and purple.

SPOONBREAD: A puddinglike bread based on cornmeal, baked in a casserole, usually served as a side dish, and often soft enough to be eaten with a spoon.

SPOON DISH: Any fish chowder served along the Atlantic and Gulf coasts.

STRATA: Any layered meat or poultry casserole that contains bread cubes and cheese.

STREAK-O'-LEAN: Salt pork with streaks of lean meat. Used to season boiled beans, peas, and vegetables.

STREUSEL: A crumbly, sweet, spicy topping on breads, muffins, cakes, and coffee cakes.

SUN TEA: Iced tea steeped in full hot sunlight.

SYLLABUB: A light-cream, sugar, lemon, and Madeira concoction sipped as a drink, eaten as a dessert, or used as a topping for fresh fruit and cakes.

TASSO: Louisiana Cajun lean, cured, smoked, spiced pork. Used mainly to flavor beans, eggs, and pastas.

TURTLE BEANS: Black beans.

VIDALIA ONIONS: Marketed only in May and June and prized for their natural sweetness, genuine Vidalias must be grown in or around Vidalia, Georgia, and carry a tag of certification by the Vidalia Chamber of Commerce.

YA YA: An African term for rice used in Louisiana Cajun cookery.

Cocktail & Tea Foods

Pimento Cheese Spread

Kentucky Beer Cheese

Basil-Avocado Cheese Spread

Jezebel

Shrimp Paste with Gin

Pearl's Chicken Liver Spread

Chilled Country Ham Mousse

Spinach and Water Chestnut Dip

Hot Shrimp and Crab Dip

Shrimp Deviled Eggs

Cajun Popcorn
with Garlic Mayonnaise

Deviled Crabmeat Balls

Glazed Chicken Wings
with Blue Cheese Dip

Sausage-Stuffed Mushrooms

Country Ham
and Broccoli Tartlets

Blue Cheese Straws

Benne Bits

Pecan-Cheese Biscuits

Shrimp Toast

Cocktail Orange Pecans

Fried Dill Pickles

Vicksburg Tomato Sandwiches

Pimento Cheese Spread

Makes about 3 cups

"RUTH, HONEY," BAWLS "HOPPIN' JOHN" MARTIN
Taylor over the phone to Ruth Fales at the Pinckney Cafe
in Charleston, South Carolina. "I'm sending two hungry
friends over for pamenuh cheese sandwiches, so pile it
on heavy." Of course, every Southerner thinks he or she
knows what constitutes perfect pimento cheese, and
even the few non-Southerners who know what the
spread is can have a very resolute idea of how it should
be made. In the South, PC is used for sandwiches,
turned into dips and festive balls, and incorporated in
burgers and breads, but never is it more popular than
when spread on crackers or stuffed into celery for
cocktail parties. While self-styled experts add everything
to it from minced onion, garlic, hot peppers, and olives
to horseradish and Tabasco, I say there's still nothing
like the simple, classic PC that I make at least once a
week and keep in the refrigerator. Without question, it's
the most distinctive and sensual of all Southern spreads.

Contrary to what most people think, the large,
red, heart-shaped pimento pepper that plays
such an important role in Southern cooking is
not the same as its humbler cousin, the red
bell pepper. (Pimentos are indigenous to the
Americas and were taken back to Spain by
Columbus.) Today, virtually all pimentos are
canned in the states of Georgia and Tennessee,
making them available nationwide.

---

*½ pound extra-sharp white Vermont cheddar
cheese*

*½ pound extra-sharp New York State cheddar
cheese*

One 7-ounce jar pimentos, drained

½ teaspoon freshly ground black pepper

Salt to taste

Cayenne pepper to taste

⅔ cup mayonnaise

Finely grate the two cheeses into a mixing bowl. On a
plate, mash the pimentos well with a fork till they're
very pulpy. Add them to the cheeses along with the
pepper, salt, and cayenne, and mix till well blended.
Using a fork, fold in the mayonnaise and mash till the
spread is smooth, adding a little more mayonnaise if it
appears too dry.

Scrape the spread into a jar or crock, cover well, and
refrigerate for at least 2 hours before serving with
crackers or using to make pimento cheese finger
sandwiches. Keeps up to 1 week tightly covered in the
refrigerator.

KENTUCKY BEER CHEESE

Makes about 2½ cups

LEGEND HAS IT THAT THIS ADDICTIVE SPREAD/DIP
was created about a century ago in a Louisville saloon
and served with crackers to any customer ordering a
five-cent lager. Today in Kentucky, there are as many
varieties of beer cheese as hot browns, some spread on
crusty bread, crackers, and rye rounds, others used as
dips for raw vegetable sticks. It can be made with all
cheddar or a combination of cheeses, and each host or
hostess has his or her favorite (and secret) seasonings.
Since beer cheese keeps well, covered, in the refrigerator
for up to a week, I usually make it (like Pimento Cheese
Spread, opposite) in large quantities, ready to serve at
last-minute cocktail get-togethers or teas.

½ pound extra-sharp aged cheddar cheese

*One 8-ounce package cream cheese, at room
    temperature*

1 garlic clove, minced

1 tablespoon minced fresh chives

½ teaspoon dry mustard

1 tablespoon Worcestershire sauce

Tabasco sauce to taste

¼ teaspoon salt

1 cup lager beer

Shred the cheddar finely into a large mixing bowl, add
the cream cheese, and mash with a fork till well
blended. Add the garlic, chives, dry mustard,
Worcestershire, Tabasco, and salt and beat with an
electric mixer till well blended. Gradually add the beer,
beating till the spread is smooth. (To transform the
spread into a dip, beat in about ¼ cup more beer.)
Scrape into a crock, cover tightly, and chill overnight.

Serve the spread with toast points, crackers, or rye
rounds (or as a dip, with raw vegetable sticks).

3

Basil-Avocado Cheese Spread

Makes about 2 cups

I HAVE TWO FRIENDS IN ST. PETERSBURG, FLORIDA, who love fresh basil so much that they grow it year round in enormous whiskey barrels and use it to make everything but ice cream. While silky avocado–cream cheese spread is certainly nothing new at Southern cocktail parties, when my obsessed friends decided to perk it up with a little basil, it was transformed into a modern wonder. Serve the spread with a wide assortment of crackers or toasted bagel chips.

2 large ripe avocados, peeled, seeded, and cut into chunks

3 scallions (part of green tops included), chopped

⅓ cup chopped fresh parsley leaves

3 tablespoons chopped fresh basil leaves

2 garlic cloves, chopped

2 tablespoons fresh lime juice

Salt and freshly ground black pepper to taste

One and one-half 8-ounce packages cream cheese, cut into pieces and softened

In a blender or food processor, blend together the avocados, scallions, parsley, basil, garlic, lime juice, and salt and pepper till smooth. Scrape the mixture down the sides, add the cream cheese, and blend 1 minute longer. Scrape the spread into an attractive serving bowl, cover with plastic wrap, and chill at least 1 hour or till firm.

JEZEBEL

Makes about 3½ cups

I ASSUME THAT THIS UNIQUE, FIERY SPREAD WAS named after the evil biblical temptress, but whatever its linguistic source, Jezebel, which has as many variations as pimento cheese and shrimp paste, seems to be indigenous to piedmont North Carolina. My sister made a wicked Jezebel, but this one, created by an old friend in Charlotte, has to be one of the best I've ever been served. I've never seen the spread even mentioned in the most comprehensive Southern cookbooks.

One 18-ounce jar pineapple preserves (or, if necessary, peach preserves)

One 10-ounce jar apple jelly

¼ cup cider vinegar

2 tablespoons prepared horseradish

1 tablespoon cracked black peppercorns

1 teaspoon dry mustard

⅛ teaspoon salt

Two 8-ounce packages cream cheese

In a large bowl, combine the preserves, jelly, and vinegar and stir till well blended. Add the horseradish, peppercorns, mustard, and salt and stir till well blended. Chill the spread, covered, at least 2 hours, then spoon it over the cream cheese on two crystal serving plates or trays and serve with assorted crackers.

SHRIMP PASTE WITH GIN

Makes about 2 cups

WHEN I TOLD SAVANNAH FOOD EXPERT DAMON LEE
Fowler that I was putting a little gin in my shrimp paste, he simply frowned. When I told Charleston's major authority on Lowcountry cookery, "Hoppin' John" Martin Taylor, he raged, "Have you gone stark raving mad?" Heaven knows what either would say if I shared my conviction that shrimp paste might be traced back to English potted shrimps! In any case, on tea tables, at formal buffets and cocktail parties, and even for breakfast, shrimp paste has to be one of the most distinctive and sublime regional creations ever devised. The spread, made locally with tiny, sweet inlet shrimp, has been around for centuries, and while it does lend itself to different seasonings, modern versions that include everything from cream cheese to mayonnaise to canned soups should be outlawed. Serve the paste on benne (sesame) crackers or toast points.

1½ pounds fresh shrimp

½ lemon

3 tablespoons gin

1 tablespoon minced scallions (white parts only)

2 tablespoons fresh lemon juice

¼ teaspoon dry mustard

⅛ teaspoon ground mace or nutmeg

Pinch of cayenne pepper

8 tablespoons (1 stick) butter, softened

Salt and freshly ground black pepper to taste

Chopped fresh parsley leaves

Place the shrimp and lemon in a large saucepan with enough water to cover and bring to a boil. Remove from the heat, let stand for 1 minute, and drain. When the shrimp are cool enough to handle, peel, devein, and cut them in half.

In a blender or food processor, combine the boiled shrimp, gin, scallion, lemon juice, mustard, mace (or nutmeg), and cayenne and process just long enough to chop the shrimp coarsely. Transfer the mixture to a large mixing bowl, add the butter and salt and pepper, and mix with a wooden spoon till the shrimp mixture and butter are well blended. Pack the mixture into a crock, cover with plastic wrap, and chill at least 2 hours.

When ready to serve, sprinkle chopped parsley over the top.

PEARL'S CHICKEN LIVER SPREAD

Makes about 3 cups

ALTHOUGH PEARL BYRD FOSTER OPERATED ONE
of the most innovative and successful restaurants in
Manhattan (Mr. & Mrs. Foster's Place) during the 1960s
and 1970s, she never forgot her roots in Virginia, a fact
that was reflected in dishes such as this simple spread
she would whip up for private cocktail and wine
receptions. What makes the spread so Southern, of
course, is the cream cheese and bourbon, and if you
want to give it even more flavor dimension, add a pinch
or so of ground nutmeg.

3 tablespoons butter

2 scallions (white part only), finely chopped

1 small garlic clove, minced

*½ pound chicken livers, trimmed of membranes
   and cut in half*

*1½ cups skinned and shredded cooked chicken
   legs or thighs*

One 3-ounce package cream cheese, softened

*1 teaspoon finely chopped fresh tarragon leaves
   (or ¼ teaspoon dried)*

½ teaspoon salt

¼ teaspoon freshly ground black pepper

2 tablespoons bourbon

In a small skillet, melt the butter over moderately low
heat, then add the scallions, garlic, and livers and
cook, stirring, till the scallions are soft and the livers
just cooked through, about 5 minutes. Remove from
the heat and let cool slightly, then transfer to a blender
or food processor. Add the remaining ingredients and
blend till very smooth. Scrape the spread into a crock
or bowl, cover with plastic wrap, and chill 2 hours.
Serve the spread with crackers or Melba toast.

Chilled Country Ham Mousse

Makes about 5 cups

ALTHOUGH THIS IS NOT TECHNICALLY A REAL MOUSSE, that's what the wife of a country ham producer in Clinton, Kentucky, called the glistening crock resting in her refrigerator. "There's not much to do with the hard ends and fatty pieces of a ham except grind them up and use them in some type of spread," she informed us as we took a knife to the concoction. "And this mousse holds up any day to a good sippin' bourbon on the rocks." Right she was, and while I'm sure she would have frowned upon my discreet addition of Madeira to the recipe, I do think the wine gives the mousse an almost elegant touch. Southerners love any molded dish— savory or sweet—and this one would enhance any cocktail buffet.

4 tablespoons (½ stick) butter

¼ cup all-purpose flour

1 cup milk, heated

1 tablespoon Dijon mustard

¼ teaspoon powdered sage

Cayenne pepper to taste

¼ cup Madeira

2 large egg yolks

½ cup heavy cream

2 tablespoons unflavored gelatin

½ cup chicken broth

1 pound country ham, trimmed of fat and cut into chunks

Watercress for garnish

In a heavy saucepan, melt the butter over moderate heat, add the flour, and whisk the roux 1 minute. Gradually add the milk, reduce the heat to low, and whisk the mixture till very thick. Add the mustard, sage, cayenne, and Madeira and stir till very well blended.

In a small bowl, combine the egg yolks and heavy cream, whisk till well blended, and stir in a little of the hot sauce. Return the mixture to the hot sauce and continue cooking over low heat, whisking, till thickened.

In another small bowl, soften the gelatin in the chicken broth for 5 minutes, then stir it into the hot sauce. Place the ham into a meat grinder or food processor, grind finely, and stir into the sauce.

Pour the mixture into a 1-quart mold, cover with plastic wrap, and chill at least 6 hours. Unmold the mousse on a large serving dish, garnish the edges with watercress, and serve with rectangles of toast.

SPINACH AND WATER CHESTNUT DIP

Makes about 3 cups

SERVED HOT OR CHILLED WITH TOASTED BREAD
or Melba toast, this dip is beloved at cocktail receptions
all over the South and couldn't be easier to prepare. The
textural contrast between the soft spinach and cream
cheese and the crunchy water chestnuts is amazing.
Perhaps best of all, the dip can be made in advance and
frozen in smaller individual ramekins for future
entertaining emergencies.

2 tablespoons butter

4 scallions (part of green tops included), minced

2 garlic cloves, minced

*Two 10-ounce packages frozen chopped spinach,
    thawed*

½ cup milk

6 ounces cream cheese

4 ounces water chestnuts, drained and chopped

½ teaspoon Worcestershire sauce

Salt and freshly ground black pepper to taste

Tabasco sauce to taste

Preheat the oven to 400°F. Grease a 1½-quart shallow
baking dish and set aside.

In a large, heavy pot, melt the butter over moderate
heat, add the scallions and garlic, and cook, stirring,
about 5 minutes. Add the spinach, cover, and cook till
the spinach is completely wilted, about 8 minutes.
Transfer to a colander and drain well, pressing to
extract all liquid.

Add the milk to the pot used to wilt the spinach,
increase the heat slightly, and whisk in the cream
cheese till melted, about 3 minutes. Add the spinach
mixture, water chestnuts, Worcestershire, salt and
pepper, and Tabasco, stir till well blended, scrape the
mixture into the prepared baking dish, and bake till
bubbly, about 20 minutes.

Serve the dip hot, or let cool, then refrigerate till ready
to serve.

9

Cocktail and Tea Foods

HOT SHRIMP AND CRAB DIP

Makes about 5 cups

SEAFOOD DIPS AT COCKTAIL PARTIES HAVE ALWAYS been popular in the coastal Southern states. The only problem is that guests tend to overindulge when a dip such as this one is particularly enticing and served hot in a dramatic chafing dish. The evaporated milk does give the dip a smooth richness, and do feel free to use a little more sherry if you love the flavor of it with seafood as much as I do. Much less expensive (and sweeter) claw crabmeat can be substituted for the lump, as folks in Louisiana and Florida are prone to do, but be warned that this type must be picked over very carefully for shells and cartilage.

8 tablespoons (1 stick) butter, plus 1 tablespoon

¼ pound fresh mushrooms, stems trimmed and caps finely chopped

½ cup all-purpose flour

1 cup milk

¼ cup evaporated milk

2 teaspoons mild paprika

½ teaspoon freshly ground black pepper

Salt to taste

2 tablespoons dry sherry

1 tablespoon Worcestershire sauce

Dash of cayenne pepper

½ pound fresh lump crabmeat, picked over for shells and cartilage

½ pound shelled cooked shrimp, coarsely chopped

1 cup finely chopped fresh parsley leaves

In a small skillet, melt 1 tablespoon of the butter over moderate heat, add the mushrooms, and stir until tender, about five minutes. Remove pan from the heat.

In a medium, heavy saucepan, melt the remaining 7 tablespoons of butter over moderate heat, then add the flour and whisk till well blended. Gradually add the regular milk and evaporated milk, whisking constantly till the mixture is thickened and smooth. Add the paprika, pepper, and salt and whisk till well blended.

Remove pan from the heat, add the sherry, Worcestershire, and cayenne, and stir well. Fold in the crabmeat, shrimp, and mushrooms, mixing gently but well. Add the parsley, stir till well blended, and heat gently over low heat. Transfer the dip to a small chafing dish and serve hot with Melba toast rounds.

SHRIMP DEVILED EGGS

Makes 1 dozen deviled eggs

DEVILED EGGS ARE TO SOUTHERN RECEPTIONS WHAT chowder is to Northern clambakes, and never in all my wanderings around Dixie have I encountered more wondrous eggs than these once served at a cocktail buffet in Avery Island, Louisiana, when I was visiting the legendary McIlhenny family to learn about the production of Tabasco sauce. Actually, the filling was made with crawfish, but since, at the time, even frozen crawfish were unavailable outside the region, I wasted no time substituting shrimp when I returned home. Equally enticing about these deviled eggs are the capers, which add as much unusual flair as the shrimp. Do make note that, in the South, the special compartmentalized plates (in ceramic or glass) used to serve deviled eggs are as important as the eggs themselves. As one hostess uttered to me not long ago, "Anybody who serves deviled eggs on a plain ole white plate is just . . . tacky."

Louisiana produces around 100 million pounds of crawfish annually, three-quarters of which come from commercial ponds. The remainder comes from Cajun rice fields that are flooded every fall just for this purpose. What is not consumed regionally is frozen and marketed in other states.

---

6 extra-large eggs

6 large shrimp

3 tablespoons mayonnaise

1 teaspoon Dijon mustard

1 teaspoon fresh lemon juice

1 teaspoon capers, drained and finely chopped

1 teaspoon finely chopped fresh parsley leaves

Tabasco sauce to taste

2 teaspoons finely chopped fresh dill

Place the eggs in a large saucepan with enough water to cover. Bring to a boil, turn off the heat, cover, and let stand 10 minutes. Drain, add cold water to cover, and let stand 5 minutes.

Meanwhile, place the shrimp in a small saucepan with enough water to cover, bring to a boil, remove from the heat, and let stand 1 minute. Drain, add cold water to cover, and let stand 5 minutes.

Carefully peel the shells from the eggs. Cut the eggs in half lengthwise, place the yolks in a mixing bowl, and reserve the whites. Shell, devein, and chop the shrimp finely, then add to the egg yolks. Add the mayonnaise, mustard, lemon juice, capers, parsley, and Tabasco and mash the mixture with a fork till smooth. Fill the whites with equal amounts of the mixture, sprinkle dill over the tops, cover with plastic wrap, and chill till ready to serve.

Cajun Popcorn with Garlic Mayonnaise

Makes 6 to 8 servings

CAJUN POPCORN, ORIGINALLY POPULARIZED IN THE 1980s by chef Paul Prudhomme at K-Paul's Louisiana Kitchen in New Orleans, has to be one of the greatest innovations in modern Southern cookery and the ideal food for stylish cocktail parties. Since Paul served the crawfish with a thick sherry wine sauce at the restaurant, I have no idea how the garlic mayonnaise dip evolved; but today this seems to be the classic dip for the dish. The key to this spicy popcorn is to fry the crawfish as crispy as possible, so by no means should the temperature of the oil drop below 350°F. Crawfish tails can now be found frozen in better markets, but if they're unavailable, small fresh shrimp can be substituted with equal success. Be warned that this popcorn becomes soggy and lifeless when allowed to cool, so make every effort to serve it immediately after frying.

1 cup mayonnaise

1 garlic clove, minced

Tabasco sauce to taste

2 large eggs, beaten

1¼ cups milk

1 cup all-purpose flour

1 teaspoon sugar

1 teaspoon salt

1 teaspoon freshly ground black pepper

½ teaspoon cayenne pepper

½ teaspoon garlic powder

½ teaspoon onion powder

¼ teaspoon dried thyme, crumbled

⅛ teaspoon dried basil, crumbled

Vegetable oil for frying

2 pounds crawfish tails or small shrimp, peeled and deveined

In a small bowl, combine the mayonnaise, garlic, and Tabasco, stir till well blended, and set aside.

In another small bowl, combine the eggs and milk and whisk till well blended. In a large bowl, combine the flour, sugar, salt, two peppers, garlic powder, onion powder, thyme, and basil and mix well. Gradually whisk in the egg mixture till well blended and let the batter stand 1 hour.

In a large, heavy skillet or deep-fat fryer, heat 1 inch of oil to about 370°F (but not below 350°F) on a deep-fat thermometer. In batches, coat the seafood with the batter, fry in the hot oil, stirring, about 2 minutes or till golden and crisp, and drain on paper towels. Serve the popcorn hot with the garlic mayonnaise.

DEVILED CRABMEAT BALLS

Makes about 18 balls

"OH HONEY, THEY'RE REALLY NOTHING BUT PLAIN OLD deviled crab turned into fancy balls," our friend Maggie almost apologized as we sipped tea in the sunroom of her modest summer house on Chesapeake Bay, just south of Annapolis, Maryland. Technically, of course, she was right, but I defy any hostess to put out a plate of these sumptuous balls and not expect to see them disappear in a matter of minutes. The balls should be served as hot as possible. I have discovered, unfortunately, that the crabmeat mixture does not freeze well—it becomes mushy—so plan accordingly.

½ pound fresh lump crabmeat, picked over for shells and cartilage

1 tablespoon finely chopped scallions

1 tablespoon finely chopped green bell pepper

1 tablespoon finely chopped celery

1 tablespoon finely chopped fresh parsley leaves

2 tablespoons mayonnaise

1 teaspoon Dijon mustard

1 large egg, beaten

1 tablespoon fresh lemon juice

Salt and freshly ground black pepper to taste

⅛ teaspoon cayenne pepper

3 tablespoons fine, dry breadcrumbs

½ cup white cornmeal

Vegetable oil for deep-frying

In a large mixing bowl, combine the crabmeat with all remaining ingredients except the cornmeal and oil and stir till well blended, adding a bit more breadcrumbs if necessary to make a firm mixture. Shape the mixture into balls, using about 1 tablespoon of mixture per ball, then coat each ball lightly and evenly in the cornmeal.

Pour about 3 inches of oil into a heavy saucepan, heat to 375°F, fry the balls in batches till golden, about 2 minutes, and drain on paper towels. Serve hot.

Glazed Chicken Wings with Blue Cheese Dip

Makes 12 to 15 wings

HOW A NORTHERN DISH CREATED AT THE ANCHOR BAR in Buffalo, New York, back in 1964 (one source gives the date as early as 1940) gradually evolved to become a Southern staple at cocktail parties and receptions is a phenomenon that staggers the imagination. And why the original fried chicken wings came to be glazed and broiled in a region that thrives on fried foods only compounds the mystery. No matter. The South now claims chicken wings with blue cheese dip as still another star in its vast culinary repertory, and if Yankees don't like it, they're invited any time to come on down and see how well the dish goes with tumblers of bourbon and branch. By the way, never is any reference made to "Buffalo Chicken Wings" in the South.

THE DIP

½ cup crumbled blue cheese (such as Clemson Blue or Maytag)

½ cup mayonnaise

½ cup sour cream

¼ cup ketchup

2 tablespoons vegetable oil

2 teaspoons white vinegar

1 tablespoon finely chopped scallions

1 tablespoon finely chopped fresh parsley leaves

1 teaspoon dry mustard

Salt and freshly ground black pepper to taste

THE WINGS

12 to 15 chicken wings

6 tablespoons ketchup

2 tablespoons Tabasco sauce

4 tablespoons (½ stick) butter, melted

Salt and freshly ground black pepper to taste

To make the dip, combine all the ingredients in a blender or food processor and blend till smooth but still thick. Scrape dip into an attractive serving bowl, cover with plastic wrap, and chill till ready to serve.

Preheat the oven broiler.

To prepare the wings, remove and discard the tips, separate the first and second joints with a sharp knife, and place the wings on a heavy baking sheet. Broil about 4 inches from the heat till golden brown, about 20 minutes, turning once. Meanwhile, whisk together the ketchup, Tabasco, butter, and salt and pepper in a small bowl till well blended.

Transfer the wings to a large bowl and drain off the fat from the baking sheet. Pour the sauce over the wings and toss well. Return the wings to the baking sheet and broil again till nicely glazed, about 3 minutes. Serve hot with the bowl of dip.

Sausage-Stuffed Mushrooms

Makes 30 stuffed mushrooms

THROUGHOUT THE SOUTH, BAKED MUSHROOM CAPS are stuffed with everything from crabmeat to ground chicken to minced country ham for cocktail and tea parties, but never was I so impressed as when these mushrooms stuffed with spicy sausage were passed on silver trays at a country club reception I attended in Birmingham, Alabama. Since you do not want the mushrooms to be at all greasy, be sure to pour off all but about 1 tablespoon of grease after frying the sausage. If I can find giant mushrooms, I also like to serve two stuffed caps per person at a sit-down dinner, the tops sprinkled with finely chopped parsley.

30 medium fresh mushrooms

½ pound bulk sausage

1 tablespoon butter

3 scallions (part of green tops included), minced

1 cup sour cream

¼ teaspoon Worcestershire sauce

¼ teaspoon salt

½ teaspoon hot red pepper flakes

Preheat the oven to 350°F.

Rinse and dry the mushrooms, remove the stems and chop them finely, and arrange the caps in a shallow baking dish.

In a large skillet, fry the sausage over moderate heat, breaking it up, till crisp, about 10 minutes. Drain on paper towels and crumble finely. Pour off all but 1 tablespoon of grease from the skillet, add the butter, and let melt. Add the chopped mushroom stems and scallions, cook over low heat, stirring, about 5 minutes, and transfer to a small mixing bowl. Add the sour cream, Worcestershire, salt, and red pepper flakes and mix till well blended.

Spoon equal amounts of the mixture into the mushroom caps and bake till the tops are golden, about 20 minutes. Serve the mushrooms with heavy toothpicks.

Country Ham and Broccoli Tartlets

Makes 12 tartlets

THESE DAINTY TEA TARTLETS CAN BE MADE WITH
just flour, but I find that the cornmeal adds not only
delectable flavor but a much more interesting texture.
This is still another way Southerners use up either the
scraggly ends of a country ham or simply leftover ham.
Fresh asparagus tips or pieces of green or red bell
pepper can be substituted for the broccoli. Miniature
12-cup metal muffin pans are widely available and
indispensable in the Southern kitchen for tiny tarts
such as these.

2 ounces cream cheese

3 tablespoons butter, room temperature

⅓ cup all-purpose flour

⅓ cup white cornmeal

⅓ cup heavy cream

1 large egg

½ cup freshly grated Parmesan cheese

⅓ cup finely chopped country ham

12 tiny, fresh broccoli florets

1 tablespoon melted butter

In a bowl, stir together the cream cheese and butter till
well blended. Add the flour and cornmeal, stir till
smooth, cover with plastic wrap, and chill 1 hour.

Preheat the oven to 400°F. Grease the cups of a
miniature 12-cup muffin pan.

With your hands, roll the dough into 12 balls, place the
balls in the prepared muffin pan cups, press evenly on
the bottoms and up the sides, and set aside.

In a bowl, whisk together the cream and egg till well
blended. Add the Parmesan cheese and country ham,
and stir till well blended. Spoon the batter evenly into
the muffin cups and bake 8 minutes. Reduce the heat
to 300°F. Top each tartlet with a broccoli floret, brush
each floret lightly with melted butter, and bake till
golden, about 18 minutes.

16

Blue Cheese Straws

Makes about 6 dozen straws

I WAS VIRTUALLY RAISED EATING THE CHEDDAR cheese straws that my grandmother, mother, and aunt would bake for cocktail receptions, teas, and other social events, but it was only many years later that my friend, colleague, and neighbor Craig Claiborne introduced me to these tangy blue cheese straws he had learned to make in his native Mississippi. Aged extra-sharp cheddar cheese can certainly be substituted in this recipe, but the blue cheese straws are truly exceptional—and different. I like to make plenty of them.

8 tablespoons (1 stick) butter, at room temperature

½ pound blue cheese, at room temperature

1¾ cups all-purpose flour

Cayenne pepper to taste

1 teaspoon Worcestershire sauce

Preheat the oven to 325°F.

In a food processor, combine all the ingredients and blend thoroughly till the mixture is smooth.

Roll out the dough ⅛ inch thick and cut into individual strips about 4 inches long. Twist the strips into corkscrews (or other shapes), arrange on ungreased baking sheets, and bake 20 to 25 minutes or till the straws are crisp and lightly browned. Let cool. Store in tightly closed tins for up to two weeks.

17

BENNE BITS

Makes about 40 bits

BENNE (OR SESAME) SEEDS PLAY AN INTEGRAL ROLE in both savory and sweet dishes throughout the coastal Carolina and Georgia Lowcountry, and rare is the Charleston or Savannah cocktail reception or tea that doesn't include a bowl of these tiny nuggets, which are eaten almost like peanuts. Benne bits are available in tins all over Charleston (and by mail), but I've yet to taste a commercial product that can equal the freshly baked nuggets. Do be very careful not to burn the benne seeds, toasting them only till they're golden brown.

— ❧ ❧ ❧ —

South Carolina legend has it that when Africans were seized to serve as slaves on Low Country rice plantations in South Carolina, some put benne (sesame) seeds in their ears and later planted them in the Carolina soil as a reminder of their homeland. Today, benne seeds still play an integral role in the sophisticated cooking of Charleston.

— ❧ ❧ ❧ —

¼ cup benne (sesame) seeds

1 cup all-purpose flour

¼ teaspoon salt

Cayenne pepper to taste

4 tablespoons (½ stick) butter, chilled and cut into pieces

1 tablespoon milk

1 tablespoon water

Preheat the oven to 350°F.

Scatter the benne seeds evenly on a baking sheet and toast in the oven, stirring, till golden brown, about 10 minutes. Let cool.

In a mixing bowl, combine the flour, salt, and cayenne pepper. Add the butter in pieces and work with your fingertips till the mixture resembles coarse meal. Add the benne seeds, milk, and water and mix with your hands till the dough is smooth.

Roll out the dough on a floured surface about ¼ inch thick and cut it into 1-inch rounds. Place the rounds on an ungreased baking sheet and bake till golden, about 12 minutes. Let cool. Store in a tightly closed tin up to 2 weeks.

Pecan-Cheese Biscuits

Makes about 75 biscuits

NO MATTER THAT THESE SUMPTUOUS, ZESTY LITTLE rounds are not really biscuits—and I have no earthly idea why they're known by everybody all over the South as "biscuits" (the one exception being a strange lady I encountered in Mobile, Alabama, who called hers cheese "cookies"). What matters is that cheese biscuits, like toasted pecans, are the backbone of any respectable Southern cocktail party or afternoon tea, and that I personally couldn't exist without a tin of them in the kitchen at all times for nibbling. This particular recipe goes back generations in my family, with the only change being my discreet addition of Parmesan cheese. Just make sure you use aged, extra-sharp cheddar, genuine Parmesan, and pecans that are not in the least rancid.

½ pound (2 sticks) butter, at room temperature

6 ounces extra-sharp cheddar cheese, finely grated and brought to room temperature

2 ounces imported Parmigiano-Reggiano, finely grated

¼ teaspoon salt

Big dash of cayenne pepper

2 cups all-purpose flour

5 ounces fresh pecan halves

Preheat the oven to 350°F.

In a large mixing bowl, combine the butter, cheeses, salt, and cayenne pepper and mix with your hands till well blended. Add the flour gradually and mix with your hands till firm and smooth, adding a little more flour if the mixture is too sticky.

Roll pieces of dough into balls the size of large marbles and place on ungreased baking sheets about 1 inch apart. Press a pecan half into the center of each and bake till slightly browned but still fairly soft, about 20 minutes. Store biscuits in tightly sealed tins for up to 2 weeks.

SHRIMP TOAST

Makes 30 toasts

I HAVE NO IDEA WHEN, WHERE, OR WHY THIS DELICATE canapé became a staple at stylish Southern cocktail receptions, but I suspect it's been around for centuries and possibly originated with the first English settlers in Charleston and Savannah. I've seen shrimp toast served at an antebellum home outside Mobile, on silver trays in the Garden District of New Orleans, at a book party on Jekyll Island, Georgia, and, indeed, on many of my own mother's buffets. The toasts couldn't be more distinctive, and I only wish they could be frozen successfully (they can't) so I could make them in large quantities for future occasions.

½ pound fresh shrimp

1 small lemon, cut in half and seeded

2 scallions (green tops included), cut in half

5 whole water chestnuts

1 teaspoon prepared horseradish

Pinch of ground nutmeg

½ teaspoon salt

Freshly ground black pepper to taste

1 large egg white, at room temperature

10 slices white toast, crusts trimmed

Preheat the oven to 400°F.

Place the shrimp in a saucepan with enough water to cover, squeeze one lemon half into the water, then drop it in. Bring to a boil, remove from the heat, and let stand 1 minute. Drain. When cool enough to handle, peel and devein the shrimp.

Place the shrimp in a blender or food processor, add the juice of the remaining lemon half, the scallions, water chestnuts, horseradish, nutmeg, salt, and pepper and blend till the ingredients are finely ground. Scrape into a mixing bowl.

In a small bowl, beat the egg white with an electric mixer till stiff peaks form, then fold into the shrimp mixture.

Cut each slice of toast into three strips, spread each strip with the shrimp mixture, place the strips on one or two ungreased baking sheets, and bake till lightly browned, about 5 minutes. Serve hot or at room temperature.

Cocktail Orange Pecans

Makes 4 cups pecans

A FORMAL SOUTHERN COCKTAIL PARTY WITHOUT
a few crystal dishes of toasted, salted pecans scattered
about the room is simply not a serious cocktail party.
(When I recently attended a cocktail book party in
Manhattan sponsored by a contingent of high-livers from
Mississippi, I felt immediately at home when I spied no
fewer than four bowls of crisp pecans on various end
tables in the apartment.) This delectable variation with
orange liqueur and orange rind comes from my old
friend Stanley Dry in Louisiana, but when I exclaimed
about the nuts to my mother in North Carolina, she
discounted the idea with "Oh honey, I've been toasting
orange pecans for years."

½ pound (2 sticks) butter

*3 tablespoons orange liqueur (such as Cointreau
or Grand Marnier)*

1 tablespoon finely grated orange rind

1½ pounds pecan halves

1 tablespoon salt

Preheat the over to 300°F.

In a large saucepan, melt the butter over moderate
heat, add the liqueur and orange zest, and stir till well
blended. Remove the pan from the heat, add the
pecans, and toss to coat well. Spread the nuts evenly
on a large baking sheet and toast in the oven,
uncovered, till golden brown, about 30 minutes, tossing
the nuts from time to time. Drain on paper towels,
sprinkle salt on top, let cool completely, and serve in
crystal bowls with cocktails. (The pecans keep in a
tightly covered container for up to 2 weeks before
possibly turning rancid.)

FRIED DILL PICKLES

Makes about 2 dozen pickle chips

AT THE HOLLYWOOD CAFE IN TUNICA, MISSISSIPPI—
where fried dill pickles were created in 1969 and where
enthusiasts still flock just to order them—this unusual
dish is served with a secret ranch dipping sauce
primarily as an appetizer before plate lunch specials of
fried catfish, fried shrimp, fried chicken, and the like.
(As for the actual conception of the specialty, "One day
we'd 'bout run out of food and were hungry, so somebody
just cut up some dill pickles, and battered 'em, and fried
'em up," explains owner "Big Man" Bobby Windham.)
Today, you'll find fried dill pickles at C.S.'s Bar in
Jackson, Mississippi, Sherman's Restaurant in
Greenville, Mississippi, Green's Barbecue in Red Level,
Alabama, and at places all over Arkansas, but don't even
bother asking about them farther north or east. These
pickles do make a great appetizer (with a dipping
sauce), but I like them even more served with cocktails
(without a sauce) in a basket lined with paper napkins.

1 cup buttermilk

1 large egg

1 cup all-purpose flour

1 teaspoon baking powder

½ teaspoon salt

Vegetable oil for deep frying

*4 large, crisp dill pickles, cut widthwise
into ¾-inch chips*

In a bowl, whisk together the buttermilk and egg till
well blended. In another bowl, whisk together the flour,
baking powder, and salt, add to the buttermilk mixture,
and stir till well blended and smooth.

In a medium cast-iron skillet, heat about 2 inches of
oil to 375°F. Dip the pickle chips in the batter, fry a few
at a time in the oil till golden brown, about 3 minutes,
drain on paper towels, and serve hot.

22

VICKSBURG TOMATO SANDWICHES

WHILE A SILVER PLATTER OF TINY TOMATO SANDWICHES has always been popular at cocktail parties and teas all over the South when summer tomatoes are at their peak, in Mississippi the "Vicksburg Tomato Sandwich" is deemed such a special delicacy that it actually takes on important social significance. There is a right and wrong way to make a Vicksburg tomato sandwich, and here's the right way in the actual words of one very fastidious hostess:

"You take a small, round cookie cutter and cut rounds of fresh white bread (no trace of crusts). These you spread liberally with real mayonnaise. Then you slice very thinly a perfectly ripened tomato (not refrigerated and with the skin removed) the exact same size as the rounds of bread, and carefully drain the slices between paper towels so they don't get runny and make the sandwich soggy. Place a slice of tomato evenly on each round of bread, salt and pepper the slices to taste, and, if you feel like being a little creative, you might add a pinch of minced garlic or, if you're very daring, even a sprinkling of curry powder. Serve the sandwiches on a polished silver plate."

She then adds, "If you don't serve tomato sandwiches at cocktail parties and gracious teas in Vicksburg during the summertime, you will be *discussed.*"

Appetizers

Crab Cakes with Mustard Sauce

Crabmeat Dewey

Mushrooms Stuffed with
Crabmeat and Pimento

Creole Crabmeat Ravigote

Florida Crab and Corn Fritters

Crabmeat au Gratin

Savannah Deviled Crab

Baltimore Bacon Oysters

Pickled Coon Oysters

Smoky Oysters

Ocracoke Clam Fritters

Shrimp Cakes with
Spicy Tartar Sauce

Georgia-Style Pickled Shrimp

Julia's Shrimp Remoulade

Creole Shrimp Ravigote

Miami Barbecued Shrimp

Paul's Coconut Beer Shrimp

Charleston Hobotee

Kentucky Hot Browns

Dilled Salmon Quiche

Deep-Dish Apple
and Cheddar Quiche

Vidalia Onion and
Goat Cheese Pie

Chicken Drumettes

Okra with Mustard Sauce

Okra Fritters with
Thousand Island Dressing

CRAB CAKES WITH MUSTARD SAUCE

Makes 6 servings

I'VE EATEN CRAB CAKES AT OBRYCKI'S IN BALTIMORE, Harris Crab House in Grasonville, Maryland, King Neptune's in Gulf Shores, Alabama, The Wreck in Mount Pleasant, South Carolina, and dozens of other celebrated Southern crab houses, but the only ones that could touch Louis Osteen's small wonders at his restaurant on Pawleys Island, South Carolina (made today with both crab and lobster) were the simple cakes served at Jimmy Cantler's Riverside Inn in Annapolis, Maryland. "Just crabmeat, mayonnaise, a few bread crumbs and onions, and seasonings," was all the waiter would volunteer in the way of a recipe, so I had to depend on my taste buds and imagination to reproduce these appetizer cakes. You can certainly serve them without the mustard sauce, but I think the sauce gives them a real flair without detracting in the least from the sweet crabmeat. To keep the cakes light as a feather, mix them very gently.

THE MUSTARD SAUCE

8 tablespoons (1 stick) butter, cut into pieces

3 tablespoons fresh lemon juice

3 large egg yolks

Freshly ground black pepper to taste

2 tablespoons water

2 tablespoons Dijon mustard

THE CRAB CAKES

1 cup mayonnaise

1 large egg white

1 tablespoon fresh lemon juice

1 tablespoon minced scallions

3 tablespoons finely crushed soda crackers

⅛ teaspoon cayenne pepper

1½ pounds fresh lump crabmeat, picked over for shells and cartilage

¾ cup fine bread crumbs

4 tablespoons (½ stick) butter

To make the mustard sauce, combine the butter, lemon juice, egg yolks, and black pepper in a heavy saucepan over low heat and whisk rapidly and constantly till the mixture thickens. Whisk in the water, remove pan from the heat, and let cool slightly. Add the mustard and whisk till the sauce is well blended and smooth. Keep warm.

To make the crab cakes, combine the mayonnaise, egg white, lemon juice, scallions, cracker crumbs, and cayenne pepper in a mixing bowl and whisk till well blended. Add the crabmeat and toss very gently. Divide the mixture into 6 equal portions and gently shape each into a small but fairly thick patty. Spread the bread crumbs on a baking sheet and coat the patties lightly but securely. Chill the patties, covered, at least 1 hour.

When ready to serve, heat the butter in a large, heavy skillet, add the crab cakes, and sauté over moderate heat 3 minutes on each side or till golden brown. Serve each cake with about 1 tablespoon of the mustard sauce spooned over the top.

Crabmeat Dewey

Makes 6 servings

CREATED OVER A CENTURY AGO AT A MARYLAND YACHT club to commemorate Commodore George Dewey's victory at Manila Bay in the Spanish-American War, Crabmeat Dewey has come down as one of the true wonders of Southern cookery. Served in handsome ramekins as the first course of a stylish meal, the dish is right up there with shrimp remoulade and hobotee. I also like to serve crabmeat Dewey in a large casserole as a main course with no more than cole slaw, pickled peaches, and hot biscuits.

3 tablespoons butter

1 pound fresh mushrooms, finely chopped

1 medium green bell pepper, seeded and finely chopped

2 scallions (white part only), finely chopped

½ cup sweet sherry

3 tablespoons chopped pimentos

1½ cups half-and-half

Salt and freshly ground black pepper to taste

1½ pounds fresh lump crabmeat, picked over for shells and cartilage and flaked

1 cup freshly grated Parmesan cheese

Preheat the oven to 350°F. Butter 6 attractive 2-cup ramekins and set aside.

In a large skillet, melt the butter over moderate heat, add the mushrooms, bell pepper, and scallions, and cook, stirring, for 3 minutes. Add the sherry and simmer till the liquid is reduced by half, about 5 minutes. Add the pimentos and half-and-half, season with salt and pepper, and bring almost to a boil. Add the crabmeat, reduce the heat to low, and stir till well blended.

Scrape the mixture into the prepared ramekins, sprinkle the cheese equally over the tops, and bake till lightly browned, 15 to 20 minutes.

27

Mushrooms Stuffed with Crabmeat and Pimento

Makes 6 servings

IN THE SOUTH, ALL SORTS OF MINCED SHELLFISH, meats, and vegetables are stuffed into large mushroom caps, baked, and served as a first course, but nothing typifies this old-fashioned practice more than these rich, full-flavored crabmeat mushrooms enhanced with pimentos and grated Parmesan. To give the mixture a bit of crunch, you might want to add a few finely chopped toasted almonds, if you have any on hand.

12 large button mushrooms (about 1 pound), wiped clean

4 tablespoons (½ stick) butter

1 tablespoon all-purpose flour

½ cup half-and-half

3 scallions (white part only), finely chopped

½ pound fresh claw crabmeat, picked over for shells and cartilage

2 tablespoons finely chopped pimentos

1 large egg, beaten

Salt and freshly ground black pepper to taste

2 tablespoons butter, melted

¼ cup freshly grated Parmesan cheese

Preheat the oven to 375°F.

Remove stems from the mushrooms and chop finely, reserving the caps.

In a small saucepan, melt 1 tablespoon of the butter over moderate heat, add the flour, and whisk for 1 minute. Add the half-and-half, whisk till the sauce is smooth, and set aside.

In another medium saucepan, heat the remaining 3 tablespoons butter over moderate heat, add the chopped mushroom stems and the scallions, and cook, stirring, for 5 minutes. Add the crabmeat and pimentos and stir to blend. Add the white sauce, egg, and salt and pepper, stir till well blended, and set aside.

Arrange the mushroom caps hollow side down in a buttered baking dish. Brush with the melted butter, bake 10 minutes, and let cool. Stuff the mushroom cavities with equal amounts of the crabmeat mixture, sprinkle the tops with cheese, and bake till golden, about 20 minutes.

CREOLE CRABMEAT RAVIGOTE

Makes 4 to 6 servings

RAVIGOTER IN FRENCH MEANS "TO INVIGORATE," and the earliest Creole cooks took the word at face value when they came up with this fiery crab salad that traditionally contains not only horseradish but two styles of hot mustard. Although a few venerable New Orleans restaurants such as Antoine's and Commander's Palace still serve crabmeat ravigote, the delectable appetizer is generally not as popular as it once was, due, most likely, to dubious efforts by certain trendy chefs to transform Creole cuisine at the expense of many classic tastes. No matter, for I'm convinced that, in the long run, dishes such as crabmeat ravigote will be around long after most of the new conceits are forgotten. And, by the way, this also makes a delightful luncheon salad.

¾ cup mayonnaise

¼ cup Creole mustard

1 teaspoon dry mustard

2 scallions (part of green tops included), minced

1 hard-boiled large egg, finely chopped

1 tablespoon chopped drained capers

1½ teaspoons prepared horseradish

2 teaspoons Worcestersire sauce

Salt and freshly ground black pepper to taste

1½ pounds fresh lump crabmeat, picked over for shells and cartilage

Bibb lettuce leaves, shredded

In a large bowl, combine the mayonnaise, two mustards, scallions, egg, capers, horseradish, Worcestershire, and salt and pepper and mix till well blended. Add the crabmeat and mix gently till well coated, taking care not to break it up. Chill, covered, about 1 hour, then serve on beds of shredded lettuce.

Florida Crab and Corn Fritters

Makes 6 servings

JOHNNY EARLES IS ONE OF THE MOST CREATIVE CHEFS in the South. At Criolla's restaurant in Grayton Beach, between Pensacola and Panama City, Florida, my friends and I sampled numerous items on his innovative menu, but what caught my attention most were the crab and corn fritters made with buttermilk and ricotta cheese. I've adapted the recipe somewhat, adding a bit of spice and adjusting some of the ingredients. The fritters are so moist and delicious by themselves that I see no need in serving them with a remoulade sauce, as the restaurant does. Do so if you like, using the recipe in Julia's Shrimp Remoulade (page 39).

1 cup yellow cornmeal

½ cup all-purpose flour

1½ teaspoons baking powder

1 teaspoon baking soda

Salt and cayenne pepper to taste

2 large eggs, beaten

1 cup ricotta cheese

⅓ cup buttermilk

1½ tablespoons fresh lime juice

4 tablespoons (½ stick) butter

1½ cups corn kernels (fresh or frozen and thawed)

½ cup finely chopped red bell pepper

2 scallions (part of green tops included), finely chopped

1 pound fresh lump crabmeat, picked over for shells and cartilage and flaked

Vegetable oil

In a large bowl, combine the cornmeal, flour, baking powder, baking soda, and salt and cayenne pepper and stir till well blended. In a small bowl, combine the eggs, cheese, buttermilk, and lime juice and stir till well blended. Add to the dry ingredients, stir till the batter is well blended and smooth, and set aside.

In a medium skillet, melt the butter over moderate heat, add the corn, bell pepper, and scallions and cook, stirring, till softened, 4 to 5 minutes. Add the cooked vegetables and crabmeat to the batter, stir gently with a fork till well mixed, and form the mixture into 6 oval patties.

In a large, heavy skillet, heat about ¼-inch of oil over moderately high heat, cook the patties about 3 minutes on each side or till golden, and drain on paper towels. Serve hot.

CRABMEAT AU GRATIN

Makes 4 servings

FOR AS LONG AS I CAN REMEMBER, CRABMEAT
au gratin has been considered the quintessential "fussy"
appetizer in upscale restaurants, gracious homes, and
country clubs throughout the South (despite there not
being one thing fussy about the dish). I readily admit
that I could eat it every day of my life. Normally, I use
only aged, extra-sharp cheddar cheese in cooking, but
not for crabmeat au gratin since it overwhelms the
crabmeat. Likewise with the sherry, which adds sensual
depth, so long as it's used discreetly. This is a rich
appetizer, so plan your meal accordingly.

1 cup half-and-half

1 cup grated mild cheddar cheese

2 tablespoons Worcestershire sauce

1 tablespoon dry sherry

1 teaspoon Tabasco sauce

Salt and freshly ground black pepper to taste

3 tablespoons all-purpose flour

2 tablespoons butter, softened

*¾ pound fresh lump crabmeat, picked over for
    shells and cartilage and flaked*

½ cup dry bread crumbs

2 tablespoons melted butter

In a heavy saucepan, combine the half-and-half,
cheese, Worcestershire, sherry, Tabasco, and salt and
pepper and bring to a simmer over moderate heat,
stirring till the cheese is melted and well incorporated.
In a small bowl, knead together the flour and butter till
a paste forms, then whisk the paste by bits into the
cream mixture till thickened. Add the crabmeat and
stir till the mixture is hot.

Preheat the oven broiler and butter four ½-cup
ramekins.

Spoon equal amounts of the mixture into the four
ramekins, lightly sprinkle bread crumbs over the top of
each, and drizzle melted butter over the crumbs. Place
the ramekins on a heavy baking sheet and run under
the broiler about 3 inches from the heat till just
golden, about 1 minute. Serve hot.

SAVANNAH DEVILED CRAB

Makes 4 servings

I'VE ALWAYS SAID THAT DEVILED CRAB CAN BE THE worst or most delicious Southern dish imaginable, depending on the quality of the crabmeat, the amount of breading (filler), and whether the texture is inexcusably dry or sumptuously moist. What I've found distinguishes the best Savannah, Georgia, deviled crab from most you find along the Carolina, Florida, and Gulf coasts is not only the use of freshly steamed whole blue crabs but also the very sensible addition of cream to the mixture. If only commercially packed fresh crabmeat is practical, opt for the claw meat over the backfin lump; it may be more difficult to pick over for shells but it's moister, sweeter, and much less expensive. Serious Savannah cooks pack their mixtures into crab backs to preserve as much moisture and sweetness as possible, but scallop shells or small ramekins work just as well, so long as you don't overbake. Wrapped tightly in aluminum foil, the packed shells can be frozen and reheated when ready to serve.

4 tablespoons (½ stick) butter

⅓ cup minced Vidalia onion

½ cup heavy cream

2 tablespoons sweet sherry

1 teaspoon minced fresh chives

½ teaspoon minced hot chile pepper

½ teaspoon dry mustard

½ teaspoon Worcestershire sauce

Salt and freshly ground black pepper to taste

½ pound fresh claw crabmeat, picked over for shells and cartilage

2 large egg yolks, lightly beaten

¼ cup dry bread crumbs

Preheat the oven to 425°F.

In a medium skillet, melt 2 tablespoons of the butter over moderate heat, add the onion, and cook, stirring, till softened, about 2 minutes. Add the heavy cream, sherry, chives, chile pepper, dry mustard, Worcestershire, and salt and pepper and cook, stirring, 2 to 3 minutes. Stir in the crabmeat, remove from the heat, then stir in the egg yolks till well incorporated.

Divide the mixture among four buttered scallop shells or small ramekins, sprinkle 1 tablespoon of bread crumbs on each serving, dot with pieces of the remaining 2 tablespoons of butter, and bake till the crumbs are golden and the mixture is bubbling, about 10 minutes. Serve hot.

32

Baltimore Bacon Oysters

Makes 6 servings

IN THE EARLY TWENTIETH CENTURY, WHEN BALTIMORE boasted more than two dozen breweries, it became a practice in the city's bars to offer free oysters to anyone ordering local beer. Usually, they were simply on the half shell, but as the tradition developed and competition for business heated up, some bars came up with novel ways to serve the oysters that would attract customers. I like to think that this is the way the blissful marriage of oysters and bacon was first conceived. Do be careful not to overcook the oysters, which toughens them.

6 slices lean bacon, cut in half crosswise

4 tablespoons (½ stick) butter

*1½ pints fresh shucked oysters, drained and
    1 cup of liquor reserved*

1½ tablespoons all-purpose flour

1 teaspoon prepared horseradish

Salt and freshly ground black pepper to taste

Toast points

In a medium skillet, fry the bacon over moderate heat till crisp, drain on paper towels, crumble, and reserve. Drain all but about 1 tablespoon of grease from the skillet, melt the butter in the grease, add the oysters, and sauté about 1 minute on each side or till the edges begin to curl. Transfer the oysters to a plate.

Add the flour to the skillet and cook over moderate heat for 2 minutes, stirring constantly. Add the reserved oyster liquor plus the horseradish and salt and pepper and cook, stirring constantly, till the sauce thickens, about 3 minutes. Remove pan from the heat, add the oysters, and heat well.

To serve, arrange the oysters on toast points, spoon a little sauce over each, and top with sprinklings of crumbled bacon.

PICKLED COON OYSTERS

Makes 6 servings

ON FLORIDA'S EAST AND WEST COASTS, COON OYSTERS (so called because raccoons are their main predator) attach their oval, ridged shells to the coral of shallow waters and are considered one of the state's great delicacies. Naturally, the oysters are often eaten on the half shell all along the two coasts, but never did I relish anything so much as the pickled ones that the wife of a retired Greek restaurateur I know in Sarasota prepared as a first course at a very fancy dinner. To prevent discoloration, be sure to use only white vinegar for this recipe.

2 pints fresh shucked oysters (liquor included)

1½ cups white vinegar

1 large onion, chopped

2 garlic cloves, crushed

6 sprigs fresh parsley

2 teaspoons mixed pickling spices

1 bay leaf

¼ cup olive oil

1 lemon, cut into quarters and seeded

Salt and freshly ground black pepper to taste

In a large, stainless-steel or enameled saucepan, combine the oysters and their liquor, bring to a brisk simmer, and cook just till their edges begin to curl, about 5 minutes. With a slotted spoon, transfer the oysters to a large bowl of cold water; let stand 5 minutes, reserving the liquor in the pan. Drain the oysters, arrange in a large, shallow ceramic or glass baking dish, and place in the refrigerator.

Add the remaining ingredients to the liquor in the pan, bring to a boil, reduce the heat to low, and simmer 30 minutes. Strain the liquid through a fine-mesh strainer into a small mixing bowl, let cool to room temperature, then pour over the refrigerated oysters. Cover with plastic wrap and chill overnight.

Remove the oysters from their marinade and serve cold with small oyster forks.

34

Smoky Oysters

Makes 6 servings

GONE ARE THE DAYS WHEN VIRGINIA OYSTERS (*Crassostrea virginica*) as big as goose eggs were plentiful from Chesapeake Bay down to Florida, and oyster houses in New Orleans, Mobile, and Biloxi overflowed with customers devouring fat Apalachicolas and Bon Secours for a dime a dozen. All Southern oysters might be scarce and expensive today compared with the bivalve's golden age 150 years ago, but this reality doesn't seem to have fazed coastal cooks in the least, one of whom, in Wilmington, North Carolina, has demonstrated for me at least half a dozen ways to cook local oysters in casseroles and at oyster roasts. These particular smoky devils might well be served as a main course, but once when I did just that, two close friends didn't hesitate to ask, "What's next?" If you don't have sherry on hand to sprinkle over the top, use a light rum.

6 strips lean bacon

1½ pints fresh shucked oysters, liquor included

1½ cups half-and-half

2½ cups crumbled soda crackers

12 tablespoons (1½ sticks) butter, melted

Salt and freshly ground black pepper to taste

Tabasco sauce to taste

Preheat the oven to 350°F. Butter a 1½-quart casserole and set aside.

In a medium skillet, fry the bacon over moderate heat till almost crisp, drain on paper towels, and crumble.

Drain the oysters, saving about ½ cup of the liquor. In a medium mixing bowl, combine the liquor and half-and-half, stir well, and set aside. In another medium bowl, combine the cracker crumbs and butter, season with salt and pepper and Tabasco, and set aside.

Sprinkle about a third of the cracker crumbs over the bottom of the prepared casserole, arrange half the oysters on top, sprinkle half the bacon over the oysters, and pour half the liquor mixture over the top. Add another third of the crumbs, arrange the remaining oysters on top, sprinkle on the remaining bacon, pour on the remaining liquor mixture, and top with the remaining crumbs. Bake till bubbly and lightly browned, about 35 minutes.

35

OCRACOKE CLAM FRITTERS

Makes 4 servings

FRESH SOFT-SHELL CLAMS ("STEAMERS") ARE STILL fried at seafood shacks all over Ocracoke Island on North Carolina's Outer Banks in much the same manner they were when the Manteo Indians inhabited the region centuries ago. However, since most clams that are iced and shipped to markets around the country tend to be tough and stringy (and often off-flavored), I've come to prefer the perfectly acceptable and tender baby ones that are canned. Be warned that the fritters will toughen quickly if fried more than about a minute on each side, and they must be served as hot as possible. Out on Ocracoke, locals eat the fritters (mounds of them!) mainly by themselves, but I must say I love to dip mine in a little tartar sauce.

THE TARTAR SAUCE

1 cup mayonnaise

1 tablespoon drained sweet pickle relish

1 tablespoon minced fresh parsley leaves

1 tablespoon minced scallion

2 teaspoons drained, minced capers

1 teaspoon Dijon mustard

THE FRITTERS

½ cup all-purpose flour

1 teaspoon baking powder

Salt to taste

Cayenne pepper to taste

*1 tablespoon finely chopped fresh dill
    (or 1 teaspoon dried dill weed)*

1 cup canned baby clams, drained

2 large eggs, separated

Vegetable oil for frying

To make the tartar sauce, mix together all the ingredients in a bowl and let stand at room temperature for 15 minutes. Chill until ready to use.

To make the fritters, sift together the flour, baking powder, salt, and cayenne pepper in a bowl and stir in the dill. Add the clams and egg yolks and mix till well blended. In another bowl, beat the egg whites with an electric mixer till stiff but not dry peaks form and fold them into the clam mixture.

In a large skillet or electric fry pan, heat 1 inch of oil to 325°F or till a small piece of bread tossed in browns quickly. Drop the clam batter by tablespoons into the oil and cook till the fritters are browned, about 1 minute. With a slotted spoon, turn the fritters over and cook till the other sides are browned, 1 minute longer. Drain on paper towels, then serve the fritters immediately with tartar sauce on the side.

SHRIMP CAKES WITH SPICY TARTAR SAUCE

Makes 6 servings

LINDA CARMAN, FORMER DIRECTOR OF MARTHA WHITE Kitchens in Nashville, Tennessee, not only knows all there is to know about Southern flour but can go on and on in her thick drawl about any particular Southern dish that sparks her passion. So when she began describing in detail the shrimp cakes with spicy tartar sauce that somebody had served as a first course at a luncheon she'd attended, I wasted no time trying to reproduce the recipe. Suffice it to say that these cakes are as sumptuous as any made with the finest crabmeat— and at a fraction of the cost.

THE SHRIMP CAKES

1½ pounds fresh medium shrimp

1 small lemon, cut in half

½ cup finely diced scallions (part of green tops included)

¼ cup finely diced celery

¼ cup finely diced green bell pepper

3 tablespoons minced fresh parsley leaves

1 tablespoon mayonnaise

1 tablespoon butter, melted

1 large egg, beaten

2 teaspoons Worcestershire sauce

Salt and cayenne pepper to taste

3 cups cornbread crumbs or soft bread crumbs

2 tablespoons butter

2 tablespoons vegetable oil

THE TARTAR SAUCE

1 cup mayonnaise

2 tablespoons minced sweet pickle

1 tablespoon minced fresh chives

1 small red chile pepper, seeded and minced

1 tablespoon drained capers, finely chopped

To make the shrimp cakes, place the shrimp and lemon in a pot with enough water to cover. Bring to a boil, remove from the heat, cover, and let stand 1 minute. Drain, discard the lemon, and when the shrimp are cool enough to handle, peel, devein, and chop them finely.

In a large bowl, combine the shrimp, scallions, celery, bell pepper, parsley, mayonnaise, melted butter, egg, Worcestershire, salt and pepper, and 1 cup of the cornbread crumbs and stir till well blended. Form the mixture into 6 round or oval cakes and coat with the remaining crumbs. Place on a platter, cover with plastic wrap, and chill 1 hour.

Meanwhile, to make the tartar sauce, combine all the ingredients in a bowl, mix till well blended, and set aside.

In a large, heavy skillet, heat the butter and oil over moderate heat till a few crumbs tossed in sputter, add the shrimp cakes, and cook 3 minutes on each side till golden. Drain on paper towels and serve hot with dollops of sauce on top of each.

Georgia-Style Pickled Shrimp

Makes 6 servings

EVERY REGION OF THE SOUTH HAS ITS OWN distinctive ways of pickling shrimp, oysters, mussels, and the like, but this Georgia method of pickling shrimp and serving them with a spicy cream sauce as an appetizer seems unique and recalls for me an incredible feast served by relatives of my mother in Monticello. "Oh honey, you do carry on," said Cuddin' Berta when I exclaimed about the dish. "You're too young to remember, but you should have tasted the buttermilk sauce Sister Tancy used to put on her shrimp over in Macon."

1½ pounds fresh medium shrimp

1 lemon, cut in half

2 tablespoons pickling spices

3 bay leaves

2 cups cider vinegar

1 cup vegetable oil

½ teaspoon dry mustard

2 teaspoons salt

1 cup sour cream

2 teaspoons prepared horseradish

1 teaspoon fresh lemon juice

Salt and freshly ground black pepper to taste

Tabasco sauce to taste

6 leaves Bibb lettuce

Place the shrimp in a large pot with enough water to cover. Add the lemon, pickling spices, and bay leaves. Bring to a boil, remove from the heat, cover, and let stand 2 minutes. Drain through a fine-mesh strainer, pick out and discard the lemon, and, when cool enough to handle, peel and devein the shrimp. Place the shrimp, pickling spices, and bay leaves in a large bowl. Add the vinegar, oil, dry mustard, and salt, and toss well. Cover with plastic wrap and chill at least 2 hours or overnight.

To make the sauce, combine the sour cream, horseradish, lemon juice, salt and pepper, and Tabasco and mix till well blended.

To serve, arrange equal amounts of shrimp on the lettuce leaves and top each portion with dollops of the sauce.

Julia's Shrimp Remoulade

Makes 6 servings

JULIA REED, AN AUTHOR WHO HAILS FROM GREENVILLE, Mississippi, but lives in New Orleans, knows a thing or two about Creole cooking in general, and everything about shrimp remoulade in particular. Remoulade dressing, of course, is one of the glories of Southern cuisine, and for years, I believed that the finest versions were found in such venerable New Orleans restaurants as Galatoire's, Broussard's, and Commander's Palace. Then, when I tasted Julia's, I flipped. "Basically, it's my take on Paul Prudhomme's dressing," she confessed, "but, you know, I do like to fiddle around a little bit." Well, her take involves substituting Dijon mustard for ordinary yellow mustard, and white wine vinegar for plain white vinegar, but the way she's really transformed the dressing is by adding capers.

THE DRESSING

2 large egg yolks

¼ cup vegetable oil

½ cup finely chopped scallions

½ cup finely chopped celery

¼ cup chopped fresh parsley leaves

¼ cup prepared horseradish

¼ lemon, seeded and cut up (including rind)

1 bay leaf, crumbled

2 tablespoons Creole mustard

2 tablespoons ketchup

2 tablespoons Worcestershire sauce

1 tablespoon Dijon mustard

1 tablespoon white wine vinegar

1 tablespoon Tabasco sauce

1 tablespoon minced garlic

3 tablespoons drained capers

2 teaspoons sweet paprika

1 teaspoon salt

THE SHRIMP

1½ pounds medium fresh shrimp

½ lemon, seeded

Thinly shredded lettuce leaves

To make the dressing, place the yolks in a blender or food processor and blend 2 minutes. With the machine running, add the oil gradually in a thin stream till the emulsion is thickened. One at a time, add the remaining ingredients and process till well blended and the lemon rind is finely chopped. Transfer the dressing to a covered container and chill at least 2 hours.

To prepare the shrimp, place them and the lemon in a large saucepan with enough water to cover, bring to a boil, remove from the heat, cover, and let stand 1 minute. Drain, discard the lemon, and when the shrimp are cool enough to handle, peel and devein them.

When ready to serve, combine the shrimp with the dressing in a bowl and toss till well coated. Make small mounds of shredded lettuce on 6 salad plates and mound shrimp over the tops.

CREOLE SHRIMP RAVIGOTE

Makes 4 to 6 servings

THIS IS A VARIATION ON CRABMEAT RAVIGOTE WITH AN altogether different sauce created years ago by Nathaniel Burton, the brilliant black chef in the Caribbean Room of New Orleans' renowned Pontchartrain Hotel. Why Nat insisted that this version of the sauce not be used for crabmeat I could never figure out—maybe because of the anchovies.

¾ cup mayonnaise

1 tablespoon minced scallions

1 tablespoon minced green bell pepper

1 tablespoon minced pimentos

1 tablespoon minced anchovies

Freshly ground black pepper to taste

Tabasco sauce to taste

1½ pounds fresh boiled shrimp, shelled and deveined

Bibb lettuce leaves, shredded

In a large bowl, combine the mayonnaise, scallions, bell pepper, pimentos, anchovies, pepper, and Tabasco and mix till well blended. Add the shrimp and mix till well coated. Chill, covered, about 1 hour, then serve on beds of shredded lettuce.

Miami Barbecued Shrimp

Makes 6 servings

QUITE FRANKLY, I'VE ALWAYS THOUGHT THAT Floridians could use a few lessons from the folks up in Tennessee and North Carolina when it comes to the art of barbecuing. On the other hand, I could only exclaim when, while judging the dishes at a March of Dimes Gourmet Gala in Miami, I popped a few of these luscious shrimp in my mouth and awarded them a top score. Old Bay seasoning, available almost everywhere in 6-ounce cans, is a strategic ingredient. Also, I find that a few chopped fresh herbs (thyme, summer savory, or tarragon) make the dish even more intriguing. As for serving the appetizer, I simply pass the platter around the table.

2 pounds fresh medium shrimp, shelled and deveined

1 tablespoon minced onions

2 garlic cloves, minced

3 tablespoons butter, melted

1 tablespoon Worcestershire sauce

1 tablespoon fresh lemon juice

1 tablespoon Old Bay seasoning

1 teaspoon medium-hot paprika

Tabasco sauce to taste

Salt and freshly ground black pepper to taste

Preheat the oven to 325°F.

In a large bowl, combine the shrimp, onions, and garlic and toss well. Add the remaining ingredients and toss till the shrimp are well coated. Arrange the shrimp in a single layer in a large, shallow roasting pan and bake about 20 minutes or till the shrimp turn pink, turning them over once or twice. Transfer the shrimp to a large platter and serve piping hot.

PAUL'S COCONUT BEER SHRIMP

Makes 6 servings

PAUL PRUDHOMME CREATED THIS AMAZING APPETIZER back in the 1970s, when he was chef at Commander's Palace in New Orleans, and long before he became so famous. I knew the second I tasted it back in the kitchen that this giant of a man would be a force to be reckoned with. To say the least, the contrasting flavors couldn't have been more innovative, and don't balk at the onion and garlic powder—they are essential to Prudhomme's unique style of Cajun cooking.

THE DIPPING SAUCE

1⅔ cups orange marmalade

5 tablespoons Creole mustard

5 tablespoons prepared horseradish

THE SHRIMP

1½ teaspoons cayenne pepper

1 teaspoon salt

1 teaspoon sweet paprika

1 teaspoon freshly ground black pepper

½ teaspoon garlic powder

¼ teaspoon onion powder

¼ teaspoon dried thyme, crumbled

¼ teaspoon dried oregano, crumbled

1 large egg

1¼ cups all-purpose flour

½ cup lager beer

1½ teaspoons baking powder

1½ cups grated fresh or frozen coconut

1½ pounds large fresh shrimp, shelled (except for the tails) and deveined

Vegetable oil for deep frying

To make the dipping sauce, combine all the ingredients in a bowl, mix till well blended, and set aside.

To prepare the shrimp, combine the cayenne pepper, salt, paprika, black pepper, garlic powder, onion powder, thyme, and oregano in a small bowl and mix thoroughly. In another bowl, combine 2 teaspoons of the seasoning mix with the egg, ¼ cup of the flour, the beer, and baking powder, and beat till smooth. In another small bowl, combine the remaining flour with 1½ teaspoons of the seasoning mix. And in a fourth bowl, place the coconut.

Sprinkle the remaining seasoning mix over the shrimp, then, holding each shrimp by the tail, dredge each in the flour, dip in the beer batter, coat generously with coconut, and place on a baking sheet.

Heat about 2 inches of oil in a small cast-iron skillet to 350°F, drop the shrimp into the oil in batches, fry 1 minute, and drain on paper towels.

To serve, divide the dipping sauce among 6 small bowls, place the bowls on small serving plates, and arrange equal amounts of shrimp around the bowls.

Charleston Hobotee

Makes 6 servings

INNOVATIVE CHARLESTON AND SAVANNAH CHEFS SEEM finally to be discovering perloo, awendaw, Huguenot torte, and any number of other distinctive dishes that once figured prominently in Carolina and Georgia Lowcountry cuisine. But, so far, not one seems to be even aware of this superlative curried meat custard that probably graced both breakfast and dinner tables during the plantation era. I can remember eating hobotee at the old Fort Sumter Hotel in Charleston and hearing my grandmother tell about fixing it for breakfast and elaborate fish dinners. A recipe for the dish is included in the classic cookbook *Charleston Receipts,* but other than that, the only recorded method for making hobotee I know of is this sacred one my mother inherited from her mother, who no doubt inherited it from hers. Served with glasses of semidry sherry as a starter to any seafood meal, small ramekins of hobotee make for a unique culinary experience that should never have been allowed to almost disappear.

3 tablespoons butter

1 medium onion, finely chopped

1 tablespoon curry powder

1½ cups finely chopped cooked beef, veal, or pork

1 slice white bread, soaked in milk and squeezed dry

2 tablespoons chopped almonds

2 tablespoons fresh lemon juice

3 large eggs

½ teaspoon sugar

Salt to taste

1 cup half-and-half

Dash of white pepper

Small bay leaves

Preheat the oven to 300°F.

In a skillet, melt the butter over moderate heat, add the onion, and cook, stirring, till softened, 2 to 3 minutes. Add the curry powder and cook, stirring, 2 minutes longer. Transfer the onions to a mixing bowl, add the meat, bread, almonds, lemon juice, one of the eggs, the sugar, and salt and blend thoroughly.

Butter six ½-cup ramekins and divide the meat mixture among them. In another bowl, combine the remaining 2 eggs, half-and-half, and white pepper and whisk till well blended. Pour equal amounts of the cream mixture into the ramekins, garnish the tops with a bay leaf, and bake till golden, about 25 minutes. Serve hot.

KENTUCKY HOT BROWNS

Makes 6 servings

ASK NATIVES OF MISSISSIPPI, SOUTH CAROLINA, OR Maryland what a hot brown is and you'll be met with a blank stare. Ask a Kentuckian, and you'll be told it's a sandwich or a baked meat dish or a casserole. Even in Kentucky nobody knows exactly how to classify a hot brown (just as nobody can say for sure what an authentic Kentucky burgoo is composed of). I've concluded it's an open-face sandwich to be served as the first course of a meal to be followed by no more than a light seafood salad. Created in the 1930s at the Brown Hotel in Louisville by a chef named Fred Schmidt, hot browns can be made with sliced or diced chicken, turkey, ham, bacon, or any combination of these ingredients. The bread can be white, rye, or pumpernickel; the cheese, cheddar or Parmesan; the sauce, thick or thin. Whatever ingredients are used, the hot brown is unquestionably one of the most distinctive and delicious regional dishes in the Southern repertory.

8 slices bacon

6 slices rye or pumpernickel bread

4 tablespoons (½ stick) butter

¼ cup all-purpose flour

1 cup half-and-half

4 ounces extra-sharp cheddar cheese, shredded

2 cups diced cooked chicken or turkey

Cayenne pepper to taste

¾ cup grated genuine Parmigiano-Reggiano cheese

6 ripe tomato slices

Preheat the oven broiler.

In a large skillet, fry the bacon over moderate heat till crisp, drain on paper towels, crumble, and reserve.

Place the bread on a baking sheet, place under broiler, toast lightly about 6 inches from the heat, and reserve. Heat the oven to 475°F.

In a large, heavy saucepan, melt the butter over moderate heat, add the flour, and whisk for 1 minute. Gradually add the half-and-half, whisking constantly till the mixture is thickened. Add the cheddar cheese and whisk till well incorporated. Add the chicken and cayenne pepper and stir till well blended.

Spread equal amounts of the chicken mixture over the toasted bread slices, sprinkle equal amounts of Parmigiano-Reggiano and half the reserved bacon over the tops, and bake till the cheese melts, about 2 minutes. Top each with a tomato slice, sprinkle the remaining bacon over the tomatoes, and bake about 2 minutes longer. Serve hot.

44

DILLED SALMON QUICHE

Makes 6 servings

UNLIKE MOST OTHER AMERICANS, SOUTHERNERS HAVE never abandoned their passion for any style of quiche since the pie was first popularized back in the fifties, and some of today's modern versions are truly remarkable. I don't recommend substituting canned salmon for the fresh in this quiche; it lacks flavor and is just too soft for my taste (poached salmon that is still slightly firm is ideal). It is not absolutely necessary to make your own pie shell if you're in a hurry and have a frozen one on hand. Do, however, make the effort to find genuine Emmenthaler cheese.

1 recipe Basic Pie Shell (page 336)

¾ pound cooked salmon, picked over and flaked

1 cup grated Swiss cheese (preferably Emmenthaler)

1 cup milk

4 large eggs

2 tablespoons all-purpose flour

2 tablespoons chopped fresh dill

1 tablespoon fresh lemon juice

Salt and freshly ground black pepper to taste

Snipped fresh dill for garnish

Preheat the oven to 425°F. Grease a 9-inch tart pan and set aside.

Place the chilled dough on a lightly floured surface and roll it out from the center with a lightly floured rolling pin to a ⅛-inch thickness. Fit the dough into the prepared tart pan and crimp the edges. Prick the bottom and sides with a fork, place on a heavy baking sheet, bake about 12 minutes or till golden, and let the shell cool. Reduce the oven to 375°F.

Spread the salmon evenly in the shell and sprinkle the cheese over the top. In a bowl, whisk together the milk, eggs, flour, chopped dill, lemon juice, and salt and pepper till well blended, pour the mixture over the cheese, and bake about 40 minutes or till a knife inserted in the center comes out clean. Let the quiche stand about 10 minutes before serving in wedges with snipped dill sprinkled over the top.

DEEP-DISH APPLE AND CHEDDAR QUICHE

Makes 6 servings

GREYFIELD INN, ON REMOTE CUMBERLAND ISLAND, Georgia, may not have the elegance and social cachet of the more fashionable hotels on Hilton Head, Kiawah, Jekyll, and other resort islands to the north, but I'd love to return there if only to sample more of the innovative Southern dishes served on a buffet in the slightly shabby but genteel dining room. I remember lots of dishes, but what really impressed me was this apple and cheddar quiche with wine, nutmeg, and just a hint of curry.

THE PASTRY SHELL

1½ cups all-purpose flour

1 teaspoon sugar

½ teaspoon salt

8 tablespoons (1 stick) butter, cut into bits

1 large egg, beaten

4 to 5 tablespoons ice water

THE FILLING

2 tablespoons butter

2 cooking apples (such as Granny Smith), peeled, cored, and chopped

6 scallions (white parts only), chopped

¼ teaspoon freshly grated nutmeg

⅛ teaspoon curry powder

1 pound sharp cheddar cheese, grated

1 cup half-and-half

4 large eggs, beaten

¼ cup dry white wine

Freshly ground black pepper to taste

To make the pastry shell, combine the flour, sugar, and salt in a large mixing bowl, add the butter, and rub with your fingertips till the mixture is mealy. Add the egg, stir well, then gradually add enough ice water to form a ball of dough. Wrap the dough in plastic wrap and chill for 1 hour.

Preheat the oven to 425°F. Grease a 9-inch deep-dish pie plate.

Place the chilled dough on a lightly floured surface and roll it out from the center with a lightly floured rolling pin to a ⅛-inch thickness. Fit the dough into the pie plate and crimp the edges. Prick the bottom and sides with a fork, place on a heavy baking sheet, bake about 12 minutes or till golden, and let the shell cool. Reduce the oven to 375°F.

To make the filling, heat the butter over moderate heat in a large stainless-steel or enameled skillet, add the apples, scallions, nutmeg, and curry powder, and cook, stirring, till the apples are softened, 3 to 5 minutes. Spread the mixture evenly over the pastry shell and sprinkle the cheese evenly over the top. In a bowl, combine the half-and-half, eggs, and wine and pepper, whisk till well blended, and pour the mixture over the cheese. Bake about 40 minutes, or till the quiche is puffed and golden. Let stand about 10 minutes before serving in wedges.

46

Vidalia Onion and Goat Cheese Pie

Makes 6 servings

YES, INDEED, CHEESE MAKING HAS MADE IMPORTANT strides in the South over the past few years, and no sooner had I received a small supply of smooth, ripe "Georgia Pecan" goat cheese, produced at Sweet Grass Dairy in Thomasville, Georgia, than I tried the obvious: a savory pie made with sweet Vidalia onions and tangy Georgia goat cheese. Suffice it that wedges of the pie are a sublime appetizer at any meal—sort of an updated quiche.

8 tablespoons (1 stick) butter

2 pounds (about 6) Vidalia onions, thinly sliced

1 unbaked 9-inch Basic Pie Shell (page 336),
*   or 1 unbaked 9-inch store-bought pie shell*

3 large eggs

1 cup half-and-half

½ teaspoon salt

½ teaspoon freshly ground black pepper

Cayenne pepper to taste

½ cup goat cheese, crumbled or chopped

Preheat the oven to 400°F.

In a large, deep, heavy skillet, heat the butter over moderately low heat, add the onions, and cook, stirring, till just soft and slightly golden, about 10 minutes. Scrape the onions evenly into the pie shell and set aside.

In a medium mixing bowl, combine the eggs, half-and-half, salt, black pepper, and cayenne pepper and whisk till well blended. Add the goat cheese and stir till well blended. Pour the mixture over the onions and bake 15 minutes. Reduce the heat to 350°F and continue to bake till the pie is puffy in the center and the top golden brown, about 25 minutes. Serve hot or at room temperature.

47

Chicken Drumettes

Makes 8 servings

SOUTHERNERS ARE ALWAYS COMING UP WITH CLEVER ways to prepare chicken wings, and my North Carolinian mother (who has always proclaimed the wings to be the tenderest and sweetest part of any bird) almost surpassed herself when she created these zesty drumettes to be served as an appetizer at informal meals as well as at picnics. Today, drumettes are often sold in packages at supermarkets, but if you can't find them there, simply remove the tips and first joint from the chicken wings and use them for stock. Take care not to overbake these drumettes, which would dry out and toughen them.

1 cup freshly grated Parmesan cheese

2 tablespoons finely chopped fresh parsley leaves

2 tablespoon dried oregano

2 teaspoons sweet paprika

2 teaspoons salt

½ teaspoon freshly ground black pepper

4 pounds chicken wing drumsticks (drumettes)

8 tablespoons (1 stick) butter, melted

Preheat the oven to 350°F. Line a large, heavy baking sheet with aluminum foil, fold up the sides to form a rim, and set aside.

On a large, flat dish, combine the cheese, parsley, oregano, paprika, salt, and pepper and mix well. Dip each drumette in the butter, roll in the cheese mixture to coat well, place on the prepared baking sheet, and bake till cooked through and lightly browned, about 1 hour, turning once. Serve at room temperature.

OKRA WITH MUSTARD SAUCE

Makes 6 servings

I CAN STILL SEE THE STUNNED EXPRESSION ON THE face of one dinner guest from Chicago when Sally was bold enough to serve this okra as a first course at a dinner in Columbia, Missouri. Born and raised in Tuscaloosa, Alabama, like me Sally had been thrust into an almost alien academic environment far from home, but, like me, she had no intention of neglecting her culinary roots just to satisfy the timid palates of the uninitiated. The irony is that after a couple of bites of this rather fancy okra dish, the shocked dinner guest was as quickly converted as are those who taste fried okra for the first time. Now, how he would have reacted to the dish without the luxurious sauce is another matter. Be sure to buy fresh, firm, small okra with no dark spots.

2½ pounds fresh okra, stems trimmed without cutting into the pods

3 large egg yolks

1½ tablespoons Dijon mustard

1 tablespoon fresh lemon juice

1 large garlic clove, minced

½ teaspoon salt

Freshly ground black pepper to taste

Tabasco sauce to taste

12 tablespoons (1½ sticks) cold butter, cut into pieces

Place the okra in a large saucepan with enough water to cover, bring to a low boil, and cook about 5 minutes or till tender but still firm. Drain and keep warm.

To make the sauce, combine the egg yolks, mustard, lemon juice, garlic, salt, pepper, and Tabasco in a medium saucepan. Over low heat, whisk in the butter gradually till it is completely incorporated and the sauce is thick.

To serve, transfer the okra to a platter and pour the sauce over the top.

Okra Fritters with Thousand Island Dressing

Makes 4 to 6 servings

THESE CRUNCHY FRITTERS (GUARANTEED TO CONVERT even the most squeamish non-Southern eater) were inspired by those included on the lazy Susan at a down-home retreat in McComb, Mississippi, called The Dinner Bell. Sorry, but these fritters simply don't work with frozen okra, so if you can't find small, firm pods in the market, choose another appetizer. And don't snicker at the Thousand Island dressing: it adds just the right zest the okra needs.

THE DRESSING

1 cup mayonnaise

¼ cup bottled chili sauce

¼ cup minced pimento-stuffed green olives

1 large hard-boiled egg, finely chopped

1 tablespoon minced fresh chives

1 tablespoon minced green bell pepper

Tabasco sauce to taste

THE FRITTERS

1½ pounds small, firm, fresh okra, rinsed

¾ cup minced onion

¼ cup minced green bell pepper

3 tablespoons all-purpose flour

½ teaspoon salt

Freshly ground black pepper to taste

2 cups yellow cornmeal

1 large egg

2 tablespoons half-and-half

Tabasco sauce to taste

Vegetable shortening

To make the dressing, combine all the ingredients in a small bowl, mix till well blended, cover, and chill till ready to serve.

To make the fritters, stem the okra and slice thinly. In a large bowl, combine the okra, onion, bell pepper, flour, salt, and pepper and toss till well blended. Add the cornmeal and toss again. In a small bowl, whisk together the egg, half-and-half, and Tabasco till well blended, pour over the okra mixture, stir gently, and let stand about 15 minutes.

In a large skillet, melt about 1 inch of shortening over moderately high heat, drop the okra mixture by tablespoons into the fat, and fry the fritters about 2 minutes on each side or till just golden brown. With a slotted spoon, transfer the fritters to paper towels to drain, then serve hot with dollops of the dressing on the side.

Eggs & Salads

Georgia Cheese and Eggs

Brains and Eggs

Egg, Sausage, and Corn Scramble

Savannah Shrimp Omelette

West Virginia
Appalachian Omelette

Spanish Omelette

Spicy Ham, Cheese,
and Mushroom Strata

Kentucky Cheese Pudding

Eggs Sardou

Eggs St. Charles

Eggs Maryland

Delta Red Eggs

Shrimp, Pea, and
Pork Cracklin' Salad

Soused Shrimp, Red Onion,
and Avocado Salad

Shrimp, Wild Rice,
and Spinach Salad

Bacon-Horseradish Potato Salad

Arkansas Caviar

Delmarva Tuna, Apple,
and Walnut Salad

Layered Club Salad

Minted Greek Chicken Salad

Buttermilk Coleslaw

Pineapple-Raisin Coleslaw

Fresh Tomato and Olive Aspic

Molded Salmon Salad

Belle Meade Frozen Tomato

Congealed Pickled Peach
and Pecan Salad

Frozen Fruit Bridge Salad

Congealed Strawberry,
Pineapple, and Banana Salad

Georgia Cheese and Eggs

Makes 6 to 8 servings

AT DINERS, CAFETERIAS, AND SIMPLE ROADSIDE CAFÉS throughout Tennessee, Kentucky, and the Deep South, I've eaten all sorts of egg and cheese dishes—since, to tell the truth, breakfast is and always has been my favorite meal of the day (and I'm not talking about bread and coffee but eggs, bacon or sausage or country ham, fresh fruit, homemade preserves, etc.). Never once, however, have I encountered anything even resembling this smooth, full-flavored, slightly tangy, almost elegant concoction that my maternal grandfather used to make in Macon, Georgia, and that today my mother and I both serve in a silver chafing dish at weekend breakfasts and brunches. For the dish to work perfectly, you absolutely must use the very finest, extra-sharp, aged cheddar you can find (I prefer a premium Vermont or Canadian cheddar), and do note that if you rush the roux or stir the eggs quickly over heat that's too high, you'll end up with a lumpy disaster. This is an easy dish to prepare, but it does require patience.

8 tablespoons (1 stick) butter

8 slices white bread, trimmed and torn into pieces

1½ cups milk

1½ pounds extra-sharp cheddar cheese, coarsely grated

10 large eggs, beaten

Salt and freshly ground black pepper to taste

Cayenne pepper to taste

In a large, heavy skillet, melt the butter, then add the bread and milk and mash steadily and thoroughly over moderately low heat with a heavy fork till the mixture has the consistency of a soft, smooth roux, adding more milk if necessary. Add the cheese and continue mashing and stirring till the cheese is well incorporated and the mixture is very smooth. Add the eggs, salt and pepper, and cayenne pepper and stir slowly and steadily with a large spoon till the eggs are set and the mixture is almost creamy. (If the mixture seems to be sticking to the bottom of the skillet, lower the heat while stirring.) Serve the cheese and eggs piping hot in a chafing dish or a large heated bowl.

52

Brains and Eggs

Makes 4 servings

NO, I WAS NOT REARED EATING BRAINS AND EGGS in North Carolina, but my mother was, as well as a friend who grew up outside Pine Bluff, Arkansas. My earliest memory of the dish is of the strong hog's brains my grandmother Maw Maw used to scramble with eggs, and it was only later, when another relative made the dish with milder, more delicate calves' brains, that I became hooked. At one time, brains were considered a great delicacy in the South (as in France), and since I've noticed recently more and more frozen ones in the better markets, I can only assume they're making a comeback with adventuresome home and professional cooks. The combination of brains and eggs produces a rich, subtle, distinctive flavor that makes the dish perfect for brunches. Just don't forget that all brains are fragile and highly perishable and must be cooked within 24 hours. Remember, also, that if brains are unavailable, calf sweetbreads make a very acceptable substitution.

1 pound calf brains (fresh or frozen and thawed)

1 tablespoon fresh lemon juice

1 tablespoon bacon grease

1 cup water

1 teaspoon salt

Freshly ground black pepper to taste

6 tablespoons (¾ stick) butter, cut into pieces

8 large eggs, beaten

To prepare the brains in advance, rinse them carefully under cold water, place in a bowl, add water to cover plus the lemon juice, and let soak for about 2 hours in the refrigerator. Drain, gently peel off and discard as much of the thin outer membrane as possible, and dry the brains carefully with paper towels.

In a large skillet, heat the bacon grease over moderately low heat, add the prepared brains, the water, salt, and pepper, and simmer, uncovered, till the water has evaporated, about 20 minutes. Remove from the heat.

When ready to serve, add the butter to the pan and, when melted around the brains, add the eggs, stir gently, and scramble over low heat just till the eggs are set and still slightly soft. Transfer to a warm bowl and serve immediately.

Egg, Sausage, and Corn Scramble

Makes 6 servings

OKAY, SO THE LADY WHO FIRST SERVED ME THIS wonderful dish was a Yankee living on Cape Cod. Her recipe came from a vintage cookbook that was as Southern as pecan pie. Curiously, since then, I've encountered similar renditions, on a luncheon buffet in Nashville and at a barbecue cook-off in Vienna, Georgia, so I conclude that the combination must be classic. Do buy the best-quality pork sausage (I'm lucky to have a steady supply of Southern whole-hog sausage, but Jimmy Dean, available nationwide, is respectable enough), and, yes, fresh corn kernels scraped from the cobs (their milk included) do make a difference. I like to serve the casserole at summer deck lunches and brunches.

5 large hard-boiled eggs, sliced

1 pound bulk pork sausage

4 tablespoons (½ stick) butter

¼ cup all-purpose flour

Salt and freshly ground black pepper to taste

2 cups half-and-half

2 cups fresh or thawed frozen corn kernels

1 cup soft bread crumbs

2 tablespoons butter, melted

Preheat the oven to 350°F. Butter a 1½-quart casserole and arrange half the egg slices over the bottom.

In a large skillet, break up the sausage, fry over moderate heat till well cooked and crumbly, and drain on paper towels.

In a large, heavy saucepan, melt the butter over moderate heat, add the flour, season with salt and pepper, and stir 1 minute. Add the half-and-half and whisk constantly till the sauce is bubbly and thickened. Stir the cooked sausage and the corn into the sauce, pour over the eggs in the casserole, and arrange the remaining egg slices over the top.

In a small mixing bowl, combine the bread crumbs and melted butter, spoon evenly over the top of the casserole, and bake till golden, about 30 minutes. Serve hot.

Savannah Shrimp Omelette

Makes 2 large omelettes (4 servings)

MY FRIEND DAMON LEE FOWLER TELLS OF FORMAL
evenings in Savannah when, after supper, guests
traditionally shed their jackets, loosen their ties, discard
earrings in empty ashtrays, open a last bottle of
Champagne, and, still not ready to call it a night, end up
taking leftover shrimp from the buffet and folding them
into midnight omelettes. It's without question one of the
most decadent scenarios imaginable—right out of
Midnight in the Garden of Good and Evil—and one that
I've emulated twice in my own home, using freshly boiled
shrimp. Since it's a bit tricky for one person to handle
two of these omelettes at the same time, the best idea is
to let other guests join in on the fun and test their skills
at the stove. If the omelettes don't turn out perfect, so
what? With these, I'd also toast a batch of buttermilk
biscuit halves, and, yes, pop another bottle of bubbly.

½ pound medium shrimp

8 large eggs

Salt and cayenne pepper to taste

6 tablespoons (¾ stick) butter

Place the shrimp in a large saucepan with enough
water to cover, bring to a boil, remove from the heat,
and let stand 2 minutes. Drain the shrimp, refresh
under cold running water, peel and devein them,
reserving the shells, and cut them in half crosswise.

Break the eggs equally into two separate bowls, season
with salt and cayenne, and beat lightly with a fork.

In two large, heavy skillets, melt equal amounts of the
butter in each over moderate heat, add equal amounts
of the reserved shrimp shells to each, and stir about 4
minutes. With a slotted spoon, lift the shells from the
pans and discard.

Increase the heat to moderately high, add a bowl of
eggs to each skillet, and stir each with a fork till soft
curds form and the eggs are just set on the bottoms.
Scatter equal amounts of the shrimp over the centers
of the eggs and lift two edges of the omelettes up over
the shrimp with a spatula. Turn off the heat and let the
omelettes stand till the shrimp are well heated but the
centers are still creamy. Cut the omelettes in half and
serve immediately on heated plates.

West Virginia Appalachian Omelette

Makes 2 omelettes

DRIVING SOUTH ON INTERSTATE 81 IN VIRGINIA, I decided to make the short detour just over the state line to have lunch at an eatery called A Taste of West Virginia, which I'd been told was operated by the nearby Greenbrier Resort renowned for its culinary excellence. The café couldn't have been more delightful or restful, and while I was tempted by a couple of hickory-smoked pork and fried seafood specialities, what intrigued me most (and made the most sense at that time of day) was this Appalachian omelette featuring genuine local country ham. Suffice it to say that I couldn't ask about the recipe fast enough.

¼ cup all-purpose flour

¼ cup white cornmeal

2 pinches onion powder

2 pinches garlic powder

Salt and freshly ground black pepper to taste

1 medium green tomato, cored and thinly sliced

9 tablespoons butter

6 large eggs

4 ounces lean country ham, chopped

1 cup grated Swiss cheese (preferably Emmenthaler)

1 teaspoon chopped fresh chives

¼ teaspoon chopped fresh parsley leaves

¼ teaspoon chopped fresh tarragon leaves

In a wide, shallow bowl, combine the flour, cornmeal, onion powder, garlic powder, and salt and pepper and stir till well blended. Dredge the tomato slices in the mixture. In a medium skillet, melt 3 tablespoons of the butter over moderate heat, add the coated tomato slices, fry till golden, about 2 minutes on each side, and set aside.

Crack 3 of the eggs into a small bowl and beat well. Melt 3 more tablespoons of the butter in the skillet over moderate heat, add the ham, and cook, stirring, 1 minute. Pour the eggs over the ham and stir till wet curds form. Scatter half the cheese and half the tomatoes over the top, sprinkle half the chives, parsley, and tarragon over the top, and cook till the eggs are just set, about 1 minute. With a spatula, flip one half of the omelette over the other half, let sit 1 minute, then transfer to a heated plate.

Repeat the process with the remaining ingredients to make a second omelette.

Spanish Omelette

Makes 1 large omelette

DON'T ASK ME HOW IN THE WORLD WHAT
Southerners call a Spanish omelette crept into the
breakfast repertory (the only ingredients remotely
associated with Spanish cuisine are onions and bell
peppers), but I've been eating this omelette at various
venues in the South ever since my grandmother fixed her
version on Sunday mornings when I was a child. Perhaps
the most famous Spanish omelette is the unfolded one
topped with a Creole sauce at Antoine's restaurant in New
Orleans, but, curiously, that luncheon omelette doesn't
even include the traditional onions and bell peppers, only
peas and mushrooms. Feel free to add a few chopped
mushrooms (and a little minced garlic), if you like.

4 tablespoons (½ stick) butter

¼ cup finely chopped onions

¼ cup finely chopped red bell pepper

3 large eggs

*¼ cup fresh or frozen and thawed boiled green
peas*

½ teaspoon salt

½ teaspoon freshly ground black pepper

In a small skillet, melt 2 tablespoons of the butter over
moderate heat, add the onions and bell pepper, and
cook, stirring, till softened, about 2 minutes. Set aside.

In a mixing bowl, beat the eggs, add the onions and
peppers, the peas, salt, and pepper and stir till well
blended.

In a medium skillet, melt the remaining butter over
low heat, add the egg mixture, and stir till the eggs
begin to set. With a spatula, flip one half of the
omelette over the other half, let sit about 1 minute,
then transfer to a heated plate. Serve immediately.

Spicy Ham, Cheese, and Mushroom Strata

Makes 6 to 8 servings

WHEN AND HOW THE STRATA EVOLVED AS A CONCEPT in Southern cooking remains something of a mystery, but it's for sure that the layered casserole in all its many variations is loved in homes from West Virginia to Georgia. Virtually any layered ingredients can be baked with different liquids to produce a strata, and probably the most classic (and popular) example is this spicy one prepared with bread cubes, ham, cheese, and mushrooms. Country ham might be substituted for regular baked ham, and herbs and other seasonings could also be added, but remember that if the primary ingredients are not arranged in alternate layers, the dish is not a genuine strata but an ordinary casserole. In the South, a strata is traditionally served on an informal dinner buffet or at a casual supper.

6 cups day-old bread cubes

3 cups cubed cooked ham

3 cups shredded extra-sharp cheddar cheese

2 cups (about 6 ounces) chopped mushrooms

3 tablespoons butter, melted

½ cup all-purpose flour

1 teaspoon dry mustard

6 large eggs

3 cups milk

Tabasco sauce to taste

In a greased 9 by 13 by 2-inch baking dish, arrange the bread cubes, ham, cheese, and mushrooms in alternate layers, beginning and ending with the bread cubes. Drizzle the butter over the top. In a small bowl, mix the flour and dry mustard and sprinkle over the top. In another bowl, whisk together the eggs, milk, and Tabasco till well blended, pour over the strata, cover with plastic wrap, and chill at least 6 hours.

Preheat the oven to 350°F.

Remove the strata from the refrigerator, let stand about 20 minutes, then bake till golden, about 1 hour. Serve hot.

KENTUCKY CHEESE PUDDING

Makes 6 servings

IN BARDSTOWN, SOUTH OF LOUISVILLE, TO LEARN more about the production of bourbon whiskey, I was utterly puzzled when my host began talking about a local dish called cheese pudding and insisted on taking me to a family-style restaurant to sample the strange casserole. I loved it, but it was not till sometime later that I read about this being the dish that President Eisenhower was once served for lunch and raved about when he went to visit Abraham Lincoln's childhood home over in Hodgenville. Apparently, he even asked for the recipe to give to Mamie, and when the press got wind of the request, cheese pudding was added to the Southern culinary pantheon. In western Kentucky, it's usually served as a main course at supper with country ham biscuits and a salad. I think it also makes a great brunch buffet dish.

8 tablespoons (1 stick) butter

6 tablespoons all-purpose flour

3 cups half-and-half

½ teaspoon salt

¼ teaspoon freshly ground black pepper

1½ cups crumbled soda crackers

6 hard-boiled eggs, chopped

3 cups grated sharp cheddar cheese

1 cup drained, chopped pimentos

Preheat oven to 325°F.

In a saucepan, melt 6 tablespoons of the butter over moderately low heat, add the flour, and whisk till the mixture is a smooth paste. Add the half-and-half, salt, and pepper, continue whisking till the sauce thickens, and remove from the heat.

Spoon about ½ cup of the sauce into a greased 1½-quart casserole, sprinkle a few of the cracker crumbs over the top, then arrange successive layers of eggs, cheese, and pimentos. Repeat till all the ingredients have been layered, ending with cracker crumbs on top. Dot with pieces of the remaining butter and bake till bubbling and golden, about 30 minutes. Serve hot.

EGGS SARDOU

Makes 4 servings

EGGS SARDOU WERE CREATED BY CHEF ANTOINE
Alciatore at Antoine's restaurant in New Orleans in the
late nineteenth century to honor the visiting French
playwright Victorien Sardou, and along with eggs
Hussarde, eggs Benedict, and a score of other elaborate
egg dishes popularized in the Crescent City, they have
become a brunch and luncheon classic. Whether the
artichokes and eggs were originally served on a bed of
creamed spinach (as they often are today) remains a
point of debate. No doubt this makes for a more dramatic
presentation, but since the basic dish is already so rich, I
prefer to leave well enough alone. Remember that this is a
restaurant dish that requires some prep work and cooking
skill. Is it worth the trouble? You bet it is, especially if
you're out to impress luncheon guests. I like to serve
these eggs (to a small group) with Pickled Peaches (page
386) and Alabama Biscuit Muffins (page 316).

THE HOLLANDAISE SAUCE

4 large egg yolks

1 tablespoon cold water

8 tablespoons butter, at room temperature

¼ teaspoon salt

Pinch of white pepper

2 tablespoons fresh lemon juice

THE ARTICHOKE BOTTOMS

8 large artichokes

THE EGGS

4 cups water

2 tablespoons white vinegar

8 large eggs

2 teaspoons butter

8 tablespoons finely chopped cooked ham

8 anchovy fillets

¼ cup finely chopped fresh parsley leaves

To make the hollandaise sauce, combine the egg yolks
and water in the top of a double boiler and beat till
thickened. Place over barely simmering water and stir
till warm, not hot. Add the butter 2 tablespoons at a
time and stir constantly till well blended. Stir 2 to 3
minutes or till the sauce thickens enough to coat the
back of a spoon. Remove from the heat, add salt, white
pepper, and lemon juice, stir about 2 minutes longer,
and keep barely warm over hot water till ready to serve.

To prepare the artichoke bottoms, cut off stems of the artichokes to produce a flat base. Remove and discard all petals and chokes and trim all around the sides and base till the base is smooth and white, with any green exterior pared away from the bottoms. Place the trimmed bottoms in a deep stainless-steel or enamel saucepan, and add enough water to cover. Bring to a boil, reduce the heat to low, cover, and simmer till the bottoms are just tender, about 25 minutes. Remove the pot from the heat but do not remove the artichoke bottoms from the pot.

To poach the eggs, pour the water into a large skillet, add the white vinegar, and bring to a simmer. Gently break the eggs into the water, spacing them so the whites do not touch and keeping the water at the simmer. Cook till the whites are set and the yolks remain runny, about 3 minutes. Remove the eggs with a slotted spoon and drain on paper towels, taking care not to break the yolks.

In a small skillet, melt the butter over low heat, add the ham, cook, stirring, 2 minutes, and set aside.

When ready to serve, drain the artichoke bottoms and distribute evenly on 4 plates. Arrange 2 anchovy fillets over each pair of bottoms, place a poached egg in the center of each bottom, and spoon 1 tablespoon of the hollandaise sauce over each egg. Sprinkle equal amounts of ham over the eggs, then sprinkle parsley over the top. Serve hot.

EGGS ST. CHARLES

Makes 6 servings

I DON'T RECALL WHETHER EGGS ST. CHARLES (NAMED after the gracious Avenue St. Charles in New Orleans' Garden District) were originally introduced to the Crescent City by the Brennan family at Brennan's Restaurant or as a new brunch dish when they took over Commander's Palace in the 1970s, but there can be no doubt that it is one of the most original and sublime creations in all of Southern cookery. The timing of the eggs and hollandaise can be tricky, but once you've mastered those techniques, the dish really couldn't be simpler to prepare. This is definitely a preparation to be served to no more than six people at a sit-down brunch or lunch, and requires little else than a tart green salad and either rolls or biscuits.

1 cup all-purpose flour

Pinch of dried, crumbled thyme

Pinch of dried, crumbled oregano

Pinch of paprika

Salt and cayenne pepper to taste

6 red snapper or striped bass fillets (6 ounces each)

8 tablespoons (1 stick) butter

12 poached eggs (see preparation of eggs in Eggs Sardou, page 60)

1 cup Hollandaise Sauce (see Eggs Sardou, page 60)

½ cup finely chopped fresh parsley leaves

On a large plate, combine the flour, thyme, oregano, paprika, and salt and cayenne pepper and mix till well blended. Lightly dredge the fish fillets in the seasoned flour on both sides and set aside.

In a large, heavy skillet, melt half the butter over moderate heat, add half the fish fillets, sauté 3 minutes on each side or till lightly browned, and transfer to warm serving plates. Repeat with the remaining butter and fish fillets.

Position 2 poached eggs on each fish fillet, spoon Hollandaise sauce over each portion, and sprinkle parsley over the tops. Serve immediately.

62

Eggs Maryland

Makes 6 servings

PROBABLY THE ONLY SOUTHERN COASTAL STATE where I've never eaten (or heard mention) eggs Maryland is the state of Maryland. I have no idea where the rich, luscious dish originated, but I've had this recipe for years and judge that its creator (in Norfolk, Virginia? Jacksonville, Florida? Brunswick, Georgia?) associated any dish that featured crabmeat with Maryland's Chesapeake Bay. Craig Claiborne (from Mississippi), barbecue maven Jeanne Voltz (from Alabama), and New York restaurateur Pearl Byrd Foster (from Virginia) all loved eggs Maryland, and I don't hesitate for a second to say that it's a luncheon egg dish that ranks right up there with the legendary ones of New Orleans. Actually, what I love to do is use even more crabmeat and just let it overflow into the sauce.

THE CREAM SAUCE

3 tablespoons butter

3 tablespoons all-purpose flour

2 cups chicken broth

¾ cup heavy cream

Salt and freshly ground white pepper to taste

THE EGGS

1 tablespoon butter

2 scallions (white part only), finely chopped

½ cup finely chopped mushrooms

½ cup flaked fresh lump crabmeat

3 tablespoons heavy cream

6 extra-large hard-boiled eggs, cut in half lengthwise, yolks pressed through a sieve, and whites reserved

1 tablespoon finely chopped parsley leaves

⅛ teaspoon grated nutmeg

Salt and fresh ground black pepper to taste

2 teaspoons dry sherry

½ cup freshly grated Parmesan cheese

Preheat the oven to 350°F.

To make the cream sauce, melt the butter in a small saucepan over moderate heat, add the flour, and whisk rapidly till well blended and smooth. Add the broth, whisking, and let simmer about 5 minutes or till thickened. Add the heavy cream and salt and pepper and let simmer 5 minutes longer, stirring. Keep the sauce warm till ready to use.

To make the eggs, melt the butter in a saucepan over moderate heat, add the scallions and mushrooms, and cook, stirring, till softened, about 2 minutes. Add the crabmeat, heavy cream, sieved yolks, parsley, nutmeg, salt and pepper, and sherry and cook, stirring, 2 minutes longer.

Stuff the egg whites with equal amounts of the crab mixture and arrange on a baking dish. Spoon the cream sauce evenly over the eggs, sprinkle the tops with cheese, and bake till slightly glazed, about 15 minutes. Serve hot.

DELTA RED EGGS

Makes 1 dozen eggs

I'D CERTAINLY EATEN ORDINARY PICKLED EGGS AT cafés, diners, and picnics while growing up in the Carolinas, but it was not till I went to Indianola, Mississippi, to visit a large catfish cooperative that I was first exposed to hard-boiled eggs pickled in vinegar and beet juice. As it turned out, red eggs are a beloved specialty in both Mississippi and Louisiana Delta households and restaurants, served not only with cold cuts but also as an appetizer at fish dinners. Some home cooks will typically use the liquid derived from boiling beets to make red eggs, but most of the locals I encountered simply open a can of cooked beets—as I do. Another popular way of serving these colorful eggs is atop a bed of wilted beet greens, with or without a few sliced beets.

3 cups cider vinegar

1 cup beet juice from canned beets

2 small red chile peppers

1 garlic clove, minced

10 dried coriander seeds

10 whole allspice

6 whole cloves

2 bay leaves

1 sliver fresh nutmeg

1 tablespoon sugar

1 teaspoon salt

12 large hard-boiled eggs

In a saucepan, combine all the ingredients except the eggs, bring to a simmer, and cook 10 minutes. Remove from the heat and let cool.

Pack the eggs into large canning jars, pour in enough of the vinegar mixture to just cover the eggs, screw on jar tops tightly, and refrigerate at least 1 week before serving.

64

SHRIMP, PEA, AND PORK CRACKLIN' SALAD

Makes 6 servings

FROM LITTLE RIVER DOWN TO GEORGETOWN, SOUTH Carolina, fishermen keep roadside markets stocked with the freshest, fattest, most beautiful white shrimp imaginable, and I must have visited every one while nesting in our cottage at Ocean Drive Beach. "With or without the heads?" is the first question most of the old salts ask before quoting prices, and if they don't ask, I'm immediately apprehensive about the freshness of the haul. Given the abundance of shrimp right out of the water (lots of which, unfortunately, is shipped north to fetch outrageous prices), I'm always coming up with new ways to prepare it, but friends still talk about this particular salad I created for lunch one sweltering day after an early-morning excursion to buy shrimp down at one market I favor in Garden City. One secret is the dill pickles.

2 cups diced streak-o'-lean cooking meat (lean salt pork)

2 pounds medium fresh shrimp

½ lemon, seeded

2½ cups cooked green peas

2 small dill pickles, diced

1 cup mayonnaise

3 tablespoons fresh lemon juice

3 tablespoons heavy cream

1 teaspoon prepared horseradish

Salt and freshly ground black pepper to taste

Curly endive (chicory) leaves

2 medium tomatoes, quartered

3 large hard-boiled eggs, peeled and quartered

In a large, heavy skillet, render the diced cooking meat over moderate heat till crisp and golden brown, about 20 minutes, watching carefully and reducing the heat if the fat threatens to burn. Drain the cracklin's on paper towels and set aside.

Place the shrimp in a large saucepan with enough salted water to cover, squeeze the lemon into the water, then toss it in. Bring to a boil, remove from the heat, let sit 1 minute, then drain and discard the lemon. When the shrimp are cool enough to handle, shell, devein, and place in a large mixing bowl. Add the peas and pickles, mix, and chill 1 hour, covered with plastic wrap.

In a small bowl, whisk together the mayonnaise, lemon juice, cream, horseradish, salt, and pepper. Add to the shrimp mixture and toss well.

Line a large salad bowl with the curly endive, mound the salad in the middle, sprinkle the top with cracklin's, and garnish with the tomatoes and eggs.

Soused Shrimp, Red Onion, and Avocado Salad

Makes 8 servings

SOUSING, A COOKING METHOD WHEREBY SEAFOOD IS completely immersed and simmered in a highly seasoned pickling liquid, can be traced back to the classical Greek kitchen and was most surely introduced to the South by the first English settlers. To souse, of course, is little more than to marinate, but from Brunswick, Georgia, to Panama City, Florida, to Gulfport, Mississippi, to virtually any other Southern coastal town, when shrimp, scallops, chunks of fish, and other seafood are prepared in this manner, *sousing* is the term you'll most likely hear. Soused seafood might well grace a formal dinner buffet in places like Wilmington and Charleston, but at fish fries, oyster roasts, and even pig pickin's, you're just as likely to see a big platter of soused shrimp as baskets of hush puppies or cornbread. One tip: to prevent the ingredients in any soused dish from becoming discolored, always use highly acidic white vinegar.

2½ cups white vinegar

2 large onions, sliced

1 large celery rib, broken into thirds

1½ tablespoons sugar

10 whole cloves

1 tablespoon salt

1 teaspoon cracked black peppercorns

2½ pounds large fresh shrimp, shelled and deveined

2 large, ripe avocados

3 tablespoons capers, drained

Red-tipped leaf lettuce

3 tablespoons chopped fresh chives

In a large enameled or stainless-steel saucepan, combine the vinegar, onions, celery, sugar, cloves, salt, and peppercorns, bring to a boil, reduce the heat to low, and simmer for 15 minutes. Add the shrimp, return the liquid to a boil, reduce the heat to moderate, cover, and simmer the shrimp for 1 minute. Remove pan from the heat and let the shrimp cool in the liquid. Pour the mixture into a large glass bowl, cover with plastic wrap, and chill overnight.

When ready to serve, peel and pit the avocados, cut into 1-inch cubes, add to the shrimp along with the capers, and toss gently. Drain the liquid from the bowl, line a large serving platter with lettuce leaves, spoon the salad in the center, and sprinkle the chives over the top. Serve chilled or at room temperature.

SHRIMP, WILD RICE, AND SPINACH SALAD

Makes 4 servings

MY SISTER GOT THIS RECIPE FROM AN OLD COLLEGE friend who lived in Fredericksburg, Virginia, and many is the time she has served the elegant salad with cold roast pork or beef, ham biscuits, a fruit cobbler, and churned ice cream. It's also a great salad for a summertime deck party, in which case you can easily double or triple the recipe. To give the salad a nice textural flair, I like to add a few crunchy pecans.

2½ cups water

1½ cups wild rice

½ pound small fresh shrimp

½ pound fresh mushrooms, sliced

1 cup firmly packed, shredded fresh spinach (tough stems removed)

2 scallions (green tops included), sliced

½ cup chopped pecans

⅓ cup dry white wine

¼ cup vegetable oil

2 teaspoons sugar

1 teaspoon salt

Freshly ground black pepper to taste

Cherry tomatoes for garnish

In a saucepan, bring the water to a boil, add the rice, reduce the heat to low, cover, and cook till the rice has absorbed all the water, about 30 minutes. Transfer to a large bowl, cover with plastic wrap, and chill.

Meanwhile, place the shrimp in another saucepan and add enough salted water to cover. Bring to a boil, remove the pan from the heat, let stand 1 minute, and drain. When the shrimp have cooled, peel, devein, and add to the rice. Add the mushrooms, spinach, scallions, and pecans and toss.

In a small bowl, combine the wine, oil, sugar, salt, and pepper, whisk till well blended, then pour over the rice and shrimp. Toss well, cover, and chill till ready to serve.

Serve the salad on salad plates garnished with cherry tomatoes.

Bacon-Horseradish Potato Salad

Makes 6 servings

SOUTHERNERS HAVE NO MONOPOLY ON CLASSIC American potato salad enhanced with all sorts of other ingredients and dressed primarily with mayonnaise, but they do draw a strict line when it comes to the variety of potato. Round, red boiling potatoes are the cardinal rule in the South (russets and other baking potatoes are considered too mealy and starchy for potato salad), with the only other acceptable type being yellow-fleshed Yukon Golds. "Tater" salad is almost as popular as coleslaw with pork barbecue in the South, and rarely will you find fried chicken or any baked ham without this salad on the side. The only other cardinal rule is never to undercook or overcook the potatoes (they're perfect when easily pierced with a small knife). Remember that they continue cooking when simply drained in a colander and do not need to be doused in cold water. All mayonnaise can be used in this recipe, but the sour cream does add a silky fluffiness to the dish.

4 slices bacon

8 medium red potatoes (about 2 pounds)

½ cup mayonnaise

½ cup sour cream

2 tablespoons prepared horseradish

½ teaspoon freshly black ground pepper

Salt to taste

4 hard-boiled large eggs, roughly chopped

4 scallions (part of green tops included), chopped

2 sweet pickles, chopped

2 tablespoons chopped pimentos

In a medium skillet, fry the bacon till crisp over moderate heat, drain on paper towels, and crumble.

Meanwhile, peel the potatoes and cut into 1-inch cubes. Place in a large saucepan with enough water to cover and bring to a boil. Reduce the heat to moderate, cover, and cook till just tender, about 10 minutes. (Do not overcook.) Drain in a colander and let cool.

In a large mixing bowl, combine the mayonnaise, sour cream, horseradish, pepper, and salt and stir till well blended. Add the crumbled bacon, potatoes, and remaining ingredients and toss gently till well blended. Cover with plastic wrap and chill till ready to serve.

Arkansas Caviar

Makes 4 servings

LOUISIANIANS, MISSISSIPPIANS, AND TEXANS LAY AS much claim to the creation of black-eyed pea "caviar" as the folks in Arkansas, but since the best version I ever tasted was at an outrageous deer, possum, bear, and partridge barbecue I once attended near Jonesboro, Arkansas, in the Ozarks, I assign credit to what I call the "Catfish State." (Arkansas is also the only state I know in the South that normally tops pork barbecue salad with Thousand Island dressing.) You can use fresh black-eyed peas if you care to go to all the trouble of soaking and boiling them and dealing with the hulls, but, frankly, canned peas are just as good for this unusual salad. Serve it at lunch with barbecue sandwiches or, in larger quantities, at fish fries or Brunswick Stew (page 110) suppers.

4 strips lean bacon

One 16-ounce can black-eyed peas, drained and rinsed

1 medium ripe tomato, diced

½ medium green bell pepper, seeded and diced

1 small jalapeño pepper, seeded and diced

2 tablespoons chopped fresh parsley leaves

3 tablespoons olive oil

1 tablespoon balsamic vinegar

2 teaspoons Worcestershire sauce

1 teaspoon chopped fresh oregano (or ⅛ teaspoon dried)

Salt and freshly ground black pepper to taste

In a medium skillet, fry the bacon over moderate heat till crisp, drain on paper towels, and crumble.

In a large serving bowl, combine the crumbled bacon and all remaining ingredients and toss till well blended. Cover with plastic wrap, chill about 1 hour, and serve on small salad plates.

DELMARVA TUNA, APPLE, AND WALNUT SALAD

Makes 4 servings

BEING VIRTUALLY UNAWARE OF (OR OBLIVIOUS TO) the fashionable fresh tuna rage elsewhere in the country, Southerners have a veritable obsession with canned tuna and have come up with every way imaginable to transform ordinary tuna salad into dishes fit for the most gracious luncheons, bridal receptions, and picnics. In Southern delis and even cafeterias, I've noticed just recently tuna salads with all sorts of unusual ingredients, but one of the most exotic and delicious I've tasted was this curried example served at a very simple restaurant (almost a diner) near Dover, Delaware, on the scenic Delmarva Peninsula. As for the tuna itself, I use only solid white albacore (never that chunk light mush) packed in oil (never water).

Two 6-ounce cans solid white tuna in oil, drained

1 large tart red apple, cored and diced

1 cup coarsely chopped walnuts

1 cup mayonnaise

1 teaspoon mild curry powder

Salt and freshly ground black pepper to taste

Bibb lettuce cups

Place the tuna in a mixing bowl and flake with a fork. Add the apple, walnuts, mayonnaise, curry powder, and salt and pepper and stir till well blended. Cover with plastic wrap and chill at least 1 hour before serving in lettuce cups.

A harder, more intensely flavored cousin of the common English walnut, the delectable American black walnut is harvested almost exclusively each fall in the state of West Virginia, and each October, some fifty thousand fans show up at a black walnut festival in Spencer to sample numerous dishes prepared with the rare nut.

Layered Club Salad

Makes 6 to 8 servings

COLORFUL LAYERED SALADS HAVE BEEN A HOLIDAY tradition in some Southern families for almost a century, served either on an elaborate Thanksgiving or Christmas buffet or, with no more than cheese toast or biscuits, at casual brunches. I've seen these salads layered with cubed ham or beef, hard-boiled eggs, various cheeses and blanched vegetables, red onions, and heaven knows what else, but this particular play on the club sandwich I find especially enticing. Obviously, leftover roast turkey breast might be substituted for the chicken—despite James Beard's proclamation to me once that "no turkey should be allowed to get close to a country club or the club car on a train."

3 cups shredded romaine lettuce

3 large ripe tomatoes, coarsely chopped

One 9-ounce package frozen peas, thawed, blanched, and drained

1½ pounds boneless chicken breast, cooked, skinned, and cubed

One 8-ounce can water chestnuts, drained

½ pound lean bacon, fried crisp and crumbled

5 scallions (part of green tops included), sliced crosswise into ¼-inch rounds

Freshly ground black pepper to taste

1½ cups mayonnaise

In a large glass salad bowl, arrange the lettuce, tomatoes, peas, chicken, water chestnuts, bacon, and scallions in separate colorful layers, season with pepper, and spoon the mayonnaise in an even layer over the top. Cover with plastic wrap and chill 1 hour.

When ready to serve, present the salad for guests to see, then toss to blend the ingredients thoroughly with the mayonnaise and serve on salad plates.

Minted Greek Chicken Salad

Makes 4 to 6 servings

WITH LARGE GREEK COMMUNITIES IN CITIES SUCH AS Tarpon Springs, Florida, Charlotte, North Carolina, and Lexington, Kentucky, a veritable Greek American style of Southern cooking has evolved over the past century that couldn't be any more distinctive. (Having been raised in a part-Greek family in North Carolina, I should know.) Composed salads, in particular, have come under this strong ethnic influence, one of many examples being this chicken creation enhanced by tangy feta cheese, briny Greek olives, fresh mint, and fiery red pepper flakes and served for lunch with plenty of toasted pita triangles. Like one Greek lady I know in Sarasota, Florida, I might also add a couple of tablespoons of capers to the salad.

3 cups shredded romaine lettuce

3 cups diced cooked chicken

2 Kirby cucumbers, peeled and thinly sliced

2 medium ripe tomatoes, cut into wedges

15 pitted Kalamata olives, sliced

4 ounces feta cheese, crumbled

1 tablespoon chopped fresh mint leaves

½ cup olive oil

3 tablespoon fresh lemon juice

1 tablespoon chopped fresh parsley leaves

Salt and freshly ground black pepper to taste

Dried red pepper flakes to taste

In a large bowl, combine the lettuce, chicken, cucumbers, tomatoes, olives, feta, and mint and toss till well blended. Cover with plastic wrap and chill 1 hour.

In a small bowl, whisk together the olive oil, lemon juice, parsley, and salt and pepper till well blended and pour over the salad. Toss till the ingredients are well coated with the dressing and serve on salad plates.

Buttermilk Coleslaw

Makes 8 servings

A RECENT BOOK ON COLESLAW (ALWAYS ONE WORD IN the South) informs us that no less than 61 percent of all coleslaw recipes in the United States are Southern; that 41 percent of the population prepare coleslaw year round; and that the salad is most often eaten with barbecue and fried chicken or fish. Without question, the major ingredient in most Southern coleslaw is shredded (not chopped, not grated) green cabbage, and the key dressings are based either on mayonnaise or vinegar. After that, the sky's the limit on what is found in coleslaws: carrots, onions, olives, poppy seeds, raisins, apples, curry powder, pineapple, sour cream, lemon juice, and Lord knows what else. I guess I've tasted them all (some superlative, some ordinary, some wretched), but this buttermilk version is hard to beat, both as a side dish and as a topping on pork barbecue sandwiches, hot dogs, and the like.

1 medium, firm green cabbage (about 1½ pounds)

1 large carrot, scraped

1 small onion

2 teaspoons sugar

1 teaspoon celery seed

Salt and freshly ground black pepper to taste

½ cup mayonnaise

½ cup buttermilk

2 tablespoons fresh lemon juice

1 tablespoon cider vinegar

Remove and discard the loose outer leaves of the cabbage, cut the head into quarters, cut out and discard the hard center core, and shred the quarters into a large bowl. Shred the carrot into the bowl, then the onion, and mix well.

In a small bowl, combine the remaining ingredients and mix till well blended and smooth. Pour the dressing over the cabbage mixture, toss till well blended, cover with plastic wrap, and chill about 2 hours before serving. (The slaw keeps about 5 days but becomes watery, and needs to be drained, after 2 days.)

PINEAPPLE-RAISIN COLESLAW

Makes 6 servings

OF THE MORE EXOTIC SOUTHERN COLESLAWS SERVED
with fried chicken and seafood, this is my favorite—at
least for the time being. Curiously, it was inspired by a
slaw I found one day in Chattanooga when a friend and I
stormed out of a pretentious restaurant that was serving
a putative Creole gumbo flavored with lemongrass (!)
and ended up at a deli down the street. I've also seen
versions of this slaw in upscale cafeterias, and, actually,
lots of Southerners like to flavor their plain, ordinary
coleslaw with just a suggestion of crushed pineapple.

*One 15-ounce can crushed pineapple, drained,
 with ⅓ cup juice reserved*

¼ cup peanut oil

2 tablespoons balsamic vinegar

½ teaspoon celery seed

½ teaspoon grated orange zest

¼ teaspoon dry mustard

Salt and freshly ground black pepper to taste

*One small, firm green cabbage head
 (about 1 pound)*

2 ounces seedless golden raisins

In a bowl, combine the reserved pineapple juice, oil,
vinegar, celery seed, orange zest, mustard, and salt and
pepper, whisk till well blended and smooth, and set
aside.

Remove and discard the outer leaves of the cabbage,
cut the head into quarters, cut out and discard the
hard center core, and shred the quarters into a large
bowl. Add the crushed pineapple and raisins and toss
till well blended.

Pour the dressing over the top, toss till well blended,
cover with plastic wrap, and chill at least 1 hour before
serving.

74

Fresh Tomato and Olive Aspic

Makes 6 to 8 servings

CONSIDERED BY MANY SOUTHERN HOSTESSES TO BE the ultimate "party dish," tomato aspic has been widely served at bridge luncheons and on buffets since the introduction of granulated gelatin more than a century ago. Unfortunately, most of the tomato aspics found today are overly sweet concoctions dependent on canned tomato juice (or V8) and Jell-O, a far cry from this classic, delectable version made with fresh, ripe tomatoes, olives, and tangy seasonings—and no trace of sugar. Since it's a bore having to wait for the aspic to set in the refrigerator, I strongly suggest you make it a day in advance and chill it overnight.

6 medium ripe tomatoes, cored and peeled

2 envelopes unflavored gelatin

2 tablespoons fresh lemon juice

1 tablespoon cider vinegar

1 tablespoon Worcestershire sauce

1 tablespoon grated onion

¼ teaspoon salt

Dash of Tabasco sauce

1 cup sliced pimento-stuffed green olives

½ cup finely chopped celery

8 leaf lettuce leaves

Mayonnaise for garnish

In a large bowl, press down the tomatoes to extract the juice and produce a wet pulp, pushing and squeezing with your fingers. Place half the pulp in a saucepan.

Pour off about 4 tablespoons of the tomato juice into a small bowl, add the gelatin, stir to soften, and stir into the pulp in the saucepan. Bring just to a boil, stirring till the gelatin is dissolved, then add the remaining pulp and stir well. Remove pan from the heat.

Add the lemon juice, vinegar, Worcestershire, onion, salt, and Tabasco to the pulp and stir well. Let cool, then chill till the mixture is slightly thickened, about 30 minutes.

Add the olives and celery and stir till well blended. Scrape the mixture into a shallow baking dish or loaf pan, cover with plastic wrap, and chill at least 3 hours or overnight to set completely.

Serve the aspic in slices on lettuce leaves and top each portion with a dollop of mayonnaise.

75

Molded Salmon Salad

Makes 4 to 6 servings

ONE OF THE BIG ENIGMAS OF MODERN SOUTHERN cookery is why fresh salmon, now so readily available even in supermarkets, has never gained the popularity of flounder, snapper, bass, and catfish in Southern homes or restaurants. Canned salmon, on the other hand, has been a staple of the Southern kitchen as long as I can remember, used from Virginia to Tennessee to Arkansas to make all sorts of dips, spreads, loaves, croquettes, mousses, and, to be sure, exotic molded salads. Is it best to use fresh, flaked, cooked salmon in this particular salad? Not really. As my mother says, "I defy anybody to notice any difference between fresh and canned salmon in molded salads."

2 envelopes unflavored gelatin

1 cup water

1 cup mayonnaise

½ cup half-and-half

1 tablespoon fresh lemon juice

½ teaspoon dry mustard

1 tablespoon snipped fresh dill (or ½ teaspoon dried dill weed)

Freshly ground black pepper to taste

2 cups canned, drained salmon

½ cup finely chopped celery

3 tablespoons seeded and finely chopped green bell pepper

1 tablespoon minced onion

4 to 6 leaves red-tipped leaf lettuce

In a small saucepan, soften the gelatin in the water for 5 minutes, then place over low heat, stirring till the gelatin is dissolved. Remove from the heat and let cool.

In a large mixing bowl, combine the mayonnaise, half-and-half, lemon juice, mustard, dill, and black pepper and stir till well blended. Add the dissolved gelatin to the mixture and stir till well blended and smooth. Add the salmon, celery, bell pepper, and onion and stir till well blended. Scrape the mixture into a greased 8-cup ring or fish-shaped salad mold, cover with plastic wrap, and chill till firm, at least 3 hours.

Serve the salad in slices on top the lettuce leaves.

BELLE MEADE FROZEN TOMATO

Makes 5 to 10 servings

CREATED AT THE EXCLUSIVE BELLE MEADE COUNTRY
Club in Nashville, this has to be the most exotic
Southern salad in the history of the Confederacy—and
one of the most mysteriously delicious. I first tasted the
salad a few years ago when my mother and I were
entertained at the club, but it was not till Julia Reed, my
food-obsessed Mississippian friend and fellow author,
persuaded an intrepid pal of hers to march into the
clubhouse kitchen and ask the chef himself for the
sacred recipe, that any of us learned just how to make
the unusual dish. This is one recipe I'd never dream of
tampering with, and I suggest you follow my example. At
the club, they serve the salad with distinctive fried hot
water corncakes, but since neither Julia nor I nor
anybody else would dare try to replicate these tricky
wonders, I settle for my more ordinary but very good Hot
Water Cornbread (page 301). (Note: if you don't add a
little red food coloring to the mixture, the salad will be
pale pink.)

3 cups tomato juice

*3 cups Hellmann's mayonnaise, plus more for
garnish*

1 small onion, finely chopped

¾ cup crushed pineapple

¼ cup cream cheese

¼ cup cottage cheese

1 tablespoon Worcestershire sauce

Tabasco sauce to taste

Red food coloring

Salt and white pepper to taste

Boston or Bibb lettuce leaves

In a blender, combine 2 cups of the tomato juice, 1 cup
of the mayonnaise, the onion, pineapple, cream cheese,
cottage cheese, Worcestershire, and Tabasco, blend till
smooth, and scrape into a bowl. In the blender, combine
the remaining tomato juice and mayonnaise and blend
till smooth, adding enough food coloring to make the
mixture the color of a very ripe tomato. Add this mixture
to the mixture in the bowl and whisk till well blended
and smooth. Season with salt and pepper and more
Tabasco if desired. Scrape the mixture into a large, 2-
inch-deep baking dish and freeze.

To serve, arrange lettuce leaves on salad plates, place
1 or 2 scoops of frozen tomato on top, and garnish each
scoop with a dollop of mayonnaise.

Congealed Pickled Peach and Pecan Salad

Makes 6 servings

WHAT COULD BE MORE SOUTHERN THAN TO COMBINE pickled peaches, pecans, and cream cheese to make a congealed salad? Of course, hostesses throughout the South love to serve this type of salad at church, bridge, and charity luncheons, but I've also discovered that nothing goes better with a glazed baked ham or virtually any meat or poultry casserole. I'm always very suspicious of commercial jars of pickled peaches and strongly urge you to learn to put up your own during the summer months (see page 386).

One 3-ounce package lemon-flavored Jell-O

¾ cup boiling water

¾ cup pickled peach juice

One 3-ounce package cream cheese, at room temperature

3 to 4 pickled peaches (cloves removed), chopped

½ cup chopped pecans

Bibb lettuce leaves

In a bowl, combine the Jell-O and boiling water and stir till dissolved. Add the peach juice, stir, and chill till the mixture begins to thicken, about 1 hour. Beat with an electric mixer till light and fluffy.

In another bowl, cream the cheese with the mixer till smooth, then add the peaches and pecans and stir till well blended. Add the cream cheese mixture to the Jell-O mixture, stir till well blended, transfer to a 1-quart mold, and chill till firm, about 2 hours.

Serve the salad on lettuce leaves.

Frozen Fruit Bridge Salad

Makes 8 servings

THERE'S NOT A PROPER LADY IN LOUISVILLE, Savannah, Montgomery, or Little Rock who wouldn't consider a frozen fruit salad such as this one the height of elegance for her bridge club or a summertime patio luncheon—served typically with trimmed finger sandwiches or tiny ham biscuits. Of course, the salad could be (and often is) made with canned or frozen fruit, but as any fastidious hostess knows, not only is it a shame not to use fresh fruit (pineapple included) when it's readily available, but the differences in taste and texture are almost radical. (One of the most spectacular frozen fruit salads I ever tasted, by the way, was made primarily with papaya, mango, and star fruit by a restaurant chef at Cypress Gardens, near Winter Haven, Florida.)

One 3-ounce package cream cheese, softened

¼ cup mayonnaise

2 tablespoons sugar

2 tablespoons fresh lemon juice

2 cups rinsed fresh raspberries

1 cup peeled, pitted, and sliced ripe fresh peaches

½ cup stemmed and rinsed fresh blueberries

2 ripe bananas, peeled and sliced

1 cup diced fresh pineapple

1 cup heavy cream, whipped to stiff peaks

8 Bibb lettuce leaves

8 rinsed and pitted ripe cherries for garnish

In a large mixing bowl, beat the cream cheese, mayonnaise, sugar, and lemon juice with a wooden spoon till well blended and smooth. Add the raspberries, peaches, blueberries, bananas, and pineapple and stir gently till well blended. Fold in the whipped cream till well blended, scrape the mixture into a large loaf pan, cover with plastic wrap, and place in the freezer overnight.

When ready to serve, slice the loaf with a sharp knife into 8 sections, place each section on a lettuce leaf on a salad plate, let stand about 10 minutes to soften slightly, and garnish each slice with a whole cherry.

Congealed Strawberry, Pineapple, and Banana Salad

Makes 6 to 8 servings

CONGEALED FRUIT SALADS HAVE BEEN A MAJOR component of Southern cuisine for at least a century, and when they're carefully layered in a glass mold, as with this colorful example, they become a true "party dish" worthy of the most elegant buffet or bridge luncheon. Diced cherries, blackberries, raspberries, crushed peaches or mangoes, and any chopped nuts can be used to make an attractive and delicious mold such as this, so feel free to experiment. In the South, this type of salad would typically be served with a variety of tea sandwiches.

One 3-ounce package strawberry-flavored Jell-O

½ cup boiling water

One 10-ounce package frozen strawberries, thawed, with the juices reserved

One 8-ounce can crushed pineapple, drained

2 bananas, mashed

½ cup chopped walnuts

½ pint sour cream

Bibb lettuce leaves

In a saucepan, combine the Jell-O and boiling water, stir till dissolved, add the strawberries plus their juice, and stir well. Transfer the mixture to a bowl, add the pineapple, bananas, and walnuts, and stir well. Scrape half the mixture into a medium-size glass mold, cover with plastic wrap, and chill about 2 hours or till just firm.

With a rubber spatula, spread the sour cream over the top, scrape the remainder of the strawberry mixture on top, cover with plastic wrap, and chill 2 to 3 hours or till fully firm.

Serve the salad on lettuce leaves.

Seafood Gumbo, page 103

Country Ham Braised
in Cider and Molasses,
page 146

Perfect Southern Fried Chicken, page 162

Fried Catfish with Pecan Sauce and
Calabash Hush Puppies, pages 209 and 309

Memphis Barbecued Baby Back Pork Ribs, page 218

Delaware Creamed Succotash, page 241

Tennessee Shrimp and Grits,
page 292

St. Augustine Shrimp and
Oyster Pilau, page 279

Cajun Red Beans and Rice, page 275

Perfect Buttermilk Biscuits, page 311

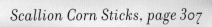
Scallion Corn Sticks, page 307

Southern Pecan Pie, page 337

Mixed Berry Cobbler, page 360

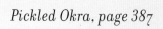
Pickled Okra, page 387

River Road Planter's Punch, page 416

Soups, Chowders, & Gumbos

She-Crab Soup

Williamsburg Peanut Soup

Beefy Okra and Tomato Soup

Delta Bean and Ham Soup

Watercress and Buttermilk Soup

Tennessee Bean, Sausage,
and Mixed Greens Soup

Creole Eggplant Soup

Pot Likker Soup

Virginia Sweet Potato
and Bourbon Soup

Kentucky Potato, Country Ham,
and Sour Grass Soup

Turtle Bean Soup

Clemson Blue Cheese Soup
with Southern Comfort

Chilled Peach
and Mango Soup

Curried Fish Chowder

Gulf Creamed Oyster
and Corn Chowder

Florida Conch Chowder

Maryland Crab Chowder

Succotash Chowder

Pumpkin, Corn, and
Bell Pepper Chowder

Cape Fear Shrimp Bisque

Pamlico Muddle

Seafood Gumbo

Gumbo Ya Ya

Carolina Gumbo

She-Crab Soup

Makes 4 to 6 servings

CREATED A CENTURY AGO AT EVERETT'S RESTAURANT in Charleston, South Carolina, by the black chef William Deas, she-crab soup is not only the quintessential dish of the Carolina and Georgia Lowcountry but the true queen of all Southern soups. And if you think debate is hot over the correct way to prepare Kentucky burgoo, Creole gumbo, and Virginia Brunswick stew, you should hear the pundits on the topic of this silky, subtle, orangish, sherry-laced delicacy made traditionally with the flesh and coral roe of female blue crabs. Should the soup be thickened with flour, puréed rice, or heavy cream? Can chopped hard-boiled egg yolks be substituted when crab roe is not available? (Roe can often be found bottled in specialty food shops.) Is it permissible to include Worcestershire sauce, grated nutmeg, or cayenne pepper? I do agree that crab roe is almost essential to round out both the flavor and texture of the soup, but beyond that, I continue to be eminently satisfied with the recipe my family and I finally acquired years ago at a restaurant called The Sea Captain in Murrell's Inlet, South Carolina. (Its sibling still exists in Myrtle Beach, but the soup's not the same.) And, oh yes, I do like at least a tablespoon of sherry in my bowl of she-crab soup. One warning: don't try to make this soup in a regular saucepan over direct heat, which could result in overheating and scorching.

- *4 tablespoons (½ stick) butter*
- *2 small onions, minced*
- *2 tablespoons all-purpose flour*
- *2 cups milk*
- *2 cups heavy cream*
- *1 teaspoon ground nutmeg*
- *2 teaspoon white pepper*
- *2 teaspoons salt*
- *2 tablespoons Worcestershire sauce*
- *2 tablespoons cornstarch*
- *1 pound fresh lump crabmeat, picked over for shells and cartilage*
- *½ cup crab roe*
- *Dry sherry to taste*

In the top of a double boiler, melt the butter over low direct heat, add the onions, and cook, stirring, till just soft, about 2 minutes. Add the flour gradually and stir till the mixture thickens. Place the pan over the bottom of the double boiler half filled with boiling water and slowly add ½ cup of the milk, stirring. When the milk is hot, add the heavy cream, nutmeg, pepper, salt, and Worcestershire and cook 5 minutes, stirring. Dissolve the cornstarch in the remaining milk, remove the pan from the hot water, and stir in the cornstarch mixture. Return the pan to the double boiler and cook the mixture till hot, 5 minutes longer. When ready to serve, add the crabmeat and roe, heat the soup thoroughly over boiling water, and lightly sprinkle each serving with sherry.

Williamsburg Peanut Soup

Makes 6 to 8 servings

MAKE NO MISTAKE ABOUT IT, DESPITE GEORGIA'S reputation as the peanut (and pecan) capital of the universe, the nuts there cannot hold a candle to the large, oily, succulent, noble goobers grown in Virginia. (I order a steady supply of 2-pound bags from Original Nut House, in Wakefield, Virginia: 1-800-913-6642.) In 1794, Thomas Jefferson's garden included no fewer than sixty-five peanut hills, and during Colonial times in Virginia, peanut soup was already considered one of the most elegant dishes served at the most refined dinners. Of course, every area of the state has its special version of the soup, and while nothing can be more soothing or delectable than a creamy peanut soup, this type based on chicken broth and a touch of tomato sauce, and found in many of the historic restaurants of Colonial Williamsburg, is hard to beat. As for the sacrilege of using peanut butter instead of freshly ground peanuts in the soup, "that's the sort of crazy thing those folks down in the Carolinas and Georgia would do," one waitress huffed.

2 cups roasted Virginia peanuts

6 cups chicken broth

3 tablespoons peanut oil

1 medium onion, chopped

2 celery ribs (including leaves), chopped

2 garlic cloves, chopped

2 tablespoons all-purpose flour mixed with 2 tablespoons cold water, stirred into a paste

1 tablespoon canned tomato sauce

1/2 teaspoon Worcestershire sauce

5 drops Tabasco sauce

Salt and freshly ground black pepper to taste

In a blender or food processor, combine 1 cup of the peanuts with 1 cup of the broth and blend to a purée. Add the remaining nuts and another cup of the broth and blend again till very smooth, then strain the mixture through a fine sieve into a bowl and set aside.

In a medium skillet, heat the oil over moderately low heat, add the onion, celery, and garlic, and cook, stirring, 5 minutes. Transfer the vegetables to the blender or food processor, add another cup of broth, blend to a purée, and scrape the mixture into a large, heavy saucepan over moderate heat. Add the flour paste to the vegetable purée, stir, and cook, stirring, 5 minutes. Add the remaining 3 cups broth, the strained peanut mixture, tomato sauce, Worcestershire, and Tabasco, season with salt and pepper, stir well, and continue to cook till the soup is velvety smooth, about 5 minutes.

BEEFY OKRA AND TOMATO SOUP

Makes 4 to 6 servings

THERE'S NOT A SERIOUS COOK IN THE SOUTH who doesn't have his or her special version of okra and tomato soup. Craig Claiborne used to add a little country ham to his Mississippi variation; Louis Osteen at Louis's in Pawleys Island, South Carolina, makes his with rice, bell peppers, and chile peppers; the chef at Woodfire Grill in Atlanta almost transforms the soup into a stew by including fresh corn and shrimp; and my own mother would never dream of preparing hers without both a marrow bone and diced beef. I make this soup only in the summer, when small, tender, fresh okra and homegrown tomatoes are available—hardly a sacrifice since the soup can be made in quantity and frozen very successfully in individual containers for the winter.

1 soup bone

One 1½-pound piece boneless beef chuck, trimmed of excess fat and cut into chunks

2 medium onions, chopped

2 celery ribs (leaves included), chopped

1 bay leaf

6 cups water

3 large ripe tomatoes, peeled and coarsely chopped

1½ pounds fresh okra (stems removed), sliced

½ teaspoon Worcestershire sauce

Salt and freshly ground black pepper to taste

In a large, heavy pot, combine the soup bone, beef, onions, celery, and bay leaf. Add the water, bring to a boil, reduce the heat to low, and simmer till the beef is tender, about 2 hours. Transfer the beef to a cutting board, cut it into small dice, and set aside. Discard the soup bone.

Strain the liquid in the pot and discard the solids. Skim the fat from the liquid, rinse out the pot, and return the liquid to the pot. Add the diced beef, tomatoes, okra, Worcestershire, and salt and pepper, return the soup to a simmer, and cook about 1 hour. Adjust the seasoning and serve very hot in soup bowls.

DELTA BEAN AND HAM SOUP

Makes 6 servings

IN ONE VERSION OR ANOTHER, I'VE HAD THIS SPICY
bean soup from the Louisiana Delta right up to the Texas
border. The most memorable I've tasted was made with
the highly spiced and smoked Cajun ham called tasso,
but since tasso is still not that easy to come by outside
the region, I've learned that aged country ham works
almost as well. While few Louisiana cooks would bother
to simmer the beans this long and turn part of them into
a purée, I find that the extra time and effort transforms
an ordinary potage into a rather refined first course.

The cuisine of Louisiana is the most complex
in the South. Traditional Southern cooking is
prevalent in most of the northern part of the
state, while the southern part is dominated
primarily by both Creole and Cajun styles of
cooking. Creole is a hybrid of sophisticated
French, Spanish, and African traditions that
evolved in New Orleans during the eighteenth
and nineteenth centuries. Cajun, developed
by French Acadians who migrated from
Canada to the Louisiana bayous in the mid-
eighteenth century, is much more plain,
robust, country food. Today, Creole and Cajun
often merge to form a single cuisine loosely
classified as "Louisiana cooking."

---

2 cups dried kidney beans

2 quarts chicken broth

1 medium onion, chopped

1 small green bell pepper, seeded and chopped

1 garlic clove, chopped

½ cup diced lean country ham

2 teaspoons chili powder

1 teaspoon dried oregano

Salt and freshly ground black pepper to taste

Place the beans in a bowl with enough water to cover
and let soak overnight.

Drain, rinse, and pick over the beans, place in a large,
heavy pot, and add the broth. Bring to a boil, reduce
the heat to low, cover, and simmer 1 hour.

Add all the remaining ingredients, bring the soup back
to simmer, cover, and cook 2 hours longer.

In a blender or food processor, purée about one-quarter
of the soup, return to the pot, and stir well. Heat the
soup thoroughly and serve in soup bowls or plates.

WATERCRESS AND BUTTERMILK SOUP

Makes 4 servings

EVER SINCE SETTLERS IN THE FIRST SOUTHERN
colonies churned butter derived from a sour milk called
clabber and drank the leftover nutritious liquid,
buttermilk has had a special status in the South that few
outsiders appreciate. Gone are the days, however, when
you can find natural buttermilk like that I drank as a
child. Today it is replaced by the very respectable
commercial product made from low-fat milk transformed
with special bacteria. For centuries, buttermilk has been
a vital ingredient in the making of certain biscuits,
cornbreads, hush puppies, pies, puddings, spoonbreads,
marinades, and salad dressings, but it's also the major
ingredient in any number of tangy soups, such as this
one, which is just as good chilled as hot. Fresh parsley
can be substituted for the watercress, and if you want to
produce a really modern soup, use arugula leaves.

1 large bunch fresh watercress, rinsed and stems removed

1 tablespoon butter

1 large onion, chopped

1 garlic clove, minced

1 medium potato, peeled and cubed

3 cups chicken broth

Salt and freshly ground black pepper to taste

¾ cup buttermilk

Cayenne pepper to taste

Tear off about ½ cup of watercress leaves for garnish
and set aside.

In a saucepan, melt the butter over moderate heat,
add the onions and garlic, and stir till soft, about 2
minutes. Add the potatoes, broth, and salt and pepper
and bring to a boil. Add the remaining watercress,
reduce the heat slightly, cover, and simmer till the
potatoes are tender, about 15 minutes.

Meanwhile, bring about 2 cups of water to a boil and
add the reserved watercress leaves. Blanch 10 seconds,
drain, and set aside.

Pour the potato-and-watercress mixture into a blender
or food processor, blend thoroughly, and return to the
saucepan. Add the buttermilk, cayenne pepper, and
blanched watercress leaves, heat thoroughly, and serve
hot or warm in soup plates.

Tennessee Bean, Sausage, and Mixed Greens Soup

Makes 6 to 8 servings

WHEN TENNESSEE WAS PART OF THE VIRGINIA Territory in the eighteenth century, settled mostly by the English and Scotch Irish, cooking in the hill country revolved mainly around roasted meats, country hams, stews, and hearty soups such as this one based on dried beans, sausages smoked at hog-killing time, and the bounty of various greens. Today, the soup might well be enriched by ramps (wild leeks), which still grow abundantly in the Tennessee mountains and are even celebrated each spring at a ramps festival in Cosby. No debate on what to serve with this type of brawny soup: cornbread.

1½ cups dried Great Northern white beans

2 tablespoons peanut oil

1 medium onion, chopped

½ red bell pepper, seeded and chopped

1 pound kielbasa, cut into ½-inch slices

4 cups chicken broth

4 cups water

1 pound turnip greens, rinsed, stems removed, and leaves shredded

1 pound mustard greens, rinsed, stems removed, and leaves shredded

Salt and freshly ground black pepper to taste

Dried red pepper flakes to taste

Place the beans in a saucepan with enough water to cover and bring to a boil. Turn off the heat, cover, and let the beans stand 1 hour.

In a large skillet, heat the oil over moderate heat, add the onion, bell pepper, and sausage, and cook till the vegetables and sausage are slightly browned, about 5 minutes. Transfer to a large pot, drain the beans, and add them to the pot. Add the broth and water, bring to a boil, reduce the heat to low, cover, and simmer 1 hour.

Add the greens to the pot, add salt and black pepper and red pepper flakes, stir well, and continue cooking over low heat, covered, till the beans are tender, about 1 hour.

Serve in deep soup bowls.

Louisiana produces two distinctly regional sausages used in gumbos, jambalayas, and other Creole and Cajun dishes: boudin (made with ground pork and chicken, rice, and onions) and smoked andouille (ground pork, garlic, and spicy seasonings). Since the sausages are rarely found outside the region, cooks often substitute kielbasa.

CREOLE EGGPLANT SOUP

Makes 6 servings

INTRODUCED TO THE AMERICAN COLONIES FROM Africa by Thomas Jefferson, eggplant is often referred to as Guinea squash in Louisiana, where the vegetable has always been much more popular than in other areas of the South—due, most likely, to the large black population there. Except, in fact, for a splendid eggplant soup that chef Bill Neal used to prepare at Crook's Corner in Chapel Hill, North Carolina, I don't recall ever eating one outside New Orleans and the Louisiana Delta. In any case, this is another of the South's great curried dishes, appropriate for a cold winter's night or, chilled and skimmed of any surface fat, at a summer luncheon.

6 tablespoons bacon grease

2 cups diced eggplant

1 cup diced onions

1 cup diced celery

1 cup diced potatoes

1 garlic clove, minced

½ teaspoon curry powder

Pinch of crumbled dried thyme

Pinch of crumbled dried basil

2½ cups chicken broth

1 cup heavy cream

In a large, heavy skillet, heat the bacon grease over moderate heat, add the eggplant, onions, celery, potatoes, and garlic, and cook, stirring, about 10 minutes. Add the curry powder, thyme, and basil and continue cooking till the potatoes start to stick to the bottom of the skillet. Add the broth, stir, and bring to a boil. Reduce the heat to low and simmer till the starch from the eggplant and potatoes thickens the liquid, about 30 minutes. When the soup is thickened, stir in the heavy cream, heat well, and serve in soup bowls.

Pot Likker Soup

Makes 6 servings

THROUGHOUT THE DEEP SOUTH AND MUCH OF Appalachia, pot likker is essentially no more than the vitamin-rich broth left over in a pot of boiled greens or peas cooked with a smoked ham bone, and it is always—I repeat, always—served with cornbread. Arguments flare up about pot likker: Is it one or two words? Can salt pork, bacon, or ham be substituted for the ham bone? Should the cornbread (or cornpone) be dunked or crumbled into the hearty broth for best results? Is it acceptable to serve the greens or peas in the broth, or must the broth stand alone? Do mustard greens, collards, turnip greens, or kale produce the most flavorful pot likker? One of the few restaurants left in the South where you can still order a bowl or cup of plain, old-fashioned pot likker is Mary Mac's Tea Room, in Atlanta, but I've learned while traveling in rural Georgia, Alabama, and Mississippi that almost any diner or roadside café that serves greens will manage to come up with a little pot likker only for the asking. This elaborate pot likker soup, on which I was virtually weaned, must have been my maternal grandmother's invention, since I've never encountered it away from home. Obviously, it's a meal in itself, and utterly wondrous. If you can't find crowder peas, just double the quantity of black-eyes.

1 pound fresh turnip greens, rinsed and stems removed

2 tablespoons peanut oil

2 cups diced cooked ham

1 large onion, chopped

1 garlic clove, minced

3 medium red potatoes, scrubbed and diced

2½ cups chicken broth

One 16-ounce can black-eyed peas, drained

One 16-ounce can crowder peas, drained

1 cup water

1½ teaspoon white vinegar

½ teaspoon salt

Freshly ground black pepper to taste

Tabasco sauce to taste

Tear the turnip greens into small pieces and place in a large pot with enough water to cover. Bring to a boil, reduce the heat to moderately low, cover, and cook 15 minutes. Drain the greens and set aside.

Heat the oil in a pot over moderate heat, add the ham, onion, and garlic, and cook, stirring, about 3 minutes. Add the turnip greens and all remaining ingredients and stir till well blended. Bring to a boil, reduce the heat to low, and let simmer about 1 hour, stirring from time to time. Serve hot in wide soup bowls.

Virginia Sweet Potato and Bourbon Soup

Makes 6 servings

FIRST, TO CLEAR UP ONE GRAVE MISCONCEPTION: genuine yams are *not* sweet potatoes, despite their resemblance to them in shape and flavor. The two are different plant species altogether—the yam a tuber found mainly in South America and Africa, the sweet potato native to the New World, especially the American South. Most likely, the confusion derives from African slaves having called the sweet potato either *njam* or *djambi*. Long before that, sweet potatoes were being cultivated in Virginia and often called the "Indian potato." Eventually, of course, the sweet potato became a major crop in the South and a major component of soul cooking, utilized in everything from puddings and pies to croquettes and casseroles to lusty soups, such as this one spiked with bourbon. (Sweet potatoes and bourbon do seem to have a natural affinity.)

2 strips bacon, cut into small pieces

1 small onion, chopped

4½ cups chicken broth

3 medium sweet potatoes (about 2 pounds), peeled and cubed

2 tablespoons molasses

½ teaspoon dried thyme

⅛ teaspoon grated nutmeg

Salt and freshly ground black pepper to taste

Cayenne pepper to taste

2 tablespoons bourbon

½ cup heavy cream

Chopped fresh chives for garnish

In a large, heavy saucepan, fry the bacon over moderate heat till crisp, drain on paper towels, and set aside. Add the onion to the fat in the pan and cook, stirring, about 2 minutes. Add the broth, sweet potatoes, molasses, thyme, nutmeg, salt and pepper, and cayenne pepper, bring to a boil, reduce the heat to low, and simmer till the potatoes are very tender, about 30 minutes. Let cool slightly.

Transfer the mixture to a blender or food processor and reduce to a smooth purée. Scrape back into the pan, add the bourbon and cream, and cook over low heat till thoroughly heated. Serve in soup bowls and sprinkle a few chives over each serving.

Kentucky Potato, Country Ham, and Sour Grass Soup

Makes 6 servings

LEGEND HAS IT THAT DURING THE FIRST YEARS ON THE Kentucky frontier, housewives followed the cows into the region's meadows and picked only the wild greens the cows ate to avoid poisonous plants, and no doubt one of these was the tangy sour grass (sorrel) that still flourishes throughout much of the state during the spring. Combine this with the area's starchy Irish potatoes and exceptional aged country ham, and you simply won't come up with a lustier soup, reminiscent of the best colonial cookery. Fresh sorrel is now available in spring and early summer in most fine markets. Look for bright, crisp, light green leaves, avoiding any that are yellowed or wilted. (A perennial, sorrel is one of the easiest and heartiest herbs to grow in the home garden, and I use mine also in all sorts of salads.) One warning: if you use a food processor to make this soup, you risk ending up with mush instead of the correct rough purée.

5 russet potatoes (about 2½ pounds), peeled and cubed

5 quarts water

6 tablespoons (¾ stick) butter

2 large Spanish onions, chopped

½ cup finely chopped country ham

3 cups chopped sour grass (sorrel) leaves, torn

1½ cups milk

Salt and freshly ground black pepper to taste

Chopped fresh chives for garnish

In a large saucepan, combine the potatoes and water, bring to a boil, reduce the heat to moderately low, and simmer till tender, about 15 minutes.

Meanwhile, in a large, heavy skillet, melt the butter over moderate heat, add the onions and ham, and cook, stirring, 5 minutes. Add the sour grass and cook, stirring, till it wilts, 1 to 2 minutes. Add this mixture to the potatoes in the pan, add the milk, stir, and simmer about 5 minutes.

Transfer the mixture to a blender, add the salt and pepper, and reduce just to a rough purée. Return to the saucepan and heat gently till piping hot. Serve in soup plates and sprinkle a few chives over the top of each portion.

TURTLE BEAN SOUP

Makes 8 servings

KNOWN ALSO AS TURTLE BEANS, BLACK BEANS HAVE been used in the Deep South to make this inimitable soup since at least the early nineteenth century, and even today, turtle bean soup is deemed to be one of the most elegant ways to begin an elaborate dinner. Ironically, the greatest version I ever tasted was prepared by the Greek owner of The Coach House in New York City, who obtained the recipe in Atlanta when he originally operated a restaurant there called The Coach & Six. The soup can be made with beef bones, salt pork, ham hocks, tomatoes, beef stock, and countless other ingredients, depending on the region. The one cardinal rule is that it must be silky smooth and contain either Madeira or sherry. There is a quick method for making the soup, whereby the beans are boiled 5 minutes and allowed to stand 1 hour instead of being soaked overnight, then slowly simmered; but I'm convinced that the texture of the soup is not the same when this shortcut is taken.

3 cups dried turtle beans (black beans)

8 cups water

¼ cup peanut oil

2 medium onions, chopped

2 celery ribs, chopped

1 garlic clove, minced

1 tablespoon all-purpose flour

1 smoked ham bone, trimmed of excess fat

2 bay leaves

Salt and freshly ground black pepper to taste

½ cup Madeira

2 tablespoons fresh lemon juice

2 hard-boiled large eggs, chopped

Thin pitted lemon slices for garnish

Rinse and pick over the beans, place in a large pot with enough water to cover, and soak overnight. Drain the beans, add the water, and bring to a boil. Reduce the heat to low, cover, and simmer 1½ hours.

In another large pot, heat the oil over moderate heat, add the onions, celery, and garlic, and cook, stirring, till softened but not browned, about 3 minutes. Sprinkle on the flour and stir 1 minute longer. Add the beans and their cooking liquid, the ham bone, bay leaves, and salt and pepper, bring to a simmer, cover, and cook 3 hours.

Remove and discard the ham bone and bay leaves and drain the beans, reserving the cooking liquid in a saucepan. In a blender or food processor, reduce the beans to a smooth purée and scrape into a large pot. Add the reserved cooking liquid, the salt and pepper, Maderia, and lemon juice and simmer till piping hot, 5 to 10 minutes.

To serve, ladle the soup into soup plates, sprinkle the eggs over the tops, and garnish each portion with a slice of lemon.

CLEMSON BLUE CHEESE SOUP
WITH SOUTHERN COMFORT

Makes 4 to 6 servings

THOUGH STILL AVAILABLE ONLY IN THE CAROLINAS, Clemson Blue Cheese, produced in relatively small quantities on the campus of Clemson University in Clemson, South Carolina, is one of the South's best-kept secrets. Compared favorably by professional turophiles (cheese lovers) with Iowa's famous Maytag Blue and many distinguished European blue-veined cheeses, Clemson Blue is strictly artisanal, not machine-made— and highly favored by Louis Osteen, Ben Barker, and many other renowned Carolina chefs. After I first tasted the rich, smooth, complex cheese, I wasted no time substituting it for English Stilton in my blue cheese soup, and eventually replaced port wine with Southern Comfort, with amazing results. Now, if only the folks down at Clemson University can figure out some way to market the cheese outside the region, great cheese making might well be recognized as still another landmark in the South's evolving culinary heritage.

2 cups chicken broth

¾ cup minced celery

½ cup minced carrots

3 tablespoons butter

2 tablespoons minced onion

¼ cup all-purpose flour

2 cups milk

½ pound Clemson Blue (or other top-grade natural blue cheese)

4 to 6 tablespoons Southern Comfort

In a saucepan, combine the broth, celery, and carrots, bring to a boil, reduce the heat, and simmer the vegetables till tender, about 10 minutes.

In a large saucepan, melt the butter over low heat, add the onion and cook, stirring, 3 minutes. Add the flour and continue cooking, stirring, 2 minutes. Gradually add the chicken broth mixture, increase the heat to moderate, and cook, stirring constantly, till bubbly and thickened.

Remove saucepan from the heat, add the cheese, and stir till the cheese is melted and well incorporated. Serve the soup with a tablespoon of Southern Comfort in each bowl.

Chilled Peach and Mango Soup

Makes 4 to 6 servings

FROM THE DAY THE FIRST CLING PEACHES FROM South Carolina and Georgia show up in Southern markets and on farm stands till the last freestone Elbertas and Georgia Belles disappear in September, cooks utilize the luscious fruit in everything from elegant soups to cobblers to preserves. Traditional chilled peach soup has always been considered an ideal starter to a light, casual summer lunch, but when, a couple of years ago, I decided to toss the flesh of a ripe mango into the blender with the peaches, a sublime revelation occurred that would affect not only my spicy peach soup but also my peach preserves, cobblers, crumbles, and pies. Simply put, it's a gustatory marriage made in heaven, and now that Florida mangoes are readily available in virtually all markets, I hope to see this combination exploited more in both Southern homes and restaurants. Just be sure that the peaches are ripe, and remember that if you're forced to buy hard mangoes, it takes a couple of days for them to ripen properly.

1½ cups sliced fresh ripe, peeled peaches

1½ cups sliced fresh ripe, peeled mangoes

1½ cups water

1½ cups dry white wine

3 thin slices fresh peeled ginger

½ cup sugar

2 tablespoons bourbon

1½ tablespoons cornstarch mixed in 1½ tablespoons cold water

3 teaspoons fresh lemon zest

¼ cup sour cream

Fresh mint leaves for garnish

In a large saucepan, combine the peaches, mangoes, water, wine, and ginger, bring to a simmer, cover, and cook 15 minutes. Add the sugar, bourbon, and cornstarch, bring to a low boil, and stir till thickened.

Transfer the mixture in batches to a blender or food processor, add the lemon zest and sour cream, and blend till smooth. Let the soup cool, then chill, covered, for at least 4 hours. Serve in chilled glass soup bowls and garnish the top of each serving with a mint leaf.

94

CURRIED FISH CHOWDER

Makes 6 to 8 servings

ANYBODY WHO BELIEVES THAT NEW ENGLANDERS
historically have a monopoly on chowder has apparently
never had Florida conch chowder, Maryland clam
chowder, Louisiana terrapin chowder, or any one of the
many hearty fish chowders that Southerners on the
Atlantic and Gulf coasts often refer to as "spoon dishes."
And those who can't associate curry powder with
Southern food have apparently never been exposed to
Charleston hobotee and curried shrimp paste,
Mississippi corn and cheese soufflé, curried cucumber
mayonnaise, or the many fish chowders enhanced by a
little curry powder from Baltimore to Mobile. As in the
old days, a spicy chowder such as this one is usually
intended today to be served as an exotic first course at a
"company" dinner, but add corn, bell peppers, carrots, or
even shellfish, and you have a more rugged chowder
that, served with skillet cornbread, is perfect for a
casual lunch or late-night supper.

3 tablespoons olive oil

1 medium onion, finely chopped

1 celery rib, finely chopped

1 garlic clove, minced

2 tablespoons curry powder

3 tablespoons all-purpose flour

1 large ripe tomato, peeled and chopped

3 cups bottled clam broth

3 cups water

1 medium potato, peeled, boiled, and mashed

*2 pounds, nonoily white fish fillets (snapper,
     bass, cod, or haddock), cut into 1-inch pieces*

1 cup heavy cream

In a large, heavy saucepan, heat the oil over moderate
heat, add the onion, celery, and garlic, and cook,
stirring, till softened, about 2 minutes. Add the curry
powder and flour, stir well, and continue cooking,
stirring, 2 minutes longer. Add the tomato, broth,
water, and mashed potato and stir till the potato is well
blended and the mixture thickened. Bring to a simmer
and cook, stirring from time to time, 20 minutes.

Add the fish to the pot and simmer 10 minutes longer.
Stir in the cream, bring the chowder almost to a boil,
and serve in wide soup plates.

Gulf Creamed Oyster and Corn Chowder

Makes 4 to 6 servings

AS ANYONE KNOWS WHO'S EVER BELLIED UP TO THE Acme Oyster House in New Orleans' French Quarter and uttered to one of the expert shuckers, "Half dozen to start," Gulf oysters are the fattest, most succulent oysters on earth. Bay Adams, Four Bayous, Baptistes, Choctawhatchees—the names go on and on, from Panama City, Florida, to Biloxi, Mississippi, to Lafayette, Louisiana. Locals love them mostly on the half shell with cocktail sauce, but they also roast them, sauté them, fry them, and incorporate them into elaborate sauced dishes and simple soups and chowders. I guess I've eaten oysters every way possible along the Gulf coast, but this creamy oyster and corn chowder I was served in Mobile is one preparation I'll never forget. Any impeccably fresh oysters can be used, but I can't emphasize enough the importance of searching for the freshest corn you can find—ears with lots of milk still in the kernels. Sure, frozen corn could be substituted if absolutely necessary (especially if you, like me, freeze your own right off the cob during late summer), but there is a difference in taste and texture.

4 ears of very fresh corn (preferably Silver Queen)

3 tablespoons butter

6 scallions (part of green tops included), chopped

1 garlic clove, minced

2 cups milk

½ cup heavy cream

Salt and freshly ground black pepper to taste

1 dozen large fresh oysters, cut in half, with liquor reserved

Chopped fresh chives for garnish

On a plate, cut the kernels from the corn (there should be about 2 cups), scrape off as much of the milk from the cobs as possible, and set aside.

In a large, heavy saucepan, melt the butter over moderate heat, add the scallions and garlic, and cook, stirring, 1 minute. Add the milk and cream and bring almost to a boil. Add the salt and pepper, the oysters plus their liquor, and the corn kernels plus their milk. Bring to a boil, remove from the heat, and let stand 5 minutes. Serve the chowder in soup plates and garnish the top of each portion with chives.

Florida Conch Chowder

Makes 4 servings

BECAUSE IT TENDS TO BE TOUGH AND STRONG-TASTING if not handled properly, conch (pronounced "conk") can be an acquired taste to all but Floridians and Gulf Coast residents accustomed to eating the mollusk fresh during the peak summer season. Fortunately for we who love a good conch chowder, the meat is available frozen or canned year round in many food shops. Whether it's fresh (perhaps from a Chinese or Italian market) or processed, I always pound conch before cooking to make absolutely sure it's tender. Also, if the ocean flavor of the meat seems a bit too aggressive, you might counter it by adding a few pinches of curry powder to the chowder, as some restaurants in Florida do. Possibly the best conch chowders I've ever tasted were in Key West, where many of the restaurants also serve a unique salad of raw conch marinated in lime juice, as well as delectable conch fritters.

4 tablespoons (½ stick) butter

1 large onion, finely chopped

2 medium carrots, scraped and finely chopped

2 garlic cloves, minced

2 medium tomatoes, finely chopped

1 pound frozen or canned conch meat, pounded with a mallet and coarsely chopped

One 6-ounce can tomato paste

1 quart water

Salt and freshly ground black pepper to taste

2 medium potatoes, peeled and cut into small cubes

In a large saucepan, melt the butter over moderate heat, add the onion, carrots, garlic, and tomatoes, and cook, stirring, till softened, about 3 minutes. Add the conch and cook, stirring, 2 minutes longer. Add the tomato paste, water, and salt and pepper and stir well. Bring to a boil, reduce the heat to low, cover, and simmer 2 hours or till the conch is tender, adding more water if necessary to keep the chowder from becoming too thick.

Add the potatoes and simmer till they are tender, 15 to 20 minutes. Serve the chowder piping hot in soup bowls.

Maryland Crab Chowder

Makes 6 to 8 servings

ONE OF THE MOST DISTINCTIVE SPECIALTIES OF Baltimore and Maryland's Chesapeake Bay area is the thick, brilliant orange, peppery crab soup found in casual restaurants such as The Chesapeake, Copsey's, and Courtney's. And it was after consuming two bowls of the fiery potage at Copsey's (followed by a little local country ham stuffed with greens) that I came up with the idea of converting the soup into a milky chowder. This, of course, changes the whole nature of the dish, but I've yet to have guests who didn't rave about the chowder. And it's equally delicious made with half crabmeat, half shrimp.

4 slices bacon, cut into small pieces

2 medium onions, chopped

3 medium red potatoes, peeled and cut into small dice

1 cup water

3 cups milk

3 cups half-and-half

1 pound fresh lump crabmeat, picked over for shells and cartilage

1 large ripe tomato, peeled and diced

½ teaspoon Worcestershire sauce

2 teaspoons chili powder

Salt and freshly ground black pepper to taste

In a large, heavy saucepan, fry the bacon over moderate heat till crisp, drain on paper towels, and reserve. Add the onions, potatoes, and water to the fat in the pan, reduce the heat to low, cover, and simmer till the potatoes are tender and most of the water is evaporated, about 15 minutes. Add the milk and half-and-half, stir, and return to a simmer. Add the crabmeat, tomato, Worcestershire, chili powder, and salt and pepper, return to a simmer, and cook slowly, stirring from time to time, about 20 minutes. Serve the chowder in soup bowls and sprinkle equal amounts of the reserved bacon over the top of each portion.

SUCCOTASH CHOWDER

Makes 6 servings

IT'S BEEN OVER A CENTURY AND A HALF SINCE Lettice Bryan showed us how to use corn in soups and chowders in her *Kentucky Housewife* "receipt" book, but at Southern chowder parties today (especially in Florida, where chowder is king) you're just as likely to find vegetable chowders such as this as you are ones based on seafood. "Since it's got both corn and limas, we just call it succotash chowder," said my host at his cottage on rustic Amelia Island, north of Jacksonville. And what did he serve with the big bowls of smoky chowder? Delightful cornets of Georgia country ham stuffed with cream cheese and, of course, cornbread dripping with butter. Personally, I don't make this chowder unless I have fresh corn, mainly because I think the milk scraped with the kernels from the ears adds even more milky richness.

¼ pound slab bacon, rind removed and cut into small dice

1 medium onion, chopped

1 red bell pepper, seeded and chopped

3 cups chicken broth

2 medium russet potatoes, peeled and cut into small dice

2 cups milk

3 cups white corn kernels (fresh or frozen and thawed)

1 cup baby lima beans (fresh or frozen and thawed)

Salt and freshly ground black pepper to taste

In a large, heavy pot, fry the bacon over low heat till the fat is rendered. Add the onion and bell pepper and cook, stirring, till softened, about 10 minutes, taking care not to brown the vegetables. Add the broth and potatoes, increase the heat to moderate, and cook till the potatoes are tender, stirring occasionally, about 12 minutes. Add the milk, corn, limas, and salt and pepper and cook till the corn and limas are tender, about 10 minutes. Serve the chowder piping hot in soup plates.

PUMPKIN, CORN, AND BELL PEPPER CHOWDER

Makes 6 to 8 servings

IF THIS CHOWDER SEEMS SOPHISTICATED ENOUGH TO come from a fine restaurant, it's because it was inspired by a creamy, amazing corn chowder with red pepper I raved about at Fearrington House, outside Chapel Hill, North Carolina (operated, as it happened, by an old high school classmate of mine, Jenny Fitch). Forever searching for new ways to use fresh pumpkin in the early fall (not to mention the last ears of summer corn), I transformed the recipe for the Fearrington corn chowder slightly to accommodate the beloved gourd. At first, I simply substituted pumpkin for the potatoes, but the texture of the chowder just wasn't right. So back in went the spuds, and I couldn't be more satisfied. Serve this robust chowder with crisp Maryland Beaten Biscuits (page 312), as the early settlers most likely would have done.

4 slices bacon, cut into small pieces

1 medium onion, finely diced

2 tablespoons all-purpose flour

6 cups chicken broth

One 12-ounce can creamed corn

*2 medium red potatoes, peeled and cut into
    ¼-inch cubes*

*1 cup fresh or canned pumpkin cut into
    ¼-inch cubes*

*½ medium green bell pepper, seeded and finely
    diced*

3 ears fresh corn

1 pint half-and-half

Salt and freshly ground black pepper to taste

*¼ cup finely diced seeded red bell pepper for
    garnish*

In a large, heavy saucepan, fry the bacon over moderate heat till almost crisp, add the onion, and cook, stirring, till softened, about 2 minutes. Sprinkle the flour over the onion and cook, stirring, 2 minutes longer.

Add the broth, stir, and bring to a boil. Add the creamed corn and bring slowly to a boil, stirring. Strain through a coarse sieve into another large, heavy saucepan, pressing on the solids to extract as much liquid as possible. Add the potatoes, pumpkin, and green pepper to the liquid, cut the kernels off the ears of corn, and add to the mixture along with any milk scraped from the ears. Bring to a low boil, reduce the heat to low, cover, and simmer till the potatoes and pumpkin are tender, 15 to 20 minutes. Add the half-and-half and salt and pepper, stir well, and bring back to a simmer. Serve the chowder in deep soup bowls and garnish the tops of each portion with the diced red bell peppers.

Cape Fear Shrimp Bisque

Makes 6 servings

MORE OFTEN THAN NOT IN THE SOUTH, A SEAFOOD bisque bears no more resemblance to the silky smooth French dish than a soufflé imitates the fluffy wonders associated with that name. (Virtually any baked casserole dish that contains eggs can be called a soufflé.) Even in Charleston and New Orleans (where crawfish bisque is thought to be the ultimate test of a great cook), few chefs today bother to make a rich shrimp, crawfish, crabmeat, or lobster stock, grind the shellfish, temper egg yolks, and carry out the other procedures necessary to produce an authentic bisque. And in Wilmington, North Carolina, a shrimp bisque such as this one is so foreign to the original concept that it's really more a chowder than a bisque. No matter what Tarheels in the area choose to call it, however, the soup is one of the most unusual and delectable you'll find anywhere in the South, a perfect prelude to any dinner that features roasted meat or fowl as the main course. With the bisque, I like to serve a bowl of Benne Bits (page 18) or maybe Scallion Corn Sticks (page 307).

6 tablespoons (¾ stick) butter

4 medium onions, finely chopped

3 medium potatoes, peeled and cut into small dice

2 cups water

3 cups milk

½ pound extra-sharp cheddar cheese, grated

1 pound shrimp, peeled, deveined, and finely chopped

Pinch of powdered fennel

Salt and freshly ground black pepper to taste

1 tablespoon dry sherry

½ cup chopped fresh parsley leaves

In a large saucepan, melt the butter over low heat, add the onions, and cook, stirring, 5 minutes. Add the potatoes and water, increase the heat to moderate, and cook till the potatoes are tender, about 10 minutes.

In a small saucepan, combine the milk and cheese over low heat, stirring, till the cheese is melted. Add to the onions and potatoes and stir well. Add the shrimp, fennel, salt and pepper, and sherry, stir, and simmer gently over moderately low heat, 10 minutes. To serve, sprinkle a little chopped parsley on the bottom of each soup bowl and fill with bisque.

Pamlico Muddle

Makes 6 servings

IT WAS THE EARLIEST ENGLISH COLONISTS WHO introduced muddles ("a mess of fish"), mulls, and other robust seafood soups and stews to the barrier islands that separate North Carolina's Pamlico Sound from the Atlantic Ocean, and today the tradition continues all along the remote Outer Banks. I've had muddles so thick with fish and shellfish you could almost eat them with a fork, but the best I've tasted were much more like this amazingly light, herby concoction, which tastes so good on a cold winter's night with coleslaw and some form of cornbread. I've heard that for one style of muddle, eggs are poached in the broth and served on top the soup. Sounds a bit bizarre to me, but I'd still love to try that.

4 slices bacon

3 medium onions, diced

2 celery ribs, diced

1 small red bell pepper, seeded and diced

2 garlic cloves, minced

3 medium ripe tomatoes, diced

2 cups bottled clam broth

2 cups water

2 teaspoons fresh lemon juice

1 teaspoon Worcestershire sauce

Tabasco sauce to taste

Salt and freshly ground black pepper to taste

1 teaspoon dried thyme, crumbled

1 bay leaf

½ pound fresh grouper, red snapper, or other nonoily white fish fillets, cut into 1-inch pieces

¼ pound medium shrimp, shelled and deveined

¼ pound fresh sea scallops, quartered

In a large, heavy pot, fry the bacon over moderate heat till crisp, drain on paper towels, crumble, and reserve. Add the onions, celery, bell pepper, and garlic to the pot and cook, stirring, till very soft, about 5 minutes. Add the tomatoes, clam broth, water, lemon juice, Worcestershire, Tabasco, salt and pepper, thyme, and bay leaf, bring to a low simmer, cover, and cook 1 hour.

Add the grouper, shrimp, and scallops, return to a simmer, and cook till the fish begins to flake, about 8 minutes. Serve the muddle in deep soup bowls with crumbled bacon sprinkled over the top of each portion.

Seafood Gumbo

Makes 6 servings

OKRA INSTEAD OF FILÉ POWDER IS USED TO THICKEN this classic Creole gumbo, but with that exception, both the ingredients and cooking technique characterize what is undoubtedly the most popular gumbo throughout the Southern Gulf states. The name *gumbo* derives from the African Congo word for okra (*guingumbo*), and legend has it that when the French settled Louisiana, it was a certain Madame Langlois who bartered with the local Choctaw Indians for the secret of filé powder (made from the leaves of the sassafras tree), used for medical purposes. With the knowledge of okra and filé powder as thickening agents, gumbo gradually evolved. The roux is what gives the soup its traditional flavor and color; the darker the roux, the toastier the gumbo. But the technique does require patience and careful attention. Roux must be cooked very carefully over low heat to prevent burning. If the roux burns, you have no alternative but to start again.

½ pound bacon, cut into small pieces

¼ cup all-purpose flour

1 pound firm fresh okra, stems removed and pods cut into small rounds (about 5 cups)

1 large onion, chopped

½ medium green bell pepper, seeded and chopped

1 large celery rib, chopped

2½ cups canned tomatoes, drained

2 quarts chicken broth

¼ cup chopped fresh parsley leaves

1 teaspoon dried thyme, crumbled

1 bay leaf

Salt and freshly ground black pepper to taste

Tabasco sauce to taste

1 pound medium shrimp, peeled and drained

1 pound fresh claw crabmeat, picked over for shells and cartilage

1 pint small fresh, shucked oysters

Boiled white rice

In a large, heavy pot, fry the bacon over moderate heat till crisp, drain on paper towels, and reserve. Add the flour to the bacon grease, reduce the heat to low, and whisk more and more steadily for about 15 minutes or till the roux is light brown, taking great care not to burn it. Add the okra and cook, stirring, till the okra is slightly browned and the roux dark brown.

Add the onion, bell pepper, and celery, stir well, cover, and let cook 3 minutes. Add the tomatoes, broth, parsley, thyme, bay leaf, salt and pepper, and Tabasco, bring to a boil, reduce the heat to low, and simmer, uncovered, 2 hours, adding a little water if the liquid is too thick.

Add the shrimp, crabmeat, oysters, and reserved bacon, stir, return to a simmer, and cook about 15 minutes longer. Taste for seasoning. Serve the gumbo over rice in deep soup bowls.

103

Gumbo Ya Ya

Makes 6 servings

IN THE EARLY 1970S, I WAS AT COMMANDER'S PALACE in New Orleans the day that head chef Paul Prudhomme came up with this chicken-and-sausage gumbo and owner Ella Brennan was searching for a catchy name for it. "We wanted to offer a nonseafood gumbo in the restaurant," Ella recalls today, "and when Paul created this one, I happened to be reading a political novel with 'Ya Ya' in the title, and said to myself, 'Why not?'" The rest is history, for today gumbo ya ya (like blackened redfish) has been imitated, modified, and transformed into a Southern classic in homes and restaurants throughout the country. As for the actual origin and meaning of the term *ya ya*, neither Ella nor I had the remotest idea till a friend informed me that *ya* means "rice" in one African dialect. The version here is the original recipe I jotted down that day in New Orleans. Do be very careful not to burn the roux; to attain the color of milk chocolate, the oil and flour should take about 4 minutes of constant whisking, though the timing can vary.

One 2- to 2½-pound chicken

½ cup vegetable oil

⅓ cup all-purpose flour

2 medium onions, chopped

½ medium green bell pepper, seeded and chopped

1 garlic clove, minced

½ pound smoked sausage (like kielbasa), thinly sliced

¼ pound baked or boiled ham, cubed

2 bay leaves

½ teaspoon dried oregano, crumbled

½ teaspoon dried thyme, crumbled

1 teaspoon salt

Cayenne pepper to taste

2 tablespoons filé powder (available in specialty food shops)

3 cups boiled white rice

Disjoint the chicken and place in a large pot or kettle with enough water to cover. Bring to a boil, reduce the heat to low, cover, and simmer till the chicken is tender, 30 to 40 minutes. Remove the chicken and, when cool enough to handle, skin, bone, and shred the meat. Strain the cooking broth into another large pot and reserve.

In a large, heavy pot or casserole, heat the oil till very hot. Add the flour gradually, stirring constantly with a whisk, and cook the roux over moderate heat, still whisking constantly, till it is the color of milk chocolate, about 4 minutes, taking special care not to burn the roux.

Add the onions, green pepper, garlic, sausage, and ham, mix thoroughly, and continue cooking, stirring, about 10 minutes. Add 2 cups of the reserved broth, the shredded chicken, bay leaves, oregano, thyme, salt, and cayenne pepper, and stir thoroughly. Add 2 more cups of the broth, bring to a boil, reduce the heat to low, and simmer 1 hour. Remove pot from the heat, add the filé powder, stir, and let stand 10 minutes.

Distribute equal amounts of the rice in the bottom of 6 soup bowls or plates and ladle gumbo over the top. Serve piping hot.

—————— ✧✧✧ ——————

The filé powder used to season and thicken many Creole and Cajun dishes in Louisiana is the ground dried leaves of the sassafras tree and has a woodsy flavor suggestive of root beer. It is now widely available.

—————— ✧✧✧ ——————

105

CAROLINA GUMBO

Makes 6 servings

EVEN MOST SOUTHERNERS DON'T REALIZE THAT EVER since the days of the great Carolina rice plantations, gumbo has been as popular in the coastal Lowcountry as in Louisiana. The main difference between the two gumbos is that the Carolina version is not based on a roux the way the Creole classic is, and depends exclusively on the okra and long-simmered major ingredients themselves to thicken the soup—an explanation for why the seafood is purposefully overcooked. Most cooks I know around Wilmington, North Carolina, always make this gumbo with both chicken and seafood, whereas down the coast, in Charleston and Beaufort, South Carolina, the tradition is to use only seafood. I love both styles. Since the gumbo freezes beautifully, you might consider making it in a larger quantity.

4 slices bacon

*4 chicken legs or thighs, boned and patted dry
    with paper towels*

2 onions, diced

½ green bell pepper, seeded and diced

2 garlic cloves, minced

⅛ teaspoon dried thyme, crumbled

Salt and freshly ground black pepper to taste

Tabasco sauce to taste

One 10-ounce package frozen okra, thawed

4 ripe tomatoes, chopped

2 pounds medium shrimp, shelled and deveined

1 pint shucked fresh oysters, with their liquor

1 quart chicken broth

2 quarts water

2 bay leaves

1 lemon, halved and seeded

Boiled white rice, buttered

In a large, heavy pot, fry the bacon over moderate heat till crisp, drain on paper towels, and crumble. Add the chicken to the pot, cook on all sides till golden, then drain on paper towels. When cool enough to handle, shred the meat. Add the onions, bell pepper, garlic, thyme, salt and pepper, and Tabasco to the pot, reduce the heat slightly, and cook, stirring, 3 minutes. Add the okra, stir, and cook another 3 to 4 minutes. Add the crumbled bacon, chicken, tomatoes, shrimp, and oysters with the liquor and stir. Add the broth, water, bay leaves, and lemon halves, plus, if necessary, enough water to just cover. Bring to a low simmer, cover, and cook 2 hours, stirring occasionally. Remove and discard the lemon halves and serve the gumbo over rice in deep soup bowls.

Stews & Casseroles

Frogmore Stew

Kentucky Burgoo

Brunswick Stew

Stewed Ham Hocks
and Butter Beans

Turkey Succotash

Plantation Oyster
and Benne Seed Stew

Memphis Quail
and Vegetable Stew

Maryland Terrapin Stew

Georgia Ham
and Cowpea Stew

Arkansas Catfish Stew

West Virginia Venison Stew

Company Turkey and Ham Casserole

Chicken and Broccoli Casserole

Sausage and
Vidalia Onion Casserole

Rutabaga, Sweet Potato,
and Orange Casserole

Hominy, Mushroom,
and Cheddar Casserole

Creole Curried Shrimp
and Mirliton Casserole

Chicken Tetrazzini

Chicken Spaghetti

Southern Mac 'n' Cheese

Spoonbread

Georgia Bereavement Casserole

Baked Fruit Casserole

FROGMORE STEW

Makes 8 to 10 servings

ONE OF THE MOST EXCEPTIONAL PHENOMENA IN THE
United States is the coastal Gullah culture that still
exists between Georgetown and Charleston, South
Carolina, and on the area's remote Sea Islands.
Historically, Gullah was the language spoken by black
slaves (also called Geechees) on the vast Lowcountry
rice plantations. While much of the African patois is now
gone, you can still buy sweetgrass baskets and mats
woven by descendants of slaves all along Highway 17
north of Charleston (I have four mats that are at least
two decades old), and on St. Helena Island (near Hilton
Head), where this hearty stew is another example of
surviving Gullah life. (Until fairly recently, Frogmore,
named after an ancestral English county estate, was the
official name of the island's town center.) Frogmore
stew, which is not unlike a Louisiana crawfish boil, is
traditionally an outdoor dish of corn on the cob, shrimp,
hot sausage, and heaven knows what else boiled in a
highly seasoned stock (or beer) and served on
newspapers at picnic tables with lots of ice-cold beer.
With any Frogmore stew, flexibility is the rule—that plus
the proviso that no ingredient should be overcooked. The
best container to use is a large, heavy stockpot, whether
the stew is prepared outside on a propane cooker or on
top of the stove.

2 gallons water

¼ cup Old Bay seasoning

4 pounds small, whole, new red potatoes

*2 pounds hot smoked link sausage (such as
kielbasa), cut into 1½-inch slices*

6 to 8 ears fresh corn, broken into 2 or 3 pieces

4 pounds large fresh shrimp, unpeeled

In a large, heavy stock pot or Dutch oven, combine the
water and Old Bay seasoning and bring to a rolling boil.
Add the potatoes, reduce the heat slightly, and cook till
almost tender, about 15 minutes. Add the sausage and
cook 5 minutes longer. Add the corn and cook about 1
minute. Add the shrimp and cook till they turn fully
pink, about 1 minute.

To serve, remove all the ingredients with a slotted
spoon onto a large serving platter or onto a newspaper-
lined picnic table set with paper plates.

KENTUCKY BURGOO

Makes 6 to 8 servings

"NO, NO, NO, THAT'S ALL WRONG," EXCLAIMED A LOCAL at a Kentucky Derby party I attended in Louisville when I began telling how I make burgoo and failed to mention pork and veal shank, chopped cabbage, okra, and a slew of seasonings. Of course, Kentuckians are as sensitive about their burgoo as Virginians are about their Brunswick stew and Louisianians their jambalaya. It's said that more than one political election has been lost in Kentucky because a candidate served some corrupt version of this sacred stew at a rally. Nobody yet knows the derivation of the stew's name—a mispronunciation of *barbecue* or *bird stew*?—but the word appeared in print as early as 1750, and, ever since, burgoo has been Kentucky's unofficial state dish, prepared at times for literally thousands of people. I do have a so-called authentic recipe, once printed in the Louisville *Courier-Journal,* but being a Carolina Tarheel, I'll stick with this same burgoo I've been stewing up for a mere eight to ten guests for at least three decades. (If I find some beautiful fresh okra, I'll also throw that in the pot.)

One 4- to 5-pound stewing hen, cut into serving pieces

2 pounds beef shank, trimmed of excess fat

1½ pounds boneless lamb shoulder or shank, trimmed of excess fat

1 medium fresh hot red chile pepper, seeded

Salt and freshly ground black pepper to taste

3 quarts water

3 medium onions, chopped

3 medium carrots, scraped and cut into rounds

1 medium green bell pepper, seeded and cut into thin slices

5 medium ripe tomatoes, chopped, with the juice retained

2 medium potatoes, peeled and diced

½ pound green beans, cut in half

3 cups fresh or frozen corn kernels

2 garlic cloves, chopped

In a large, heavy pot, combine the chicken, beef shank, lamb, chile pepper, salt and pepper, and water and bring to a boil, skimming any foam from the top. Reduce the heat to low, cover, and simmer till the meats are almost tender, 2 to 2½ hours. With a slotted spoon, transfer the meats to a cutting board and discard the pepper. Add the remaining ingredients to the pot and stir. Bring to a boil, reduce the heat to low, cover, and simmer 1 hour longer, adding a little more water if the liquid looks too thick.

Remove and discard the skin and bones from the chicken and cut the meat into bite-size pieces. Remove the beef from the bone, discard the bone, and cut the meat into bite-size pieces. Cut the lamb into bite-size pieces. Return all the meats to the pot and stir well. Return the stew to a simmer, cover, and cook till the meats are very tender, 30 to 45 minutes.

BRUNSWICK STEW

Makes 6 servings as a main course; 12 servings as a side dish

IT SEEMS THAT I'VE SPENT A LIFETIME INVESTIGATING the origins of Brunswick stew, not to mention cooking and eating it. Georgia crackers are fully convinced that the lusty stew was created in Brunswick, Georgia, in 1898 at a July Fourth celebration, and to make the claim official, the town has mounted the original pot at its Welcome Center on Highway 17. Tarheels point to Brunswick County, North Carolina, as the stew's birthplace, by virtue of its integral association with the region's legendary pork barbecue. But only Virginians have documents to prove that the stew can be traced back to 1828, when a certain "Uncle Jimmy" Matthews first prepared it in Brunswick County for a large hunting party. Well, I've eaten Brunswick stew everywhere, but all modesty aside, I still think it's hard to beat the one I've been making for my Brunswick stew parties thrown maybe three times a year, where guests eat only stew, salad, and cornbread and drink beer. (I also can't imagine serving any Carolina pork barbecue without small bowls of this stew on the side.) The only cardinal rule in cooking any Brunswick stew is that the heat must be at the lowest simmer and the stew stirred repeatedly to prevent scorching. And what about that squirrel you hear some use in the stew? All I can say is I haven't seen a stew made with squirrel since I was a child.

½ cup vegetable oil

One 4-pound chicken (preferably a hen), quartered

1 cup chopped onions

1 cup chopped celery (leaves included)

1 medium ham hock, trimmed

3 large ripe tomatoes, chopped

1 small red chile pepper, seeded and minced

Salt and freshly ground black pepper to taste

Paprika to taste

2½ quarts water

1½ cups fresh or frozen corn kernels

1½ cups fresh or frozen sliced okra

1½ cups fresh or frozen lima beans

1½ cups cooked potatoes, mashed

In a large, heavy skillet, heat ¼ cup of the vegetable oil over moderate heat, add the chicken, brown on all sides, and transfer to a large plate. In a large stew pot, heat the remaining ¼ cup oil over moderate heat, add the onions and celery, and cook, stirring, 2 minutes. Add the browned chicken, ham hock, tomatoes, chile pepper, salt and pepper, paprika, and water, bring to a boil, reduce the heat to low, cover, and simmer 1 hour. Remove the chicken with a slotted spoon and simmer the mixture 1 hour longer. When the chicken has cooled, skin, bone, and shred the meat, and set aside.

Bring the mixture in the pot to a boil, add the corn, okra, and lima beans, reduce the heat to low, and cook for 30 minutes, stirring from time to time. Remove the ham hock with a slotted spoon and, when cool enough to handle, bone, shred the meat, and return the meat to the pot along with the reserved chicken. Add the mashed potatoes to the pot, stir well, and continue to cook, stirring, till nicely thickened, about 15 minutes. Serve the stew by itself in large soup bowls or in small bowls as a side dish to pork barbecue.

Stewed Ham Hocks and Butter Beans

Makes 6 servings

ALTHOUGH SOUTHERN BUTTER BEANS ARE technically a variety of lima beans (native to the Americas), make no mistake that the appearance and flavor of the two are distinctly different. Speckled butter beans (or "specs"), in particular, with their white skins dotted with red and purple, are the most popular type, turning a beautiful copper color and boasting dense richness when simmered slowly, as in this lusty stew. Unfortunately, real butter beans are becoming more and more difficult to find in all but the most rural areas, still another example of a unique Southern staple falling victim to modern marketing practices and public apathy. Fresh or frozen Fordhook limas can be substituted in this stew, but if you do see speckled butter beans at farm stands during the summer months, grab them. And for heaven's sake, when you bake a smoked ham (shank portion), be sure to saw off and freeze the hock.

3 ounces streak-o'-lean (lean salt pork),
cut into small pieces

1 large onion, chopped

1 celery rib, chopped

½ green bell pepper, seeded and chopped

2 garlic cloves, minced

2 large ripe tomatoes, chopped,
with the juices retained

1 tablespoon chopped fresh thyme leaves

1 tablespoon chopped fresh sage leaves

1 tablespoon Dijon mustard

Salt and freshly ground black pepper to taste

6 meaty smoked ham hocks, trimmed of skin

5 cups water

1 pound fresh or frozen butter beans
(or Fordhook lima beans)

In a large, heavy pot, fry the streak-o'-lean over moderate heat till crisp, drain on paper towels, and reserve. Add the onion, celery, bell pepper, and garlic to the pot and cook, stirring, till softened, about 3 minutes. Add the tomatoes and their juice, the thyme, sage, mustard, and salt and pepper and stir well. Add the ham hocks and water, bring to a boil, and skim any froth from the top. Reduce the heat to a gentle simmer, cover, and cook about 2 hours. Add the reserved streak-o'-lean and the beans, return to a simmer, and cook about 30 minutes longer.

With a slotted spoon, transfer the hocks to a large platter and arrange the beans around them.

TURKEY SUCCOTASH

Makes 4 servings

DESPITE A VERY STRANGE RECIPE FOR DELAWARE
succotash containing tomatoes and nutmeg that
appeared in *The American Heritage Cookbook* in 1980,
succotash has been an almost sacred blend of corn and
lima beans ever since the early settlers in Virginia
learned from the Powhatan Indians how to make it. So
popular is the stew throughout the South, in fact, that
it's almost always featured even in cafeterias right along
with black-eyed peas, stewed tomatoes, and string beans
cooked with ham hock. And so obsessed am I with
succotash that, years ago, I began turning it into a main
course by adding either leftover chicken or turkey plus a
few other vegetables and seasonings. At first, a few
eyebrows were raised, but after most guests tasted my
creation, I was hounded for the recipe. Think about this
stew after Thanksgiving or Christmas, when you're
confronted with a mound of leftover turkey and need to
come up with a simple but toothsome supper.

4 slices bacon

1 medium onion, finely chopped

1 celery rib, finely chopped

½ green bell pepper, seeded and finely chopped

3 cups chicken broth

*One 10-ounce package frozen corn kernels,
thawed*

One 10-ounce package frozen lima beans, thawed

*2 medium potatoes, peeled and cut into small
cubes*

*2 cups diced cooked turkey (preferably dark
meat)*

½ teaspoon dried tarragon, crumbled

Salt and freshly ground black pepper to taste

In a large, heavy pot, fry the bacon over moderate heat
till almost crisp, drain on paper towels, crumble, and
set aside. Add the onion, celery, and bell pepper to the
pot and cook, stirring till softened, about 3 minutes.
Add the remaining ingredients plus the reserved bacon
and bring to a boil. Reduce the heat to low, cover, and
simmer gently till the beans and potatoes are tender,
about 20 minutes. Serve piping hot.

Plantation Oyster and Benne Seed Stew

Makes 4 servings

THIS IS NOT ONLY ONE OF THE MOST UNUSUAL BUT also one of the oldest antebellum stew recipes in the South Carolina Lowcountry repertory. I first read about the dish in a book that related tales about the food served on the old rice plantations between Georgetown and Charleston, but the author never revealed the name of the plantation at which it was served. Was it Bellefield, Arcadia, Waverly, Litchfield, or another of the surviving estates that I've been visiting since I was a child? No matter, for none other than Louis Osteen, the chef at Louis's on Pawleys Island, also knew about this dish and came up with a brilliant modern interpretation, which we discussed in detail. Louis includes pancetta in his recipe, but since I feel that cured Italian bacon detracts from the stew's authenticity, I use what was surely used in the old plantation kitchen: namely, salt pork.

¼ cup benne (sesame) seeds

1 tablespoon peanut oil

1 ounce salt pork, finely diced

2 tablespoons finely minced onion

2 tablespoons all-purpose flour

24 small fresh oysters, with the liquor reserved

1¾ cups bottled clam juice

1 teaspoon chopped fresh thyme

1¼ cups heavy cream, warmed

1 tablespoon fresh lime juice

1 teaspoon sesame oil

2 tablespoons chopped fresh chervil

Salt and freshly ground black pepper to taste

In a small, heavy skillet, dry-roast the benne seeds over moderate heat till they become dark, 8 to 9 minutes, stirring often and taking care not to burn them. Transfer the seeds to a cutting board, roughly crush half of them with a spoon and reserve separately from the whole seeds.

In a large, heavy saucepan, heat the peanut oil over moderate heat, add the salt pork, fry till lightly browned and crisp, and drain on paper towels. Add the onion and crushed benne seeds to the pan and stir till the onion browns slightly, about 3 minutes. Add the flour, stir, and cook 2 minutes longer. Add the oyster liquor, clam juice, and thyme and whisk 2 minutes. Add the cream and simmer 5 minutes. Add the oysters, whole benne seeds, lime juice, sesame oil, chervil, and salt and pepper and leave on the heat till the oysters just begin to curl, about 4 minutes. Remove from the heat.

Ladle the stew into soup bowls, sprinkle crisp salt pork over each portion, and serve piping hot.

Memphis Quail and Vegetable Stew

Makes 6 servings

WHEN I WAS GROWING UP IN NORTH CAROLINA, GOING quail hunting on Saturday mornings was almost a rite of passage, and a certain guarantee of roasted or fried birds or a rich stew that same evening. Of course, in some areas of the South, quail are generally called *bobwhites* (a name supposedly derived from the sound the birds make), while in others the term is *partridge*, despite the fact that America has no true partridge like that found in Europe. About the only person I know who still shoots his own quail is an old friend in Memphis, and when Henry comes back with a half dozen or so birds, you can be sure they'll end up in a pot and simmered slowly with whatever fresh vegetables he has on hand. Today, what both professional and home cooks alike use are farm-raised quail (fresh or frozen). While they are less robust in flavor than their wild cousins, they're nevertheless succulent birds that deserve more attention.

Long before the current rage over ramps (wild leeks) in America's trendy food fraternity, the bulbs were foraged in Tennessee's mountain country and used in all sorts of soups, stews, and casseroles. Every spring, in fact, there's a ramp festival in Cosby, Tennessee, with hill-billy music and numerous dishes prepared with ramps.

8 quail, dressed

2 cups all-purpose flour

4 slices bacon, cut into bits

2 tablespoons vegetable oil

2 large onions, finely chopped

1 carrot, scraped and finely chopped

3 ripe tomatoes, chopped

2 large potatoes, peeled and cut into small cubes

2 cups fresh or frozen lima beans

2 cups fresh or frozen corn kernels

½ teaspoon dried thyme, crumbled

1 bay leaf

Salt and freshly ground black pepper to taste

Cayenne pepper to taste

3 quarts water

On a plate, dredge the quail in the flour, tapping off any excess. In a large, heavy pot, fry the bacon over moderate heat till crisp, drain on paper towels, and set aside. Add the oil to the pot, add the onions and carrot, and cook, stirring, 2 minutes. Add the reserved bacon plus the remaining ingredients, bring to a low simmer, cover, and cook 2 hours, adding a little more water if the stew thickens too much.

MARYLAND TERRAPIN STEW

Makes 4 to 6 servings

PERHAPS NO DISH IN SOUTHERN COOKERY WAS EVER more relished or respected than the rich terrapin stews prepared in Baltimore's "turtle-soup houses" in the early nineteenth century—to such a degree that by the middle of the century, the stew had become the pride of the city's Maryland Club and other elite social venues. Small diamondback terrapins from the fresh or brackish waters of the region were the aristocrats of the turtle world, but such was the popularity of this stew that by the twentieth century the species was nearly extinct. Thanks to conservation measures, terrapins were restored to some extent in Maryland waters, but today, fresh turtle meat is still a rare and expensive commodity, and even down in Louisiana, where the reptile is revered as much as in Maryland, turtle stew and soup are usually reserved for only special occasions. Fresh turtle meat can sometimes be found in Chinese markets, but much more available (and completely acceptable) are the canned and frozen products sold in many specialty food shops—at a price. Is it worth the effort and cost? One spoonful of this sublime delicacy is enough to answer that question.

1½ quarts canned terrapin meat

Chicken broth as needed

¾ cup (1½ sticks) butter

1 large onion, finely chopped

½ cup dry sherry

Salt and freshly ground black pepper to taste

Cayenne pepper to taste

2 hard-boiled eggs, peeled and chopped

Drain the terrapin meat, reserving the liquid in a bowl, and mince the meat. Measure the liquid and add enough chicken broth to yield 1¾ cups. In a saucepan, heat the mixture.

In a large pot, melt 4 tablespoons (½ stick) of the butter over moderate heat, add the onion, and cook, stirring, till very soft, about 3 minutes. Add the hot broth mixture, stir in the remaining butter and the sherry, add the salt and pepper and cayenne pepper, and simmer over low heat about 5 minutes. Add the terrapin meat and chopped eggs, return to a simmer, and cook to heat through and mingle the flavors, 10 to 15 minutes. Transfer the stew to a large, heated serving tureen and serve piping hot.

GEORGIA HAM AND COWPEA STEW

Makes 6 servings

IN MOST RURAL AREAS OF GEORGIA, BLACK-EYED PEAS are still called cowpeas. I can remember this hearty stew one of my great aunts outside Macon once threw together for dinner after we'd spent much of the day picking Elberta peaches in a neighbor's orchard. I often use fresh or frozen peas in this stew, the single advantage of dried peas being the flavorful liquid in which they must be soaked at least an hour (even overnight), which can be substituted for the fresh water. The traditional way to serve the stew in Georgia is over boiled rice.

¾ pound shelled fresh or frozen cowpeas (black-eyed peas), rinsed and picked over

1 pound cooked smoked ham, cut into small cubes

1 large onion, chopped

1 celery rib, chopped

½ green bell pepper, seeded and chopped

1 bay leaf

¼ teaspoon dried sage, crumbled

Salt and freshly ground black pepper to taste

3 cups water

2 tablespoons tomato ketchup

Worcestershire and Tabasco sauces to taste

1 tablespoon all-purpose flour mixed with 1 tablespoon water

In a large, heavy pot, combine the cowpeas, ham, onion, celery, bell pepper, bay leaf, sage, and salt and pepper, add the water, and stir well. Bring to a boil, reduce the heat to a gentle simmer, cover, and cook 1 hour. Add the ketchup, Worcestershire, and Tabasco, and cook till the peas are tender, about 30 minutes longer. Add the flour-and-water mixture and stir till the stew is thickened. Serve hot.

Arkansas Catfish Stew

Makes 4 to 6 servings

WHILE LIVING IN MISSOURI, I ATE MY FIRST ARKANSAS catfish stew when I visited a friend one weekend at his family's home in Carson. What I remember most was that the stew was cooked outdoors in a heavy washtub—evidently an old tradition in towns all along the Mississippi River. I also recall that the catfish were the most gigantic I'd ever seen—maybe ten pounds each—and that the stew itself was probably the best I'd ever tasted. Yes, I know that Mississippi is now the leading producer of catfish in the nation, thanks to modernized fish farms and processing methods throughout its Delta region, but after all, pond cultivation began in Arkansas back in the 1950s, and . . . well, the memory of that delicious washtub stew made with wild, huge, ugly, bottom-feeding river catfish lingers. This recipe is tame compared with the stew I was served, so if you want to give it real character, buy a large, whole, hideous fish and use the head, tail, and bones to make a rich catfish stock to replace all or part of the water.

5 slices meaty bacon, cut into tiny cubes

2 medium onions, finely chopped

3 medium ripe tomatoes, chopped, with the juice retained

2 large potatoes, peeled and cut into 1-inch cubes

2 cups water (or, preferably, catfish stock)

¼ teaspoon ground cloves

2 tablespoons Worcestershire sauce

Tabasco sauce to taste

Salt and freshly ground black pepper to taste

2 pounds catfish fillets, cut into 1½-inch pieces

117

In a large, heavy pot, fry the bacon over moderate heat till crisp, drain on paper towels, and set aside. Add the onions to the pot and cook, stirring, till very soft, about 4 minutes. Add the tomatoes, potatoes, water, cloves, Worcestershire, Tabasco, and salt and pepper and bring to a boil. Reduce the heat to a low simmer, cover, and cook 30 minutes. Add the catfish and reserved bacon, stir, cover, and continue to simmer till the fish flakes, 10 to 12 minutes. Serve hot.

West Virginia Venison Stew

Makes 6 servings

EVEN BEFORE THE WESTERN PART OF VIRGINIA broke away from the state in 1861 to form a separate Union government, frontier settlers, who depended heavily on wild game for survival, organized church and civic get-togethers called "soups" or "stews," where everybody contributed some corn, potatoes, onions, and various meats to a huge stew pot. Today, in the mountain regions dotted with isolated cabins and low-income housing, small communities continue to celebrate wild game, huckleberry, maple sugar, and pumpkin seasons by throwing a festive "soup" or "stew," and in the most remote areas of the state (as in the mountains of North Carolina and Tennessee), it's not unusual to see a little illegal moonshine being poured.

1 cup all-purpose flour

Salt and freshly ground black pepper to taste

Cayenne pepper to taste

2 pounds boneless venison shoulder, trimmed of excess fat and cut into 1½-inch pieces

4 tablespoons (½ stick) butter

1 cup sweet vermouth

2 tablespoons red currant jelly

2 celery ribs (leaves included), chopped

½ teaspoon dried thyme, crumbled

½ teaspoon dried rosemary, crumbled

1 bay leaf

3 cloves

2 cups beef broth

12 tiny new potatoes, scrubbed but not peeled

6 small white onions, peeled and scored on the root ends

3 medium carrots, scraped and cut into rounds

2 medium parsnips, peeled and cut into 1-inch cubes

In a bowl, combine the flour, salt and pepper, and cayenne pepper and dredge the venison in the mixture, tapping off any excess flour. In a large, heavy pot, melt the butter over moderately high heat, add the venison, and brown on all sides. Add the vermouth and jelly and stir well, scraping any browned bits off the bottom of the pot. Add the celery, thyme, rosemary, bay leaf, cloves, and broth, reduce the heat to a low simmer, cover, and cook 1 hour. Add the potatoes, onions, carrots, parsnips, and salt and pepper to taste, return to a simmer, cover, and cook till the venison is very tender, about 1 hour longer, adding more broth if necessary.

Company Turkey and Ham Casserole

Makes at least 12 servings

IN THE SOUTH, A "COMPANY CASSEROLE" ALWAYS implies a dish that will serve at least a dozen guests, and none of these elaborate preparations is more popular than a crusty one featuring ham and chicken or turkey. This makes an ideal buffet casserole, it's basically a cinch to prepare, and, frankly, I know of no better way to use up leftover turkey and ham during and after the Thanksgiving and Christmas holidays. Southern cooks might easily substitute grated sharp cheddar or Parmesan cheese for the Swiss, but if you do opt for Swiss, make the effort to use genuine Emmenthaler and not that underaged, bland domestic stuff. Any leftover casserole, by the way, freezes beautifully in an airtight container.

6 tablespoons (¾ stick) butter

1 cup finely chopped onions

6 tablespoons all-purpose flour

1 teaspoon salt

½ teaspoon freshly ground black pepper

2½ cups milk

½ pound fresh mushrooms, sliced

5 tablespoons dry sherry

5 cups chopped cooked turkey breast

2 cups chopped cooked ham

Two 5-ounce cans water chestnuts, drained and sliced

1 cup shredded Swiss cheese

2 cups fresh bread crumbs

6 tablespoons (¾ stick) butter, melted

Preheat the oven to 400°F. Grease a large, shallow baking dish and set aside.

In a large, heavy skillet, melt 4 tablespoons of the butter over moderate heat, add the onions, and cook, stirring, till soft but not browned, about 3 minutes. Sprinkle the flour, salt, and pepper over the onions and stir about 2 minutes longer. Reduce the heat to low and gradually add the milk, stirring constantly till the mixture is thickened and smooth. Remove the pan from the heat.

In a small skillet, melt the remaining 2 tablespoons butter over moderate heat, add the mushrooms, and cook, stirring, till golden, about 5 minutes. Add the mushrooms to the milk mixture, then add the sherry, turkey, ham, and water chestnuts and stir till well blended. Spoon the mixture into the prepared baking dish and sprinkle the cheese over the top. In a small mixing bowl, combine the bread crumbs and melted butter, spoon the mixture evenly over the cheese, and bake till the casserole is lightly browned, about 35 minutes. Serve hot.

119

Chicken and Broccoli Casserole

Makes 6 servings

ATTEND ANY SOUTHERN CHURCH FUND-RAISING benefit, bereavement, informal weekend buffet lunch, or even wedding reception, and this is exactly the style of casserole that's likely to be served—along with a couple of others. Leftover turkey and a different vegetable can be substituted for the chicken and broccoli, other cheeses might be used, and one or more herbs might be added for more intense flavor. Just make sure the cheese sauce is smooth, with no lumps, and that the casserole is served as piping hot as possible.

4 tablespoons (½ stick) butter

1 medium onion, finely chopped

1 cup sour cream

1 cup milk

1 cup shredded Swiss cheese

½ cup freshly grated Parmesan cheese

2 tablespoons chopped pimentos

Salt and freshly ground black pepper to taste

¼ pound egg noodles, boiled according to package directions and drained

3 cups cubed cooked chicken

One 1-ounce package frozen chopped broccoli, thawed

1 cup pimento-stuffed green olives, drained and cut in half

½ cup dry bread crumbs

2 tablespoons butter, melted

Preheat the oven to 350°F. Grease a 2-quart casserole and set aside.

In a large, heavy saucepan, melt the butter over moderately low heat, add the onion, and stir 2 minutes. Add the sour cream, milk, cheeses, pimentos, and salt and pepper and stir slowly till the cheeses melt and the sauce is smooth. Remove the pan from the heat.

In the prepared casserole, combine the noodles, chicken, broccoli, and olives and pour the cheese sauce over the top. In a small mixing bowl, combine the bread crumbs and melted butter, spoon evenly over top of the casserole, and bake till slightly crusty, 35 to 40 minutes. Serve hot.

Sausage and Vidalia Onion Casserole

Makes 10 to 12 servings

THE STORY GOES THAT WHEN A TOOMBS COUNTY, Georgia, farmer named Moses Coleman planted some Bermuda onion seeds in the sandy loam around Vidalia in the spring of 1931, the onions he harvested were not just mild in aroma but "sweet as Coca-Cola." The reason, it was later discovered, was the low sulfur content of the region's soil. Today, coveted Vidalia onions, widely available only in May and June, are a thirty-million-dollar business in Georgia and protected under a registered trademark (Yumion). Southerners fry, grill, and bake Vidalia onions, and even eat them whole, raw like apples, but I know of no preparation that highlights their exquisite sweetness and unique savor like this succulent casserole intended for an elaborate buffet. (For a less auspicious occasion, just cut the recipe in half and use a 2-quart casserole.) It is essential to serve this casserole piping hot.

1½ pounds bulk pork sausage

4 tablespoons (½ stick) butter

6 Vidalia onions, sliced

2 garlic cloves, minced

1½ cups heavy cream

Large pinch of ground nutmeg

Salt and freshly ground black pepper to taste

½ cup dry bread crumbs

4 tablespoons (½ stick) butter, melted

Preheat the oven to 375°F. Butter a shallow 3½-quart casserole and set aside.

In a large, heavy skillet, break up the sausage meat with a fork and fry over moderate heat till well browned all over. Drain on paper towels and set aside.

In a large, heavy saucepan, melt the solid butter over moderate heat, add the onions and garlic, and cook, stirring, till softened, about 4 minutes. Add the cream, nutmeg, and salt and pepper and cook, stirring, till the onions are tender, about 10 minutes. Scrape the mixture into the prepared casserole and spoon the sausage evenly over the top. Sprinkle the bread crumbs over the sausage, drizzle the melted butter over the crumbs, and bake till golden, about 35 minutes. Serve hot.

Rutabaga, Sweet Potato, and Orange Casserole

Makes 6 servings

THOUGHT TO BE A CROSS BETWEEN A CABBAGE AND A globe turnip, the smooth, heavy, pale yellow rutabaga has been a popular root vegetable in the South since it migrated from Europe with the early settlers in the seventeenth century. Small, relatively tender, and slightly sweet rutabagas can be boiled and mashed or simply cut into strips and blanched for salads, but since the more common large ones tend to be pithy and bitter, most Southern cooks prefer to bake them slowly with sweet potatoes, carrots, Vidalia onions, oranges, and other sweet ingredients in a casserole. Rutabagas are available year round, but winter is the peak season. They can be the dickens to peel, but are well worth the effort.

2 pounds rutabagas (yellow turnips), peeled and cut into 2-inch chunks

1 pound sweet potatoes, peeled and cut into 2-inch chunks

1 orange, peeled, white pith removed, seeded, and cut up

4 tablespoons (½ stick) butter, softened

½ cup heavy cream

¼ teaspoon grated nutmeg

Salt and freshly ground black pepper to taste

Preheat the oven to 350°F. Butter a 2-quart casserole or baking dish and set aside.

Place the rutabagas in a large pot and add enough water to cover by 1 inch. Bring to a boil, reduce the heat to moderate, cover, and cook 15 minutes. Add the sweet potatoes, return the heat to moderate, and cook 15 minutes longer or till the vegetables are tender.

Transfer the cooked vegetables to a food processor, add the orange, 2 tablespoons of the butter, the cream, nutmeg, and salt and pepper, and reduce to a coarse purée. Scrape the mixture into the prepared casserole, dot the top with the remaining butter, and bake 20 to 25 minutes. When ready to serve, run the casserole under the broiler momentarily to glaze the top.

122

HOMINY, MUSHROOM, AND CHEDDAR CASSEROLE

Makes 4 servings

EVER SINCE THE ORIGINAL SETTLERS OF JAMESTOWN, Virginia, were greeted by Indians in 1607 with bowls of softened maize with salt and hog fat ("rockahomini"), there's been confusion even in the South over the difference between hominy and grits. In short, hominy is whole, dried corn kernels soaked in water and lye to remove the outer hulls; dry and grind hominy, and you have grits (or, in Charleston, South Carolina, "hominy grits"). The only old-fashioned hominy I've encountered was made by a Tennessee housewife, but fortunately the canned beads of corn are not only much easier to handle but just as good as the handmade product. Today, hominy is used to make all sorts of breads and puddings, but it's also a major ingredient in homey casseroles such as this one, intended to be served alongside roasted meats and fowl and even barbecued pork ribs.

2 tablespoons butter

2 scallions (white parts only), minced

1 garlic clove, minced

¼ pound mushrooms, finely chopped

One 28-ounce can hominy, drained

2 tablespoons chopped pimentos

1 cup grated extra-sharp cheddar cheese

½ cup sour cream

Salt and freshly ground black pepper to taste

Cayenne pepper to taste

½ cup half-and-half

Preheat the oven to 350°F. Butter a 1-quart casserole and set aside.

In a small skillet, melt the butter over moderately low heat, add the scallions, garlic, and mushrooms, stir till the mushrooms give up their liquid, about 5 minutes, and remove from the heat.

Arrange the hominy across the bottom of the prepared casserole and layer the mushrooms, pimentos, ¾ cup of the cheese, and sour cream on top. Season with salt and pepper and cayenne pepper and pour half-and-half over the top. Sprinkle the remaining cheese evenly over the top and bake till golden, about 25 minutes. Serve hot.

123

CREOLE CURRIED SHRIMP AND MIRLITON CASSEROLE

Makes 6 servings

CHAYOTE, A GOURDLIKE, PALE GREEN, DELECTABLE fruit about the size and shape of a large, scraggly pear, is called mirliton in Louisiana, where, as in Florida, it flourishes and is much loved. Over the years in New Orleans and around Cajun country, I've eaten mirliton fried, stuffed with seafood, and incorporated into salads, but since the fruit itself is pretty bland, it makes lots of sense to combine it with other ingredients, as in this popular curried casserole served at brunches throughout Louisiana. Just ten years ago, yellow squash, zucchini, or eggplant would have to have been substituted for the mirlitons outside the region, but now that chayotes (often called "vegetable pears") are widely available in markets (especially during the winter months), there's no excuse for not aiming for authenticity.

3 tablespoons butter

3 tablespoons all-purpose flour

Salt and freshly ground black pepper to taste

1¼ cups chicken broth

½ cup heavy cream

1 teaspoon curry powder

1 tablespoon light brown sugar

1 tablespoon fresh lemon juice

½ pound fresh small shrimp, peeled and deveined

2 tablespoons olive oil

1 medium onion, chopped

1 small green bell pepper, seeded and chopped

4 medium mirlitons (chayotes), peeled and chopped

½ cup dry bread crumbs

½ cup freshly grated Parmesan cheese

2 tablespoons butter, melted

Preheat the oven to 350°F. Butter a 2-quart casserole and set aside.

In a large saucepan, melt the butter over moderate heat, add the flour and salt and pepper, and whisk till the mixture bubbles. Add the broth and whisk till well blended and smooth. Add the cream, curry powder, brown sugar, and lemon juice and stir till well blended. Add the shrimp, stir, and remove from the heat.

In a small skillet, heat the oil over moderate heat, add the onion and green pepper, cook, stirring, about 5 minutes to soften, then remove from the heat.

Layer half the mirlitons over the bottom of the prepared casserole, layer half the onion and green pepper evenly over the mirlitons, and spoon half the cooked shrimp mixture over the top. Repeat with the remaining mirlitons; onion and green pepper; and shrimp mixture. Cover the casserole, and bake 20 minutes.

Meanwhile, in a small mixing bowl, toss the bread crumbs and cheese with the melted butter. Spread evenly over top of the casserole and continue to bake, uncovered, till golden brown, about 20 minutes more. Serve hot.

Chicken Tetrazzini

Makes 6 servings

THERE ARE SOME (MAINLY IN SAN FRANCISCO) WHO
refute the claim that this rich, creamy casserole was
created in Charleston, South Carolina, shortly after the
turn of the twentieth century for the famous coloratura
soprano Luisa Tetrazzini, but whatever the dish's
regional origin, it has come down as one of the South's
most classic and beloved casseroles. Unlike most
casseroles, a tetrazzini is never layered but simply
tossed, and what gives the dish its distinct identity over
its obvious Italian cousin (spaghetti with a *ragù* sauce)
are not only the diverse ingredients but also the way it's
baked till crusty. Leftover turkey, ham, or a mixture of
meats can be used to make this tetrazzini, and no
unbaked casserole freezes so beautifully till ready to be
thawed, baked, and served.

6 tablespoons (¾ stick) butter

¼ pound fresh mushrooms, chopped

¼ cup all-purpose flour

1 teaspoon salt

Freshly ground black pepper to taste

¼ teaspoon ground nutmeg

1 cup chicken broth

1 cup half-and-half

2 pounds cooked chicken, cubed

1 cup black olives, drained, pitted, and chopped

½ cup slivered almonds

½ cup freshly grated Parmesan cheese

1 large egg yolk, beaten

*7 ounces spaghetti, cooked according to package
directions (but not more than 8 minutes) and
drained*

Preheat the oven to 350°F. Butter a 2- to 2½-quart
casserole.

In a small skillet, melt 2 tablespoons of the butter over
moderate heat. Add the mushrooms, stir for 5 minutes,
and remove from the heat.

In a large, heavy pot over moderate heat, melt the
remaining 4 tablespoons of butter, add the flour, salt,
pepper, and nutmeg, and cook, stirring, 1 minute.
Gradually add the broth and half-and-half and cook,
stirring, till the sauce begins to thicken, about 5 minutes.
Remove pot from the heat, add the chicken, olives,
almonds, cheese, and egg yolk, and stir till well blended.

Place the cooked spaghetti in the casserole, pour the
chicken mixture over the top, toss to mix well, and
bake till crusty, 25 to 30 minutes. Serve hot.

CHICKEN SPAGHETTI

Makes at least 12 servings

I HAVE SEEN AND HEARD ABOUT OTHER SOUTHERN recipes for chicken spaghetti, but Craig Claiborne always swore that the dish was created by his mother and talked about up and down the Mississippi Delta. The elaborate preparation was his pride and joy, and there can be no doubt that it is a masterpiece of Southern casserole art. (The only explanation for the name is the dish's remote similarity to classic Italian spaghetti sauce.) The casserole is, without question, something of an ordeal to prepare—Craig used to spend an entire day on the job—so to justify all the time and effort, wait for the occasion to invite at least a dozen hungry guests. With the casserole, you need to serve no more than a tart green salad and plenty of sturdy red wine.

One 3½-pound chicken, with giblets

Salt to taste

3 cups canned peeled Italian plum tomatoes, coarsely chopped, with the juice retained

7 tablespoons butter

3 tablespoons all-purpose flour

½ cup heavy cream

⅛ teaspoon ground nutmeg

Freshly ground black pepper to taste

½ pound fresh mushrooms, quartered

2 cups finely chopped onions

1½ cups finely chopped celery

1½ cups seeded and chopped green bell pepper

1 tablespoon minced garlic

¼ pound ground beef round

¼ pound ground pork

1 bay leaf

½ teaspoon red pepper flakes

1 pound dried spaghetti

½ pound sharp cheddar cheese, shredded

Freshly grated Parmesan cheese

Preheat the oven to 350°F. Butter a 5- to 6-quart casserole and set aside.

Place the chicken and giblets in a kettle with enough water to cover and add salt. Bring to a boil, reduce the heat to low, cover, and simmer till tender, about 45 minutes. Remove the chicken and, when cool enough to handle, shred the meat and set aside. Return the skin and bones to the pot, cook the broth down over moderate heat till reduced to 5 cups, about 30 minutes, strain into a bowl, and set aside. Discard the skin and bones.

Meanwhile, place the tomatoes in a medium saucepan and cook down over moderate heat to half the original volume, stirring often.

Melt 3 tablespoons of the butter in another medium saucepan over moderate heat, add the flour, and whisk till well blended and smooth. Add 1 cup of the broth plus the cream, whisking rapidly, and when smooth, add the nutmeg and season with salt and pepper. Reduce the heat to low and continue to cook, stirring often, about 10 minutes. Remove the white sauce from the heat.

In a large skillet, melt the remaining 4 tablespoons of butter over moderate heat, add the mushrooms, and cook, stirring, till golden, about 5 minutes. Add the onions, celery, and bell pepper and cook, stirring, till the vegetables are crisp yet tender, about 5 minutes. Add the garlic, beef, and pork and cook, stirring and breaking the meat apart with a large, heavy spoon, till the meats lose their pink color. Add the bay leaf, pepper flakes, reduced tomatoes, and white sauce and stir till well blended.

In a large pot of boiling salted water, cook the spaghetti till just tender, drain, and rinse under cold running water.

Spoon enough of the meat sauce over the bottom of the prepared casserole to cover it lightly and add about one-third of the cooked spaghetti. Add one-third of the shredded chicken, another layer of meat sauce, and a layer of one-third of the cheddar. Continue making layers, ending up with a layer of spaghetti topped with a thin layer of meat sauce and cheddar. Pour in about 2 cups of the broth to almost cover the top layer of spaghetti, place the casserole on top of the stove, and bring it just to a boil. Cover with a lid or aluminum foil, place in the oven, and bake 15 minutes. Uncover and bake till lightly browned on top, about 15 minutes longer. Serve immediately with Parmesan cheese on the side.

Southern Mac 'n' Cheese

Makes 6 servings

ANYBODY WHO DOUBTS THAT MACARONI AND CHEESE has a Southern pedigree need only be directed to any cafeteria from Virginia to Alabama to observe the heaping spoonfuls being plopped on virtually every plate that passes down the line. History has not recorded whether this was the dish Thomas Jefferson had in mind when he sent an emissary to Naples for a macaroni machine, but it's for sure that by the mid-nineteenth century, the casserole was evolving from layered macaroni and cheddar cheese baked with an egg-and-milk custard to a much more elaborate production involving different cheese sauces and all sorts of seasonings. Today, Southerners still argue whether mac 'n' cheese should be made with a custard or a sauce, as well as whether it is correct to bake it in a cast-iron skillet or casserole. Personally, I couldn't care less, as long as the dish contains plenty of cheese, is never allowed to overcook and dry out, and is served piping hot. To give the casserole a bit of zest, add about ½ teaspoon of dry mustard.

4 tablespoons (½ stick) butter

¼ cup all-purpose flour

2¼ cups milk, heated

1 teaspoon salt

⅛ teaspoon grated nutmeg

Freshly ground black pepper to taste

Cayenne pepper to taste

3½ cups grated extra-sharp cheddar cheese

½ pound elbow macaroni

½ cup freshly grated Parmesan cheese

Preheat the oven to 375°F. Butter a 1½-quart casserole and set aside.

In a large, heavy saucepan, melt the butter over moderate heat, add the flour, and whisk 1 minute. Whisking constantly, gradually add the milk till the mixture bubbles and thickens. Remove the pan from the heat, add the salt, nutmeg, two peppers, and cheddar cheese, and stir till the cheese melts completely. Set aside.

Fill another large saucepan with water, bring to a boil, add the macaroni, and cook according to package directions. Drain the macaroni well in a colander.

Stir the drained macaroni into the cheese sauce till well blended, scrape into the prepared casserole, and sprinkle Parmesan over the top. Bake till golden brown on top, about 30 minutes, and serve piping hot.

SPOONBREAD

Makes 6 to 8 servings

SPOONBREAD IS, WITHOUT QUESTION, THE LIGHTEST, richest, and most elegant of all Southern cornmeal dishes, a custardlike, versatile miracle that approaches the texture of a soufflé and is as appropriate at breakfast with fried country ham and red-eye gravy as on the grandest dinner table or buffet. Of course, Virginia, Maryland, the Carolinas, Tennessee, and Kentucky all lay claim to the dish, but since history records an Indian porridge introduced to the first Virginia settlers called *suppone,* which appears to be the ancestral source of spoonbread, perhaps that state deserves the most credit. (In any case, the dish was not refined with butter, milk, and eggs till well into the nineteenth century.) Depending on the region, spoonbread can be enhanced with everything from cheese to bacon or ham to dainty vegetables, but in its most pristine form, there can be no doubt that it's one of the country's (indeed the world's) most distinctive and delicious culinary creations. And, yes, the dish is so soft that it can be and often is eaten with a spoon.

3 cups milk

1½ cups white cornmeal

8 tablespoons (1 stick) butter, softened and cut into pieces

2 teaspoons baking powder

5 large eggs, separated

Preheat the oven to 350°F. Butter a 2-quart casserole and set aside.

In a large saucepan, bring the milk to a boil and gradually add the cornmeal, stirring rapidly with a spoon as you slowly pour it in. Reduce the heat to low and cook, stirring constantly, till the mixture is thick, about 10 minutes. Remove the pan from the heat, add the butter and baking powder, stir till the butter has melted, and set aside to cool.

In a small mixing bowl, beat the egg yolks with a fork till light, then stir them into the cooled cornmeal mixture. In a large mixing bowl, beat the egg whites with an electric mixer till stiff peaks form, then fold them into the mixture till all traces of white have disappeared. Scrape the mixture into the prepared casserole and bake till a knife inserted in the center comes out clean, about 40 minutes. Serve hot.

GEORGIA BEREAVEMENT CASSEROLE

Makes 10 to 12 servings

AT NO OCCASION IN THE SOUTH IS THE ART OF casserole baking more evident than at the bereavements following funerals, which are, quite frankly, as social as they are solemn. It's not unusual, in fact, to see at least half a dozen casseroles (savory and sweet) contributed to a bereavement table by relatives and friends, but I don't think I had ever seen such a display as the one I saw in Monticello, Georgia, at the home of a cousin who had "passed." One of the casseroles was this elaborate beauty made with full-flavored brown rice (which is unpolished, with only the husks removed) instead of the standard white long-grain variety—served, no less, in an exquisite silver chafing dish. All that ceremony lacked was a four-piece jazz combo like the one featured at another bereavement I once attended at a country club in Charlotte, North Carolina.

5 cups water

2 teaspoons salt

2 cups brown rice

8 tablespoons (1 stick) butter

1 large onion, chopped

2 celery ribs, chopped

1 pound fresh mushrooms, chopped

½ cup all-purpose flour

2 cups chicken broth

2 cups half-and-half

6 cups cubed cooked chicken

1 cup slivered toasted almonds

One 4-ounce jar pimentos, drained and chopped

½ teaspoon dried tarragon, crumbled

Salt and freshly ground black pepper to taste

2 tablespoons dry sherry

In a large saucepan, bring the water and salt to a brisk boil, add the rice, and stir. Cover the pan, reduce the heat to a simmer, and cook till all the water has been absorbed and the rice is tender, 40 to 45 minutes. Fluff the rice with a fork and keep warm.

Meanwhile, preheat the oven to 350°F. Grease an attractive 3- to 3½-quart casserole and set aside.

In a large, heavy skillet, melt the butter over moderate heat, add the onion, celery, and mushrooms, and cook, stirring, 5 minutes. Sprinkle the flour over the top and cook, stirring, 3 minutes longer. Add the broth and half-and-half and stir steadily till the mixture thickens, about 10 minutes. Pour the mixture into the prepared casserole, add the cooked rice, the chicken, almonds, pimentos, tarragon, salt and pepper, and sherry, stir till well blended, and bake, covered, till bubbly, about 30 minutes. Serve immediately.

Baked Fruit Casserole

Makes 8 to 10 servings

HOT FRUIT CASSEROLES HAVE BEEN SERVED AT breakfasts, luncheons, and as a side dish on lavish buffets throughout the South ever since canned fruits acquired a certain cachet in the 1920s. They can contain any number of fruits (I once counted eight at a country club luncheon in Nashville), be enhanced with everything from curry powder to fresh mint to nuts, and boast such boozy flavorings as sherry, Madeira, brandy, and dry vermouth. Don't ask me why fresh fruits should not be used in place of canned; all I can say is I've tried it repeatedly, and the casserole always ended up mushy. Since this is one casserole that can be successfully reheated over and over, there's no reason not to make it in large quantities.

One 16-ounce can pineapple rings

One 16-ounce can peach halves

One 16-ounce can pear halves

1 cup seedless golden raisins

One 14-ounce jar spiced apple rings

2 tablespoons all-purpose flour

½ cup firmly packed light brown sugar

1 tablespoon mild curry powder

1 cup semidry sherry

¾ cup (1½ sticks) butter

Butter a 2- to 2½-quart casserole and set aside.

Drain all the fruits and cut the pineapple rings in half. Arrange the fruits in alternating layers in the prepared casserole, saving the apple rings for the top, and set aside.

In a medium heavy saucepan, combine the flour, brown sugar, curry powder, sherry, and butter over moderate heat and stir till the mixture is thickened and smooth, about 10 minutes. Pour the mixture over the fruit, cover with plastic wrap, and let stand in the refrigerator overnight.

Preheat the oven to 350°F.

Place the casserole in the oven and bake till bubbly hot and slightly glazed on top, 20 to 30 minutes. Serve immediately.

Meats

Pork and Apple Pie
with Biscuit Crust

Roast Pork Loin with Plums
and Mushroom Sauce

Florida Glazed Pork Chops
with Carambola

Fresh Country Sausage

Biscuits with Sausage Gravy

Alabama Hot Pot

Country-Style Chitlins

Ham Croquettes

Ham and Sweet Potato Hash

Smithfield Ham and Veal Rolls

Beverly's 500-Degree Country Ham

Country Ham Braised in Cider
and Molasses

Stuffed Maryland Ham

Meat Loaf Deluxe

Beer-Braised Short Ribs of Beef

Bourbon Beef and Oyster Pot

Chilled Spiced Beef

Virginia Ginger Ale Chili

Chicken-Fried Steak
and Gravy

Greenbrier Deviled Oxtails

Chilled Mobile Thyme Tongue

Mountain Sweetbreads in
Mushroom Cream Sauce

Natchitoches Meat Pies

South Carolina Hash

Pork and Apple Pie with Biscuit Crust

Makes 6 servings

THE SOUTH'S LOVE OF CRUSTED SAVORY PIES CAN MOST
likely be traced back to the dramatic "raised" pies baked
by the first English settlers all along the East Coast.
Prepared with suet crusts, short pastry, puff pastry, and
various batters, those hefty meat and fish pies must
have been a sight to behold. Today the only vestiges
of the tradition in this country are chicken and beef
potpies, lobster and clam pies, and the Southern meat,
fowl, and game pies prepared with the same distinctive
biscuit crusts often used also to make fruit cobblers.
For this particular recipe, leftover beef, chicken, or
turkey could be substituted for the pork, minus the
apples, which might be replaced with green peas and
perhaps a few chopped pimentos. Actually, the filling
lends itself to endless experimentation.

THE PIE FILLING

3 slices bacon

1 large onion, chopped

1 celery rib, chopped

*1 medium green bell pepper, cored, seeded, and
  chopped*

1 garlic clove, minced

2 pounds lean cooked pork, cut into small cubes

2 tart apples, peeled, cored, and sliced

2 cups beef broth

2 tablespoons yellow cornmeal

2 tablespoons tomato paste

2 tablespoons Worcestershire sauce

Tabasco sauce to taste

1 teaspoon salt

Freshly ground black pepper to taste

THE BISCUIT CRUST

2 cups all-purpose flour

2 teaspoons baking powder

1 teaspoon salt

3 tablespoons vegetable shortening

¾ cup milk

1 large egg, beaten

Preheat the oven to 350°F.

To make the pie filling, fry the bacon in a large heavy
skillet over moderate heat till almost crisp and drain
on paper towels. Add the onion, celery, bell pepper, and
garlic to the skillet and cook, stirring, about 3 minutes.
Crumble the cooked bacon over the vegetables, then
add the remaining ingredients, stirring. Reduce the
heat to low, simmer, stirring from time to time, about
30 minutes, then transfer to a 2-quart baking dish or
casserole.

To make the crust, combine the flour, baking powder,
salt, and shortening in a mixing bowl and work mixture
with fingers till mealy. Add the milk and egg and stir
till well blended and smooth.

Spoon the batter over the top of the pork-and-apple
mixture and bake till golden, 40 minutes.

Roast Pork Loin with Plums and Mushroom Sauce

Makes 8 servings

LIKE NOBODY ELSE, SOUTHERNERS STILL CHAMPION the noble pig that has sustained us through four centuries of glory and misfortune. While our unique styles of bacon, sausage, salt pork, country hams, and pork barbecue remain the envy of much of the world, on a day-to-day basis we love nothing more than a beautiful pork roast. We stuff loins and shoulders with everything from apples to greens to dried apricots; we devise gravies, sauces, and glazes enhanced by oranges, raisins, mushrooms, and cranberries; and we baste our roasts with bourbon, sweet wines, cider, and even sorghum and molasses. I don't suppose anybody is as expert at dealing with pork roast as Emeril Lagasse in New Orleans, and it is he who gave me the simple idea of doing a cider and pork wine sauce and serving the meat with slightly glazed purple plums.

One 3-pound boneless pork loin

2 teaspoons dried sage, crumbled

½ teaspoon salt

¼ teaspoon freshly ground black pepper

1½ cups apple cider

1 cup chicken broth

¼ cup port wine

1 cup heavy cream

4 tablespoons (½ stick) butter

6 to 8 purple plums, seeded and cut into wedges

1 pound fresh mushrooms, sliced

Preheat the oven to 450°F.

Rub the pork loin all over with the sage, salt, and pepper and position, fat side up, on a rack in a large roasting pan. Pour 1 cup of the cider into the pan, cover, and bake 15 minutes. Reduce the heat to 325°F, bake the loin 1½ hours longer, transfer to a platter, and let stand.

Place the roasting pan over moderate heat, add the remaining ½ cup cider, and stir to scrape up any browned bits. Add the broth, port, and cream and cook, stirring often, till the sauce is thickened, about 20 minutes. Turn off the heat, cover, and keep warm.

In a large skillet, melt 2 tablespoons of the butter over moderate heat, add the plums, and cook, stirring and turning, till softened and slightly golden, about 5 minutes. Transfer to a plate, and keep warm. Melt the remaining 2 tablespoons butter in the skillet, add the mushrooms, and cook, stirring occasionally, till they release most of their liquid and are tender, about 10 minutes. Add the cream mixture, reduce the heat, and cook till thoroughly heated.

To serve, place two or three slices of pork on individual plates, spoon mushroom sauce over each portion, and garnish each with a few plums.

FLORIDA GLAZED PORK CHOPS WITH CARAMBOLA

Makes 6 servings

NOW CULTIVATED IN FLORIDA, THE GLOSSY, GOLDEN, sweet carambola (also known as star fruit) is but one of the new exotic tropical fruits being used to add depth to one style of Southern cooking. Available in many specialty food markets and some upscale supermarkets from early fall to midwinter, carambolas range from three to five inches in length, are easily identified by their five distinctive ribs (the broader the rib, the sweeter the fruit), and require no peeling. Floridians use carambolas not only in salads and desserts but also to enhance any number of otherwise ordinary dishes, such as these glazed pork chops.

2 tablespoons butter

6 medium-thick loin pork chops, trimmed of excess fat

½ cup orange juice

¼ cup sugar

2 teaspoons cornstarch

¼ teaspoon ground allspice

⅛ teaspoon ground cloves

3 teaspoons fresh orange rind

Salt and freshly ground black pepper to taste

1 large carambola, rinsed well and thinly sliced

Fresh watercress for garnish

In a large heavy skillet, melt the butter over moderate heat, arrange the pork chops in the pan, and brown well on both sides. Add 3 tablespoons of the orange juice, reduce the heat to low, cover, and simmer the chops till tender, 40 to 45 minutes.

Meanwhile, combine the sugar, cornstarch, allspice, cloves, orange rind, and salt and pepper in a small saucepan, add the remaining orange juice, and stir over low heat till well blended and smooth. Add the carambola slices and simmer about 3 minutes.

To serve, place the pork chops on plates, spoon a little glaze over each portion, top each with carambola slices, and garnish with watercress.

136

Fresh Country Sausage

Makes 3 pounds sausage meat

ONE OF MY EARLIEST MEMORIES OF GROWING UP IN North Carolina was the ritual Saturday morning drive to a large farm to stock up on fresh eggs and chickens, buttermilk, slab bacon, and, to be sure, the best whole-hog country sausage ever made. Throughout the South, bulk sausage has always been part of the fall hog-killing tradition, and even out of season, many serious cooks (myself included), wary of most commercial products, still grind and blend their own sausage on a regular basis. I find some store-bought brands (Neese's in North Carolina, George Jones in Tennessee, and even widely available Jimmy Dean) to be acceptable, but more often than not, what you find in supermarkets (especially in the North) are frozen rolls of fatty, underseasoned, disgusting sausage that even my beagle would reject. Since sausage plays such an important role in Southern cookery (the array of brands in supermarkets is staggering), I urge everybody to buy a good meat grinder and follow this basic recipe. (Do not use a food processor to make sausage.) The sausage freezes well up to 2 months.

2 pounds boneless pork shoulder, chilled

1 pound fresh pork fat, chilled

1 tablespoon salt

1 teaspoon freshly ground black pepper

2 teaspoons ground sage

1 teaspoon dried red pepper flakes

2 tablespoons cold water

Cut the pork and pork fat into 2-inch chunks and pass first through the coarse blade, then through the fine blade of a meat grinder into a large mixing bowl. Add the remaining ingredients, moisten both hands with water, and knead the mixture till well blended and smooth. Wrap the sausage in plastic wrap and store in the refrigerator at least 2 hours before using.

BISCUITS WITH SAUSAGE GRAVY

Makes 4 to 6 servings

AT DINERS, ROADSIDE RESTAURANTS, AND FAMILY
restaurants throughout the South, "biscuits 'n' gravy"
refers either to fried sausage patties between split
biscuits covered with a thickened pan brown gravy or to
fried country ham and split biscuits with red-eye gravy.
Both are quintessential breakfast dishes that uphold the
Southern tradition of starting the day with "serious
food." No matter where I travel, I never fail to search for
places that serve one or the other—with, of course, some
style of eggs. Unless you can find decent bulk sausage,
I strongly suggest you grind your own (page 137), and
unless you want tasteless, revolting, milky white gravy,
I can't emphasize enough the importance of frying the
sausage and making the gravy in a cast-iron skillet (never
a nonstick one) so that as much browned sausage debris
as possible can be scraped from the bottom. And do
consider doubling the biscuit recipe so there'll be plenty
of extra ones to spread with fruit preserves.

THE BISCUITS

1½ cups all-purpose flour

2 teaspoons baking powder

½ teaspoon salt

3 tablespoons chilled vegetable shortening

¾ cup milk

1 pound bulk sausage (page 137)

THE GRAVY

4 tablespoons (½ stick) butter

¼ cup all-purpose flour

2½ cups milk

Salt and freshly ground black pepper to taste

Preheat the oven to 475°F.

To make the biscuits, whisk together the flour, baking powder, and salt in a large mixing bowl. Add the shortening and cut it in with a pastry cutter or rub with your fingertips till the mixture is mealy. Gradually add the milk and stir just till the dough holds together and is still sticky. Transfer to a lightly floured work surface, knead about 8 times, and form the dough with your hands into 8 smooth rounds about 1 inch thick. Arrange the rounds on a baking sheet about 1 inch apart, bake in the upper third of the oven till golden brown, about 15 minutes, and keep warm.

With your hands, form the sausage meat into 8 patties, fry the patties on both sides in a large skillet over moderate heat till nicely browned and cooked through, about 5 minutes, drain on paper towels, and keep warm on a plate. Set the skillet with the fat aside.

To make the gravy, pour off about half the fat from the skillet, add the butter to the skillet, and stir over moderate heat till the fats are incorporated, scraping the browned bits off the bottom. Gradually add the flour, stir till it has absorbed the fats, and cook, stirring constantly, till the flour turns golden brown, about 2 minutes. Gradually add the milk, stirring constantly, till the gravy is thickened, smooth, and slightly browned. Season with salt and pepper and stir well.

To serve, split 4 to 6 of the biscuits in half and place the bottoms on warm serving plates. Top each bottom with a sausage patty, arrange the biscuit tops at an angle, spoon hot gravy over the tops, and serve immediately.

Alabama Hog Pot

Makes 6 to 8 servings

ONCE WAS THE TIME THROUGHOUT MUCH OF THE South when hog pots featuring at least four types of pork were just as popular at big church suppers, political rallies, and fund-raising cookouts as pit-cooked barbecue. Today, however, you don't see many old-fashioned hog pots in our cholesterol-obsessed society, which I find sad, since people who've never eaten pig's feet and ears slowly simmered with pork shoulder, lean salt pork, sausage, cabbage, and numerous other greens and seasonings don't know what they've been missing. This particular hog pot, which I've adapted for my own home kitchen, was inspired by a spectacular one fired up at a huge church benefit that a friend invited me to attend in Greenville, Alabama. In the South, you'll have no trouble finding packaged pig's feet and perfectly cleaned pig's ears in most supermarkets; elsewhere, any good butcher should be able to fill your order and prepare the cuts for cooking. This hearty dish requires nothing more than a tart green salad or vinegary coleslaw, some form of cornbread, and plenty of cold beer.

2 pig's feet, cleaned

2 pig's ears, cleaned

¼ pound lean salt pork

¼ cup vegetable oil

1 pound boneless pork shoulder, trimmed of excess fat and cut into 1-inch cubes

1 large onion, chopped

1 celery rib, chopped

1 carrot, scraped and chopped

Salt and freshly ground black pepper to taste

1 medium head green cabbage (discolored leaves discarded), cored, quartered, and coarsely chopped

½ pound smoked pork sausage (such as kielbasa), sliced

1 cup dry white wine

Place the pig's feet in a large, heavy pot with enough water to cover, bring to a simmer, skimming off any scum from the surface, cover, and cook for 2 hours. Add the ears and salt pork to the pot, add more water to cover if necessary, return to a simmer, and cook till the feet and ears are tender, 1 to 1½ hours. Drain and, when cool enough to handle, remove any loose bones from the feet, cut the ears and salt pork into thin strips, and set aside.

Wash out and dry the pot. Add the oil over moderate heat, brown the pork cubes in the oil on all sides, and add to the pig's feet and other meats. Add the onion, celery, and carrot to the pot, season with salt and pepper, and cook, stirring, till the vegetables soften, about 5 minutes. Add the meats to the vegetables, scatter the cabbage over the top, arrange the sausage slices over the cabbage, and season with salt and pepper. Add the wine plus enough water to cover the ingredients, bring to a simmer, cover, and cook till the pork cubes are tender and the cabbage very soft, about 1 hour.

COUNTRY-STYLE CHITLINS

Makes 6 to 8 servings

CHITLINS (OR, IN YANKEE LANGUAGE, CHITTERLINGS)
are the small intestines of hogs, and are considered a
delicacy in country kitchens throughout the Deep South.
Whether slowly simmered or boiled, battered, and fried,
chitlins can be an acquired taste for some, but when
they're prepared carefully and served with the right
condiments (some style of vinegar, chopped onions,
mustard, corn relish, etc.), it's easy to understand why
they have been prized for centuries as a major
component of soul food. Pig intestines are also used in
Louisiana to make Cajun smoked andouille sausage, and
if you've ever eaten and enjoyed the classic French
sausages called *andouilles,* you'll probably love the
flavor of Southern chitlins. Chitterlings are widely
available in Southern markets and at some pork shops
throughout the country.

10 pounds chitlins (chitterlings), fresh or frozen

1 large onion, quartered

1 large celery rib, cracked in thirds

1 garlic clove, smashed

¼ cup cider vinegar

Salt and freshly ground black pepper to taste

Hot pepper vinegar (available in bottles)

Chopped red onions

Under cold running water, clean the chitlins to remove
fat and any foreign matter, place them in a large kettle
or casserole, and add the onion, celery, garlic, vinegar,
and salt and pepper. (Do not add water, since the
chitlins will create their own liquid.) Bring to a boil,
reduce the heat to low, cover, and simmer till tender,
2½ to 3 hours, adding a little water if the liquid level
begins to drop. Test the chitlins for tenderness. If
necessary, continue simmering about 30 minutes
longer. Serve with hot pepper vinegar and chopped
onions on the side.

Ham Croquettes

Makes 6 servings

WHY HAM CROQUETTES, ONCE A PRIZED STAPLE IN every Southern department store tearoom, country club clubhouse, and smart home dining room, fell into disfavor years ago continues to baffle me. "It's a disgrace," says renowned Southern food writer Jean Anderson, "and I suspect it's because the health police tried to frighten people away from anything fried. I loved ham and chicken croquettes as a child, and I love them now." Well, I haven't seen much evidence lately that Southerners are very frightened of fried foods. Like Jean, I love any style of croquettes, and I think it's high time this sapid dish underwent a rebirth—in homes and restaurants. These ham croquettes were traditionally served with mustard or tomato sauce on the side. If you really want something exceptional, make them with well-aged country ham—minus the salt in the recipe. For perfect texture, the ham mixture really should be refrigerated overnight before being formed into patties.

4 tablespoons (½ stick) butter

3 scallions (white parts only), finely chopped

3 tablespoons all-purpose flour, plus extra for dredging

1½ cups milk

4 cups coarsely chopped cooked ham

3 large egg yolks

¼ teaspoon dried sage, crumbled

Salt and freshly ground black pepper to taste

1 large egg, beaten with 2 tablespoons water

2 cups fine bread crumbs

Peanut oil for frying

In a saucepan, melt the butter over moderate heat, add the scallions and flour, and whisk till soft and well blended, about 2 minutes. Whisking rapidly, add the milk till well blended, add the ham, stir well, and remove from the heat. Whisking rapidly, add the egg yolks, return to the heat, add the sage and salt and pepper, and whisk till well blended. Scrape the mixture into a dish, cover, and refrigerate overnight.

With your hands, divide the mixture into 6 balls and roll lightly in the flour. Pat the balls into smooth oval patties, dip briefly into the egg wash, dredge in the bread crumbs, and place on a plate till ready to fry.

In a large, heavy skillet, heat about 1 inch of oil over moderately high heat about 1 minute, fry the patties till golden brown, about 3 minutes on each side, and drain on paper towels. Serve piping hot.

Ham and Sweet Potato Hash

Makes 4 servings

EXCEPT IN SOUTH CAROLINA, WHERE THE TERM *HASH* most often refers to a thick meat gravy served over rice (usually with pork barbecue), any dish of chopped meat, vegetables, and seasonings that is formed into a cake, fried till crispy, and topped with a fried or poached egg has been known to all Southerners as hash, ever since the lowly concept was popularized by diners, lunch counters, and cafeterias early in the twentieth century. By far the most beloved hash is that made with either leftover ham or pork and diced sweet potatoes, and in the past few years I've encountered upscale variations of this traditional dish even in a few fine restaurants. If you see "Ham & Sweet" listed on a diner or cafeteria menu, you can be sure the reference is to this hash (which might also contain a little spiced apple).

1 pound cooked ham, cut into ½-inch cubes

1½ cups diced cooked sweet potatoes (slightly firm in texture)

2 medium onions, minced and sautéed in 2 tablespoons butter for 2 minutes

½ large green bell pepper, cored, seeded, and finely chopped

½ teaspoon ground sage

Salt and freshly ground black pepper to taste

¾ cup heavy cream

4 tablespoons (½ stick) butter

4 large eggs

Minced fresh parsley leaves

In a large mixing bowl, combine the ham, sweet potatoes, onions, bell pepper, sage, salt and pepper, and cream, stir till well blended, and, with your hands, form into a large cake.

In a large, heavy skillet, melt half of the butter over moderately high heat, add the ham cake, and press down evenly with a spatula to form a compact oval cake. Reduce the heat to moderate and cook the hash about 5 minutes or till the underside is browned and crusty. Loosen the hash with the spatula and invert onto a plate. Add the remaining butter to the skillet and increase the heat slightly. Slide the other side of the hash into the skillet, reduce the heat to moderate, and cook about 5 minutes or till the other side is browned and crusty. Transfer the hash to a heated platter and keep warm.

Break the eggs gently into 1 or 2 saucepans of boiling water, poach for 2 minutes, and transfer with a slotted spoon to a clean cloth to drain. Top the hash with the poached eggs and sprinkle with minced parsley.

Smithfield Ham and Veal Rolls

Makes 6 servings

SMITHFIELD, VIRGINIA, HAS BEEN CONSIDERED THE undisputed birthplace of Southern-style country hams for at least three hundred years, and today, still, a legal statute protecting the tradition dictates that a genuine Smithfield ham must be cured, treated, smoked, and processed within the small town's borders. Of course, producers of ham from the commercial giant Gwaltney to the smallest farmer have come up with every way imaginable to cook the noble ham and use it in numerous recipes, but nothing impressed me more on one of my visits to the area than the way the mother of a relatively minor ham producer teamed the ham with veal to make these delectable rolls fit for the most distinguished formal dinner. Since Smithfield hams can be exorbitantly expensive these days, by all means feel free, as I do, to substitute any respectable baked country ham.

> 8 tablespoons (1 stick) butter
>
> ½ cup finely chopped scallions (white and light green parts)
>
> 2 garlic cloves, minced
>
> 2 cups soft bread crumbs
>
> 1 cup finely chopped parsley leaves
>
> 1 large egg, beaten
>
> 2 tablespoons chicken broth
>
> Four boneless veal steaks (about 2 pounds)
>
> 2 teaspoons Dijon mustard
>
> ½ pound thinly sliced cooked Smithfield ham
>
> 1 tablespoon butter, melted
>
> ½ cup dry white wine

Preheat the oven to 325°F.

In a large skillet, melt the butter over moderate heat, add the scallions and garlic, and cook, stirring, till softened, about 2 minutes. Remove from the heat, add the bread crumbs, parsley, egg, and broth, stir till well blended, and set aside.

With a mallet or rolling pin, pound the veal steaks to a ½-inch thickness, spread each with equal amounts of mustard, and top each with a ham slice. Roll up jelly-roll style and secure with wooden toothpicks. Place the rolls, seam side down, on a rack in a shallow baking pan, brush each with melted butter, and bake till tender, 30 to 35 minutes.

Transfer the rolls to a serving platter, remove the toothpicks, and cut each into ½-inch slices. Add the wine to the pan over moderately high heat, stir to loosen the pan drippings, and pour over the slices.

144

Beverly's 500-Degree Country Ham

Makes one baked country ham (at least 12 servings)

WHEN MY FRIEND BEVERLY, WHO WAS BORN IN
Mississippi and raised in North Carolina, outlined for me
the way she'd always baked "the greatest country ham
on earth," I told her in no uncertain terms that she'd
lost her mind. Then, when my curiosity finally got the
best of me, I resolved to try her technique—insane as it
sounded—and followed the directions to the letter.
Suffice it to say that I'm not sure it's the greatest
country ham on earth, but it turns out to be one of the
most sublime examples I've ever cooked. This should be
great country ham in its most pristine, unadorned,
simple style, so be sure to use the best cured, well-aged
ham you can find.

*One 12- to 14-pound premium cured, aged
country ham*

5 cups water

Under running water, scrub well the entire exterior
surface of the ham, place skin side up in a large
roasting pan, add enough water to cover, and let soak
about 12 hours or overnight—soak for less time if you
prefer your ham to be saltier—at room temperature.

Preheat the oven to 375°F.

Drain the ham, add the 5 cups of water, cover tightly,
and place in the oven. Increase the heat to 500°F, bake
10 minutes, then turn off the oven for 3 hours, never
opening the oven door.

Return the heat to 500°F, bake 15 minutes, turn off the
oven, and let the ham stand for 6 to 8 hours, never
opening the oven door.

Transfer the ham to a large platter or cutting board
and slice according to need.

COUNTRY HAM BRAISED IN CIDER AND MOLASSES

Makes at least 12 servings, with leftovers for ham biscuits and other dishes

WILKES COUNTY, LOCATED HIGH IN THE MOUNTAINS of North Carolina, produces some of the greatest country hams in the entire South, and without question the best in the county hang in Clayton Long's ham house at Glendale Springs, about ten miles from West Jefferson. Like his daddy ("Mr. G") before him, Clayton is a maverick who would no more compromise the quality of his exquisite hams to streamline and increase production than he'd neglect the acres of Christmas trees he grows while the hundreds of hams are slowly aging under natural weather conditions in the ham house. Unlike most producers, he cures his hams with only salt and brown sugar; he uses no preservatives or coloring agents; he wouldn't dream of aging a ham less than nine months; and he refuses to ship his hams across the state line, since this would require subjecting them to ludicrous federal regulations that might alter their quality. If you want a Long ham, you have no alternative but to make a special detour, as hundreds of loyal customers do every fall. The reward is the finest and least expensive country ham to be found anywhere (about thirty dollars, compared with seventy-five dollars and up elsewhere, for a 16-pound ham). I've cooked Clayton's ham every way imaginable (besides simply frying it with red-eye gravy for breakfast), but perhaps the most unforgettable method is with this braise using apple cider and molasses.

One 14- to 16-pound cured country ham

1 cup molasses

1 cup firmly packed light brown sugar

1 gallon apple cider

3 medium onions, chopped

3 medium carrots, scraped and chopped

2 cups dry bread crumbs mixed with 2 cups firmly packed light brown sugar

Scrub the ham well with a stiff kitchen brush under running water, then position it in a large, deep, oval pan. Add cool water to cover and let the ham soak for 12 hours at room temperature, changing the water twice.

Remove the ham from the pan, rinse the pan well, return the ham to the pan, and add enough fresh water to come halfway up the sides. Add the molasses and brown sugar to the water, stir as well as possible, then add enough cider to just cover the ham. Add the onions and carrots and bring the liquid to a very low simmer. Cover partially and simmer slowly for 3 hours. Let the ham cool completely in the liquid.

Preheat the oven to 425°F.

Place the ham on a work surface, remove the skin and all but ¼ inch of the fat, and score the fat in diamonds with a sharp knife. Rinse the roasting pan well after discarding the contents, then place the ham in the pan on a rack fat side up and coat with the bread-crumb/brown-sugar mixture, pressing down with your fingers. Bake, uncovered, till the crumbs are browned, 20 to 30 minutes.

To serve, position the ham on a large, heavy wooden or ceramic platter and carve into thin slices with an electric or serrated knife.

STUFFED MARYLAND HAM

Makes 12 to 15 servings

MOST TRAVELERS VISIT BALTIMORE AND THE
Chesapeake Bay area strictly to eat steamed blue crabs
and other seafood, unaware that in southern Maryland,
especially around Mechanicsville, in St. Mary's County,
another great regional specialty is served in cozy taverns
and small restaurants: spicy braised fresh or lightly
cured ham stuffed with cabbage, celery, kale, watercress,
or a variety of other greens. Typically, customers begin a
meal with a crab cake, but the real treat is the colorful
ham bursting with different flavors and washed down
with plenty of local beer. One of the secrets of this
unique dish is to allow the ham to cool in its broth
overnight—so plan accordingly. Unlike braised country
ham, this style of ham is usually served in thick slices.

*2 large green cabbages (about 3 pounds each),
    cored and finely chopped*

2 bunches watercress (stems removed), rinsed

3 medium onions, finely chopped

4 celery ribs (leaves included), finely chopped

1 teaspoon dry mustard

1 teaspoon salt

½ teaspoon freshly ground black pepper

½ teaspoon cayenne pepper

One 10-pound precooked ham shank

Place the cabbage, watercress, onions, celery, dry
mustard, salt, pepper, and cayenne pepper in a
stockpot or roasting pan large enough to fit the ham.
Add enough water to reach within 1 inch of the top of
the vegetables, stir, and bring to a boil. Turn off the
heat, cover the pot, and let the vegetables stand 10
minutes in the hot water. Drain the vegetables in a
colander over a bowl to catch the broth, let cool, and
reserve the broth.

With a sharp knife, cut Xs about 1 inch square and 2
inches deep all over the ham and fill each X with
vegetable stuffing. Wrap the ham in a wide double
thickness of cheesecloth and tie the ends to secure it
tightly.

Place the ham in the pot along with the reserved broth
and add enough water to cover. Place a lid on the top,
bring the liquid to a boil, reduce the heat to low, and
simmer the ham for 2 to 2½ hours, adding water as
needed to keep it covered. Turn off the heat and let the
ham cool in the liquid, preferably overnight.

When ready to serve, reheat the ham in its liquid,
transfer to a cutting board or large platter, remove and
discard the cheesecloth, and cut in thick slices.

MEAT LOAF DELUXE

Makes 8 servings

WHILE IT TOOK THE REST OF THE COUNTRY DECADES to bring all-American meat loaf out of the closet as a dish worthy of even the snazziest homes and restaurants, Southerners have always not only loved and respected the loaf but also debated every aspect of its preparation to the point of obsession. The various types of meat, the ingredients that yield the most flavor and moisture, the best fillers for binding, the mixing and baking techniques—no facet of meat loaf escapes intense scrutiny and challenge. There's a lot that distinguishes Southern meat loaf from most other styles (the cardinal importance of bulk pork sausage, the use of bacon as a flavoring and moisturizing agent, free-form baking for even crustiness, etc.), but perhaps the most defining principle is that great meat loaf requires no gravy—that, in fact, it would be desecrated by gravy. My own recipe for the ultimate meat loaf seems to be slightly modified from year to year, but for the time being, this deluxe version should satisfy even the most finicky Reb.

5 tablespoons butter

½ pound large fresh mushrooms, stems finely chopped and caps reserved

1 large onion, finely chopped

½ medium green bell pepper, seeded and finely chopped

2 celery ribs, finely chopped

2 garlic cloves, minced

½ teaspoon dried thyme, crumbled

½ teaspoon dried rosemary, crumbled

1 pound ground beef round

1 pound ground pork

1 pound ground veal

½ pound bulk pork sausage

1 tablespoon Dijon mustard

½ cup tomato ketchup

3 tablespoons Worcestershire sauce

½ teaspoon Tabasco sauce

Salt and freshly ground black pepper to taste

3 large eggs, beaten

1 cup bread crumbs soaked in ½ cup heavy cream

3 strips bacon

Pimento-stuffed green olives, cut in half, for garnish

Preheat the oven to 350°F.

In a medium skillet, melt 3 tablespoons of the butter over moderate heat, add the mushroom stems, and cook, stirring, about 5 minutes or till most of their liquid has evaporated. Stir in the onion, bell pepper, celery, garlic, thyme, and rosemary, reduce the heat to low, cover, and simmer about 15 minutes or till the vegetables are soft and the liquid has evaporated.

Place the meats in a large mixing bowl, add the sautéed vegetables, and mix lightly. Add the mustard, ketchup, Worcestershire, Tabasco, salt and pepper, eggs, and breadcrumbs and mix with your hands till blended thoroughly. Shape the mixture into a firm, thick oval loaf, place in a shallow baking or gratin dish, drape bacon over the top, and bake 1 hour in the upper third of the oven. Remove the bacon strips and continue baking 15 to 20 minutes longer, depending on how thick the loaf is and how crusty you want the exterior to be.

Shortly before the meat loaf is removed from the oven, melt the remaining 2 tablespoons butter in a small skillet over moderate heat, add the reserved mushroom caps, and cook, stirring, about 2 minutes or till nicely glazed. Transfer the meat loaf to a large, heated platter, arrange olives over the top, and garnish the edges with the mushroom caps.

Beer-Braised Short Ribs of Beef

Makes 4 to 5 servings

WHAT TRENDY YOUNG RESTAURANT CHEFS TODAY HAVE yet to learn, but what Southern home cooks have known for centuries, is that there's one way and only one way to transform tough, cartilage-laden short ribs of beef (like lamb shanks) into a culinary wonder: braising them slowly in liquid for hours. No dry-heat cooking, no marinating and grilling, no quick method whatsoever will break down the meat fibers and soften up the fat as braising does. Cooking short ribs correctly is a long but easy process. The technique I've used for years involves both boiling and braising the ribs with vegetables for optimal succulence and tenderness. Most Southerners cook short ribs simply in water, but, just recently, I've found that beer provides a slight bitterness that beautifully balances the sweetness of the meat and onions. Do shop very carefully for short ribs, rejecting any that have more bone than meat. What you're looking for are meaty ribs at least 4 inches wide and 3 inches thick. Remember that nothing freezes as well as uncooked short ribs.

6 meaty short ribs of beef

Three 12-ounce cans beer or ale

Salt and freshly ground black pepper to taste

12 small onions, scored on the root ends

10 small red potatoes, peeled

One 16-ounce can whole tomatoes with juice

Place the short ribs in a large saucepan or pot, add the beer and, if necessary, enough water to cover, and season with salt and pepper. Bring to a boil, reduce the heat to low, cover, and simmer at least 3 hours, adding more beer or water if necessary to cover. During the last hour of simmering, add the onions. During the last 30 minutes, add the potatoes.

Meanwhile, preheat the oven to 375°F.

With a slotted spoon, transfer the meat to a large, shallow baking dish, place the onions and potatoes around the meat, and add the tomatoes and their juice. If the juice does not fill the baking dish by three quarters, add a little of the cooking liquid. Season with salt and pepper and bake till the top is slightly crusted, about 45 minutes. Serve directly from the baking dish.

BOURBON BEEF AND OYSTER POT

Makes 8 servings

CREATED BY ONE OF MY MENTORS, PEARL BYRD FOSTER of Virginia, this is possibly the best example I know of truly innovative Southern cookery. Illogical as it may sound, beef and oysters make a brilliant marriage, enhanced especially by the use of a less tender but more flavorful cut of meat simmered slowly for a long time for optimum succulence. The ideal vessel for preparing this is an enameled cast-iron pot. Pearl always served the dish with simple parsleyed new potatoes and corn sticks, and I've never found a reason not to follow her practice.

½ cup vegetable oil

2 tablespoons butter

One 3-pound bottom or top round beef roast, trimmed of all fat and cut into 1½-inch cubes

3 ounces bourbon

2 cups beef broth

1 cup water

1 medium onion, chopped

1 celery rib, cut into 1-inch pieces

1 large carrot, scraped, halved lengthwise, and cut into 1-inch pieces

1 large russet potato, peeled and cut into cubes

2 tablespoons tomato paste

1 garlic clove, crushed

1 small bay leaf

2 cloves

¼ teaspoon dried thyme, crumbled

Worcestershire and Tabasco sauces to taste

Salt and freshly ground black pepper to taste

1 quart fresh, shucked oysters, liquor included

½ cup peeled and freshly grated horseradish

In a heavy 4-quart pot, heat the oil and butter together over moderate heat till the butter melts, then add the beef and brown it on all sides. Pour off any excess fat, add the bourbon, carefully ignite, and when the flames die out, add the broth and water and scrape the bottom to loosen all the browned bits. Add the onion, celery, carrot, potato, tomato paste, garlic, bay leaf, cloves, and thyme, season with Worcestershire, Tabasco, and salt and pepper, and stir to blend well. Bring to a boil, reduce the heat to moderately low, and simmer till the meat is very tender, about 2 hours.

With a slotted spoon, transfer the meat to a platter, carefully pour the liquid and vegetables into a food processor or blender (in batches, if necessary), and reduce to a purée, adding a little more broth if the mixture is too thick. Return the meat and puréed vegetables to the pot, arrange the oysters over the top, and pour the oyster liquor over them. Bring to a simmer, cover, and cook just till the edges of the oysters curl, 5 to 6 minutes. Serve the beef and oysters with a little horseradish on the side.

Chilled Spiced Beef

Makes 8 servings

WHETHER IT'S CALLED SPICED ROUND IN NASHVILLE, spice roll in Tidewater Virginia, or *daube de boeuf* in New Orleans, chilled spiced beef served in thin slices has been deemed one of the South's most elegant dishes since the mid-nineteenth century. While it's been said that the cooking process originated at meat-packing companies in Nashville as a way of preserving beef before refrigeration came along, I've always suspected that it goes back much further, to England and France, where I've been eating cold, spicy beef dishes for as long as I can remember. While the dish is time-consuming and slightly tricky to prepare, it's one that can highlight a formal buffet table like nothing else. Bottom or top beef round is often used, but I find that no cut has more flavor than brisket. With the beef, I like to serve an assortment of mustards.

One 4-pound brisket of beef (thin cut)

2 tablespoons finely chopped fresh parsley

1 tablespoon minced fresh rosemary

1 tablespoon minced fresh thyme

½ teaspoon ground cloves

½ teaspoon ground allspice

½ teaspoon ground nutmeg

Salt and cayenne pepper to taste

Rinse the brisket well under cold running water. In a small bowl, combine the herbs and spices, add the salt and cayenne pepper, mix well, and rub the herb/spice mixture over all the surfaces of the meat. Roll up the meat lengthwise as tightly as possible, firmly bind with kitchen string, then wrap in cheesecloth and tie securely. Wrap in plastic wrap and place in the refrigerator for 6 hours.

Remove the plastic wrap, place the rolled beef in a kettle just large enough to hold the bundle, and cover with cold water. Bring the water to a boil, reduce the heat to low, cover, and simmer till the beef is fork tender, about 5 hours, adding more water if necessary to keep the beef covered.

Transfer the beef to a deep bowl, pour a little cooking broth on top, fit a plate atop the meat, then place 8 to 10 pounds of weight (large canned goods, bricks, etc.) on the plate to press the meat down. Place the bowl in the refrigerator and chill 12 hours.

To serve, remove the cheesecloth and string, cut the cold beef against the grain in thin slices, and serve on an attractive platter.

152

Virginia Ginger Ale Chili

Makes 6 to 8 servings

IF GEORGIANS CAN HAVE THEIR BELOVED COCA-COLA Baked Beans (page 242), Virginians in the western part of the state are certainly entitled to their ginger ale chili spiced with both hot red peppers and dry mustard. Southerners (who have never, ever considered Texas to be a legitimate Confederate state, partly because those folks barbecue beef brisket, goat, snake, and other strange meats instead of pig) generally don't pay much attention to chili con carne, but when they do, rest assured they always manage to give it a unique twist that would make most Texans cringe. Even I raised an eyebrow when an old college mate told me the unique way his family and friends around Roanoke had always made chili, but when I tried this unusual recipe, I had to admit it was one of the best versions ever conceived.

2 pounds ground beef chuck

¼ pound ground pork shoulder

1 large Spanish onion, chopped

1 green bell pepper, seeded and chopped

3 garlic cloves, minced

One 28-ounce can tomatoes, juice included

1 cup ginger ale

1 small hot red chile pepper, chopped

2 tablespoons chili powder

1 tablespoon ground cumin

1 tablespoon dried oregano, crumbled

2 teaspoons dry mustard

1 tablespoon salt

1 teaspoon freshly ground black pepper

One 20-ounce can kidney beans, drained

Grated sharp cheddar cheese for garnish

Diced red onion for garnish

In a large heavy pot, brown the beef and pork, stirring, till no pink color remains in the beef. Pour off most of the grease. Add the onion, bell pepper, and garlic and cook, stirring, till vegetables are softened, about 5 minutes. Add the tomatoes plus their juice, the ginger ale, red chile pepper, chili powder, cumin, oregano, dry mustard, salt, and pepper and stir well. Bring to a simmer, cover, and cook 1 hour. Add the beans and simmer 1 to 1½ hours longer, stirring from time to time.

Serve the chili in deep soup bowls and garnish each portion with grated cheese and diced red onions.

Chicken-Fried Steak and Gravy

Makes 4 servings

IN ARKANSAS AND KENTUCKY, THEY TEND TO CALL IT country-fried steak; in Maryland, Virginia, and the Carolinas, it's smothered steak; but down in Mississippi and Alabama, folks generally know it as chicken-fried steak. Whatever term is used, cube steaks that are battered and fried in oil and bacon drippings and served with a creamy gravy ("smothered") were a Southern specialty long before western pioneers and Texas cattlemen corrupted the dish's reputation by producing meat that was not unlike whitleather in taste and texture. As anybody from Dixie knows, the secret to any superb chicken-fried steak is not only the quality of the beef and gravy but the principle of never overcooking the meat—rarely more than about two minutes on each side. Technically, the best cube steak is cut from top or bottom beef round (not chuck) and tenderized (or cubed) by running it through a tenderizing machine once or twice. When buying these steaks, I don't hesitate a second to ask the butcher which cut of meat was used, refusing any that is not top or bottom round.

FOR THE STEAKS

> ¼ cup milk
>
> 1 large egg
>
> 1 cup dry bread crumbs
>
> Salt and freshly ground black pepper to taste
>
> Cayenne pepper to taste
>
> Four 4-ounce beef cube steaks
>
> 2 tablespoons vegetable oil
>
> 2 tablespoons bacon drippings

FOR THE GRAVY

> 2 tablespoons bacon drippings
>
> 1 large onion, minced
>
> 1 tablespoon all-purpose flour
>
> 1 cup heavy cream
>
> 1 cup milk
>
> Salt and freshly ground black pepper to taste

To fry the steaks, combine the milk and egg in a small bowl and whisk till well blended. In another bowl, mix the bread crumbs, salt and pepper, and cayenne pepper till well blended and transfer the mixture to a plate. Dip each steak into the liquid, coat with bread crumbs on each side, and place on a plate.

In a large heavy cast-iron skillet, heat the oil and bacon drippings over moderately high heat till quite hot. Add 2 of the steaks to the pan, cook about 2 minutes on each side or till golden brown, transfer to a plate, and keep warm. Repeat with the other 2 steaks and reserve the pan drippings.

To make the gravy, heat the bacon drippings over moderate heat, add the onion, and cook, stirring, about 1 minute. Sprinkle the flour over the onion and stir 1 minute longer, scraping up any brown bits from the pan. Add the heavy cream, milk, and salt and pepper and whisk briskly till the gravy is thickened and smooth, 6 to 7 minutes.

To serve, place the steaks on individual plates and ladle gravy over each.

154

Greenbrier Deviled Oxtails

Makes 4 servings

THE FACT THAT BEEF HAS NEVER PLAYED THE SAME leading role as pork or poultry in Southern cooking explains partly why the tough, bony, but extremely flavorful oxtail has not been used more (despite the wide popularity of short ribs). Today, however, oxtails are much more available in supermarkets than in the past, and since they lend themselves so beautifully to soups and slow braising, it's a shame not to exploit their potential. I remember one exceptional oxtail and vegetable soup I ate at a friend's home in Oxford, Mississippi, but without question, these crusty deviled oxtails I relished at the renowned Greenbrier Resort in White Sulphur Springs, West Virginia, serve to illustrate just how glorious this lowly cut of beef can be.

4 pounds oxtails, cut into 2-inch sections and trimmed of excess fat

3 cups water

1 large onion, quartered

1 celery rib, cracked in thirds

1 carrot, scraped and cut into thirds

½ teaspoon dried thyme

1 bay leaf

½ cup sour cream

¼ cup Dijon mustard

2 teaspoons Worcestershire sauce

Salt and freshly ground black pepper to taste

Cayenne pepper to taste

2 cups dry bread crumbs

4 tablespoons (½ stick) butter, melted

Preheat the oven to 350°F.

In a large casserole, combine the oxtails, water, onion, celery, carrot, thyme, and bay leaf, cover, and braise in the oven till the oxtails are tender but not falling apart, about 2½ hours. Uncover and let cool.

In a small bowl, combine the sour cream, mustard, Worcestershire, salt and pepper, and cayenne pepper, stir till well blended, and set aside. Place the bread crumbs in a wide, shallow bowl and set aside.

Preheat the oven broiler.

With a slotted spoon, transfer the oxtails to paper towels and pat dry. Coat completely with the sour cream mixture, dredge in the bread crumbs, and arrange in a single layer in a greased baking pan. Drizzle the butter over the oxtails and broil about 4 inches from the heat, turning once, till golden brown and crusty, 12 to 15 minutes. Serve piping hot.

Chilled Mobile Thyme Tongue

Makes 6 to 8 servings

OVER THE YEARS, I'D SAY I'VE BEEN TO MY SHARE OF gracious garden parties in Mobile, Alabama (perhaps the most memorable one during the annual forty-day carnival preceding Lent), and so often have I seen platters of what locals call thyme tongue among the smoked turkey, rolled veal, creamed oysters in patty shells, and vegetable aspic on the buffet that I'm ready to believe it's the city's signature dish. Nobody seems to know when or how thyme tongue became so popular, or why it is religiously served with watermelon rind pickles, but if you've always balked at eating beef tongue, this aromatic way of preparing it will dispel any blind prejudice. Just make sure to cook the tongue till it is fork tender, and slice it almost paper thin. The tongue is also delicious stuffed in biscuits with Dijon mustard in place of the more traditional country ham.

One 3½- to 4-pound fresh beef tongue

2 cups white vinegar

1 cup dry red wine

1 cup dark brown sugar

1 tablespoon dry mustard

2 teaspoons dried thyme, crumbled

2 teaspoons salt

1 teaspoon freshly ground black pepper

1 bay leaf

4 cloves

1 large onion, thinly sliced

1 garlic clove, thinly sliced

½ lemon, cut in half and seeded

Watermelon Rind Pickles (page 383)

With a sharp paring knife, make small indentions all over the tongue, then place the tongue in a deep ovenproof baking dish or enameled casserole just large enough to hold it.

In a medium saucepan, combine all remaining ingredients except the watermelon rind pickles and stir till the sugar and mustard are dissolved. Bring to a boil for about 1 minute, stirring, then pour the marinade evenly over the tongue. Let cool, cover, and let the tongue marinate in the refrigerator for 24 hours, turning it two or three times.

Preheat the oven to 325°F.

Return the tongue to room temperature, cover tightly with aluminum foil or a lid, and bake till easily pierced with a fork, about 3 hours.

Let the tongue cool to room temperature in its liquid, then transfer to a cutting board, slit the skin on the underside and peel off, and cut away root, small bones, and any gristle. Return the tongue to the marinade and refrigerate, covered, till ready to serve.

To serve, transfer the chilled tongue to a platter or cutting board, carve in thin slices, and arrange the slices on a chilled platter garnished with watermelon rind pickles.

156

Mountain Sweetbreads in Mushroom Cream Sauce

Makes 6 servings

NEVER ONES TO SHY AWAY FROM ORGAN MEATS LIKE most other Americans, rural Southerners relish sweetbreads (the thymus glands of calves, lambs, and pigs) as much as chitlins, liver, heart, and even "mountain oysters" (pig's testicles). Never was I served more sublime veal sweetbreads than at a cozy retreat called The Orchard Inn, up in Highlands, North Carolina, almost on the intersecting borders of South Carolina and Georgia. Without question, the most delicate, creamy sweetbreads are from young calves and lambs; those from older animals and hogs are tougher and much stronger in flavor. Today, veal sweetbreads are available fresh or frozen in more and more markets. Do remember not only that they must be soaked overnight in acidulated water and the tough membranes removed before cooking, but also that they are the most perishable of all organ meats and should be prepared within 24 hours of purchase. Since nothing seems to enhance sweetbreads like fresh lemon juice, I like to serve a bowl of seeded lemon wedges on the side.

2 pounds veal sweetbreads, soaked overnight in acidulated water and cleaned

⅓ cup fresh lemon juice

Salt and freshly ground black pepper to taste

8 tablespoons (1 stick) butter

4 scallions (white parts only), chopped

2 cups sliced mushrooms

3 tablespoons all-purpose flour

1 cup chicken broth

1 cup half-and-half

Toast points

Drain the soaked sweetbreads and place them in a large saucepan with the lemon juice and enough salted water to cover. Bring to a boil, reduce the heat to low, simmer 10 minutes, and transfer to a bowl of ice water. Cut away all membranes, then separate the sweetbreads into 2-inch pieces. Pat dry with paper towels, cut into ½-inch slices, and season with salt and pepper.

In a large skillet, melt 4 tablespoons of the butter over moderate heat, add half the sweetbreads, brown 2 minutes on each side, and transfer to a plate. Repeat with the remaining sweetbreads.

Add the remaining butter to the skillet, add the scallions and mushrooms, and cook, stirring, till softened, about 3 minutes. Add the flour and continue to cook, stirring, 2 minutes. Add the broth and half-and-half, bring to a simmer, and cook about 3 minutes. Add the browned sweetbreads, simmer 10 minutes, and serve on toast points arranged on individual plates.

NATCHITOCHES MEAT PIES

Makes about 18 small pies

AT NATCHITOCHES, A SMALL TOWN IN CENTRAL Louisiana, black locals used to sell meat pies from carts on the street till the authorities cracked down on food made outside commercial kitchens. Subsequently, a sharecropper and local butcher by the name of James Lasyone revived the tradition in 1966, the news spread, the world flocked to his eatery to sample the pies, and today Lasyone's produces no fewer than two hundred thousand of the half-moon pies per year—all eaten at the restaurant or ordered over the phone (318-352-3353). The patented recipe is undisclosed to everyone but James and his two daughters, but he does concede that "the main secret is in the fried dough, not the filling." And I do find it amazing that the delectable pies are not very greasy. The stuffed, unfried pies freeze beautifully in Ziploc bags, so you might want to double this recipe.

FOR THE FILLING

2 tablespoons peanut or vegetable oil

¾ pound ground beef chuck

¾ pound ground pork

½ cup chopped scallions (part of green tops included)

1 garlic clove, minced

1 teaspoon salt

1 teaspoon freshly ground black pepper

¼ teaspoon cayenne pepper

2 tablespoons all-purpose flour

FOR THE PASTRY

1 cup all-purpose flour

1 teaspoon baking powder

½ teaspoon salt

3 tablespoons vegetable shortening

1 large egg, beaten

⅓ cup milk

1 cup peanut oil for deep frying

To make the filling, heat the oil in a large skillet over moderate heat, add the beef, pork, scallions, and garlic, and cook, stirring and breaking up the meats, till the beef loses its red color. Add the remaining ingredients and continue to cook, stirring, till the mixture is almost dry, about 10 minutes. Transfer to a bowl, let cool, then chill.

To make the pastry, sift the flour, baking powder, and salt into a mixing bowl, add the shortening, and cut with a pastry cutter till the mixture resembles coarse cornmeal. Add the egg and milk and stir till a ball of dough forms. Transfer the dough to a lightly floured surface, roll out about ½ inch thick, and, using the lid of a coffee can, cut out rounds of dough.

To assemble the pies, place a heaping tablespoon of filling on one side of each round of dough. With your fingertips, dampen the pie edges with water, fold the other sides of dough over the filling, and seal the edges with a fork dipped in water. Prick twice with a fork on top.

To fry, heat the oil in a medium cast-iron skillet to about 350°F, quickly fry each pie till golden, about 2 minutes on each side, and drain briefly on paper towels. Serve hot.

South Carolina Hash

Makes 8 servings

WHEREAS IN NORTH CAROLINA NO PORK BARBECUE restaurant worth its peppery vinegar sauce would serve "que" without a little Brunswick stew on the side, the age-old tradition at barbecue pits in South Carolina is a side dish of thick meat gravy over rice or grits simply called hash. Depending on the area of the state, hash can be made with all beef, all pork, organ meats, or a combination of these primary ingredients, and while nobody agrees on just what constitutes an authentic hash, at hash cook-offs held everywhere from Gaffney to Union to the Sea Islands near Charleston, at least there seems to be a consensus that any hash must be cooked slowly in a cast-iron pot till it's the consistency of a smooth meat purée (or, as one expert put it, "thick baby food"). Adventurous travelers in the state will look for the hash at Willard's Hash and Barbecue in Gaffney, Maurice's Piggy Park in Columbia, and Mr. B's Barbecue on Johns Island. At home, you might want to try my version, served over boiled rice or grits or simply on a bun.

2 pounds lean beef round or rump, trimmed of excess fat

1 pound lean pork, trimmed of excess fat

¼ pound pork liver (optional)

1 large onion, diced

8 tablespoons (1 stick) butter

2 tablespoons tomato paste

Salt and freshly ground black pepper to taste

Place the beef, pork, and optional liver in a heavy cast-iron pot and add enough water to cover. Bring to a boil, reduce the heat to low, cover, and simmer till the meats are almost falling apart, about 3 hours. Transfer the meats to a large pan and, when cool enough to handle, pull into bits.

Place the meats and onion in a food processor, grind coarsely, and return to the pot. Add the butter, tomato paste, and salt and pepper, bring to a simmer, and cook till the mixture resembles a thick gravy, 2½ to 3 hours, stirring frequently.

Poultry & Game

Perfect Southern Fried Chicken

Beer-Battered Fried Chicken

Maryland Fried Chicken with
Cream Gravy

Arkansas-Style Buttermilk
Fried Chicken

Old Hen Chicken Pot Pie

Mississippi Smothered Chicken

Maw Maw's Chicken
and Dumplings

Country Captain

Louisiana Chicken and
Sweet Potato Hash

Chicken and Hominy Chili

Bourbon Chicken

Curried Orange Chicken

Curried Turkey Hash Cakes

Roast Turkey with Sausage
and Pecan Dressing

Turkey Cutlets with Red Cabbage

Turkey Croquettes

Fried Rabbit with Madeira Gravy

Braised Rabbit with
Wild Mushrooms

Braised Duck with Leeks
and Onions

Duck with Red Cabbage

Edna's Virginia Roast Pheasant
with Chestnut Dressing

Smothered Quail

Roasted Quail Stuffed
with Oysters

Braised Venison
and Root Vegetables

PERFECT SOUTHERN FRIED CHICKEN

Makes 8 servings

WHY PEOPLE GET SO WORKED UP ABOUT COOKING good fried chicken is a real mystery to Southerners, and quite frankly I'm getting a little tired of all the helpless moaning and groaning. Nothing on earth is simpler than frying great chicken, so long, that is, as you observe a few basic cardinal rules: (1) Learn to cut up your own whole chickens, which allows not only more uniform pieces than those hacked to death in supermarkets but also the freedom to cut out the pully bone (wishbone) from the breast, if you wish; (2) use only a black, cast-iron skillet or heavy steel electric fry pan for even heat distribution, as well as high-quality vegetable shortening such as Crisco; (3) Never crowd the skillet with too many pieces of chicken or turn the pieces more than once; (4) maintain the heat of the fat exactly no matter what temperature is indicated, except when, due to the nature of the batter or a heating malfunction, the chicken is obviously burning; (5) never, ever cover fried chicken once it has drained unless you want soggy skin. For truly luscious, beautifully flavored and textured fried chicken, I first soak the raw pieces in buttermilk, add a little bacon grease to the fat, and fry the dark-meat pieces a few minutes longer than the white. And if you're wondering if great Southern fried chicken should involve only organic birds, or can be skinless, or really needs salt, or might be undercooked at the bone, you shouldn't be frying chicken in the first place.

Two 3-pound fryer chickens

Buttermilk

2 cups all-purpose flour

1 teaspoon salt

Freshly ground black pepper to taste

Vegetable shortening (preferably Crisco), for deep frying

1 tablespoon bacon grease

Cut the chicken carefully and evenly into serving pieces, taking care to keep the skin of each piece intact, and rinse under cold running water. Place the pieces in a bowl, add enough buttermilk to just cover, and let soak about 30 minutes.

In a heavy brown paper bag, combine the flour, salt, and pepper and shake till well blended. Add the chicken pieces to the bag, shake vigorously to coat evenly, tap excess flour off each piece back into the bag, and stack the pieces on a large plate.

Place a large cast-iron skillet over moderate heat or set an electric fry pan at 375°F, fill half full of melted shortening, and add the bacon grease. When a drop of water flicked into the fat sputters, arrange the dark-meat pieces of chicken in the fat, making sure not to overcrowd the pan. Fry the chicken till golden brown and crisp, 15 to 20 minutes, turn with tongs, and fry till golden brown, about 15 minutes longer. (Turn the chicken only once.) Drain on another brown paper bag and repeat the procedure with the white-meat pieces.

Transfer the chicken to a large serving platter. Do not cover to keep warm. Serve warm or at room temperature.

BEER-BATTERED FRIED CHICKEN

Makes 4 to 6 servings

SOUTHERN COOKS HAVE BEEN BANTERING OVER FRIED chicken ever since Mary Randolph proffered the first (and, in many respects, still definitive) recipe in her *Virginia House-Wife* in the early nineteenth century, one of the latest twists being this tangy version using a slightly fermented beer batter. If an extra-crispy skin and very moist interior is what you're looking for in fried chicken, this could be the perfect formula. Do note, however, that the chicken is cooked about 10 minutes less than in the traditional method, since this batter tends to burn more quickly than one made with a milk product. Just watch the chicken very carefully as it cooks. If it seems to be browning too rapidly, reduce the heat to 325°F.

Kentucky fried chicken, as opposed to ordinary Southern fried chicken, is no more than a technique perfected by Colonel Harland Sanders in the late 1930s, whereby chicken seasoned with a secret formula of herbs and spices is not actually fried but cooked in a pressure cooker.

¾ cup all-purpose flour

6 ounces lager beer

½ teaspoon salt

Tabasco sauce to taste

Vegetable shortening (preferably Crisco), for deep frying

One 3- to 3½-pound chicken, cut into serving pieces

In a bowl, whisk together the flour, beer, salt, and Tabasco till smooth and let the batter stand for 1 hour.

In a large cast-iron skillet or electric fry pan, heat about 2 inches of shortening to 350°F or till a few drops of water flicked in with the fingers sputters. Whisk the batter again, dip the dark-meat pieces of chicken in the batter, letting the excess drip off, and fry in the fat till golden, about 10 minutes on each side, turning once with tongs. Drain on paper towels, then repeat the procedure with the white-meat pieces of chicken. Do not cover to keep warm.

Serve the chicken hot or at room temperature.

MARYLAND FRIED CHICKEN WITH CREAM GRAVY

Makes 4 to 6 servings

ALTHOUGH MARYLAND FRIED CHICKEN IS A TOTALLY different culinary concept from traditional Southern fried chicken, it certainly qualifies as one of the classic glories of our cookery. Actually, it's not "fried chicken" at all, since the pieces are just lightly browned before being simmered in liquid and served covered with a cream gravy. When, how, and why the dish evolved remains a secret of history, but it is true that Marylanders have always argued about whether the gravy should be poured over the chicken or served in a sauceboat, and that they've always eaten the dish with Maryland Beaten Biscuits (page 312). Although not meaning to buck tradition, I must confess that sometimes I've made this gravy with buttermilk instead of half-and-half, and love it.

1 cup plus 1 tablespoon all-purpose flour

1 teaspoon salt

¼ teaspoon freshly ground black pepper

¼ teaspoon cayenne pepper

1 cup whole milk

One 3- to 3½-pound chicken, cut into serving pieces

Vegetable oil for frying

½ cup water

1 cup half-and-half

In a paper bag, combine the 1 cup of flour, salt, black pepper, and cayenne pepper and shake till well blended. Pour the milk into a shallow bowl, dip the chicken pieces in the milk, then shake them in the paper bag to coat evenly, tapping off excess flour.

In a large, heavy skillet, heat about ½ inch of oil over moderately high heat, add the chicken, cover, and fry till golden, about 5 minutes on each side, turning the pieces with tongs. Uncover and continue to fry till the pieces are slightly browned all over. Pour off the fat, add the water, reduce the heat to moderate, cover, and cook till tender, 15 to 20 minutes. Transfer the chicken to a platter and keep warm.

Pour off all but 1 tablespoon of liquid from the skillet, reduce the heat to low, add the 1 tablespoon flour, and stir for 3 minutes. Add the half-and-half, increase the heat to moderate, and cook till the gravy is thickened, scraping up any brown bits from the pan. Remove from the heat.

Strain the gravy over the chicken and serve immediately.

164

ARKANSAS-STYLE BUTTERMILK FRIED CHICKEN

Makes 8 to 10 servings

THIS RECIPE COMES FROM A BLUE-BLOODED FARMING family in Tuckerman, Arkansas, who are as well known for their political parties as for the rice and pecans they grow and the dishes they serve famous and humble guests alike. So renowned is this buttermilk fried chicken, in fact, that Hillary Clinton included it in *The Clinton Presidential Center Cookbook.* When I learned that the chicken is fried in covered skillets and turned over and over, I bolted, but after I tried it I had to admit, except for it not being as crisp as I think Southern fried chicken should be, it was nonetheless utterly delicious—full flavored, silky, slightly tangy, and, yes, different.

Two 3½-pound chickens, cut into serving pieces

Kosher salt

4 large eggs

1 quart regular buttermilk

1 cup mayonnaise

¾ cup amber ale

½ cup finely chopped fresh basil

1 tablespoon finely chopped fresh oregano

1 tablespoon sweet paprika

4 cups all-purpose flour

Salt and freshly ground black pepper to taste

2 quarts peanut oil

Season the chicken with the salt, let stand for 20 minutes, rinse, and pat dry with paper towels.

In a large bowl, whisk together the eggs, buttermilk, mayonnaise, ale, basil, oregano, and 1 teaspoon of the paprika. Add the seasoned chicken pieces to the bowl, turn to coat them, and refrigerate for 2 hours. In another large bowl, combine the flour, salt and pepper, and remaining 2 teaspoons of paprika and stir till well blended.

When ready to fry, dredge the chicken pieces well in the seasoned flour and place them on a platter. In 2 large, heavy skillets with tight-fitting lids, heat the oil to moderate, add the chicken, cover, and fry about 12 minutes. With tongs, turn the pieces over, cover, and fry 10 minutes longer. Remove the lids and continue frying, turning once or twice, till the chicken is deep golden and crisp, about 10 minutes. Drain on paper towels and serve hot or at room temperature.

OLD HEN CHICKEN POT PIE

Makes 6 servings

WHAT MAKES MANY SOUTHERN CHICKEN POT PIES different from all others is not only the use of a full-flavored fowl (or stewing chicken), but also the layer of pastry strips within the pie itself, which provide a delectable contrast with the crispy top crust. Even in the South, it seems that old hens are harder and harder to find in supermarkets or even specialty food markets, so whenever I find one (especially on sale), I grab it and freeze it till I'm ready to make this pie—or the best chicken soup on earth. Notice that the chicken must be simmered at least 2½ hours to become tender.

One 4-pound fowl (stewing hen), cut into servings pieces

1 medium onion, quartered

2 ribs celery (leaves included), each broken into 3 pieces

Salt and freshly ground black pepper to taste

2 cups all-purpose flour

¼ teaspoon salt

1 cup vegetable shortening

¼ cup ice water

2 medium carrots, scraped, cut into thin rounds, blanched 5 minutes in boiling water, and drained

1 cup fresh or thawed frozen green peas

2 tablespoons butter, melted

Place the chicken pieces in a large pot, add the onion and celery, and season with salt and pepper. Add enough water to cover, bring to a boil, reduce the heat to low, cover, and simmer till tender, 2½ to 3 hours.

While the chicken is cooking, combine the flour and salt in a large mixing bowl, and cut in the shortening with a pastry cutter till the mixture is mealy. Stirring with a spoon, gradually add the ice water till a ball of dough forms. On a lightly floured work surface, roll out half the dough about ⅛ inch thick and line the bottom and sides of a greased 2-quart baking dish with it, tucking the crust into the corners. Roll out the remaining dough about ⅛ inch thick and cut half of it into 1-inch-thick strips, reserving the remainder for top of the pie.

Transfer the chicken pieces to a cutting board and, when cool enough to handle, bone and cut the meat into bite-size pieces. Strain the broth into a bowl and set aside. Preheat the oven to 350°F.

Arrange half the chicken pieces over the bottom of the baking dish, half the carrots and peas over the chicken, and top with the pastry strips. Arrange the remaining chicken, carrots, and peas on top of the strips, season with salt and pepper, and pour in enough reserved chicken broth to almost cover the top layer. Fit the remaining pastry over the top of the pie, pressing down the edges and trimming off the excess. Brush the top with the melted butter, poke a couple of vent holes in the pastry with the tip of a knife, and bake till the top is golden brown, 30 to 40 minutes.

Mississippi Smothered Chicken

Makes 4 to 6 servings

I'VE HAD DELICIOUS "SMOTHERED" POULTRY AND game in Kentucky and Creole Louisiana, but when it comes to smothered chicken, Mississippians have made almost an art of one technique. Basically, a chicken is split down the back and opened up as if for broiling. It's then cooked in a iron skillet with several weights on top, turned over, and cooked further in a gravy till the meat is almost falling off the bones. The chicken can either be cooked by itself or enhanced with any number of vegetables and seasonings. Whatever adjustments are made, the technique produces one of the most unusual and toothsome chicken preparations you'll ever taste. For weights on top of the plate, I use several canned goods or a smaller cast-iron skillet.

One 3½-pound chicken, split down the backbone, with the breast left unsplit

Salt and freshly ground black pepper to taste

4 tablespoons (½ stick) butter

½ pound fresh mushrooms, sliced

16 very small white onions, peeled and scored on the root ends

½ cup dry white wine

½ cup chicken broth

1 bay leaf

¼ teaspoon dried thyme, crumbled

2 tablespoons finely chopped garlic

2 tablespoons finely chopped fresh parsley leaves

Season the chicken with salt and pepper and fold the wings under to hold them secure.

In a large cast-iron skillet, melt 2 tablespoons of the butter over low heat, add the chicken, skin side down, cover firmly with a heavy plate that fits inside the skillet, and add several weights (such as canned goods) to top of the plate. Cook 25 minutes. Pour off most of the fat from the skillet and add the remaining 2 tablespoons butter. Turn the chicken skin side up and scatter the mushrooms and onions over and around the chicken. Add the wine, broth, bay leaf, thyme, and garlic, replace the plate and weights on top, and continue cooking, over low heat, 45 minutes longer or till the chicken is very tender.

Transfer the chicken to a warm platter and spoon the mushrooms and onions over the top. Cook until the liquid in the skillet is reduced by half, pour over the chicken and vegetables, and sprinkle parsley on top.

Maw Maw's Chicken and Dumplings

Makes 6 servings

I CAN STILL SEE OUR NEIGHBOR IN CHARLOTTE,
Mr. Nunn, bring the hatchet down precisely on the neck of an old hen from his chicken coop, sending the bird flopping about the sandy yard like the proverbial chicken with its head cut off. After scalding, plucking, and dressing the fowl, he wrapped it in newspaper, handed it to me, and said, "Here, son, take this to your mamma and grandmamma and they'll make you a good Brunswick stew or pot of chicken and dumplings." If I learned nothing else from watching Maw Maw make her chicken and dumplings and tasting the sumptuous result, it was that it's almost pointless to make this dish with anything but a stewing hen, since a rich broth is obligatory to give the dumplings full flavor. Also, for just the right texture, the dumplings must be cooked *before* the chicken and vegetables are thickened. Properly made, chicken and dumplings is one of the true glories of authentic Southern cookery, a dish fit for both an informal family supper and the most elegant dinner party.

FOR THE CHICKEN

One 4- to 5-pound fowl (stewing hen), cut into serving pieces

1 large onion, quartered

2 ribs celery (leaves included), chopped

4 carrots, scraped and cut into thick rounds

Salt and freshly ground black pepper to taste

1 quart water

1 cup whole milk

¼ cup all-purpose flour blended with ¼ cup water

FOR THE DUMPLINGS

1 cup all-purpose flour

1 teaspoon baking powder

½ teaspoon salt

2 tablespoons chilled vegetable shortening

½ cup whole milk

To cook the chicken, combine all the ingredients for the chicken except the flour-and-water mixture in a large, heavy pot over moderately high heat. Bring to a slow boil and skim the surface of any froth. Reduce the heat to a simmer, cover, and cook till the chicken is very tender, about 2½ hours.

Meanwhile, to make the dumplings, sift the flour, baking powder, and salt together into a bowl and cut in the shortening with a pastry cutter till the mixture is mealy. Add the milk and mix lightly till the dough just holds together. (Do not overmix.)

With the chicken gently bubbling, drop the dough by rounded tablespoons into the liquid and simmer, uncovered, about 10 minutes. Cover and simmer the dumplings 10 minutes longer. With a slotted spoon, transfer to a plate, and keep warm.

To finish the dish, drain the cooking liquid into a bowl, skim off the fat, and pour 3 cups of the liquid into a saucepan, adding a little water if necessary. Add the flour-and-water mixture and stir over moderately high heat till the sauce is thickened. Pour the sauce over the chicken and vegetables and reheat about 10 minutes.

Serve the chicken and dumplings together on heated plates.

The modern poultry industry began in Delaware in the 1920s and '30s, and by 1939 poultry became so important to the state that that "Blue Hen Chicken" was declared the official state bird by the state legislature. Today, no single county in the U. S. produces more chickens than Sussex County, Delaware.

Country Captain

Makes 4 to 6 servings

A CORRUPTION OF THE WORD *CAPON?* A REFERENCE to a certain army officer involved in the Savannah spice trade in the eighteenth century? A colonial navy captain who brought the recipe back from India to Virginia? The legends abound over the origins of this mysterious chicken dish that has been a Southern classic for nearly two hundred years. What's important to know is that a genuine country captain is not the quick fricassee you find in many restaurants, but rather a preparation that's braised in a baking dish or casserole slowly enough to allow all the varied flavors to meld. I wouldn't dream of cooking a country captain (on top of the stove or in the oven) for less than an hour, and since I like my chicken almost falling off the bones, I might let it simmer for up to 1½ hours.

¼ cup all-purpose flour

Salt and freshly ground black pepper to taste

Pinch of ground allspice

One 3- to 3½-pound chicken, cut into serving pieces

2 tablespoons butter

1 tablespoon peanut oil

2 medium onions, finely chopped

1 small green bell pepper, seeded and finely chopped

1 garlic clove, minced

2 teaspoons medium curry powder

4 medium ripe tomatoes, chopped (juice included)

3 tablespoons seedless golden raisins

1 cup chicken broth

1 cup sliced blanched almonds

Preheat the oven to 350°F. Butter a 2-quart baking dish or casserole and set aside.

In a paper bag, combine the flour, salt and pepper, and allspice, add the chicken pieces, and shake well, tapping off the excess flour. In a large, heavy skillet, heat the butter and oil together over moderate heat, brown the seasoned chicken pieces on all sides, and transfer to a plate. Add the onions, bell pepper, garlic, and curry powder to the skillet and cook, stirring, till the vegetables are softened, about 5 minutes. Add the tomatoes plus their juices and the raisins, stir till slightly thickened, and remove from the heat.

Arrange half the chicken pieces in the prepared baking dish and spoon half the vegetables evenly over the top. Repeat with the remaining chicken and vegetables, add any remaining juices from the skillet plus the broth, and bake 30 minutes. Uncover, sprinkle the almonds evenly over the top, and bake, uncovered, till the chicken is tender and the almonds browned, about 30 minutes.

Louisiana Chicken and Sweet Potato Hash

Makes 4 servings

BEING FROM NORTH CAROLINA, THE SWEET POTATO capital of the South, I found it hard to admit that the relatively new variety of sweet potato called Beauregards (developed at Louisiana State University) was without question the most succulent sweet potato I'd ever tasted. Today, Louisiana is one of the few states that grades its sweet potatoes by size and quality and, to my knowledge, it's the only state that actually cures the potatoes for ultimate sweetness and moistness. Such potatoes are delicious simply roasted and smeared with butter, but when you combine them with poached chicken to make this hash—which Louisianians are just as likely to serve for breakfast (topped with a poached or fried egg) as for supper—the result is sublime. One tip: Never buy "green" (freshly harvested) sweet potatoes during the summer months, since they don't yet have the enzyme that converts starch to sugar when cooked. The best tubers are stored by growers and marketed during the winter months.

2 whole, boneless, skinless chickens breasts (about 1½ pounds), cut in half

3 medium sweet potatoes (about 1½ pounds), scrubbed and cut into ½-inch cubes

3 tablespoons butter

1 large onion, finely chopped

1 medium green bell pepper, seeded and finely chopped

1 garlic clove, minced

1 teaspoon hot paprika

½ teaspoon dried thyme, crumbled

Salt and freshly ground black pepper to taste

3 scallions (part of green tops included), chopped

¼ cup chopped fresh parsley leaves

1 cup half-and-half

Place the chicken breasts in a large, deep skillet, add enough water to barely cover, and bring to a low boil. Reduce the heat to low, poach the chicken till tender, about 10 minutes, transfer to a work surface, and cut into ½-inch cubes. Set aside.

Place the sweet potatoes in a large saucepan with enough water to cover, and bring to a low boil. Reduce the heat to low, cover, and cook till the potatoes are tender, about 15 minutes. Drain and set aside.

In a large, heavy skillet, melt the butter over moderate heat. Add the onion, bell pepper, and garlic, and cook, stirring, till the vegetables are softened, about 3 minutes. Add the paprika, thyme, and salt and pepper and stir for 1 minute. Add the chicken, sweet potatoes, scallions, parsley, and half-and-half and cook, stirring, till the liquid is reduced and the hash is thickened and "tight."

171

CHICKEN AND HOMINY CHILI

Makes 6 servings

AT FIRST I CRINGED WHEN MY HOSTESS IN NASHVILLE said she was serving a more modern, much "healthier" chili that she'd read about in some local newspaper, made not only with chicken instead of beef but with hominy. I'm still not sure that this chili will supplant the more traditional concoction, but I did ask for a second helping, and yes, I did love the innovative, brilliant addition of hominy. When I reproduced the chili at home, I found that the perfect finishing touch was a few shakes of the Tabasco bottle.

2 tablespoons corn oil

2 pounds chicken thighs

1 large onion, chopped

½ green bell pepper, seeded and chopped

2 garlic cloves, minced

1 jalapeño chile pepper, seeded and chopped

2 tablespoons chili powder, or to taste

3 cups chicken broth

Two 15-ounce cans navy beans, drained

One 15-ounce can hominy, drained

Salt and freshly ground black pepper to taste

In a large, heavy pot, heat the oil over moderate heat, add the chicken, brown on both sides, and transfer to a plate. Pour off all but about 1 tablespoon of fat from the pot, add the onion, bell pepper, garlic, chile pepper, and chili powder, and cook, stirring, till the vegetables are softened, about 3 minutes. Remove from the heat.

Remove and discard the skin and bones of the chicken and cut the meat into small pieces. Add the chicken and the broth and beans to the pot, bring to a boil, reduce the heat to low, and cook till the chicken is very tender and the chili has thickened, 30 to 35 minutes. Add the hominy and salt and pepper, stir well, and cook about 10 minutes longer. Serve hot.

172

Bourbon Chicken

Makes 4 servings

ALTHOUGH I WAS SERVED THIS SIMPLE BUT beautifully flavored dish at a colleague's home in Atlanta, it's the sort of no-nonsense chicken preparation that might well appear in one guise or another on dinner tables in Kentucky and Tennessee, where so much of the South's favorite spirit is produced. At various times, I've thrown pieces of okra, butter beans, or green peas into the skillet, with maybe a little more chicken broth. Once, I even altered the dish's texture by adding about half a cup of chopped pecans. So, by all means, feel free to experiment, the way many Southern home cooks do.

2 tablespoons butter

2 tablespoons peanut oil

One 3- to 3½-pound chicken, cut into serving pieces

½ cup bourbon

1 medium onion, finely chopped

½ small green bell pepper, seeded and finely chopped

½ teaspoon dried thyme, crumbled

½ teaspoon dried rosemary, crumbled

Salt and freshly ground black pepper to taste

½ cup chicken broth

¼ cup heavy cream

In a large, heavy skillet, heat the butter and oil over moderate heat, add the chicken pieces, and brown on all sides. Add ¼ cup of the bourbon, carefully ignite with a match, and let burn till the flames die. Add the onion, bell pepper, thyme, rosemary, and salt and pepper and cook, stirring, till the vegetables are softened, about 5 minutes. Add the remaining ¼ cup of bourbon and the chicken broth, bring to a boil, reduce the heat to low, cover, and simmer till the chicken is tender, 30 to 40 minutes.

With a slotted spoon, transfer the chicken and vegetables to a serving platter. Add the cream to the skillet, return the heat to moderate, and cook, stirring, till the gravy is thickened, about 3 to 5 minutes depending on desired consistency. Pour over the chicken and serve immediately

Curried Orange Chicken

Makes 6 servings

NOBODY IS MORE SOUTHERN THAN MY SISTER, AND when I complimented her on the "Indian" chicken dish she once served at her home in Wilmington, North Carolina, she looked at me with puzzlement and said, "Honey, I don't know what on earth you're talking about. This recipe goes back almost three hundred years, to the Cape Fear rice planters, and every friend I have in Wilmington has her special version." So much for this particular ethnic influence on Southern cooking, I figured, fully bewildered. Naturally, Hootie served the simple dish with rice, as I now do, and, without fail, guests rave as if I'd been cooking half a day.

3 whole chicken breasts on the bone, split

2 tablespoons butter, cut into pieces

Salt and freshly ground black pepper to taste

1½ cups orange juice

½ cup dark raisins

½ cup chopped almonds

½ teaspoon curry powder

¼ teaspoon dried thyme, crumbled

Chopped fresh parsley leaves for garnish

Preheat the oven to 425°F.

Arrange the chicken breasts in a greased shallow baking dish, dot with the butter, season with salt and pepper, and bake 15 minutes.

Meanwhile, combine the orange juice, raisins, almonds, curry powder, and thyme in a saucepan, bring to a simmer, and cook 10 minutes.

Pour the orange juice mixture evenly over the chicken, reduce the heat to 325°F, and bake till tender and nicely glazed, about 30 minutes.

CURRIED TURKEY HASH CAKES

MAKES 4 to 6 servings

WHEN MISSISSIPPI-BORN CRAIG CLAIBORNE USED TO come to my home for Thanksgiving dinner, the first words he'd utter at the door were, "Save me a few slices of turkey breast for sandwiches and some dark meat to make my mamma's hash." Sometimes I think Southerners roast a turkey mainly to use the leftovers in all sorts of soups, stews, salads, hashes, casseroles, croquettes, gumbos, and Lord knows what else. Leftover turkey dishes almost constitute a cuisine in itself. Different types of curried hashes are prevalent in the Carolina Lowcountry and Louisiana and Mississippi bayous, but the idea of turning ordinary turkey hash into crusty cakes like those made with crabmeat is my own.

2 medium boiling potatoes, peeled, boiled till very tender, and roughly chopped

8 tablespoons (1 stick) butter, room temperature

3 cups chopped cooked turkey

1 medium onion, chopped

1 rib celery, chopped

½ green bell pepper, seeded and chopped

3 large eggs, 2 beaten

½ cup heavy cream

1½ teaspoons salt

Freshly ground black pepper to taste

1 teaspoon curry powder

¾ cup all-purpose flour

2 cups fine bread crumbs

4 to 5 tablespoons vegetable oil

In a mixing bowl, mash the potatoes to a purée with a potato masher or fork, add 4 tablespoons of the butter in pieces, and beat with a wooden spoon or electric mixer till smooth and the butter is completely absorbed.

In a blender or food processor, grind the turkey, onions, celery, and bell pepper to a medium texture and transfer to the bowl with the potatoes. Add the whole egg and stir till well blended. Add the cream, salt, pepper, and curry powder and beat well till the mixture is smooth. Cover the bowl with plastic wrap and chill 30 minutes to firm up the texture and allow the flavors to develop.

Shape the hash into oval cakes, dust each evenly in the flour, dip in the beaten eggs, roll in the bread crumbs, and chill 30 minutes.

Heat the remaining butter with the oil in a large, heavy skillet, add the cakes, and cook on both sides over moderate heat till golden brown and crusty, about 10 minutes in all.

Roast Turkey with Sausage and Pecan Dressing

Makes at least 8 servings

OF THE MYRIAD STYLES OF DRESSINGS THAT Southerners make to stuff a turkey for roasting (cornbread and apple, oyster and almond, rice and liver, prune and chestnut, onion and sage, ham and wild mushrooms), none is more popular than a classic sausage and pecan stuffing redolent of sage and any number of other seasonings. Traditionally, the mixture is "tightened" (bound) with either dried bread crumbs or crumbled cornbread, and of course, stuffed roast turkey simply wouldn't be the same without dark (never white) giblet gravy. Nor would the feast be complete without extra dressing baked till crusty in a pan right alongside the turkey—reason enough to double this stuffing recipe. The only cardinal rule is that the turkey must never be allowed to dry out and toughen from overbaking, so keep a sharp eye after about 2½ hours.

FOR THE DRESSING

1 pound bulk sausage

8 tablespoons (1 stick) butter

5 medium onions, finely chopped

3 ribs celery, finely chopped

4 cups crumbled cornbread or dry bread crumbs

1 teaspoon dried sage, crumbled

½ teaspoon dried thyme, crumbled

Salt and freshly ground black pepper to taste

⅔ cup hot water

½ pound pecans, coarsely chopped

FOR THE TURKEY AND GRAVY

One 10- to 12-pound turkey, giblets included

Salt and freshly ground black pepper to taste

1 cup water

Preheat the oven to 325°F.

To make the dressing, break up the sausage in a large skillet, fry till all traces of pink are gone, and drain the fat from the skillet. Add 2 tablespoons of the butter, the onions, and the celery, and cook, stirring, till softened, about 5 minutes. Add the remaining butter plus all remaining dressing ingredients, stir till the butter is melted and the ingredients are well blended, and set aside to cool.

Set the giblets aside. Season the turkey inside and out with the salt and pepper, stuff the cavity loosely with the dressing, and truss the bird. (Place any extra dressing in a buttered baking pan, keep it refrigerated till the last 45 minutes of roasting, and place it in the oven with the turkey.) Position the turkey breast side up on a rack in a large roasting pan, pour the water into the pan, cover, and cook 2½ hours, basting from time to time. Uncover and continue roasting till the turkey is golden, 15 to 20 minutes longer. Transfer to a large serving platter, remove the trussing, and cover the bird loosely with aluminum foil till ready to carve. Reserve the pan with the drippings.

To make the gravy, while the turkey is roasting, place the giblets in a large saucepan with enough water to cover, and simmer, covered, 1 hour. Transfer the giblets to a chopping board, chop coarsely, and reserve the cooking liquid. When the turkey has finished roasting, place the pan over moderately high heat and cook down the drippings till nearly burned, scraping the pan. Gradually add the cooking liquid from the giblets, stirring and scraping, till the gravy is slightly thickened and darkened. Stir in the chopped giblets, season with salt and pepper to taste, heat well, and pour the gravy into a sauceboat.

To serve, spoon the dressing into a heated bowl, carve the turkey, and serve with giblet gravy.

TURKEY CUTLETS WITH RED CABBAGE

Makes 4 servings

WITHOUT QUESTION, THE ORGANIC TURKEYS RAISED on large farms in eastern North Carolina are the tenderest, sweetest, most succulent in the entire South. So revered are these birds that a special turkey festival is held each year in Raeford (just south of Fayetteville), where cooks from all over the state prepare various turkey dishes and compete for sizeable cash prizes. This particular dish was a first-prize winner at one festival, and while the cabbage shows obvious German influence, the turkey cutlets themselves couldn't be more Southern. Every time I see whole turkey breasts on sale, I think about making this sensational dish.

FOR THE CABBAGE

6 bacon slices, cut into small pieces

2 tablespoons sugar

1 small onion, chopped

1 small head red cabbage (coarse outer leaves discarded), cored and shredded

2 red apples, cored and thinly sliced

2 tablespoons cider vinegar

½ teaspoon caraway seeds

Salt and freshly ground black pepper to taste

½ cup dry red wine

FOR THE CUTLETS

¼ cup all-purpose flour

1 teaspoon salt

¼ teaspoon freshly ground black pepper

1 large egg

1 tablespoon milk

1 pound turkey breast cutlets, each cut ½ inch thick

1 cup fine dry bread crumbs

2 tablespoons butter

2 tablespoons peanut oil

4 seeded lemon wedges for garnish

To make the cabbage, fry the bacon in a large skillet over moderate heat till crisp and transfer to a plate. Pour off all but 4 tablespoons of the bacon drippings, add the sugar to the skillet, and stir till it begins to brown, about 4 minutes. Reduce the heat to low, add the onion, and cook, stirring, till golden, about 5 minutes. Add the cabbage, apples, vinegar, and caraway seeds and stir well. Season with salt and pepper, add the wine, bring to a simmer, cover, and cook 30 to 40 minutes. Keep warm.

To make the cutlets, combine the flour, salt, and pepper in a shallow dish and mix well. In a small bowl, combine the egg and milk and beat till well blended. Place the bread crumbs in another shallow dish.

Place the cutlets between 2 pieces of waxed paper and pound each about ⅛ inch thick. Dredge each cutlet in the flour mixture, shaking off excess flour, then dip each into the egg mixture and coat with bread crumbs.

In a large, heavy skillet, heat the butter and oil over moderate heat, add the cutlets, and cook about 3 minutes on each side or till golden. Serve the cutlets on heated plates with cabbage and a lemon wedge on the side.

179

TURKEY CROQUETTES

Makes 6 to 8 servings

THERE'S HARDLY A SOUTHERN ANTEBELLUM COOKBOOK that does not include at least a few croquettes, made with everything from chicken and turkey to ham and seafood to mashed potatoes and boiled grits or rice. Served at breakfast, as a practical midday meal, or even as a side dish for roasts and stews at more formal affairs, the versatile croquette (like the fritter) has been not only the perfect way to use various leftovers but a means for the cook to experiment with all sorts of ingredients and techniques. I was raised eating salmon, crabmeat, ham, chicken, and turkey croquettes on a fairly regular basis (at country clubs, in department store tearooms, at diners, and of course at home), and after a hiatus of some forty years, when the croquette fell into disfavor everywhere except cafeterias, it's encouraging to see these wonderful oval patties reappearing (often as fritters or "cakes") in a few upscale Southern restaurants and on dinner tables—sometimes with a creamy mushroom or spicy tomato sauce.

3 tablespoons butter

1 small onion, minced

3 tablespoons all-purpose flour

½ cup chicken broth

½ cup whole milk

2 tablespoons dry sherry

3 cups coarsely chopped cooked turkey

¼ teaspoon ground nutmeg

Salt and freshly ground black pepper to taste

Tabasco sauce to taste

2 large egg yolks

All-purpose flour for dredging

1½ cups fine bread crumbs

1 large egg beaten with 3 tablespoons water

Vegetable oil for frying

In a large saucepan, melt the butter over moderate heat, add the onion, sprinkle on the flour, and whisk till softened, about 3 minutes. Whisking rapidly, add the chicken broth, milk, and sherry and whisk till well blended. Add the turkey, nutmeg, salt and pepper, and Tabasco and stir till well blended. Remove the pan from the heat and, whisking constantly, add the egg yolks and whisk till well blended. Return the pan to the heat, cook, stirring, for about 2 minutes, and remove from the heat. Transfer the mixture to a bowl, let cool, then refrigerate 2 to 3 hours.

Spread the flour and bread crumbs on two separate plates. Shape the turkey mixture into 6 to 8 balls, roll lightly in the flour, and pat into oval patties. Dip the patties in the egg wash, then in the bread crumbs. Place on a large plate, cover with plastic wrap, and chill about 30 minutes before cooking.

In a large, heavy skillet, heat about 1 inch of oil over moderate heat till a little water flicked with the fingers sputters. Add half the patties, fry till golden brown and crispy, about 3 minutes on each side, and drain on paper towels. Repeat with the remaining patties. Serve hot.

Fried Rabbit with Madeira Gravy

Makes 6 to 8 servings

NO DISH IS MORE PRIZED IN THE SOUTH THAN FRIED rabbit with a cream or wine gravy, and while the idea makes me shudder a bit today, I can still remember as a young boy catching wild rabbits in traps, helping my grandfather skin and dress them, then watching my mother cut them up and fry them for dinner. Today, of course, frozen dressed rabbits are available in more and more markets as Americans shed their prejudices over eating "bunnies," and restaurant chefs come up with ever new preparations. Basically, rabbit is fried just like chicken, meaning that care must be taken not to overcook it to avoid dry toughness. And yes, fried rabbit does taste almost like fried chicken (and, for that matter, like fried squirrel). Madeira gravy goes back a long way in the South, but if you don't have a bottle of the wine, substitute either port or sweet vermouth.

1¼ cups all-purpose flour

½ cup yellow cornmeal

Salt and freshly ground black pepper to taste

1 cup lard or vegetable shortening

Two 3-pound rabbits, dressed and cut into serving pieces

1 cup buttermilk

1½ cups chicken broth

1 cup Madeira

In a paper bag, combine 1 cup of the flour, the cornmeal, and salt and pepper and shake well. In a large cast-iron skillet, melt the lard over moderate heat. Dip the rabbit pieces in batches into the buttermilk, dredge by shaking in the paper bag, add to the skillet, and brown evenly on all sides in the fat (in batches, if necessary). Reduce the heat slightly and continue to cook, turning frequently with tongs, till the rabbit is tender, 30 to 35 minutes. Drain on another paper bag or paper towels.

Pour off all but about 2 tablespoons of fat from the skillet, add the remaining ¼ cup flour, and stir over moderate heat till smooth, scraping up drippings from the bottom of the pan. Add the chicken broth and Madeira, season with salt and pepper, increase heat slightly, and stir constantly till the gravy is nicely thickened.

Serve the rabbit on a platter and pass the gravy separately.

Braised Rabbit with Wild Mushrooms

Makes 4 to 6 servings

LARGE, MEATY, MATURE RABBITS (AVAILABLE FROZEN in better supermarkets) are ideal for slow braising, so when shopping, check carefully to make sure the rabbit is not too small and bony—as many tend to be. Generally, a 3½-pound meaty rabbit will serve at least four people; if you have any doubt, your best bet is to buy two. I love the earthy flavor of fresh morels with this rabbit, but if these mushrooms are not available (or too expensive for your budget), substitute either chanterelles or shiitakes. The rabbit should be fork tender after about a half hour of braising. If it's not, cook it longer.

4 tablespoons (½ stick) butter

One 3½-pound rabbit, dressed and cut into serving pieces

1 large onion, chopped

½ pound fresh wild mushrooms, rinsed and sliced

1 garlic clove, minced

1 cup dry white wine

3 large ripe tomatoes, peeled, seeded, and chopped

1½ cups beef broth

2 teaspoons chopped fresh tarragon leaves (or ½ teaspoon dried and crumbled)

1 teaspoon chopped fresh chervil leaves (or ¼ teaspoon dried and crumbled)

Salt and freshly ground black pepper to taste

Preheat the oven to 350°F.

In a large, heavy skillet, melt the butter over moderate heat, add the rabbit pieces (in batches, if necessary), brown on all sides, and transfer to a plate. Add the onion, mushrooms, and garlic to the skillet and cook, stirring, until the onion is softened, about 5 minutes. Add the wine and continue cooking till most of the liquid has evaporated, about 5 minutes. Add the tomatoes, beef broth, tarragon, and chervil, season with salt and pepper, bring to a boil, and allow to boil till the sauce begins to thicken, 5 to 7 minutes. Remove from the heat.

Arrange the rabbit pieces in a large, greased baking dish, pour the sauce over the top, cover, and bake till the rabbit is fork tender and the sauce nicely thickened, 30 to 35 minutes.

Braised Duck with Leeks and Onions

Makes 4 servings

WHEN SOUTHERNERS SPEAK OF DUCK, THEY'RE talking about wild ducks, and more specifically, about the green-headed, grain-eating mallards that migrate south from Canada each year searching for warmer waters and for feeding grounds. I had lots of exposure to early-morning duck hunting when I was growing up in the Carolinas, but never have I witnessed such passion over the meaty birds and such communal sport than around the marshy flatlands of western Mississippi and the rice fields of eastern Arkansas. Most of the natives in the region prefer simply to roast their mallards, but one of the most memorable preparations I have eaten was this slowly braised duck with two styles of onion, served by none other than the talented wife of an Episcopal priest I knew who had been transferred from North Carolina to Mississippi. The two most widely available ducks in the United States today are the Long Island and Muscovy species, both adequately flavorful, even if fattier than wild mallards or ringnecks. A rule of thumb is that one 4-pound duckling feeds two people—so plan accordingly.

1 cup all-purpose flour

1 teaspoon salt

Freshly ground black pepper to taste

Two 4-pound ducks, dressed, pricked all over with a fork, cut into serving pieces, and patted dry with paper towels

4 tablespoons (½ stick) butter

2 medium leeks, rinsed well and chopped

6 cups dry red wine

½ teaspoon dried thyme, crumbled

2 bay leaves

Salt and freshly ground black pepper to taste

20 tiny white onions, peeled and scored on the root ends

2 tablespoons cornstarch dissolved in ½ cup water

On a plate, combine the flour, salt, and pepper and mix well. Dredge the duck pieces in the flour, shaking off the excess.

In a large, heavy stainless-steel or enameled pot or casserole, melt the butter over moderately high heat till it is pale brown. Add the duck pieces, brown on all sides, and transfer to a platter. Pour off all but about 3 tablespoons of the fat, reduce the heat to moderate, add the leeks, and cook, stirring, till golden, about 5 minutes. Return the duck to the pot, add the wine, thyme, bay leaves, and salt and pepper, bring to a simmer, cover, and cook 1 hour. Add the white onions and simmer till the onions are tender, about 30 minutes longer. Stir in the cornstarch mixture, increase the heat to moderate, and cook till the sauce is thickened. Taste for salt and pepper, transfer the duck and onions to a serving platter, and serve piping hot.

DUCK WITH RED CABBAGE

Makes 6 servings

AT HIS RENOWNED RESTAURANT ON PAWLEYS ISLAND, South Carolina, Louis Osteen serves as many highly creative dishes as Southern classics, and none has impressed me more than his succulent seared duck breasts with buttery Savoy cabbage. If you can find Savoy cabbage, fine; if not, I've learned that the more common red cabbage works just as well—or perhaps even better—for the dish. Louis rubs the duck breasts with olive oil and black pepper and lets them "cure" overnight before cooking, but, frankly, I can't detect any difference in flavor this extra step makes. Today, more and more markets carry boneless duck breasts (at a hefty price), but if you can't find them, any good butcher should be able to fill the order. The other option is to buy whole ducks and cut away the breasts yourself. Whatever you do, remember that the breasts should be seared no more than medium-rare, and that overcooking only toughens them.

2 tablespoons peanut oil

3 whole boneless duck breasts, split, skinned, and trimmed of excess fat and membrane

Salt and freshly ground black pepper to taste

8 tablespoons (1 stick) butter

1 large head red cabbage (discolored outer leaves discarded), cored and roughly diced

In a large, heavy skillet, heat the oil till very hot but not smoking. Season the duck breasts with salt and pepper, add to the hot oil, and sear 1 minute on each side. Reduce the heat to moderate, continue to cook the breasts 5 minutes on each side, transfer to a platter, and keep warm in the oven.

Add the butter to the skillet and stir, scraping the bottom to collect any bits of debris. Add the cabbage, cook till slightly browned, 2 to 3 minutes, turn over, and cook until lightly browned on the other side, about 2 minutes more. Add any juices collected on the platter of duck breasts, toss the cabbage well, and season with salt and pepper to taste.

To serve, divide the cabbage evenly among 6 serving plates, cut the duck breasts into 4 slices each, and place on top of the cabbage. Spoon the juices from the pan over the duck and cabbage and serve immediately.

Edna's Virginia Roast Pheasant with Chestnut Dressing

Makes 4 servings

DURING COLONIAL TIMES AND THROUGHOUT THE nineteenth century, wild game birds were so abundant and relished in America that Benjamin Franklin suggested we adopt the wild turkey as our national bird. Hunting turkeys, quail, partridge, pheasant, canvasback ducks, and guinea hens was particularly fancied in the South, to such an extent that by the turn of the twentieth century, passenger pigeons were totally extinct and many other species of fowl on the verge of disappearing. One lady who remembered when pheasants were still relatively plentiful in and around her home village of Freetown, Virginia, was the renowned chef Edna Lewis. And "Miss Edna" always said she would much prefer to roast a brace of plump wild pheasants for Thanksgiving dinner than a big commercial turkey. ("We used to raise turkeys on our farm and ship every one of them up to the Yankees," she would recall, laughing.) If you're lucky enough to know a fervent huntsman, all the better for the fresh pheasant you can obtain; otherwise, the farmed frozen ones can be almost as flavorful, so long as they're not overcooked and dry.

4 cups finely torn fresh bread

1 cup finely diced celery (leaves included)

½ cup finely diced onion

1 cup peeled, cooked chestnuts (sold in cans and jars), coarsely chopped

1 teaspoon dried sage, crumbled

1 teaspoon dried thyme, crumbled

Salt and freshly ground black pepper to taste

1 cup chicken broth

8 tablespoons (1 stick) butter, melted

Two plump, young 2½-pound pheasants, dressed

Preheat the oven to 375°F.

In a large mixing bowl, combine the bread, celery, onion, chestnuts, sage, thyme, salt and pepper, half the chicken broth, and 6 tablespoons of the butter and stir till the dressing is well blended.

Pack the cavity of each pheasant with as much dressing as it will hold, secure the cavities with small metal skewers, and brush each bird with the remaining 2 tablespoons melted butter. Spoon the remaining dressing into a baking dish and set aside.

Place the pheasants breast side down in a roasting pan, cover, and roast for 30 minutes. Meanwhile, moisten the dressing with just enough of the remaining broth to make a compact mixture.

Reduce the oven to 350°F, uncover the pheasants, place both the birds and pan of dressing in the oven, and cook till the pheasants are tender and the dressing is crusted, 30 to 40 minutes.

To serve, cut each pheasant in half lengthwise with a sharp knife and serve hot, with the additional dressing on the side.

185

SMOTHERED QUAIL

Makes at least 6 servings

SOUTHERNERS LIKE TO "SMOTHER" EVERYTHING FROM chicken to rabbit to quail—meaning they either simply bake their meat slowly in a vessel with a tight-fitting lid or cook it in an iron skillet with a heavy weight on top. You really don't have to tenderize quail, but marinating it briefly in a mixture of gin, oil, and seasonings does add a bit of mystery to its slightly gamey flavor. One nice thing about smothering quail in this manner, instead of frying, roasting, or grilling it, is that the likelihood of the tiny bird drying out is minimized.

12 dressed quail (fresh or frozen)

Salt and freshly ground black pepper to taste

½ cup gin

½ cup vegetable oil

1 large onion, chopped

1 cup chopped celery leaves

1 teaspoon dried tarragon, crumbled

Tabasco sauce to taste

8 tablespoons (1 stick) butter

12 strips bacon

12 toast triangles

Season the quail inside and out with salt and pepper and arrange them in a single layer in a large baking dish. In a medium mixing bowl, whisk together the gin and oil till well blended. Add the onion, celery leaves, and tarragon, season with Tabasco, and stir. Pour the marinade over the quail, cover with plastic wrap, and refrigerate at least 6 hours, turning the quail twice.

Preheat the oven to 350°F.

Remove the quail from the marinade and wipe dry with paper towels. Melt 4 tablespoons of the butter in a large cast-iron skillet over moderate heat, add half the quail, brown them lightly on all sides, and transfer to a large, shallow baking dish or casserole. Repeat with the remaining butter and quail. Wrap each quail snugly with a strip of bacon, strain the marinade over the birds, cover them with a sheet of aluminum foil, and bake till the quail are very tender, about 45 minutes.

On a large serving platter, arrange each quail on a toast triangle and serve.

Roasted Quail Stuffed with Oysters

Makes 4 servings

ALL ALONG THE CAROLINA AND GULF COASTS, COOKS have been aware for ages of the natural affinity between game birds and oysters, and never is this marriage more successful than when plump fresh oysters are stuffed inside tender, flavorful quail (or, in some Southern parlance, "partridges" or "bobwhites") and gently roasted. Since quail are so small and delicate, overcooking them is nothing less than disastrous, so watch the timing carefully to make sure they don't dry out and toughen. When I once attended a quail roast at a restored plantation in South Carolina, a big to-do was made about the difference between hunted quail, which feed on berries, and those given chicken feed on commercial farms. No doubt the wild birds have more flavor, but I have absolutely no objection to the frozen farm-raised quail now available in many markets. I like to serve the quail in this recipe with plenty of wild rice.

8 dressed quail (fresh or frozen)

½ lemon

12 tablespoons (1½ sticks) butter, melted

1½ tablespoons dried tarragon, crumbled

Salt and freshly ground black pepper to taste

Tabasco sauce to taste

16 fresh oysters, shucked

2½ cups yellow cornmeal

8 strips bacon

Preheat the oven to 450°F.

Rinse the quail well inside and out and pat dry with paper towels. In a bowl, squeeze the lemon into the butter, add the tarragon, salt and pepper, and Tabasco, and stir till well blended. Dip the oysters into the butter mixture, dredge lightly in the cornmeal, and stuff 2 into the cavity of each quail. Tie or skewer the birds with the wings and legs close to the bodies, and wrap each with a strip of bacon.

Place the quail on a rack in a large, shallow roasting pan and roast for 15 minutes. Remove the bacon, baste the birds with the pan juices, and return to the oven for 10 minutes, basting once more. Serve piping hot.

BRAISED VENISON AND ROOT VEGETABLES

Makes 6 servings

SOUTHERN HUNTERS HAVE BEEN STALKING THE whitetail deer for centuries. I can still remember my uncle Robert showing up periodically at the house with a side of dressed venison, which Mother would cut into steaks or roasts or use to make various stews and braised dishes. Mature fresh venison must be marinated to tenderize the meat and tame the gamey flavor, but since the frozen venison available in most markets today is much younger, it really needs no initial marination. And, besides, just the long, slow simmering in this recipe is enough almost to guarantee succulent, tender meat. When there's an option on cuts, I always choose shoulder of venison over round or rump, since the proportion of fat in the former produces both ideal flavor and texture.

1 cup all-purpose flour

Salt and freshly ground black pepper to taste

Cayenne pepper to taste

2 pounds boneless venison shoulder, trimmed of excess fat and cut into 1½-inch pieces

4 tablespoons (½ stick) butter

1 cup sweet vermouth

2 tablespoons red currant jelly

2 ribs celery (leaves included), chopped

½ teaspoon dried thyme, crumbled

½ teaspoon dried rosemary, crumbled

1 bay leaf

3 cloves

2 cups beef broth

12 tiny new potatoes, scrubbed but not peeled

6 small white onions, peeled and scored on the root ends

3 medium carrots, scraped and cut into rounds

2 medium parsnips, peeled and cut into 1-inch cubes

In a bowl, combine the flour, salt and pepper, and cayenne pepper, mix well, and dredge the venison in the mixture, tapping off the excess flour. In a large, heavy pot, melt the butter over moderately high heat, add the floured venison, and brown on all sides. Add the vermouth and jelly and stir well, scraping up any browned bits off the bottom of the pan. Add the celery, thyme, rosemary, bay leaf, cloves, and beef broth, reduce the heat to a low simmer, cover, and cook for 1 hour. Add the potatoes, onions, carrots, parsnips, and salt and pepper to taste, return to a simmer, cover, and cook till the venison is very tender, about another hour, adding more broth if necessary.

Seafood

Shrimp Creole

Shrimp and Tomato Pie

Crawfish Etouffée

Crab Norfolk

Creole Crab Imperial

Maryland Deviled Crab Cakes

Buster Crabs with
Lemon-Pecan Sauce

Joe's Stone Crabs
with Mustard Sauce

Lowcountry Oyster Roast

Fried Oysters

Baked Oysters with
Mustard Greens and Bacon

Deviled Oysters
with Mustard Sauce

Aunt Toots's Oyster
and Almond Pie

Salmon Croquettes

Baked Tuna-Stuffed Bell Peppers

Jekyll Island Fish Cakes

Key West Conch Fritters

Creamed Shad Roe

Baby Flounder with
Mushrooms and Pecans

Fried Catfish with Pecan Sauce

The Original Blackened Redfish

Baked Pompano
Stuffed with Crabmeat

Stuffed Red Snapper Demos

Gulf Coast Frogs' Legs

SHRIMP CREOLE

Makes 6 servings

ALONG WITH SEAFOOD GUMBO, JAMBALAYA, AND beignets, shrimp creole is a signature dish of New Orleans, but I don't think I've ever had two versions there that tasted exactly alike. Carelessly prepared (as it usually is outside the region), shrimp creole can be bland, banal, and downright ghastly, but when made with real care, according to traditional culinary principles, it qualifies as one of the South's greatest creations. Bottles of filé powder (ground sassafras leaves) are now available almost everywhere, and this unique thickening agent does have a very special flavor. Just make sure to add it off the heat; otherwise, the dish will be offensively stringy.

3 tablespoons peanut oil

4 medium onions, chopped

2 ribs celery, chopped

1 large green bell pepper, seeded and chopped

3 garlic cloves, minced

½ teaspoon dried thyme, crumbled

½ teaspoon dried fennel, crumbled

1 bay leaf

Salt and freshly ground black pepper to taste

½ teaspoon cayenne pepper

2 cups bottled clam juice

One 28-ounce can crushed tomatoes

2 tablespoons tomato paste

2 pounds medium fresh shrimp, peeled and deveined

2 teaspoons filé powder

Hot cooked rice

In a large, heavy pot, heat the oil over moderate heat, add the onions, celery, bell pepper, and garlic, and cook, stirring, till the vegetables are softened, about 3 minutes. Add the thyme, fennel, bay leaf, salt and pepper, cayenne pepper, and clam juice, stir well, return to a simmer, and cook for about 5 minutes. Add the tomatoes and tomato paste, stir, cover, and cook 15 to 20 minutes longer.

Add the shrimp, stir well, and cook just till the shrimp turn pink, about 2 minutes. Remove the pot from the heat, sprinkle the filé powder over the top, and stir gently till the liquid has thickened.

To serve, spoon about a cup of rice into wide soup bowls and ladle the shrimp over the top. Serve hot.

SHRIMP AND TOMATO PIE

Makes 4 to 6 servings

JUST AS SOUTHERNERS OFTEN REFER TO ANY BAKED dish that contains eggs as a *soufflé,* so can they loosely use the word *pie* to describe both savory and sweet baked concoctions with a bread crumb or cornbread crust. Throughout the South, the affinity of shrimp and tomatoes manifests itself in all sorts of soups, stews, casseroles, salads, aspics, and sandwiches, but never does the marriage seem so well defined and perfect as in this pie, which is just as likely to show up on a bridge luncheon in Kentucky as on a deck buffet in coastal Florida. I've never seen this pie made with anything but firm, fresh shrimp; when I once tried to substitute crabmeat, the result was a mushy disaster. Needless to say, the ideal time to make the pie is summer, when juicy ripe tomatoes are at their peak. To add a little more depth, you might want to fold into the mixture a little fried, crumbled bacon along with the shrimp.

2½ cups dry bread crumbs

1 cup milk

2 tablespoons butter

1 small onion, minced

½ small green bell pepper, seeded and minced

2 medium ripe tomatoes, peeled, seeded, and chopped

4 tablespoons (½ stick) butter, melted

1 tablespoon Dijon mustard

1 tablespoon Worcestershire sauce

1 tablespoon dry sherry

Salt and freshly ground black pepper to taste

Tabasco sauce to taste

1½ pounds medium fresh shrimp, shelled and deveined

Preheat the oven to 350°F.

In a large bowl, combine 2 cups of the bread crumbs and the milk and let soak.

In a large skillet, melt the 2 tablespoons of butter over moderate heat, add the onion, bell pepper, and tomatoes and cook, stirring, till the mixture softens and the tomatoes lose most of their juices, about 10 minutes. Add the mixture to the soaked bread crumbs, add 2 tablespoons of the melted butter, the mustard, Worcestershire, sherry, salt and pepper, and Tabasco and stir till well blended. Fold the shrimp into the mixture, then scrape into a buttered 1½- to 2-quart baking dish. Scatter the remaining bread crumbs evenly over the mixture, drizzle the remaining melted butter over the top, and bake till golden brown, 35 to 40 minutes.

CRAWFISH ETOUFFÉE

Makes 4 servings

WITHOUT QUESTION, LOUISIANA CRAWFISH (AND never say "crayfish" in Creole/Cajun country, unless you want eyebrows to rise) is one of the most noble delicacies of the South, and never are "crawdaddies," or "mudbugs," or "yabbies" more appreciated than when used to make a rich, aromatic, classic étouffée. For me, no trip to New Orleans is complete without a visit to the venerable Bon Temps Cafe for the crawfish étouffée, and on the rare occasion when I can find fresh crawfish outside the region, my thoughts are automatically directed to making this sumptuous dish. Frozen, peeled crawfish tails in 1-pound bags are increasingly available in finer seafood markets around the country, but if you can't find them, small fresh shrimp are almost as good—and sometimes even better (if frozen crawfish tails are not processed exactly right, they can have a fishy taste).

¼ cup peanut oil

¼ cup all-purpose flour

1 medium onion, finely chopped

½ medium green bell pepper, seeded and finely chopped

2 ribs celery, finely chopped

1 large ripe tomato, peeled, seeded, and chopped

2 garlic cloves, minced

1½ cups bottled clam juice

2 tablespoon butter, melted

½ teaspoon dried basil, crumbled

3 scallions (part of green tops included), chopped

¼ teaspoon cayenne pepper

2 tablespoons fresh lemon juice

1 pound frozen peeled crawfish tails (or small fresh shrimp), peeled and deveined

4 cups cooked rice

In a large, heavy saucepan, heat the oil over high heat till it begins to smoke, about 5 minutes. Add the flour and, whisking briskly and constantly, cook till the roux is reddish brown and smooth, 3 to 5 minutes. (Do not let it burn.)

Remove the pan from the heat, add the onion, bell pepper, celery, tomato, and garlic and stir till well blended. Return the pan to the heat, reduce the heat to low, and gradually add the clam juice, stirring. Add the butter, basil, scallions, cayenne pepper, and lemon juice, stir well, and simmer till the vegetables are tender and the sauce has thickened, about 20 minutes. Add the crawfish, stir, and cook about 10 minutes longer or till the crawfish are pink and tender.

To serve, mound equal amounts of rice in the middle of 4 serving plates and spoon the crawfish mixture around the rice.

CRAB NORFOLK

Makes 6 servings

ONE OF THE SIMPLEST DISHES IN THE SOUTHERN crabmeat repertory, crab Norfolk was created in 1924 by W. O. Snowden at the Snowden and Mason restaurant in Norfolk, Virginia, and served in small, specially designed, oval aluminum pans. The original did not contain either chives or sherry, but I find that both ingredients add a delightful complexity to the dish. If you can't find small oval aluminum pans, substitute small ramekins or simply bake the crabmeat in a 1½-quart casserole.

1½ pounds fresh lump crabmeat, picked over for shells and cartilage

2 tablespoons cider vinegar

1 tablespoon sweet sherry

6 tablespoons (¾ stick) butter, melted

¾ teaspoon Worcestershire sauce

3 tablespoons minced fresh chives

Salt and freshly ground black pepper to taste

Tabasco sauce to taste

Preheat the oven to 350°F.

In a large bowl, combine all the ingredients and toss till well blended, taking care not to break up the crabmeat. Divide the mixture evenly among six 1½-cup oval aluminum pans and bake just till bubbly, about 20 minutes. Serve hot.

CREOLE CRAB IMPERIAL

Makes 4 servings

CLASSIC CRAB IMPERIAL USUALLY INVOLVES LUMP
crabmeat combined with mayonnaise or a sherried white
sauce, spooned into shells, sprinkled with cheese, and
baked till golden brown. Indeed, there is no more
impressive, richer dish in all of Southern cookery. In
Louisiana, however, cooks often transform the dish
completely by incorporating additional ingredients,
including a spicy Creole mustard, and serving it chilled on
a bed of lettuce or red cabbage leaves. I still love to serve
traditional hot crab imperial for an intimate, rather formal
dinner any time of the year, but when the warm weather
comes, nothing is more appropriate for a deck luncheon
than this zesty chilled version. The measurements for
these ingredients are precise, so don't tamper.

4 tablespoons (½ stick) butter

*½ cup minced scallions (part of green tops
     included)*

4 tablespoons minced green bell pepper

4 tablespoons minced celery

Salt and freshly ground black pepper to taste

1½ cups mayonnaise

½ cup Creole mustard

1½ tablespoons Worcestershire sauce

1 cup well-drained and minced pimento

Tabasco sauce to taste

*1 pound lump crabmeat, picked over for shells
     and cartilage*

4 leaves red cabbage

¼ cup chopped fresh parsley leaves

In a large skillet over low heat, melt the butter. Add the
scallions, bell pepper, celery, and salt and pepper, and
cook, stirring, till the vegetables are softened
completely, about 10 minutes. Transfer the mixture to
a large mixing bowl and let cool slightly. Add the
mayonnaise, mustard, Worcestershire, pimento, and
Tabasco, mix lightly, and let cool further.

Place the crabmeat in another large bowl, add the
mayonnaise mixture, and blend gently to coat the
crabmeat without breaking up the lumps. Chill for 1 hour.

To serve, spoon equal amounts of the crabmeat onto
the cabbage leaves arranged on 4 salad plates and
sprinkle each serving with chopped parsley.

MARYLAND DEVILED CRAB CAKES

Makes 4 servings

HEAVEN KNOWS I'VE EATEN MY FILL OF FRIED OR broiled deviled crab in the shell at seafood houses along the Carolina and Florida coasts, but only in a couple of Maryland's Chesapeake Bay restaurants have I encountered (and swooned over) deviled crab cakes gently sautéed to a golden finish. "Egg white," one cook informed me when I asked how she made her cakes so light, "and not too many bread crumbs—inside or outside the patties." The only problem with eating crab cakes that have been correctly "deviled" is that, afterward, you might find ordinary crab cakes bland by comparison. I like to pat this mixture into tiny rounds and, in fine Southern style, serve the cakes at cocktail parties—with or without tartar or mustard sauce.

½ cup half-and-half

½ cup mayonnaise

1 large egg white

1½ teaspoons dry mustard

2 teaspoons Worcestershire sauce

2 teaspoons fresh lemon juice

Tabasco sauce to taste

2 scallions (part of green tops included), minced

1 small red bell pepper, seeded and minced

½ teaspoon salt

1 pound fresh lump crabmeat, picked over for shells and cartilage

1 cup fine dry bread crumbs

1 tablespoon butter, melted

¼ cup peanut oil

2 tablespoons butter

In a bowl, whisk together the half-and-half, mayonnaise, and egg white till well blended. Add the dry mustard, Worcestershire, lemon juice, Tabasco, scallions, bell pepper, and salt and stir till well blended. Gently fold in the crabmeat and ½ cup of the bread crumbs till well blended.

Divide the mixture into 4 equal parts and shape each into an oval patty. In a small bowl, combine the remaining bread crumbs with the melted butter, mix well, and turn each patty in the mixture to coat lightly.

In a large, heavy skillet, heat the oil and the 2 tablespoons butter over moderate heat, add the crab cakes, and cook till lightly browned, about 3 minutes per side. Drain briefly on paper towels and serve immediately.

Buster Crabs with Lemon-Pecan Sauce

Makes 4 to 6 servings

ALL ALONG THE EASTERN AND GULF COASTS, SOFT-shell blue crabs are often referred to as "busters," most likely a reference to a molting crab "busting" loose from its old shell. Why the buster crabs in and around New Orleans always seem to me to be much larger and more succulent than those found elsewhere I can't explain—especially since, generally, small busters are supposed to be the tenderest and most flavorful. Soft-shell crabs are now widely available in markets from spring to mid-summer. Despite my preference for the hefty Gulf busters, the safest bet is to buy the smallest crabs you can find.

12 soft-shell crabs, cleaned

3 cups whole or 2 percent milk

1 cup all-purpose flour

Salt and freshly ground black pepper to taste

¾ cup vegetable oil

8 tablespoons (1 stick) butter

1 cup peanuts, coarsely chopped

2 tablespoons finely chopped fresh parsley leaves

Juice of 1 lemon

Tabasco sauce to taste

Arrange the crabs in a large, shallow baking dish, add the milk, and let soak for 30 minutes.

On a plate, combine the flour and salt and pepper, mix till well blended, and dredge the crabs lightly in the mixture. In a large skillet, heat the oil over moderate heat, add the crabs in batches, and cook till golden brown and slightly crusty, about 3 minutes on each side. Drain on paper towels, transfer to a platter, and keep hot.

Pour off the excess oil from the skillet, add the butter, and heat over moderate heat till the butter foams. Add the peanuts and shake the skillet 2 minutes to coat and brown them slightly. Add the parsley, lemon juice, and Tabasco, stir well, and pour the hot sauce over the crabs.

JOE'S STONE CRABS WITH MUSTARD SAUCE

Makes about 1½ cups sauce

WHEN TRAVELING IN THE SOUTH, THERE ARE EXACTLY two no-reservations restaurants where I'm willing to tolerate long waits to eat the food: Galatoire's in New Orleans and Joe's Stone Crab in Miami Beach. Joe's, which has been around since 1913 and is now a historic landmark, still serves succulent stone crab claws with coleslaw, hash-brown potatoes, and this sublime mustard sauce. In my opinion, the only crabmeat as sweet and delicate as that of the huge stone crabs indigenous to Florida is that of the Dungeness crab of the Pacific Northwest. (Since only the claws of stone crabs are eaten, fishermen in Florida twist them off and throw back the crab, which grows new claws in a little over a year.) Until fairly recently, boiled stone crabs were simply not available outside the region, but now the finest fish markets carry them fresh (at a hefty price) during the fall and winter months, and frozen the rest of the year. At Joe's, the creamy mustard sauce is as important as the crabs, so simply buy the claws precooked (about 5 per person), crack them with a mallet or hammer, and serve them cold with this unique dipping sauce.

3½ teaspoons dry mustard

1 cup mayonnaise

¼ cup half-and-half

1 teaspoon Worcestershire sauce

1 teaspoon A.1. steak sauce

⅛ teaspoon salt

In a mixing bowl, combine all the ingredients and beat with an electric mixer 3 full minutes or till creamy. Cover with plastic wrap and chill well before serving.

197

Since Florida law prohibits the harvesting of whole stone crabs along the Keys and Gulf coast, their bodies are never eaten—only their huge claws. When fishermen take the crabs, only one large claw is removed, and the crab is returned to the water. It takes about eighteen months for a claw to grow back to legal size, and a typical crab can regenerate a claw three or four times in its life cycle.

LOWCOUNTRY OYSTER ROAST

OKAY, SO THIS IS NOT THE PROCEDURE FOR AN
authentic oyster roast such as those I've attended all
along the Carolina and Georgia coasts or for any number
of social or political occasions. But unless you care to
dig an outdoor pit or construct a cinder-block oven with
a sheet-metal grid, purchase oysters by the bushel, and
soak burlap bags in water to create steam over a live fire,
my method of roasting oysters on an ordinary grill will
have to suffice to give you some idea of what this
glorious age-old coastal tradition is all about. And,
actually, the procedure couldn't be any less complicated,
the idea being simply to let the oysters cook in smoky
steam till the shells open. Gauge the number of oysters
you buy according to what you think appetites will be,
assuming that the average guest will consume at least a
dozen oysters. If you have help steaming the oysters and
are particularly adept with an oyster knife, you might
choose to open and loosen the oysters yourself, saving
guests the trouble. On the other hand, opening oysters is
a ritual that can be lots of fun for all. Traditionally, bowls
of coleslaw and hot rice and baskets of biscuits are
served at most oyster roasts—along with, of course,
tubs of ice-cold beer.

Charcoal briquets

Wood chips, soaked in water

*Live oysters in the shell, scrubbed under running
water*

Oyster knives

Work gloves

Small bowls of warm clarified butter

Small bowls of cocktail sauce

Seeded lemon wedges

Cover the bottom of a large outdoor grill with charcoal
briquets, ignite them, and let them burn till they turn
gray, about 30 minutes. Toss a few handfuls of soaked
wood chips over the charcoal, place a rack on the grill,
and spread oysters over the rack. Close the grill's lid
and let the oysters steam just till the shells open
(discard any that do not open), about 5 minutes. Pile
the oysters in a bucket or on a large platter, serve hot
with oyster knives and gloves, and place bowls of the
three condiments on the table. Repeat the steaming
procedure with as many oysters as are needed, tossing
more chips on the fire to maintain the steam.

FRIED OYSTERS

Makes 4 to 6 servings

I ALWAYS THOUGHT THAT THE GREATEST FRIED
oysters on earth were found in New Orleans—until, that
is, somebody took me to Wintzell's in Mobile, Alabama,
and I ordered a jumbo oyster loaf. Wintzell's, alas, is no
more, but at least I had the chance to learn how they
fried their glorious oysters—one secret being to always
wait for the fat to heat back up to the right temperature
before frying another batch. For these oysters, buy the
largest grade available, and, for heaven's sake, do not
commit the cardinal sin of overcooking them—not one
second more than 2 minutes. The oysters can be served
with tartar sauce, mayonnaise, or horseradish cocktail
sauce—or, in typical Gulf Coast fashion, can be stuffed
into a baguette sliced lengthwise and spread with
mayonnaise and pickle relish.

1 cup yellow cornmeal

½ cup dry bread crumbs

1 teaspoon freshly ground black pepper

¼ teaspoon sweet paprika

¼ teaspoon cayenne pepper

Salt to taste

4 dozen fresh oysters, shucked and drained

*8 tablespoons (1 stick) butter, melted and poured
    into a bowl*

Peanut oil for frying

On a plate, combine the cornmeal, bread crumbs, black
pepper, paprika, cayenne pepper, and salt and mix well.
Dip the oysters briefly into the butter, dredge lightly in
the cornmeal mixture, and place on a large platter.

In a large, heavy skillet, heat about 1-inch of oil to
375°F on a thermometer or till a morsel of bread
tossed into the pan sizzles quickly. Drop the oysters, a
few at a time, into the oil, fry them no more than 2
minutes or till golden brown, turning once, and drain
on paper towels. (To prevent sogginess, always wait
briefly between batches for the fat to heat back up to
the right temperature.)

Serve the oysters piping hot in a cloth-lined basket.

BAKED OYSTERS WITH MUSTARD GREENS AND BACON

Makes 4 servings

HIGHLANDS BAR & GRILL IN BIRMINGHAM, ALABAMA, has been a virtual school of modern Southern cookery ever since the early 1990s, and not a week passes that owner/chef Frank Stitt doesn't create yet another innovative dish displaying Southern and Mediterranean techniques applied to the ingredients of his native Alabama. There's a baby flounder stuffed with shrimp and crabmeat, and a grilled pompano with roasted pumpkin and orange hollandaise sauce, but his Apalachicola oysters baked with a topping of peppery mustard greens and bacon is a wonder of contrasting flavors. Fresh, young, winter mustard greens are not that easy to find, even in parts of the South. If they are available, buy only those with crisp young leaves with a deep green color. A good substitute for the greens in this recipe is a combination of fresh spinach and watercress. And don't balk at all the bacon grease; that's what gives the dish much of its true Southern flavor.

¼ pound bacon, finely diced

1 medium onion, finely diced

2 garlic cloves, finely diced

1 small hot red chile pepper, seeded and finely chopped

4 cups washed, drained, finely chopped, loosely packed mustard greens

1 lemon, lightly zested, seeded, and juiced

8 tablespoons (1 stick) butter

Salt and freshly ground black pepper to taste

2 dozen fresh oysters on the half shell

1 cup coarse white bread crumbs

Preheat the oven to 500°F.

In a large skillet, fry the bacon over moderate heat till almost crisp, drain on paper towels, and finely crumble. Add the onion to the skillet, reduce the heat to low, and stir till very soft but not browned, about 7 minutes. Add the garlic and chile pepper and stir 2 minutes longer. Add the mustard greens, lemon zest and juice, bacon, and butter, toss well about 1 minute, and season with salt and pepper.

Place a small mound of greens on each oyster and sprinkle bread crumbs on top of each. Arrange the oysters on a heavy baking sheet and bake till the crumbs are golden and the oysters heated through, about 5 minutes. Serve immediately.

Deviled Oysters with Mustard Sauce

Makes 6 servings

IT'S NO SECRET THAT SOUTHERNERS EAT MAYONNAISE on practically everything but chocolate, but one unique trait of Southern cookery that often goes unnoticed by those outside the region is the use of mayonnaise in place of milk and cream products in numerous toppings for baked dishes—large casseroles included. No doubt this would make some cringe, but the truth is that mayonnaise not only binds other topping ingredients like nothing else but it also produces a nice glaze on dishes, such as these deviled oysters. Typically, the ramekins would be served with small country ham biscuits at a genteel luncheon.

2 cups mayonnaise

2 tablespoons Dijon mustard

1 tablespoon prepared horseradish

1 tablespoon fresh lemon juice

Salt and freshly ground black pepper to taste

8 strips bacon

½ pound fresh mushrooms, chopped

2 dozen fresh oysters, shucked and drained

1 cup freshly grated Parmesan cheese

Preheat the oven to 375°F.

In a bowl, combine the mayonnaise, mustard, horseradish, lemon juice, and salt and pepper, mix till well blended, and set aside.

In a large skillet, fry the bacon over moderate heat till crisp, drain on paper towels, and crumble. Pour off all but 2 tablespoons of the grease, add the mushrooms to the pan, and cook over moderate heat, stirring, till they release most of their moisture, about 3 minutes. Remove from the heat.

Butter the bottom and sides of 6 individual 4-ounce ramekins and place 4 oysters in each. Add equal amounts of mushrooms to each ramekin, then spoon on equal amounts of the mayonnaise mixture. Add the crumbled bacon to each, sprinkle each with cheese, and bake till slightly puffy and the cheese begins to brown, about 12 minutes. Serve piping hot.

201

Seafood

Aunt Toots's Oyster and Almond Pie

Makes 6 servings

THIS RECIPE HAS BEEN IN MY GEORGIA–NORTH Carolina family for at least three generations. As a child, nothing thrilled me more than to learn that my great aunt Toots would be serving this pie at one of her Sunday afternoon "suppers." Be warned: even though the pie bakes at a slow 300°F, you must watch it carefully after about 25 minutes to make sure it remains moist and the oysters don't overcook.

½ cup slivered almonds

2 cups crushed soda crackers

¼ teaspoon ground nutmeg

Salt and cayenne pepper to taste

1 quart freshly shucked oysters, liquor reserved

½ cup dry sherry

1 teaspoon Worcestershire sauce

4 tablespoons (½ stick) butter, cut into small pieces

1 cup half-and-half

Preheat the oven to 300°F.

To toast the almonds, spread them evenly on a baking sheet and bake, stirring several times, till slightly browned, 10 to 15 minutes. Set aside.

In a bowl, combine the crackers, nutmeg, and salt and cayenne pepper and mix well. In another bowl, mix together the reserved oyster liquor, sherry, and Worcestershire. In a 2-quart baking dish, arrange alternate layers of seasoned crackers and oysters, drizzling the oyster liquor mixture over each layer, dotting each layer with pieces of butter, and finishing with a layer of crackers dotted with butter. Pour the half-and-half around the sides and bake 20 minutes. Scatter the reserved almonds over the top, baste with a little of the cooking liquid, and bake till the top is nicely browned but the pie is still moist, about 10 minutes longer. Serve hot.

SALMON CROQUETTES

Makes 4 to 5 servings

SALMON CROQUETTES HAVE BEEN A SOUTHERN STAPLE at bridge and charity luncheons, on country club buffets, and even at fancy dinner parties for as long as I can remember. When they're made with the best ingredients and handled with care, nothing is more delicious; when they contain cheap canned salmon and mashed potatoes and are overcooked to the consistency of tennis balls, they're inedible. So long as it's top-grade pink or red salmon (which can be quite expensive), the canned product can be used, but once you've had these subtly flavored, delicately mixed, correctly sautéed ovals made with tender poached or grilled fresh salmon, there can be no substitute. For a nice variation, you might add a little chopped fresh dill or tarragon to the mixture in place of the pickle. Traditionally, the croquettes are served with a bowl of tartar sauce on the side, coleslaw, and piping hot hush puppies.

2 cups finely flaked poached or grilled salmon

Juice of 1 lemon

1 tablespoon dry mustard

¼ cup chopped fresh parsley leaves

1 tablespoon chopped fresh chives

1 tablespoon finely chopped sweet pickle

1 tablespoon finely chopped capers

½ cup mayonnaise

1 to 1½ cups fresh bread crumbs

¼ cup chicken broth

Paprika to taste

Fine dry bread crumbs, for dredging

6 tablespoons (¾ stick) butter

In a large mixing bowl, combine the salmon, lemon juice, dry mustard, parsley, chives, pickle, capers, and mayonnaise and toss till well blended. Add enough of the fresh bread crumbs to tighten the mixture, then add enough chicken broth to produce a firm but moist consistency.

Using your hands, form the mixture into 4 or 5 oval croquettes and brush both sides of each with a little chicken broth. Sprinkle each with paprika and roll lightly in the dry bread crumbs.

In a large, heavy skillet, melt the butter over moderate heat, add the croquettes, and cook till golden brown, 4 to 5 minutes on each side. Drain on paper towels. Keep warm till ready to serve.

Baked Tuna-Stuffed Bell Peppers

Makes 4 servings

BAKED STUFFED BELL PEPPERS HAVE ALWAYS BEEN A staple of the Southern diet, the perfect medium for all sorts of ground meats, chopped leftover poultry and seafood, and, for health fanatics, diced fresh vegetables and mushrooms. Much as I love canned albacore tuna in salads or by itself, just about the only way I'll prepare it hot is when it's mixed with other ingredients, stuffed into green, red, or yellow bell peppers, and baked with a golden cheese topping. Actually, any cooked, flaked, leftover oily fish, such as mackerel, bluefish, or fresh tuna, makes a wonderful stuffing for these peppers (or large poblano chile peppers), but if you're curious about what Southerners might point to on a diner menu or whip up for close friends on a cold night, do try the canned tuna (solid white only).

4 large green bell peppers

1 cup raw long-grain rice, cooked according to package directions

One 6-ounce can solid white tuna packed in oil, drained

1 small onion, finely chopped

One 10-ounce package frozen corn kernels, thawed

½ cup finely chopped fresh mushrooms

Salt and freshly ground black pepper to taste

Paprika to taste

1 ripe tomato, peeled, seeded, and finely chopped

½ cup shredded sharp cheddar cheese

3 cups hot water

Preheat the oven to 350°F.

Cut a wide circle around the stems of the peppers, lift off the lids, and discard. Scoop out and discard the seeds and membranes, trim the bottoms of the peppers so they will stand upright, and arrange in a 2-quart baking dish.

In a large mixing bowl, combine the rice, tuna, onion, corn, and mushrooms, season with salt and pepper and paprika, and mix till well blended. Stuff equal amounts of the mixture into the peppers, spoon equal amounts of the chopped tomato over the mixture, and sprinkle equal amounts of cheese over the tops. Pour the hot water around the peppers and bake till the tops are golden, 30 to 35 minutes. Carefully lift the peppers out of the dish with a slotted spoon, place on a large plate, and serve piping hot.

Jekyll Island Fish Cakes

Makes 4 to 6 servings

I WAS IN BRUNSWICK, GEORGIA, TO FOLLOW UP ON the town's claim to be the home of Brunswick stew (dubious), to view the putative "original pot" mounted at the Welcome Center (impressive), and to sample as many bowls of stew as possible (good and bad), when somebody began raving about the fish cakes served at some family-style restaurant over on Jekyll Island. Perched in a faded Naugahyde booth, I was indeed stunned by the light, crispy, flavor-packed cakes, and when I hopped up and asked the hefty woman cook back in the small kitchen what her secret was, she simply muttered, "Mixed fish and clean oil." What she meant by mixed fish was a combination of lean and fat fish for the right flavor and texture—a principle that had never dawned on me but that made a lot of sense. Sea bass and salmon make a perfect union for these cakes, but you could also combine halibut and bluefish or grouper and trout.

1 pound sea bass fillets

½ pound salmon fillets

1 whole lemon, cut in half and seeded

3 peppercorns

½ bay leaf

3 scallions (part of green tops included), minced

½ cup finely chopped fresh parsley leaves

1 large egg, beaten

3 tablespoons mayonnaise

1 tablespoon fresh lemon juice

2 tablespoons Dijon mustard

1 tablespoon Worcestershire sauce

Tabasco sauce to taste

Salt and freshly ground black pepper to taste

½ cup dry bread crumbs

⅓ cup vegetable oil

Lemon wedges, for garnish

Arrange the fish fillets in a large nonreactive skillet, add enough water to barely cover them, squeeze the lemon halves into the water, and add the peppercorns and bay leaf. Bring water to a low simmer, cover, and cook till the fish flakes, about 10 minutes. Transfer the fish to a plate, let cool completely, remove any skin, then flake well with a fork.

Place the flaked fish in a mixing bowl, add all remaining ingredients except the vegetable oil and lemon wedges, and mix gently till the ingredients just hold together. Form the mixture into 4 to 6 oval cakes and place on a plate.

In a large, heavy skillet, heat the oil over moderate heat till a morsel of bread tossed in the pan sizzles, add the fish cakes, and cook till golden brown, about 4 minutes per side. Drain on paper towels and serve hot with the lemon wedges to be squeezed over the fish cakes.

KEY WEST CONCH FRITTERS

Makes about 14 fritters

PRONOUNCED "CONK," THE SMALL MOLLUSK IN THE large pink shell called conch has been associated with and revered in Key West, Florida, since the mid-nineteenth century. Most often used to make sapid chowders and crispy fritters, conch must be tenderized by being either pounded or finely chopped, to overcome its natural toughness, but few who've ever wandered down Duval Street in Key West and stopped in places like Sloppy Joe's or Bo's Fish Wagon for a few slightly chewy but wonderful conch fritters are aware of the care that goes into producing this unique delicacy. All sorts of exotic sauces come with the fritters, but I've yet to find one that can equal a few squeezes of fresh lime juice. Although you might find fresh conch in Chinese or Italian markets during the summer, you're probably better off buying the canned or frozen product, since fresh conch is highly perishable after only a couple of days in the refrigerator.

½ pound canned or frozen conch meat (if fresh, foot and orange fin removed)

2 tablespoons fresh lime juice

1 small onion, minced

½ small green bell pepper, seeded and minced

1 garlic clove, minced

Salt and freshly ground black pepper to taste

Cayenne pepper to taste

1 large egg, beaten

1 cup whole milk

1 cup all-purpose flour

1 teaspoon baking powder

Vegetable oil for frying

Lime wedges for garnish

Dice the conch finely, place in a food processor, and grind till finely minced. Transfer to a glass bowl, add the lime juice, and toss well. Cover with plastic wrap and refrigerate 30 minutes.

Add the onion, bell pepper, garlic, salt and pepper, cayenne pepper, egg, and milk to the minced conch, stir till well blended, and set aside.

In a large bowl, combine the flour and baking powder and stir till well blended. Gradually add to the conch mixture, stir till a thick batter forms, cover, and refrigerate 1 hour.

To fry the fritters, heat the oil in a large, heavy saucepan over moderately high heat and, in batches, drop tablespoons of the conch batter into the oil. Turning frequently, fry till golden brown, 4 to 5 minutes. Drain on paper towels and keep warm in the oven till all the fritters are fried. Serve immediately with lime wedges to be squeezed over the fritters.

CREAMED SHAD ROE

Makes 4 servings

MUCH PRIZED BY THE EARLY INDIANS AND PILGRIMS for its sweet (if terribly bony) flesh and the delectable roe, the large American shad that migrated each spring from the Atlantic to spawn in eastern fresh-water rivers was so popular by the nineteenth century that it was fished almost to extinction (and, later, almost driven out of certain waters by industrial pollution). Today, the shad have rebounded, and while, in my experience, it's rare to find the annoyingly bony fish itself except in the best seafood markets of Maryland, Delaware, and Virginia, Southerners relish the roe and have come up with numerous creative ways to prepare it: roasted with wild sorrel, stuffed into other fish, poached with various vegetables, and creamed, as in this rather elegant recipe retrieved from an old Annapolis, Maryland, church cookbook. (Marylanders, by the way, have also devised a way to bake or steam shad five or six hours, till the bones literally disintegrate.)

4 slices bacon

2 pairs shad roe (about 1 pound)

2 cups water

½ cup whole milk

1 tablespoon fresh lemon juice

1 bay leaf

3 tablespoons butter

3 scallions (part of green tops included), minced

3 tablespoons all-purpose flour

½ cup heavy cream

2 tablespoons dry sherry

Salt and freshly ground black pepper to taste

Tabasco sauce to taste

4 pieces toast

2 tablespoons minced fresh parsley leaves for garnish

In a large, heavy skillet, fry the bacon over moderate heat till crisp, drain on paper towels, crumble, and reserve. Drain the grease from the skillet and let the skillet cool.

Arrange the shad roe in the skillet and add the water, milk, lemon juice, and bay leaf. Bring the liquid to a boil, reduce the heat to low, cover, and simmer for 10 minutes. Transfer the roe to a plate and reserve the liquid in the pan, removing the bay leaf.

In a large saucepan, melt the butter over low heat, add the scallions, and cook, stirring, for 1 minute. Sprinkle on the flour and whisk till well blended, about 1 minute longer. Increase the heat to moderate, add the reserved cooking liquid, and whisk rapidly till thickened and smooth. Add the cream, sherry, salt and pepper, and Tabasco and stir till well blended. Cut the roe into bite-size pieces, add to the sauce, and stir till well heated.

To serve, place a piece of toast on individual plates, spoon equal amounts of creamed roe on the toast, and garnish the tops with the bacon and parsley.

BABY FLOUNDER WITH MUSHROOMS AND PECANS

Makes 4 servings

WHILE THE REST OF THE COUNTRY SEEMS TO BE embracing every exotic and trendy fish from Arctic char to Moroccan tuna to Chilean sea bass, flounder is what Southerners still perceive as the ideal fish to simply broil with lemon and butter, stuff with all sorts of shellfish, flavored rice, and vegetables, or gently sauté with a creamy wine sauce. This particular dish, which might also be made with small red snapper, sole, and even trout fillets, can be prepared literally in a matter of minutes. What's equally appealing is that it lends itself to endless experimentation with whatever ingredients you have in the kitchen—chopped ripe tomatoes or leeks, minced garlic or chile peppers, other nuts and wild mushrooms, fresh broccoli florets or diced asparagus, raisins or capers, and all sorts of herbs and spices. Frankly, I've never understood how food snobs can consider flounder a boring fish, given its amazing versatility.

6 tablespoons (¾ stick) butter

1 cup coarsely chopped fresh mushrooms

½ cup all-purpose flour

Salt and freshly ground black pepper to taste

4 small fresh flounder fillets (about ½ pound each), skinned

1 cup dry white wine

Pinch of ground fennel

¼ cup heavy cream

1 cup coarsely chopped pecans

In a small skillet, melt 2 tablespoons of the butter over moderate heat. Add the mushrooms, cook, stirring, for about 3 minutes, and remove from the heat.

On a plate, combine the flour and salt and pepper and mix till well blended. Dredge the fish fillets lightly in the mixture and place on another plate. In a large skillet, melt the remaining butter over moderate heat, add the floured fillets, and sauté 2 minutes on one side. Turn the fillets over, scatter the mushrooms on top and around the sides, and cook 2 minutes longer. Add the wine and fennel, cook 1 minute longer, then pour on the cream, stirring gently but taking care not to break up the fish. Reduce the heat to low, cover the skillet, and let the fish rest in the cooking liquid several minutes.

To serve, transfer the fillets to a heated serving platter, reduce the sauce over moderately high heat till just thickened, about 3 minutes, pour the mushrooms and sauce over the fish, and scatter pecans over the top. Serve hot.

Fried Catfish with Pecan Sauce

Makes 4 to 6 servings

ONE OF MY EARLIEST CHILDHOOD MEMORIES IS catching hideous catfish in the Catawba River outside Charlotte, North Carolina, watching my grandfather and mother clean the fish and fry them in a huge cast-iron skillet, and eating them with coleslaw, hush puppies, and, by all means, ketchup. Of course, catfish was considered "common" in those days, and I still snicker today when I read about the sweet fish being so fashionable in restaurants or watch trendy chefs preparing and saucing it as if it were Dover sole. Although pond cultivation of catfish began in Arkansas, the Mississippi Delta is now the major producer, supplying the national markets with no less than 250 million pounds annually and elevating the lowly fish to a lofty status unheard of just twenty years ago. Fortunately, catfish is one fish that remains as white, firm, and sweet when frozen as when fresh. Fried catfish served with nothing but a few squeezes of lemon or ketchup, or crusted with ground cornmeal and pecans, is still as popular with Southerners as when I was a boy. For a more updated and sophisticated dish, serve the fish with this buttery pecan sauce.

Arkansas is not only a major rice-producing state but second only to Mississippi in catfish farming. It is also the home of Tyson, one of the world's largest poultry-processing companies.

THE SAUCE

½ cup toasted pecans, chopped

4 tablespoons (½ stick) butter, melted

1 teaspoon fresh lemon juice

¼ teaspoon Worcestershire sauce

Tabasco sauce to taste

THE CATFISH

1 cup white cornmeal

¼ cup all-purpose flour

¼ teaspoon salt

¼ teaspoon freshly ground black pepper

2 pounds fresh catfish fillets, rinsed and patted dry with paper towels

Vegetable oil for frying

To make the sauce, in a bowl combine all the ingredients and stir till well blended.

To make the catfish, combine the cornmeal, flour, salt, and pepper on a plate and mix well. Dredge the catfish fillets in the mixture and place on another plate.

In a large cast-iron skillet, heat about ¼ inch of oil over moderate heat and, in batches if necessary, fry the fillets about 5 minutes on each side or till nicely browned. Drain on paper towels.

To serve, spoon a little sauce over each fillet and serve hot.

THE ORIGINAL BLACKENED REDFISH

Makes 4 servings

POPULARIZED BY THE GREAT CAJUN CHEF PAUL Prudhomme, blackened fish became a rage around the entire country in the 1980s after he served it at K-Paul's Louisiana Kitchen, in New Orleans. In truth, frying fish outdoors in this manner had been a Cajun tradition for decades; what Prudhomme did was demonstrate how the smoky ritual could be executed in the restaurant or home kitchen. Of course, the technique has been abused by cooks from coast to coast, with some using the wrong types of fish, others cooking the fish on grills instead of in blazing-hot cast-iron skillets, and still others tampering with strange seasonings that transform the flavor altogether. Here is the original method I learned from Prudhomme at his restaurant and at one front-yard cookout, and believe me, it shouldn't be modified if you want to see how brilliant the dish can be. Nothing is as succulent as fresh redfish indigenous to Louisiana, but since it's available only in the most upscale, expensive fish markets, you can also use small fillets of red snapper, pompano, tile fish, or grouper. Do be warned that cooking fish in this manner creates lots of smoke, so if you can get a cast-iron skillet extremely hot outside over an open fire or on a grill, so much the better. (Note: Prudhomme has marketed a seasoning mix called Cajun Magic, available at 1-800-457-2857 or www.chefpaul.com, which contains, and therefore can be substituted for, the seasonings in this recipe.)

3 teaspoons salt

2 teaspoons medium-hot paprika

½ teaspoon cayenne pepper

¼ teaspoon freshly ground black pepper

¼ teaspoon dried thyme, crumbled

¼ teaspoon dried oregano, crumbled

¼ teaspoon dried basil, crumbled

12 tablespoons (1½ sticks) butter, melted

8 boneless, skinless fish fillets (about ¼ pound each)

On a deep plate, combine all the seasonings and mix till well blended. Pour the butter into a bowl. Dip the fish fillets in the butter, sprinkle the seasoned mixture on both sides, and place on a platter.

Heat a large cast-iron skillet over high heat for about 8 minutes or till smoking hot. Add half the fish fillets, drizzle about 1 teaspoon butter over each, and cook about 1½ minutes. (The butter may flame up, so be careful.) Turn the fish, drizzle each fillet with another teaspoon of butter, cook 1½ minutes longer, and transfer to the platter. Repeat the procedure with the remaining fillets, then serve immediately.

210

BAKED POMPANO STUFFED WITH CRABMEAT

Makes 4 servings

IN MY OPINION, POMPANO IS THE MOST DISTINCTIVE and succulent of all Southern fish. While I've caught them myself in the surf as far north as the Outer Banks of North Carolina, by far the finest, fattest specimens are landed off the Florida and Gulf coasts. Perhaps the most famous pompano dish is richly sauced pompano en papillote (baked in parchment), created many decades ago at Antoine's restaurant in New Orleans. But since the white, slightly oily fish is so sturdy, it also lends itself perfectly to being stuffed and baked in the manner relished by all Southerners. Since the heads and tails are left on the fish in this recipe, the dish makes a very dramatic presentation worthy of the most stylish dinner party.

> *8 tablespoons (1 stick) butter*
>
> *6 scallions (part of green tops included), cut into thin rounds*
>
> *1 cup fresh bread crumbs*
>
> *¾ pound fresh lump crabmeat, picked over for shells and cartilage*
>
> *¼ cup finely chopped fresh parsley leaves*
>
> *¼ cup dry sherry*
>
> *Four 1½-pound pompanos, gutted but with heads and tails left on*
>
> *Salt and freshly ground black pepper to taste*
>
> *Chopped fresh parsley leaves for garnish*

Preheat the oven to 375°F.

In a heavy skillet, melt 2 tablespoons of the butter over moderate heat. Add the scallions, cook, stirring, till softened, about 3 minutes, and transfer to a mixing bowl. Melt 2 more tablespoons of the butter in the skillet, add the bread crumbs, stir till golden and crisp, and add to the scallions. Add the crabmeat, parsley, and sherry to the bowl and gently mix till the stuffing is well blended. Remove from the heat.

Season the pompanos inside and out with salt and pepper, spoon equal amounts of stuffing into the cavities, and secure the edges with small skewers or heavy toothpicks. Arrange the pompanos in a large buttered baking pan, dot the tops with the remaining 4 tablespoons of butter, and bake till the fish feel firm to the touch, about 30 minutes. Arrange on a heated platter, sprinkle parsley over the tops, and serve immediately.

211

Stuffed Red Snapper Demos

Makes 4 servings

STANLEY DEMOS CREATED THIS SPECTACULAR DISH at his legendary Coach House in Lexington, Kentucky, before retiring to Florida and turning the restaurant over to his children. Quite frankly, I don't think I've ever eaten better Southern stuffed fish. I've used this stuffing for boned striped bass, flounder, and pompano, but for truly distinctive flavor and ideal texture, it's hard to beat a large red snapper so fresh that you can almost taste the sea.

One 4- to 5-pound fresh red snapper

Salt and freshly ground black pepper to taste

8 tablespoons (1 stick) butter

½ cup finely chopped scallions (part of green tops included)

⅓ cup finely chopped celery

1 cup fresh bread crumbs

6 large fresh shrimp, peeled, deveined, and diced

6 fresh oysters, shucked and chopped

3 tablespoons fresh lemon juice

½ cup dry white wine

2 strips bacon

2 lemons, quartered and seeded

Watercress for garnish

Preheat the oven to 350°F.

Bone the snapper by first cutting open the belly all the way to the tail. Using a boning knife, carefully loosen the flesh from the ribs to the backbone, discard the bones, spread the fish out in butterfly fashion, and season with salt and pepper.

In a skillet, melt 4 tablespoons of the butter over moderate heat. Add the scallions and celery and cook, stirring, till softened, about 2 minutes. Transfer to a mixing bowl, add the bread crumbs, shrimp, oysters, lemon juice, wine, and salt and pepper to taste, and mix till well blended.

Place the stuffing in the center of the spread snapper and fold the sides up and over till the edges come together. Remove any excess stuffing. Starting at the head of the fish, sew the edges securely with a large threaded trussing needle (or secure tightly with small metal skewers). Place the fish on a rack in a roasting pan, make 3 or 4 incisions in the flesh on top with a sharp knife, place the bacon strips lengthwise on top, and bake till the fish is flaky but still juicy, about 45 minutes.

To serve, transfer the fish to a heated serving platter and remove and discard the bacon and trussing. In a small saucepan, melt the remaining butter, pour over the fish, and garnish the platter with lemon wedges and watercress.

212

Gulf Coast Frogs' Legs

Makes 4 to 6 servings

UNBEKNOWNST TO MOST AMERICANS, FROGS' LEGS are a treasured delicacy all along the Gulf Coast, from Florida to Louisiana—as well as in much of Arkansas. Both the green frogs and bullfrogs that proliferate in this region form the basis for a veritable small industry. While I've had very elegant frogs' legs braised in white wine at finer restaurants, frying or sautéing them in oil or butter is by far the most popular preparation. Although nothing equals the sweet, delicate flavor of fresh frogs' legs, frozen ones, usually packaged in connecting pairs ranging from 4 to 6 ounces a piece, are more and more available in specialty food markets. (If, by chance, you do find fresh ones, choose those that are plump and slightly pink.) Since their flavor is so subtle, frogs' legs should be cooked as simply and briefly as possible; overcooking only causes them to toughen.

½ cup cider vinegar

½ cup water

1 medium onion, sliced

2 garlic cloves, chopped

12 pairs dressed, plump frogs' legs, each pair tied together with twine at the first joints

1 cup all-purpose flour

½ teaspoon salt

½ teaspoon freshly ground black pepper

Cayenne pepper to taste

1 large egg, beaten

½ cup regular buttermilk

Vegetable oil for frying

Seeded lemon wedges for garnish

In a large bowl, combine the vinegar, water, onion, and garlic and stir till well blended. Add the frogs' legs, cover with plastic wrap, and let marinate in the refrigerator about 2 hours.

In another bowl, combine the flour, salt, pepper, cayenne pepper, egg, and buttermilk and stir till a soft batter forms.

Drain and rinse the frogs' legs and pat dry with paper towels. In a large, heavy skillet, heat about ¼ inch of oil over moderately high heat, dip the frogs' legs in the batter, and, in batches, fry them 3 to 4 minutes on each side or till golden brown. Drain on paper towels, remove and discard the twine, and serve the frogs' legs hot with lemon wedges.

Both frogs' legs and alligator meat are considered great delicacies in Florida and marketed frozen in some other states. Mild in flavor, alligator meat has almost the same delicate flavor and texture as chicken and veal; the prime cuts come from the animal's jaw and tail.

Barbecue

Carolina Chopped
or Pulled Pork 'Cue

Memphis Barbecued
Baby Back Pork Ribs

Oven-Barbecued Spareribs

Barbecued Country-Style
Pork Ribs

Barbecued Spareribs
with Plum Sauce

Barbecued Shredded Pork

Georgia Barbecued Pork Chops

Honey-Barbecued Pork Loin

Birmingham Barbecued Veal

Dry-Rub Barbecued Chicken

Edisto Barbecued
Mustard-Sesame Chicken

Creole Barbecued Shrimp

Barbecued Bluefish

Florida Barbecued Swordfish

Barbecued Quail

Arkansas Barbecued Duck

Lynchburg Barbecued Rabbit
with Raisin-Whiskey Sauce

Basic Vinegar Barbecue
Moppin' Sauce

Basic Tomato Barbecue Sauce

Basic Dry-Rub Barbecue Mix

Carolina Chopped or Pulled Pork 'Cue

Makes at least 10 servings

BARBECUE (OR 'CUE) IN NORTH CAROLINA MEANS HOG and hog only (preferably whole hog), and this, in all my Tarheel prejudice, is the king of all barbecue: pit-cooked, hickory-smoked, spicy, vinegary, moist, slightly crackly, incredibly succulent chopped or pulled pork shoulder that is cooked at least 8 hours—a Carolina hallmark for centuries. Debate rages all over the state about the virtues of Lexington-style barbecue (with a slightly sweet vinegar-tomato sauce) versus those of Eastern style (a tart vinegar and red pepper sauce). I love them both and refuse to argue. Ideally, you need an outdoor pit to produce genuine North Carolina barbecue (especially at a traditional pig pickin'), but years ago I perfected a method using an ordinary kettle grill, which continues to impress even the most nagging experts. Just follow the directions to the letter, make sure the pork cooks over a drip pan and not the coals, and, above all, be patient. Also, since this is an all-day affair, and since the chopped barbecue freezes beautifully up to about 4 months without losing its savor and moisture, I strongly suggest you barbecue two shoulders.

1 small bag hickory chips (available at nurseries and hardware stores)

One 10-pound bag charcoal briquets

One 8- to 9-pound boneless fresh pork shoulder (all skin and fat left on)

4 cups cider vinegar

¼ cup Worcestershire sauce

1 cup ketchup

2 tablespoons prepared mustard

2 heaping tablespoons dark brown sugar

2 tablespoons salt

1 tablespoon red pepper flakes, or to taste

Freshly ground black pepper to taste

216

Soak 6 handfuls of hickory chips in a pan of water for 45 minutes.

Open one bottom and one top vent on a kettle grill, place an aluminum drip pan in the bottom of the grill, stack charcoal briquets evenly around the pan (not in the center), and ignite the coals. When the coals are ashen (30 to 45 minutes), sprinkle 2 handfuls of the soaked chips evenly over the hot coals. Place the rack on the grill about 6 inches over the coals.

Position the pork shoulder, skin side up, in the center of the grill directly over the drip pan (not over the hot coals), lower the lid, and cook 3 hours, replenishing the coals and chips as they burn up. Turn the pork over, lower the lid, and cook 3 hours longer.

Meanwhile, prepare the sauce by combining all remaining ingredients in a large stainless-steel or enameled saucepan. Stir well, bring to a simmer over moderate heat, and cook 5 minutes. Remove from the heat and let stand about 2 hours.

Transfer the pork to a large platter or cutting board, make deep gashes in the meat with a sharp knife, and baste liberally with the sauce. Replenish the coals and chips as needed, replace the pork, skin side down, on the grill, and cook 2 to 3 hours longer or till the meat is tender when stabbed with a large fork, basting with the sauce from time to time.

Transfer the pork to a chopping board, remove and discard most (but not all) of the crisp skin and excess fat, and either chop the meat coarsely with a hatchet or cleaver or pull into shreds. Add just enough sauce to moisten the meat, toss till well blended, and either serve the barbecue immediately with the remaining sauce on the side or refrigerate and reheat in the top of a double boiler over simmering water when ready to serve.

Serve the barbecue with Carolina Barbecue Coleslaw (page 269), Brunswick Stew (page 110), and hot Calabash Hush Puppies (page 309) or Beer Hush Puppies (page 310), or heaped on a hamburger bun with coleslaw and sauce.

MEMPHIS BARBECUED BABY BACK PORK RIBS

Makes 4 to 6 servings

SOUTHERN BARBECUE ENTHUSIASTS MIGHT DEBATE vehemently over which region, state, or city produces the best chopped pork barbecue, pulled pork, barbecued shrimp, or dry-rub chicken, but when it comes to barbecued pork ribs, only a fool denies that the undisputed capital is Memphis, Tennessee. Pitmasters may win distinguished prizes in Richmond, Virginia, Lynchburg, Tennessee, Tryon, North Carolina, or Jonesboro, Arkansas, but until they garner at least a "First Place Ribs" prize at the annual Memphis in May World Championship, they really haven't made the grade. Memphis is all about smoky barbecued ribs, and at least in my gluttonous experience, the city's leading exponent is the original Corky's barbecue house, which has been around since 1982 and which utilizes both a dry-rub and a tangy-sweet moppin' sauce for its pit-cooked ribs. Naturally, both recipes are big secrets, but I think my approximation, based on many visits and cagey conversations with cooks and waiters, comes pretty close to the magic.

FOR THE GRILL

1 small bag hickory chips (available at nurseries and hardware stores)

One 10-pound bag charcoal briquets

Vegetable oil for brushing

FOR THE DRY-RUB

¼ cup firmly packed dark brown sugar

2 tablespoons chili powder

2 tablespoons paprika

2 teaspoons dried thyme, crumbled

2 teaspoons dried oregano, crumbled

1 teaspoon ground cumin

1 teaspoon dry mustard

1 teaspoon cayenne pepper

Salt and freshly ground black pepper to taste

FOR THE MOPPIN' SAUCE

½ cup cider vinegar

½ cup tomato sauce

2 tablespoons fresh lemon juice

1 tablespoon molasses

1 tablespoon Worcestershire sauce

1 teaspoon Tabasco sauce

FOR THE RIBS

4 racks baby back pork ribs (about 2 pounds each)

Salt and freshly ground black pepper to taste

To set up the grill, soak 2 to 3 handfuls of hickory chips in a pan of water for 45 minutes. Arrange a thick layer of charcoal briquets over the bottom of an outdoor grill, ignite, and when the coals are ashen (30 to 45 minutes), sprinkle the soaked chips evenly over the coals.

Meanwhile, combine all the ingredients for the dry-rub in a bowl and mix till well blended. In another bowl, combine all the ingredients for the moppin' sauce and whisk briskly till well blended. Using a sharp knife and, if necessary, a pair of pliers, cut and pull off the membrane from the back of each rack of ribs. Season the ribs with salt and pepper, then rub each with about 2 tablespoons of the dry-rub mixture.

When ready to grill, brush the grill rack with oil, place the ribs on the rack bone-side down, and grill about 15 minutes. Turn the ribs over with tongs and grill 15 minutes. Brush with a little moppin' sauce, turn the ribs over, and grill 15 minutes. Brush again with sauce, turn, and grill 15 minutes longer or till very tender. (Replenish the coals and chips if necessary, and if the dripping fat causes flare-ups, move the ribs around or flick a little water over the coals.)

Transfer the ribs to a cutting board, brush them with more sauce, then sprinkle enough dry-rub over the surfaces to form a crust. Serve as whole racks or cut into sections, with extra dry-rub on the side.

It's a veritable ritual throughout the South to prepare and serve some form of pork, boiled greens, black-eyed peas, and cornbread on New Year's Day for good luck. The reasoning? A hog can look backward, so pork is the optimistic choice for a prosperous future; turnip greens, collards, and mustard greens represent folding money; black-eyed peas look like little coins and swell when cooked; and cornbread is the color of gold. What could make more sense?

219

Oven-Barbecued Spareribs

Makes 4 to 6 servings

THIS RECIPE PROVES THAT PORK SPARERIBS DON'T necessarily have to be cooked on a grill over a wood or charcoal fire—a good thing to know when the weather bureau is predicting torrential rain and you've promised guests barbecued ribs. Alas, the ribs won't have that inimitable smoky flavor of the grill, but this complex sauce almost makes up for the loss. Some cooks defat the ribs (and reduce the baking time) by parboiling instead of roasting them, a procedure that, in my opinion, robs them of much of their flavor and defeats the whole purpose of barbecued ribs.

5 to 6 pounds meaty pork spareribs, cut into individual ribs

Salt to taste

1 cup ketchup

1 cup molasses

2 medium onions, finely chopped

Juice of 1 orange

3 tablespoons minced orange rind

2 tablespoons butter

2 tablespoons white vinegar

2 tablespoons peanut oil

2 garlic cloves, minced

5 cloves

1 teaspoon Worcestershire sauce

1 teaspoon Dijon mustard

½ teaspoon Tabasco sauce

Freshly ground black pepper to taste

Preheat the oven to 325°F.

Sprinkle salt lightly over the spareribs, place them on a rack in a large roasting pan, cover the pan, and bake the ribs 1 hour.

Meanwhile, in a stainless-steel or enameled saucepan, combine the remaining ingredients plus salt to taste, bring to a boil over moderate heat, reduce the heat to low, and cook, stirring, for about 10 minutes. Remove the pan from the heat.

Increase the oven heat to 400°F. Brush the ribs with some of the sauce and continue baking till tender, about 45 minutes, turning the ribs about every 15 minutes and brushing with the sauce.

To serve, pile the ribs on a large platter and serve hot.

220

Barbecued Country-Style Pork Ribs

Makes 6 to 8 servings

IF THE HIGH RATIO OF FAT TO LEAN MEAT IS WHAT makes baby back pork ribs so ideal for the barbecue grill, lean, meaty country-style ribs, cut from the shoulder end of the pork loin, are the perfect candidate for slow parboiling, before being finished in the oven with a robust barbecue sauce to give them plenty of character. Beautiful as these ribs might look in the market, be warned that if you simply plop them on a hot grill and baste them with sauce, not only will the meat most likely be tough, but by the time they're halfway edible the sauce might have burned. I have successfully barbecued these ribs slowly over very low heat on a covered grill, but the long procedure is just not worth the time and effort—not when this alternate method produces such succulent results.

8 meaty country-style pork ribs

¼ cup peanut oil

1 medium onion, finely chopped

1 garlic clove, minced

1½ cups water

1 cup ketchup

½ cup cider vinegar

3 tablespoons Worcestershire sauce

1 tablespoon chili powder

1 tablespoon firmly packed dark brown sugar

1 teaspoon dry mustard

½ teaspoon dried oregano

Salt and freshly ground black pepper to taste

Arrange the ribs in a large pot, add enough water to cover, and bring to a boil, skimming any scum off the top. Reduce the heat to low, cover, and simmer the ribs till tender, about 1½ hours.

Meanwhile, preheat the oven to 350°F.

In a large, heavy, stainless-steel or enameled saucepan over moderate heat, heat the oil, add the onion and garlic, and cook, stirring, about 3 minutes. Add the remaining ingredients and stir till well blended. Bring the sauce to a simmer and cook, uncovered, stirring from time to time to prevent sticking, about 20 minutes.

With a slotted spoon, transfer the ribs to a large, shallow baking dish, pour the sauce over the top, and bake till slightly browned, about 20 minutes. Turn the ribs over and bake, basting several times with the sauce, till the other sides are slightly browned and the meat is very tender, 15 to 20 minutes.

Serve the ribs and sauce on a large, deep platter.

Barbecued Spareribs with Plum Sauce

Makes 4 to 6 servings

THE GREAT BARBECUE TRADITION CONTINUES TO evolve in the South, and one fairly recent innovation is the popular use of relatively thick, sometimes syrupy basting sauces flavored with any number of fresh fruits and berries. Mangoes, oranges, guavas, apricots, plums, blackberries, raspberries—all can transform an ordinary barbecue sauce into a whole new, often exotic complement to pork, chicken, game, and even fish. I like to serve these particular ribs with smoky baked beans, a red cabbage coleslaw, oniony corn sticks, and, of course, plenty of ice-cold beer or ale.

> *8 fresh purple plums, peeled, seeded, and diced*
>
> *4 scallions (white part only), diced*
>
> *2 garlic cloves, diced*
>
> *½ cup ketchup*
>
> *½ cup molasses*
>
> *¼ cup white vinegar*
>
> *3 tablespoons soy sauce*
>
> *1 tablespoon Dijon mustard*
>
> *Salt and freshly ground black pepper to taste*
>
> *2 racks meaty pork spareribs (about 3 pounds each)*
>
> *Peanut oil for brushing*

Ignite a thick layer of charcoal briquets in an outdoor grill, let them burn till ashen (30 to 45 minutes), and place the grill rack about 6 inches from the coals.

Meanwhile, in a stainless-steel or enameled saucepan, combine all the ingredients except the spareribs and oil, bring to a boil, reduce the heat to low, and simmer, stirring from time to time, 15 to 20 minutes. Remove the pan from the heat, let cool slightly, then purée the sauce in a blender or food processor. Scrape into a bowl and set aside.

Brush the spareribs with oil, place on the grill, lower the lid on the grill, open the vents, and cook about 20 minutes. Uncover, turn the ribs, brush with the sauce, and continue cooking, uncovered, turning and brushing the ribs with the sauce, till tender, 25 to 30 minutes.

Transfer the racks to a cutting board, cut into individual ribs, and serve hot with remaining sauce on the side.

222

BARBECUED SHREDDED PORK

Makes about 4 cups

LIKE SEVERAL OTHER MODERN INNOVATIONS IN MY
Southern kitchen, this one was inspired by Louis
Osteen's modification of classic French rillettes at his
renowned restaurant on Pawleys Island, South Carolina.
The dish is quite simply pork cooked partly in its own
fat, shredded, to an almost unctuous consistency, and
served with a barbecue sauce. So unless you use a fatty
pork shoulder (or an equal combination of lean pork and
white pork fat or leaf lard), the purpose is defeated.
Served on toast as a cocktail appetizer or a first course
at an earthy country meal, this pork is one of the most
delicious creations ever devised. You can make the dish
spicier and even more interesting by adding a minced
fresh chile pepper to the sauce. Do remember that the
consistency of the meat should be slightly coarse, almost
stringy. And when you've mastered this technique with
pork, try next using a fatty duck or goose.

> *3 pounds boneless pork shoulder (skin removed but fat left on), cut into 2-inch cubes*
>
> *2 garlic cloves, minced*
>
> *1 tablespoon salt*
>
> *2 tablespoons freshly ground black pepper*
>
> *3 cups water*
>
> *1½ cups Basic Tomato Barbecue Sauce (page 236)*
>
> *Toasted bread rounds*

The day before you plan to serve this dish, in a large,
heavy pot, combine the pork, garlic, salt, pepper, and
water and bring to a low boil, skimming scum from the
top. Reduce the heat to low and simmer, stirring from
time to time, to prevent the pork from browning on the
bottom of the pot, for 2 to 2½ hours.

When the pork starts to come apart, break it into
shreds with a fork. When the water and other juices
have evaporated, transfer the pork and rendered fat to
a large bowl and shred the pork into very small pieces.
Add the barbecue sauce and stir till well blended with
the pork. Let cool, cover with plastic wrap, and
refrigerate overnight.

Place the pork in a large baking pan and, using 2 heavy
forks, shred it further in long pulling motions till it is
bound by its own fat and the mixture is slightly coarse.
Scrape into a crock or bowl, cover again, and
refrigerate at least 4 hours.

Remove the pork from the refrigerator about 1 hour
before serving and spread on toasted bread rounds.
Tightly covered, the pork will keep in the refrigerator
for up to a week.

223

Georgia Barbecued Pork Chops

Makes 6 servings

SOME SAY THAT IN THE COMPLEX WORLD OF BARBECUE sauces, North Carolina is the vinegar–hot pepper state, South Carolina the mustard state, and Georgia the ketchup state. While the theory is a bit too hypothetical, what is true is that Georgians do seem to prefer their sauces considerably sweeter than do their northern neighbors. And I must say I've rarely tasted a barbecue sauce in the Peach Tree State that didn't contain at least a little mustard. (The mustardy barbecue sauce at Johnny Harris in Savannah, for example, is legendary). Do remember that any sauce with both ketchup and brown sugar tends to burn if the meat or fowl being barbecued is not watched carefully.

1 cup cider vinegar

1 cup ketchup

½ cup peanut oil

2 tablespoons Worcestershire sauce

½ cup firmly packed light brown sugar

2 tablespoons prepared mustard

1 garlic clove, minced

Salt and freshly ground black pepper to taste

6 center-cut loin pork chops about 1-inch thick

Ignite a layer of charcoal briquets in an outdoor grill, let them burn till ashen (30 to 45 minutes), and place the grill rack about 6 inches over the coals.

In a stainless-steel or enameled saucepan, combine all the ingredients except the pork chops and stir till well blended. Bring to a simmer over low heat, stirring, let simmer about 15 minutes, and pour the sauce into a wide bowl to cool.

Dip the pork chops into the sauce, place on the grill, and cook till both sides are nicely browned, about 30 minutes, turning and basting with a little sauce from time to time. Transfer the chops to a platter and serve immediately.

Honey-Barbecued Pork Loin

Makes 6 to 8 servings

OKAY, I KNOW THAT PORK LOIN IS NOT THE BEST CUT of meat for barbecuing, since it's so lean and lacks the flavor and sturdiness of a fatty, husky shoulder or rack of ribs, but at least some prejudice went out the window when I tasted this luscious loin prepared by a few good folks at a church barbecue down in Marietta, Georgia. One trick was to minimize the risk of the pork's drying out by butterflying the loin, marinating it in this almost sour-sweet mixture, and cooking it for less time than usual (or just till the meat was nicely glazed). Do check the texture of the pork with a knife or fork after about 30 minutes to make sure it's tender but not falling apart.

1 cup peanut oil

1 cup soy sauce

½ cup honey

¼ cup firmly packed light brown sugar

1 small onion, minced

2 garlic cloves, minced

Salt and freshly ground black pepper to taste

One 3-pound boneless pork loin

In a saucepan, combine all the ingredients except the pork, whisk over low heat till the marinade is well blended, about 10 minutes, and set aside.

Place the pork loin on a cutting board and butterfly it with a sharp knife by cutting lengthwise to within ½ inch of the other side. Open the loin and place in a large, shallow dish or pan. Pour the marinade over the top, cover with plastic wrap, and marinate in the refrigerator for 2 hours, turning once.

Ignite a layer of charcoal briquets in an outdoor grill, let them burn till ashen (30 to 45 minutes), and place the grill rack about 6 inches over the coals.

Remove the loin from the marinade and place, opened up, on the grill. Brush with the marinade and cook 30 to 40 minutes, turning twice and basting often.

Transfer the loin to a large platter, let rest about 5 minutes, then carve into serving slices. Serve hot.

Birmingham Barbecued Veal

Makes at least 6 servings

THE ONLY TIME I EVER HAD BARBECUED VEAL IN THE South was at a lavish wedding reception in Birmingham, Alabama, but it was a dish I'll never forget. Generally, veal has never been a popular meat in Dixie, possibly because, till just a few years ago, Southern veal was more often "baby beef" than the young, delicate, milk-fed calf's meat prized by gourmands the world over. The irony, I learned, is that no meat (other than pork) lends itself better to the barbecuing process than a primal veal shoulder of an older calf that is boned, unrolled, marinated, and either grilled slowly over a very low charcoal fire or grilled briefly over charcoal and then baked in the oven. Once in a while, I do see veal shoulder (and breast) in better markets, but more than likely you'll have to depend on a good butcher for this cut.

1 large onion, coarsely chopped

8 scallions (part of green tops included), coarsely chopped

1 medium green bell pepper, seeded and coarsely chopped

6 sprigs fresh parsley leaves, coarsely chopped

2 garlic cloves, coarsely chopped

½ cup peanut oil

½ cup canned tomato sauce

¼ cup honey

3 tablespoons wine vinegar

3 tablespoons Worcestershire sauce

1 tablespoon capers, drained

Salt and freshly ground black pepper to taste

Tabasco sauce to taste

One 4- to 5-pound boneless veal shoulder, trimmed of excess fat

In a blender or food processor, combine the onion, scallions, bell pepper, parsley, and garlic and chop till just blended but not puréed. In a large skillet, heat the oil over moderate heat, add the blended vegetables, and cook, stirring, for 5 minutes. Add the tomato sauce, honey, vinegar, Worcestershire, capers, salt and pepper, and Tabasco, stir, reduce the heat to low, and simmer till very soft, 15 to 20 minutes. Set aside to cool.

Unroll the veal shoulder in a deep baking dish, spoon the cooled vegetable marinade over the top, cover with plastic wrap, and refrigerate at least 6 hours or overnight, turning the veal once or twice.

Remove the veal from the refrigerator. Ignite a layer of charcoal briquets in an outdoor grill, let them burn till ashen (30 to 45 minutes), and place the grill rack about 5 inches over the coals. When the grill is ready, preheat the kitchen oven to 325°F. Remove the veal from the marinade, place on the grill rack, and grill about 15 minutes on each side, turning from time to time and brushing lightly with the marinade.

Transfer the veal to another deep baking dish or casserole, pour the remaining marinade over the top, cover, and bake in the oven till very tender, about 1½ hours. Serve the veal hot in slices with the sauce on the side.

Dry-Rub Barbecued Chicken

Makes 4 to 6 servings

SINCE YOUNG BATTERY CHICKENS ARE SO BLAND today, they need to be either marinated or, as I learned at a barbecue competition in Huntsville, Alabama, seasoned with a spicy dry-rub before being grilled. (Even organic chickens, which may or may not have a bit more flavor, benefit from a dry-rub when being barbecued.) Indirect, slow cooking over fairly mild wood chips (not hickory) is the best way to produce optimum flavor and maintain the chicken's moistness, so be sure to use a drip pan and to push the coals as far to the edges of the grill as possible. The chicken is ready when, pricked with a fork, the juices run clear and are not in the least pink. For crisper skin, move the chicken directly over the coals during the final minutes of cooking.

Today, Alabama is still known for its elaborate parties, monumental barbecues, and gracious Southern hospitality, but no festivity has ever equaled the formal ball a certain Samuel B. Moore sponsored in the late nineteenth century at his plantation in Huntsville to honor his prize-winning cow, Lily Flag.

One 3- to 3½-pound fryer chicken, cut into serving pieces

3 tablespoons Basic Dry-Rub Barbecue Mix (page 237)

One good handful of apple or oak wood chips, soaked in water 30 minutes

Vegetable oil for brushing

Lightly rub the chicken pieces with the dry-rub mix, place in a large bowl, cover with plastic wrap, and refrigerate 4 to 5 hours or overnight.

Ignite a layer of charcoal briquets in an outdoor grill and let them burn till ashen (30 to 45 minutes). Push the hot coals to the sides of the grill, position a drip pan in the center, and sprinkle the wood chips over the coals. Place the grill rack about 6 inches from the coals and brush with oil.

Place the chicken pieces, skin side up, in the center of the grill, close the lid of the grill, open the vents, and cook about 20 minutes. Turn the chicken over, cover again, and cook till the juices run clear when the breasts and thighs are pierced with a fork and the chicken is tender, 20 to 25 minutes longer.

Transfer the chicken to a platter and serve immediately.

Edisto Barbecued Mustard-Sesame Chicken

Makes 4 to 6 servings

OF ALL THE SEA ISLANDS OFF THE SOUTH CAROLINA coast, only Edisto has resisted, indeed rejected, the massive development that has completely transformed Hilton Head, Kiawah, St. Helena, and most others. To attend a family oyster roast or barbecue on pristine Edisto Beach, as I have several times, is not only to move back a century in time but to witness the culinary rituals in their most primitive forms. Typically, barbecuing is done on grates over live wood or charcoal fires in open pits, and when the menu involves pork or chicken, the sauce is almost guaranteed to include mustard (so scorned up in North Carolina) and a few of the benne (sesame) seeds indigenous to so much coastal South Carolina cookery. Bottles of benne seeds are available in most health food and specialty food shops, but beware that, due to their high oil content, they turn rancid rapidly if not frozen. Also, since bennes become slightly bitter when overcooked, remember to turn this chicken regularly on the grill.

> *1 cup dry white wine*
>
> *½ cup sesame oil*
>
> *1 tablespoon sesame seeds*
>
> *½ teaspoon dried thyme, crumbled*
>
> *½ teaspoon dried oregano, crumbled*
>
> *Salt and freshly ground black pepper to taste*
>
> *One 3- to 3½-pound fryer chicken, cut into*
>   *serving pieces*
>
> *1 tablespoon Dijon mustard*
>
> *1 tablespoon honey*

In a large bowl, combine the wine, oil, sesame seeds, thyme, oregano, and salt and pepper and whisk till well blended. Add the chicken pieces, toss to coat well, cover the bowl with plastic wrap, and let marinate at room temperature about 1 hour, turning the pieces once.

Ignite a layer of charcoal briquets in an outdoor grill, let them burn till ashen (30 to 45 minutes), and place the grill rack about 6 inches from the coals.

Drain the chicken and reserve the marinade. Place the chicken on the grill and cook on both sides till almost tender, about 30 minutes in all, turning and basting with the marinade from time to time. In a small bowl, combine the mustard and honey with 2 tablespoons of the remaining marinade, whisk till well blended, brush over the chicken, and continue cooking till the chicken is fully tender, 10 to 15 minutes longer.

Transfer the chicken to a platter and serve immediately.

228

CREOLE BARBECUED SHRIMP

Makes 4 servings

OPEN ONLY A FEW YEARS, MURIEL'S JACKSON SQUARE restaurant in New Orleans may not have the historic pedigree of Galatoire's or Commander's Palace, but if you want to see where many locals go for no-nonsense turtle soup, classic seafood gumbo, and these remarkable Creole barbecued shrimp, look no further. Basted and served with an herby, highly reduced beer-and-butter sauce, the jumbo Gulf shrimp are rich, satisfying, just as good prepared on an inside grill as over charcoal outdoors, and beautiful on the plate. To avoid toughness, be sure to grill the shrimp just till they're opaque; and since they're served with plenty of sauce, there's no need to baste them repeatedly.

2 cups beer

1 cup Worcestershire sauce

1 scallion (white part only), minced

1 garlic clove, minced

½ cup heavy cream

1 pound (4 sticks) butter, cut into pieces

1 tablespoon fresh lemon juice

1 teaspoon dried thyme, crumbled

1 teaspoon dried rosemary, crumbled

1 teaspoon dried oregano, crumbled

1 teaspoon hot paprika

Salt and freshly ground black pepper to taste

16 fresh jumbo shrimp (about 1 pound), shelled and deveined

Cooked white rice

Ignite a layer of charcoal briquets in an outdoor grill, let them burn till ashen (30 to 45 minutes), and place the grill rack about 5 inches from the coals.

Meanwhile, in a large saucepan, combine the beer, Worcestershire, scallion, and garlic, bring to a boil, and cook till almost all the liquid is evaporated, about 10 minutes. Reduce the heat to moderate, add the cream, and cook till thickened, about 10 minutes. Add the butter and lemon juice and stir till well incorporated. Reduce the heat to low and, whisking, add the herbs, paprika, and salt and pepper, let cook about 5 minutes, and keep warm.

Brush each shrimp with a little of the butter sauce, thread 4 shrimp each on 4 wooden or metal skewers, place the skewers on the grill, and cook, turning several times, till the shrimp are opaque, 8 to 10 minutes.

Heat the sauce to hot. Make a small mound of rice on each of 4 serving plates, position the skewered shrimp over the rice at an angle, and spoon sauce over and around the shrimp and rice.

BARBECUED BLUEFISH

Makes 4 servings

EVERY OCTOBER, MY FAMILY AND I, ALONG WITH hundreds of other zealous fishermen, head for the South Carolina coast for the sole purpose of challenging the huge schools of ferocious bluefish migrating down the Atlantic. Like mackerel and tuna, fresh bluefish, with its fatty, well-textured flesh, is a perfect fish to barbecue, the one stipulation being that it must be dressed literally within a few hours of being caught and the dark, oily underbelly removed to eliminate a strong, fishy flavor. When buying bluefish fillets at the seafood market (never touch bluefish that has been frozen), always sniff them carefully for offensive odors, and be sure to cook them that same day. A little extra care should always be taken when dealing with bluefish, but once it's been properly barbecued, you'll agree it's one of the most delicious fish imaginable.

1 cup ketchup

¼ cup white vinegar

¼ cup peanut oil

2 tablespoons butter

2 tablespoons Worcestershire sauce

2 tablespoons fresh lemon juice

1 garlic clove, minced

¼ teaspoon dried hot red pepper flakes

Salt and freshly ground black pepper to taste

Paprika to taste

4 fresh bluefish fillets (about ½ pound each)

Peanut oil, for brushing

Ignite a layer of charcoal briquets in an outdoor grill, let them burn till ashen (30 to 45 minutes), and place the grill rack about 6 inches from the coals.

In a bowl, combine all the ingredients except the fish and peanut oil, whisk till the sauce is well blended, and set aside.

Brush the fish lightly with the oil, place on the grill, and cook 10 to 12 minutes on each side or till lightly browned and flaky, basting once or twice per side with the sauce.

Transfer the fish to a platter and serve immediately.

Florida Barbecued Swordfish

Makes 4 servings

BECAUSE OF ITS FIRM, MEATY, MODERATELY FATTY texture, fresh swordfish is an ideal fish for barbecuing. During the summer months, when most of the gigantic fish are landed all along Florida's east coast, there's not a serious grill cook from Jacksonville to Key West who doesn't boast a favorite marinade, moppin' sauce, or dry-rub to enhance swordfish steaks. (Equally superb, but very hard to come by, is the genuine dolphin fished in the same waters—not to be confused with the very similar and much more available mahi mahi.) Frozen swordfish steaks are marketed year round, but I've yet to encounter a frozen slab that has either the mellow flavor or dense texture of the fresh.

Four 6-ounce center-cut fresh swordfish steaks

3 tablespoons Basic Dry-Rub Barbecue Mix (page 237)

Vegetable oil, for brushing

4 tablespoons (½ stick) butter, melted

Seeded lemon wedges, for garnish

Season the steaks lightly on both sides with the dry-rub mix, rubbing it gently into the flesh. Place on a platter, cover with plastic wrap, and let stand at room temperature for about 20 minutes.

Ignite a layer of charcoal briquets in an outdoor grill, let burn till they are ashen (30 to 45 minutes), place the grill rack about 6 inches from the coals, and brush the rack with oil.

Place the steaks on the grill and sear 1 minute on each side. Brush with the butter and cook 5 minutes. Turn, brush again with the butter, and cook about 5 minutes longer or till the fish is opaque and almost flakes. (Do not overcook.) Brush again with butter and serve immediately with lemon wedges, to be squeezed over the fish.

BARBECUED QUAIL

Makes 4 servings

BARBECUED QUAIL CAN BE ONE OF THE MOST
succulent game birds on earth, but Southerners learned
long ago that, unless the delicate creatures are wrapped
in bacon and basted constantly with some other liquid
fat to prevent them from drying out, the best method is
to braise them slowly in barbecue sauce on top of the
stove. Some cooks like to split the quail up the back and
flatten them for easier browning, but I much prefer to
cook and serve the birds intact. Nothing goes better with
barbecued quail than wild rice.

1 large onion, minced

½ cup dry white wine

½ cup cider vinegar

¼ cup ketchup

¼ cup firmly packed dark brown sugar

3 tablespoons Worcestershire sauce

1 teaspoon dry mustard

Salt and freshly ground black pepper to taste

Tabasco sauce to taste

4 tablespoons lard or peanut oil

*8 dressed quail (fresh or frozen and thawed),
    rinsed inside and out and patted dry with
    paper towels*

In a stainless-steel or enameled saucepan, combine
the onion, wine, vinegar, ketchup, brown sugar,
Worcestershire, dry mustard, salt and pepper, and
Tabasco, bring to a simmer, stirring, and cook the
sauce 10 minutes. Remove the pan from the heat.

In a large, heavy enameled skillet or casserole, heat
the lard over moderately high heat, add the quail, cook
till golden, 2 to 3 minutes on each side, and remove
the pan from the heat. Pour off all the fat, pour the
barbecue sauce over the quail, cover, and simmer over
low heat about 20 minutes, turning the birds once.

Transfer the quail to a heated platter, pour on the
sauce, and serve hot.

232

ARKANSAS BARBECUED DUCK

Makes 4 servings

BECAUSE OF ITS AMPLE FAT, DUCK (LIKE GOOSE) HAS been barbecued in the South for centuries, and none is so prized as the noble, green-headed mallards that migrate by the millions each year to the marshy rice fields of eastern Arkansas. Barbecue, in fact, is as much a religion in Arkansas as in North Carolina, and legend has it that at one particular Fourth of July feast, where everything from oxen to venison to bear was thrown on the grate over an open fire, barbecued duck was served for dessert! Flames do tend to leap up when duck is barbecued, so if you're not yet adept at moving the pieces away from the "hot spots" on the grill, you might want to push the coals to the edges and cook the duck over an aluminum drip pan positioned in the center.

1 small onion, minced

½ cup red wine vinegar

½ cup orange juice

2 teaspoons Dijon mustard

2 teaspoons chili powder

1 teaspoon sweet paprika, or to taste

Salt and freshly ground black pepper to taste

One 5- to 6-pound dressed duck, quartered

In a bowl, combine all the ingredients except the duck, whisk till the sauce is well blended, and set aside.

Place the duck quarters on a cutting board and, using a sharp knife, remove and discard part of the excess fat. Place the quarters with the skin side down and pound them with a mallet as flat as possible. Arrange in a deep dish or pan, pour the sauce over the top, cover with plastic wrap, and let marinate 1 hour.

When the duck has marinated about 30 minutes, ignite a single layer of charcoal briquets in an outdoor grill, let them burn till ashen (30 to 45 minutes), and place the grill rack about 6 inches from the coals.

Remove the duck quarters from the marinade, place skin side down on the grill, and cook about 40 minutes or till the flesh is tender and the skin crisp, turning the pieces often and basting with the marinade. (Do not overcook or allow the coals to flare up.)

Transfer the duck to a serving platter and serve immediately.

LYNCHBURG BARBECUED RABBIT
WITH RAISIN-WHISKEY SAUCE

Makes 6 servings

BARBECUE FESTIVALS AND COMPETITIONS ARE HELD
in virtually every Southern state, but I've yet to attend one
that has the seriousness of purpose or the prestige of the
Jack Daniel's Invitational, sponsored by the famous
distillery every October in Lynchburg, Tennessee. Here,
maybe fifty pitmasters from all over compete for
recognition and sizeable cash prizes, and while most
demonstrate their expertise with whole hogs, pork
shoulders, and spareribs, a few are not averse to throwing
a few chickens, rabbits, catfish, and even beef ribs on the
grill. What you will *never* be served at the J.D. Invitational
is one drop of what I consider to be the world's greatest
sour mash whiskey. The reason? The small town of
Lynchburg is still legally dry as a bone. Go figure.

234

1 cup golden raisins

1 cup orange juice

½ cup fresh lemon juice

*¼ cup Jack Daniel's whiskey (or other fine
   bourbon)*

¼ cup water

6 tablespoons sugar

1 teaspoon grated orange peel

*Two 2½-pound meaty rabbits, fresh and dressed
   or frozen and thawed*

Vegetable oil, for brushing

Ignite a layer of charcoal briquets in an outdoor grill,
let them burn till ashen (30 to 45 minutes), and place
the grill rack about 6 inches from the coals.

Meanwhile, in a saucepan, combine all the ingredients
except the rabbit and oil, bring to a boil, reduce the
heat to low, and simmer till the raisins are soft and the
sauce is almost syrupy, about 15 minutes. Remove the
pan from the heat.

Cut the rabbits into serving pieces and brush each with
oil. Place the pieces meaty side down on the grill, baste
lightly with the sauce, and cook till lightly browned,
about 10 minutes. Turn the pieces with tongs, baste
lightly again, and continue turning and basting till the
rabbit is nicely browned all over and tender. (Do not
overcook, which would toughen the meat.)

Transfer the rabbit to a platter and serve hot with the
remaining sauce on the side.

Basic Vinegar Barbecue Moppin' Sauce

Makes about 3 cups

USE THIS ALL-PURPOSE SAUCE TO BASTE, MIX INTO, and serve with any form of chopped, shredded, or pulled barbecued pork. It's the style of sauce you're likely to find at a typical North Carolina pig pickin'. In a tightly sealed jar, the sauce keeps up to 2 months in the refrigerator.

Avery Island in western Louisiana is actually a gigantic hill on a swampy base of pure salt, and it is here that generations of the McIlhenny family have been producing Tabasco Sauce since shortly before the War Between the States. Originally grown by Edmund McIlhenny from seeds given him by a Mexican friend, the small red pepper plants that flourish here were the only survivors when the island was flooded by Union troops in 1863. Two years later, McIlhenny decided to grind and blend some of the peppers with the island's salt, let the mash ferment, then add vinegar to make a zesty sauce. The basic formula has never changed, but today the mash is fermented and aged for years in special white oak barrels before being blended with premium distilled vinegar and periodically stirred for a month with wooden paddles. When the pepper skins and seeds are filtered out, the result is the unique sauce known worldwide as Tabasco. Many, many other hot sauces are produced around the South, but none has the subtle mysteries of Tabasco. Do keep Tabasco in the refrigerator; if it turns reddish brown, it's lost its flavor and zing and needs to be replaced.

---

1 cup white vinegar

1 cup cider vinegar

4 tablespoons (½ stick) butter, cut into pieces

1 tablespoon sugar

1 tablespoon salt

1 tablespoon crushed red pepper flakes

1 teaspoon dry mustard

1 tablespoon Worcestershire sauce

Tabasco sauce to taste

In a stainless-steel or enameled saucepan, combine all the ingredients over low heat and simmer, stirring. Cook, stirring, for about 15 minutes. Remove from the heat and let cool.

Basic Tomato Barbecue Sauce

Makes about 3 cups

THIS ROBUST, SLIGHTLY SWEET RED SAUCE IS IDEAL for either barbecued pork ribs or beef brisket, both of which take on a nice glaze when basted with the sauce. In the Deep South, cooks might also use a sauce like this one for barbecued venison, lamb, or duck. Be warned that the sauce does tend to burn if used over coals that are too hot, so any meat being basted with the sauce should be cooked at least 6 inches from the coals. In a tightly sealed jar, the sauce keeps well about a month in the refrigerator.

1½ cups cider vinegar

1 cup ketchup

1 medium onion, minced

3 tablespoons firmly packed dark brown sugar

2 tablespoons Worcestershire sauce

1 teaspoon chili powder

Salt and freshly ground black pepper to taste

Tabasco sauce to taste

In a stainless-steel or enameled saucepan, combine all the ingredients and bring to a boil. Reduce the heat to low and simmer, stirring, till the sauce is slightly thickened, about 20 minutes. Remove from the heat and let cool.

236

Basic Dry-Rub Barbecue Mix

Makes about 2 cups

THIS DRY-RUB CAN BE USED ON PORK, BEEF, POULTRY, and even sturdy fish such as swordfish and salmon, and it's especially effective at sealing the juices of chicken. The mix can be stored up to about 3 months without losing its savor.

½ cup salt

½ cup firmly packed light brown sugar

½ cup freshly ground black pepper

¼ cup hot paprika

1 tablespoon dry mustard

1 tablespoon freshly grated lemon zest

1 teaspoon garlic powder

In a bowl, combine all the ingredients, whisk till well blended, and store in a tightly covered jar till ready to use.

237

Vegetables

Kentucky Pole Beans and Potatoes

Delaware Creamed Succotash

Coca-Cola Baked Beans

Hoppin' John

Alabama Crowder Peas
and Butter Beans

Scalloped Potatoes and Fennel

Buttermilk-Horseradish
Mashed Potatoes

Glazed Party Potatoes

Louisiana Sweet Potato
and Pecan Pudding

Candied Sweet Potatoes

Cornwallis Yams

Corn Fritters

Vanilla Corn Pudding

Cheddar Spoonbread

Cajun Maque Choux

Two-Cheese Squash Soufflé

Acorn Squash and Pimento Bake

Spicy Carrot and Pecan Soufflé

Mama Dip's Eggplant Casserole

Spiced Rutabega, Potato,
and Apple Purée

Nashville Turnip Greens
with Ham Hock

Virginia Turnip and
Red Onion Soufflé

Stewed Okra and Tomatoes

Batter-Fried Okra

Baked Vidalia Onions Stuffed with
Country Ham and Chanterelles

Vidalia Onion and Rice
Casserole

Fried Green Tomatoes

Calabash Coleslaw

Carolina Barbecue Coleslaw

Appalachian Cabbage
and Bacon Pudding

KENTUCKY POLE BEANS AND POTATOES

Makes 6 to 8 servings

WHEN I WAS A CHILD GROWING UP IN NORTH CAROLINA, one of my kitchen duties was to string and snap the Kentucky Wonder pole beans that climbed up tall stakes in my grandaddy's large garden. I hated the chore, but how I loved eating those tender, delicious string beans, which Mother would simmer with ham hock or streak-o'-lean for maybe three hours before adding a few tiny new red potatoes to the pot. Today, genuine Kentucky Wonders have almost disappeared everywhere but in their home state (and even there are grown mostly in home gardens), replaced by the stringless, more fragile Blue Lakes found in most supermarkets, which require little more than about 20 minutes of simmering to become tender. I suppose this relatively new hybrid is okay, the only problem being that the beans hardly have enough time to absorb the flavor of the cooking meat—and no serious Southern cook would dream of simmering green beans without a little pork side meat. Broad, flat pole beans can still be found in most Southern markets during the summer months, and these must indeed be simmered at least 1 hour for optimal flavor and texture. When forced to buy Blue Lakes, what I do is pick out—literally going bean by bean—the largest, fattest ones possible and simply pray they're sturdy enough to undergo lengthy cooking without becoming mushy. What you do not want for this classic Southern dish are young, thin, delicate, fashionable French-style green beans, which cook in as little as 5 minutes. Just be careful not to scorch these beans and potatoes, adding a little extra water if necessary till the beans are meltingly tender.

2 pounds fresh green beans (not *thin French-style beans*)

One 1-inch-thick chunk streak-o'-lean (lean salt pork) cooking meat

½ teaspoon salt

Freshly ground black pepper to taste

1 dozen tiny new red potatoes

Pinch off the ends of the beans and, if necessary, remove any strings. Snap the beans into 1½-inch pieces, rinse well in a colander, and transfer to a large pot. Add the cooking meat, salt, and pepper and enough water to cover by 1 inch. Bring to a boil, reduce the heat to low, cover, and simmer the beans slowly till tender but still slightly firm, about 1 hour.

Meanwhile, rinse the potatoes lightly to remove any grit and cut away a strip of skin around the center of each with a vegetable peeler. Add the potatoes to the beans, stir with a spoon, and simmer till tender, about 30 minutes, adding more water if necessary. Drain the beans and potatoes and serve hot in a large bowl.

Delaware Creamed Succotash

Makes 8 servings

DESPITE THERE BEING A SMALL TOWN IN RHODE
Island named Succotash Point, Southerners have always
claimed that the corn-and–lima bean dish called
sukguttahash by the early Powhatan Indians originated
in seventeenth-century Virginia and eventually spread
throughout the South. Subsequently, each state or
region developed its own style of succotash, one of the
most distinctive being this creamed Delaware version,
made with tomatoes and nutmeg. My own mother in
North Carolina, of course, would never have dreamed of
adding tomatoes to succotash till I virtually forced her to
taste this version. And there was a man in Alabama who
once told me I'd lost my mind when I mentioned making
succotash with milk or cream. I am pretty adamant
about using only fresh corn (naturally, with the milk
scraped from the cobs) and limas (or, even better, real
butter beans, if they're available), and I can't emphasize
enough the importance of stirring succotash while it's
thickening over heat, to prevent scorching. (One burnt
kernel or bean can ruin the entire pot.)

2½ cups fresh lima beans

6 strips bacon, diced

2 large onions, finely chopped

2½ cups fresh corn kernels (plus milk scraped from the cobs)

2 cups peeled and chopped ripe tomatoes, juices included

¾ cup half-and-half

⅛ teaspoon ground nutmeg

Salt and freshly ground black pepper to taste

Tabasco sauce to taste

Place the lima beans in a medium saucepan with
enough salted water to cover, bring to a moderate
simmer, cover, cook till tender, about 15 minutes, and
drain.

Meanwhile, in a large, heavy pot, fry the bacon over
moderate heat till almost crisp and pour off all but
about 3 tablespoons of the bacon grease. Add the
onions and stir till softened, about 2 minutes. Add the
lima beans, the corn plus the milk from the cobs, the
tomatoes and their juices, and the half-and-half, stir
well, and continue to cook another 5 minutes. Season
with salt and pepper and Tabasco and continue to
cook, stirring carefully to prevent sticking, till the
mixture has thickened slightly. Transfer the succotash
to an earthenware tureen or deep serving dish and
serve hot.

Coca-Cola Baked Beans

Makes 6 servings

EVEN BEFORE ELIZABETH CANDLER GRAHAM published her offbeat *Classic Cooking with Coca-Cola* in 1994, one of the South's quintessential beverages had been used far and wide not only to baste hams and make all sorts of casseroles, puddings, and even cookies, but also to produce these unique baked beans. I've had the beans sweetened with molasses or sorghum instead of brown sugar and doctored with bell peppers or pickle relish. Whatever the concoction, there was always that special zing of Coke. Are the beans really good? You bet they are. And can Pepsi be used? Not in the South.

Originally concocted from extracts of coca leaves and cola nuts in 1886 by an Atlanta druggist as a remedy for headaches and hangovers, the secret formula for Coca-Cola syrup is now valued at more than 100 millions dollars and kept in a bank safe.

Two 15-ounce cans baked beans with pork

1 medium onion, finely chopped

1 cup loosely packed light brown sugar

½ cup ketchup

½ cup Coca-Cola

2 teaspoons dry mustard

Salt and freshly ground black pepper to taste

6 slices bacon

Preheat the oven to 325°F.

In a large bowl, combine the beans, onion, sugar, ketchup, Coke, dry mustard, and salt and pepper and stir till well blended. Scrape the mixture into a large, shallow baking dish, drape the bacon slices evenly over the top, and bake, uncovered, till the bacon is thoroughly cooked and the beans are bubbling, 1 to 1¼ hours. Serve the beans directly from the baking dish.

HOPPIN' JOHN

Makes 8 servings

WANNA KNOW WHY THIS AGE-OLD DISH OF BLACK-eyed peas and rice is eaten all over the South on New Year's Day to bring good luck? Because the peas look like little coins that swell when cooked, that's why. (Some say for ultimate success and prosperity, you should eat exactly 365 peas.) Stories abound about the obscure origins of the name hoppin' John, one being that, in antebellum days, a certain lame black cook named John hopped about a plantation kitchen on one leg while preparing the dish. Of course, the debate rages from region to region over the correct approaches to hoppin' John. Must the peas be served with rice? Should they actually be cooked with rice? Are tomatoes a key ingredient, and if so, should they be stewed and spooned over the peas and rice or simply chopped raw over the top? Should the peas be cooked till they're almost mushy or just al dente? Herbs added? Everything cooked in a saucepan or cast-iron skillet? Here's the way I do hoppin' John, which is wonderful with baked spareribs or braised country ham or chitlins—or anything else you can think of.

¼ pound slab bacon, cut into ¼-inch cubes

1 small onion, finely chopped

1 celery rib, finely chopped

1 garlic clove, minced

2 pounds black-eyed peas (fresh or frozen)

Salt and freshly ground black pepper to taste

Red pepper flakes to taste

3 cups water

Hot cooked rice

3 large ripe tomatoes, chopped or stewed

In a large saucepan, fry the bacon over moderate heat till almost crisp and pour off all but about 1 tablespoon of the grease. Add the onion, celery, and garlic and cook, stirring, for 2 minutes. Add the peas, salt and pepper, red pepper flakes, and water, bring to a boil, reduce the heat to low, cover, and simmer till the peas are tender but not mushy, about 1 hour. Drain the peas, then serve them in small bowls over mounds of hot rice with a few spoonfuls of tomatoes on the tops.

Alabama Crowder Peas and Butter Beans

Makes 6 servings

IN GEORGIA AND ALABAMA, THEY'RE USUALLY CALLED crowder peas; in Kentucky and Tennessee, cowpeas; in Maryland and Delaware, lady peas; and throughout the South, just black-eyed peas (whether they have the distinctive dark spot or not). No matter the size, shape, or color, they're all what Southerners term field peas in general, and when they're simmered together with fresh speckled butter beans, a little seasoning meat, and a hot red pepper (as I've observed more than once at the tables of Alabama friends), and served with chopped raw onions and cornbread, there's simply no greater side dish in the entire repertory. Today, fresh crowder peas are becoming as difficult to find (even in the South) as fresh genuine butter beans. Of course, fresh or frozen black-eyed peas and baby limas can be substituted in this recipe with delicious results, but since crowders and "specs" do have special flavor, watch for them in restaurants and diners when traveling in the South. (Traditionally, the fresh peas are cooked with a few of the tender green pods, or "snaps.")

In the South, "side meat" refers to any form of pork used in cooking to flavor peas, beans, greens, and some stews. The most popular types are salt pork, streak-o'-lean (meaty salt pork), ham hock, and cured country ham ends and pieces.

---

2 cups shelled fresh crowder peas (or fresh or frozen and thawed black-eyed peas)

2 cups shelled fresh butter beans (or frozen and thawed baby limas beans)

2 ounces streak-o'-lean (lean salt pork), diced

1 small hot red pepper, seeded and minced

Salt and freshly ground black pepper to taste

Chopped red onion, for garnish

Place the peas and beans in a large bowl of water and, stirring around with your fingers, pick them over and discard any blemished ones or foreign particles. Drain, place in a large saucepan, and add the streak-o'-lean, red pepper, salt and pepper, and enough water to cover. Bring to a boil, reduce the heat to low, cover, and simmer till the peas and beans are tender but not mushy, about 20 minutes. (Frozen peas and beans might need less cooking time.)

Drain the peas and beans, transfer to a serving bowl, and serve hot with onions sprinkled over the top or served on the side.

SCALLOPED POTATOES AND FENNEL

Makes 6 servings

SOUTHERNERS LAY CLAIM TO SCALLOPED POTATOES as if the French *gratin dauphinois* never existed, but it's only recently that we've embraced fresh fennel as a wonderful vegetable to braise, stuff into baked fish, eat raw in salads and with dips, or use to enhance our beloved scalloped potatoes. (Of course, if, like many Southerners, you have a natural prejudice against licorice, you probably won't like fennel, although its flavor is very light and delicate when the bulb is cooked.) Fresh fennel is now widely available throughout the winter months and keeps well, tightly wrapped, in the refrigerator for about a week. When shopping, look for crisp, unblemished bulbs, and refuse any with wilted, feathery tops. Check this dish carefully after about 40 minutes. If it appears to be baking and browning too rapidly, add a little milk around the sides and baste the potatoes and fennel well before adding the remaining cheese.

3 medium russet potatoes (about 1½ pounds), peeled

2 medium fennel bulbs (about 1 pound), cut in half and cored

½ cup chopped fresh chives

Salt and freshly ground black pepper to taste

¾ cup freshly grated Parmesan cheese

3 tablespoons butter, cut into pieces

1 cup heavy cream or half-and-half

Preheat the oven to 375°F.

Cut the potatoes and fennel into ⅛-inch slices and arrange in alternate layers in a 1½- to 2-quart gratin or baking dish, sprinkling a few chives over each layer and seasoning the layers with salt and pepper. Sprinkle ¼ cup of the cheese over the top, dot with the butter, pour the cream over the top, and bake till the potatoes are tender, about 45 minutes. Sprinkle the remaining cheese over the top and bake 10 to 15 minutes till golden brown. Serve hot.

BUTTERMILK-HORSERADISH MASHED POTATOES

Makes 6 servings

EVERYBODY THINKS OF MAKING MASHED POTATOES with milk, cream, half-and-half, or sour cream, but only in the South will you find them whipped with tangy buttermilk, just as they were when folks still churned their own butter. Horseradish is a much more modern innovation—and, in my opinion, a great one. I'd just as soon not eat mashed potatoes if they're not served immediately after being beaten. Reheating them in a double boiler or wrapped in foil in the oven may keep them hot, but they're still almost guaranteed to be lumpy.

5 to 6 russet potatoes, peeled and cut into chunks

4 tablespoons (½ stick) butter, cut into pieces and softened

¾ cup regular buttermilk

2 tablespoons prepared horseradish

1 teaspoon salt

Freshly ground black pepper to taste

Place the potatoes in a large saucepan with enough water to cover, and bring to a boil. Reduce the heat to moderate, cover, cook till the potatoes are very tender, 20 to 25 minutes, and drain.

Transfer the potatoes to a large, heavy saucepan over low heat, add the butter, and beat with an electric mixer till the potatoes are mashed and the butter well incorporated. Add the remaining ingredients and continue beating over low heat till the potatoes are light and fluffy and not at all lumpy. Serve piping hot.

Glazed Party Potatoes

Makes 6 to 8 servings

IT SOMETIMES SEEMS THAT EVERY FORMAL DINNER buffet I attend, from Maryland to Arkansas, includes what are commonly called "party potatoes." Some versions are smooth as silk or slightly chunky, others are relatively bland or overly spicy, and still others are appropriately moist or so dry they should be put down the disposal. Simple to prepare, party potatoes can be utterly delicious when they remain creamy yet have a crusty top. If I have any suspicion that the potatoes might be drying out (I poke them with a knife or fork), I add a little more milk or, if they feel cooked, take them out of the oven momentarily, then run them quickly under the broiler till the top is glazed.

6 medium russet potatoes (about 3 pounds), peeled and diced

4 tablespoons (½ stick) butter, softened

1¼ cups whole or 2-percent milk

3 large egg yolks, beaten

6 scallions (part of green tops included), finely chopped

2 cups grated extra-sharp cheddar cheese

Salt and freshly ground black pepper to taste

Pinch of ground nutmeg

Preheat the oven to 375°F.

Place the potatoes in a large pot and add enough water to cover. Bring to a boil, reduce the heat to low, cover, and simmer till the potatoes are very tender, about 20 minutes.

Drain the water from the pot, add the butter, and mash the potatoes with a potato masher till they are smooth. Add the milk, egg yolks, scallions, 1½ cups of the cheese, salt and pepper, and nutmeg, and stir till well blended and creamy. Scrape the mixture into a 1½-quart buttered dish or shallow casserole, sprinkle the remaining cheese evenly over the top, and bake till the top is glazed and slightly crusty, with a few dark spots, but the potatoes are still creamy and moist, 25 to 30 minutes. Serve piping hot.

Louisiana Sweet Potato and Pecan Pudding

Makes 6 to 8 servings

NORTH CAROLINA AND GEORGIA MIGHT PRODUCE more sweet potatoes and pecans, respectively, than any other states in the South, but a good case can be made that the "cured" Beauregard sweet potatoes and buttery Centennial pecans grown in Louisiana offer a flavor that is in a class by itself. In my experience, this spicy, vanilla-flavored pudding, traditionally served with roasted meat and game dishes, is unique to Louisiana. Just remember never to buy freshly harvested "green" sweet potatoes in the summer, since they still lack the enzyme that converts starch to sugar, and that the best fresh Southern pecans are never available till around October. If ever there was a Southern dish that depended on the season for optimal savor, it's this noble pudding.

6 medium sweet potatoes (about 3 pounds)

2 large eggs, beaten

½ cup half-and-half

1 teaspoon pure vanilla extract

⅛ teaspoon ground cinnamon

1 cup firmly packed light brown sugar

⅓ cup all-purpose flour

6 tablespoons (¾ stick) butter

1 cup chopped pecans

Preheat the oven to 350°F.

Place the potatoes in a large pot with enough salted water to cover, bring to a boil, reduce the heat to low, cover, and simmer till very tender, about 25 minutes. Drain the potatoes and, when cool enough to handle, peel, place in a large mixing bowl, and mash with a potato masher. (Do not use a food processor.)

Add the eggs, half-and-half, vanilla, and cinnamon to the mashed potatoes, stir till well blended, and transfer the mixture to a large baking dish or casserole. In a bowl, combine the brown sugar and flour and stir till well blended. Add the butter and cut in with a pastry cutter till the mixture is mealy. Add the pecans and stir till well blended. Distribute the pecan mixture evenly over top of the pudding and bake till golden brown, about 30 minutes. Serve hot.

Candied Sweet Potatoes

Makes 4 to 6 servings

OFTEN MADE WITH A HEAVY, CLOYING, CANNED commercial syrup and covered with sickening melted marshmallows, candied sweet potatoes have earned a bad reputation throughout the South. Today, however, cooks are learning to respect the dish more, and when candied sweet potatoes are prepared properly, there's no more luscious addition to the holiday table—or, for that matter, to any formal or informal buffet. I knew one lady in Chattanooga, Tennessee, who always sprinkled a big handful of crushed pecans over her potatoes before baking them, an idea I still borrow when I want to highlight the rich dish.

4 medium sweet potatoes (about 1½ pounds)

1 cup firmly packed light brown sugar

½ teaspoon ground cinnamon

¼ teaspoon ground cloves

¼ cup water

4 tablespoons (½ stick) butter, cut into pieces

1 teaspoon pure vanilla extract

Preheat the oven to 350°F.

Place the sweet potatoes in a large saucepan with enough water to cover, bring to a boil, reduce the heat to low, cover, and simmer till the potatoes are barely tender, about 20 minutes. Drain and, when cool enough to handle, peel the potatoes, cut into ½-inch rounds, and arrange the slices overlapping in a shallow 1½-quart buttered baking dish.

In a saucepan, combine ¾ cup of the brown sugar, the cinnamon, cloves, water, and butter, bring to a simmer, stirring, and cook for about 5 minutes. Add the vanilla and stir till the syrup is well blended.

Pour the syrup evenly over the potatoes, sprinkle the remaining ¼ cup of brown sugar over the top, cover tightly with aluminum foil, and bake for about 20 minutes. Uncover and continue baking till the potatoes are tender and nicely glazed, about 10 minutes, basting once with the syrup.

Serve the potatoes hot, directly from the baking dish.

Cornwallis Yams

Makes 4 to 6 servings

TO DINE AT THE REMOTE COLONIAL INN IN HISTORIC Hillsborough, North Carolina, when I was a student at the university in nearby Chapel Hill was to go back two hundred years, when Southern cuisine was just beginning to establish a unique identity. And to sample a dish such as these spicy Cornwallis yams was to get some idea just how different and exotic early cookery could be. Since genuine yams from South America and parts of Africa and Asia were no more available then than now (and I do wish people could finally let that fact sink in), the tubers would have been native sweet potatoes, but since both dried coconut from Pacific islands and West Indian pineapples were gaining popularity in Colonial days—coconut cake has been known in the South since at least the early nineteenth century, and records show that George Washington loved pineapple—it's highly likely that both ingredients could have been used to make innovative dishes such as this one. Whether the "yams" would have been served as a side vegetable with fried country ham or roast pork, or as a dessert, remains open to debate. Either way, they're delicious.

4 medium sweet potatoes (about 1½ pounds)

1 cup whole milk

½ cup sugar

¼ cup crushed canned pineapple

4 tablespoons (½ stick) butter

2 large eggs, beaten

¼ teaspoon salt

¼ teaspoon ground cinnamon

¼ cup packaged flaked unsweetened coconut

Preheat the oven to 350°F.

Place the sweet potatoes in a large saucepan with enough water to cover, bring to a boil, reduce the heat to low, cover, and simmer till the potatoes are tender, about 30 minutes. Drain the potatoes.

When cool enough to handle, peel the potatoes, place in a mixing bowl, and mash well with a heavy fork. Add all remaining ingredients except the coconut and continue mashing and mixing till the mixture is well blended and almost smooth. Scrape into a buttered 1½-quart baking dish and bake till nicely glazed on top, 40 to 45 minutes.

Sprinkle the flaked coconut evenly over the top and serve hot.

CORN FRITTERS

Makes about 16 fritters

SOMETIMES CALLED "CORN OYSTERS" IN SOUTHERN coastal states, since they can resemble fried oysters, corn fritters have been a staple all over the South for at least two hundred years. I once watched some folks in Mississippi make an entire lunch of nothing but corn fritters and spinach salad. Even more telling, I've served the fritters with eggs and bacon for breakfast more than once when confronted with sacks of Silver Queen corn fresh from the field that I knew would lose its sweetness if kept too long. What you don't want are soggy fritters, so unless you plan to serve them immediately, one solution is to keep them hot and crisp on a wire rack in the oven once they've been drained briefly on paper towels. I also like to serve these fritters with roast pork and chunky apple sauce.

4 ears fresh corn, shucked

½ small green bell pepper, seeded and minced

2 large eggs, beaten

6 tablespoons all-purpose flour

Salt and freshly ground black pepper to taste

½ cup half-and-half

¼ cup peanut oil

2 tablespoons butter

Place the corn in a large pot with enough water to cover, bring to a boil, cook 2 minutes, and drain. When cool enough to handle, cut the corn kernels off onto a plate, scraping the cobs with the back of the knife to extract as much of the corn milk as possible. Place the kernels and corn milk in a mixing bowl, add the bell pepper, eggs, flour, salt and pepper, and half-and half, and stir till the mixture is well blended and thick.

In a large skillet, heat the oil and butter over moderately high heat, spoon about 4 mounds of the batter into the fat, and cook till golden on one side, 3 to 4 minutes. Turn with a slotted spoon, cook 3 to 4 minutes or till golden on the other side, and drain on paper towels. Repeat with the remaining batter, keeping the fritters hot on a large plate or wire rack in the oven till ready to serve.

Vanilla Corn Pudding

Makes 6 servings

WHEN I LEARNED YEARS AGO THAT THE FAMOUS Virginian chef Edna Lewis seasoned her corn pudding with a little vanilla extract, the connection between sweet New England Indian pudding and the savory one that evolved in the South immediately became apparent. Indeed, in certain nineteenth-century Southern cookbooks, the term *Indian pudding* (referring to Indian maize) was often used to describe a savory corn custard served both with roasted meats and as a dessert, thus compounding the confusion. Today, of course, corn pudding is strictly a savory side dish in the South, and when truly fresh sweet corn from the field is used (before the natural sugar begins to convert to starch), very little if any sugar is needed. You can certainly make the traditional pudding without the touch of vanilla, but I find that the flavoring adds a sense of mystery to the dish that is elusively captivating. When cutting the kernels of corn from the ears, be sure to scrape any milk from the cobs and add it to the mixture.

3 large eggs

3 cups fresh corn kernels (plus any milk scraped from the cobs)

2 teaspoons minced onion

3 tablespoons all-purpose flour

½ teaspoon salt

1 tablespoon sugar

Cayenne pepper to taste

Ground nutmeg to taste

4 tablespoons (½ stick) butter, melted and cooled

1½ cups half-and-half

¼ teaspoon pure vanilla extract

Preheat the oven to 350°F.

In a large mixing bowl, beat the eggs with an electric mixer till frothy, then stir in the corn plus any corn milk and the onion. In a small bowl, combine the flour, salt, sugar, cayenne pepper, and nutmeg, stir till well blended, and add to the corn mixture, stirring. Add the butter, half-and-half, and vanilla and stir till well blended.

Pour the mixture into a well-greased 1½- to 2-quart baking dish, place the dish in a large roasting pan, place the pan in the oven, and pour enough boiling water into the pan to come one-quarter of the way up the sides of the baking dish. Bake the pudding for 15 minutes, stir gently to distribute the corn as evenly as possible, and continue baking till the top is golden brown and a knife inserted into the center comes out clean, about 30 minutes longer.

Cheddar Spoonbread

Makes 4 to 6 servings

IS SOUTHERN SPOONBREAD A PUDDING, A CUSTARD, a casserole, or a veritable bread? Should it contain baking powder, salt, and sugar? Can it actually be prepared as a bread, or is it always served as a vegetable side dish and eaten with a spoon? No Southern dish is shrouded in such mystery. Although the name supposedly derives from an Indian word for porridge (*suppone*), there's really no mention of spoonbread in cookbooks till the turn of the twentieth century. Did the cornmeal dish evolve from the much earlier mush breads or batter breads? Whatever its origins, I was raised eating spoonbread, both at breakfast (with fried country ham and red-eye gravy) and as a dinner side dish, and I've had it at various locales in the South enhanced with everything from diced ham to bell peppers to bourbon to different cheeses. I must have a dozen recipes for spoonbread, but this one with extra-sharp cheddar cheese is probably my favorite. I usually serve the dish with any meat and gravy, fried seafood, or plain roast chicken, and on brunch buffets, but the truth is that spoonbread is wonderful with everything and at any time.

1 cup white cornmeal

2 cups water

1 teaspoon salt

½ cup grated extra-sharp cheddar cheese

1 cup whole milk

2 large eggs, beaten

3 tablespoons butter, melted

Preheat the oven to 350°F.

In a large, heavy saucepan, combine the cornmeal, water, and salt, bring to a boil, reduce the heat to moderate, and cook, stirring constantly, for 5 minutes. Remove the pan from the heat, add the cheese, and stir till the cheese has melted; the mixture will be quite thick. Add the milk, eggs, and butter and stir till the mixture is smooth. Scrape into a medium buttered baking dish and bake till the inside is firm but still moist and the top is golden brown, about 45 minutes. Serve hot.

Cajun Maque Choux

Makes 6 to 8 servings

STILL ANOTHER SOUTHERN DISH SHROUDED IN mystery is this simple Cajun concoction, which can be traced back three hundred years and which, today, is often enriched throughout Louisiana with everything from crawfish to chicken to spicy tasso ham. You won't find this dish mentioned in even the most comprehensive food dictionaries, much less in any all-purpose cookbook, and had not the legendary Commander's Palace in New Orleans almost singlehandedly revived maque choux years ago, chances are it would have simply disappeared from restaurant menus. This rather sophisticated recipe (adapted from the Commander's version) is for plain vegetable maque choux, intended to be served as a side dish to roasted or grilled meats and poultry. If you'd like to transform it into an unusual main course for four, simply add about 2 cups of diced cooked chicken, cured ham, or raw shrimp and adjust the amount of water accordingly.

½ pound bacon, cut into small pieces

1 medium onion, finely chopped

1 small green bell pepper, seeded and finely chopped

4 garlic cloves, minced

1 small hot chile pepper, seeded and minced

¼ pound small fresh okra (stems removed), cut into rounds

8 ears fresh corn, shucked, kernels removed, and milk scraped from the cobs and reserved

¼ cup water

Salt and freshly ground black pepper to taste

4 scallions (part of green tops included), chopped

1 tablespoon butter

In a large, heavy skillet over moderate heat, fry the bacon till crisp, drain on paper towels, and reserve. Add the onion, bell pepper, garlic, and chile pepper to the skillet and cook, stirring, about 3 minutes. Add the okra, the corn plus its milk, the water, and salt and pepper, reduce the heat to low, cover, and simmer, stirring once or twice, till the vegetables are tender, 10 to 15 minutes.

With a slotted spoon, transfer the vegetables to a serving dish, stir in the scallions and butter, and garnish the top with the bacon.

254

Two-Cheese Squash Soufflé

Makes 6 servings

EVERY SERIOUS SOUTHERN COOK HAS HIS OR HER special crookneck squash soufflé. This is mine, in its most recent reincarnation. For years, I made the soufflé with no garlic and only sharp cheddar cheese, then decided it had to be more aggressive. Now I'm convinced that a combination of well-aged, extra-sharp cheddar (preferably Vermont or Canadian) produces the ultimate soufflé. For the right texture, do not use a food processor for this dish, and when shopping, buy only bright yellow, firm, medium-size yellow squash with no dark spots. The soufflé is ideal with short ribs of beef, meat loaf, and baked ham stuffed with greens. I wish I could say that this soufflé can be mixed and frozen, then thawed and baked, like so many others, but it has never tasted right when I've tried this. Don't ask me why. I don't even like leftover soufflé that's refrigerated in foil and reheated for another meal.

> 8 medium yellow squash (about 3 pounds), scrubbed and cut into 1-inch cubes
>
> 2 large onions, coarsely chopped
>
> 2 garlic cloves, chopped
>
> 6 tablespoons (¾ stick) butter, softened
>
> 2 large eggs, beaten
>
> ½ cup minced fresh parsley leaves

> ½ cup dry bread crumbs
>
> ½ teaspoon salt
>
> Freshly ground black pepper to taste
>
> Pinch of ground nutmeg
>
> ½ cup grated extra-sharp cheddar cheese
>
> ½ cup freshly grated genuine Parmesan cheese

Preheat the oven to 350°F.

In a large saucepan, combine the squash and onions, add enough salted water to cover, and bring to a boil. Reduce the heat to low, cover, and simmer till the squash is tender, about 30 minutes. Drain in a colander and mash well with a potato masher or heavy fork to extract excess liquid.

Place the vegetables in a large mixing bowl, add all the remaining ingredients except about 3 tablespoons of the grated Parmesan, and mix thoroughly with a heavy spoon. Transfer the mixture to a well-buttered medium-size baking or gratin dish, sprinkle the remaining Parmesan over the top, and bake till golden, about 30 minutes. Serve hot.

255

Acorn Squash and Pimento Bake

Makes 6 to 8 servings

EVIDENCE OF SQUASH DATING BACK SOME TWO thousand years has been found in Indian burial grounds in Virginia and Kentucky. Today, one of the most popular winter varieties in most states is the oval-shaped, dark green, orange-fleshed acorn squash, which, because of its relatively bland flavor, is almost always baked either with spices or other distinctive ingredients. Unlike soft, yellow crookneck summer squash, which is very perishable, hard acorn squash needs no refrigeration and can be stored in a cool, dark place for at least a month. As for the pimentos in this dish, sometimes I think the only thing Southerners don't do with pimentos is make ice cream. This classic squash and pimento bake is just one of the ways the large pepper indigenous to the Americas is used to enhance literally dozens of dishes. Do note that the red, heart-shaped pimento pepper (produced and packed almost exclusively in the South today) is *not* the same as its humbler red bell cousin—in either flavor or texture. I hear people complain that genuine pimentos are next to impossible to find in markets outside the South, but I've never had any problem finding at least the 4-ounce jars (throughout the South, both 4- and 7-ounce jars are stocked in all supermarkets). If you have no luck, have a serious word with the store manager. For a nice textural variation on this dish, I often add about half a cup or so of crushed Brazil nuts, pecans, or walnuts to the squash and pimento mixture before baking.

2 large acorn squash

8 tablespoons (1 stick) butter, cut into pieces

2 large eggs

¼ cup mayonnaise

One 4-ounce jar diced pimentos, drained

1 small onion, finely chopped

½ small green bell pepper, seeded and finely chopped

2 teaspoons light brown sugar

Salt and freshly ground black pepper to taste

½ cup fine bread crumbs

2 tablespoons butter, melted

½ cup grated extra-sharp cheddar cheese

Preheat the oven to 325°F.

Place the whole squash on a heavy baking sheet and bake till tender when stuck with a fork, 1½ to 2 hours. When cool enough to handle, cut the squash into quarters, remove and discard the seeds and skin, place the flesh in a large mixing bowl along with the butter, and mash well with a potato masher. Add the eggs, mayonnaise, pimentos, onion, bell pepper, brown sugar, and salt and pepper, beat the mixture with an electric mixer till well blended and smooth, and scrape into a buttered 2-quart baking dish or casserole.

Sprinkle the bread crumbs over the top, drizzle melted butter over the crumbs, and bake 30 minutes. Sprinkle the cheese evenly over the top and bake till the top is golden brown, 10 to 15 minutes longer. Serve piping hot directly from the baking dish.

Spicy Carrot and Pecan Soufflé

Makes 6 servings

SOUTHERNERS HAVE BEEN PAIRING CARROTS AND pecans for ages, aware of how the large amount of oil in the nuts neutralizes the sugar in the carrots. Carrots, however, are basically bland, so when they're cooked, it's common practice to perk them up with a few spices. Since this is actually a very elegant soufflé that goes perfectly with most ham and pork dishes, try to use an attractive soufflé dish if at all possible.

2 pounds carrots, scraped and quartered

8 tablespoons (1 stick) butter, cut into chunks and softened

¼ cup sugar

¼ cup whole milk

3 large eggs

½ cup chopped pecans

2 tablespoons all-purpose flour

1 teaspoon baking powder

¼ teaspoon ground cinnamon

⅛ teaspoon ground nutmeg

Preheat the even to 350°F.

Place the carrots in a large saucepan with enough water to cover, and bring to a boil. Reduce the heat to moderate, cook till the carrots are tender, about 20 minutes, and drain.

Place the carrots in a food processor, add the butter and sugar, and process till well blended. Add all remaining ingredients and process till the mixture is smooth, stopping to scrape down the sides. Scrape the mixture into a 1½- to 2-quart soufflé dish or casserole and bake till set, about 45 minutes. Serve hot.

MAMA DIP'S EGGPLANT CASSEROLE

Makes 6 servings

MILDRED COUNCIL, BETTER KNOWN AS MAMA DIP at her legendary restaurant in Chapel Hill, North Carolina, has been nourishing everybody from Craig Claiborne to Garrison Keillor to Michael Jordan to flocks of UNC students for the past thirty years. A mecca of classic Southern dishes, Mama Dip's Kitchen turns out platters of fried chicken, beef short ribs, and chitlins, pots of succotash and okra and tomatoes, and rich fruit cobblers and puddings, but sometimes I think I could devote an entire meal to this eggplant casserole made, yes, with canned mushroom soup. I had to learn the hard way that certain vegetable dishes (traditional string bean and almond casserole, my mother's broccoli casserole, and certainly this eggplant casserole) never turn out right when a fresh sauce is substituted for canned soups. For heaven's sake, don't ask me why; it's simply a fact of life—like it or not. When I once broached the subject with Mama Dip, she just looked me straight in the eye and said, "Aw, honey, don't be such a snob. If something's good, it's good, and that's all that matters." Case closed. Mama Dip makes this casserole with both sliced and mashed eggplant, depending on her mood. Both are delicious.

2 medium eggplants, peeled and cut into ¼-inch slices

4 tablespoons (½ stick) butter, melted

¼ cup whole milk

One 10¾-ounce can cream of mushroom soup

2 large eggs, beaten

½ cup freshly grated Parmesan cheese

½ teaspoon salt

¼ teaspoon freshly ground black pepper

¼ cup cracker crumbs mixed with 2 tablespoons melted butter

Preheat the oven to 375°F.

Place the eggplant in a large pot with enough salted water to cover, bring to a boil, reduce the heat to low, and cook till tender, about 15 minutes.

Drain all the water from the pot, add the butter, milk, soup, eggs, cheese, salt, and pepper and stir till well blended. Scrape the mixture into a 1½-quart casserole or baking dish, sprinkle the buttered cracker crumbs evenly over the top, and bake till golden, about 30 minutes. Serve hot.

SPICED RUTABAGA, POTATO, AND APPLE PURÉE

Makes 6 servings

I'VE ALWAYS SUSPECTED THAT WHEN SCARLETT O'HARA holds up a root vegetable in *Gone with the Wind* and proclaims defiantly, "I'll never be hungry again," what she's cursing is not really a white turnip but an old, pithy, yellow rutabaga. Which is too bad since, when this member of the turnip family, neglected everywhere outside the South, is bought and prepared with care, no vegetable can be as flavorful or delicious. "Big yellows," which, when young, have a thin, pale yellow skin and sweet, firm flesh, are best from about July through April. Buy them off season and, as with white turnips and parsnips, you risk tubers that are woody, strong tasting, and next to impossible to peel. In this purée, the potatoes add a starchy-smooth texture, while the apple serves to neutralize any bitterness of the rutabaga. For just the right texture, I don't recommend using a food processor for this purée.

1 medium rutabaga (about 1½ pounds), peeled and diced

1 large russet potato, peeled and diced

1 large apple, peeled, cored, and diced

1 cup chicken broth

⅛ teaspoon dried thyme, crumbled

Pinch of ground nutmeg

Pinch of ground cinnamon

2 tablespoons heavy cream

In a medium, heavy saucepan, combine the rutabaga, potato, apple, chicken broth, thyme, nutmeg, and cinnamon and bring to a boil. Reduce the heat to low, cover, and simmer till the vegetables and fruit are very tender, about 20 minutes. Uncover the pan and cook a little longer or till the ingredients lose most of their liquid, stirring periodically to make sure they don't scorch. Transfer the ingredients to a large mixing bowl, add the cream, and mash with a potato masher or beat with an electric mixer till smooth and fluffy. Serve hot.

Nashville Turnip Greens with Ham Hock

Makes 8 servings

ONE ALFRED LELAND CRABB, WRITING ABOUT
Nashville, Tennessee, some fifty years ago, proclaimed
the city the turnip green and hog jowl center of the
universe, and traced its obsession with the dish back to
1810. While I'm not sure the turnip greens I've eaten in
Nashville are necessarily superior to those simmered
with ham hock or other side meat in every other state of
the Confederacy, I must say that a mess of greens once
included on a "meat-n-three" platter at Nashville's
venerable Loveless Cafe is a memory that lingers. What
is for sure is that boiled turnip greens (like collards)
have been one of the backbones of authentic Southern
cookery for centuries, a staple that has survived every
social, economic, and culinary crisis imaginable and
that, to this day, is still served, along with hoppin' John,
as a harbinger of good luck each and every New Year's
Day (the very logical reason being that the green color
and crisp texture of the leaves before cooking represent
folding money). A cardinal sin is not to remove the stems
and ribs of the leaves, and do remember that, for
ultimate flavor, the greens must be simmered with the
meat long and slowly—and to hell with texture. As for
the ham hock, most Southerners like to trim it, chop the
meat, and serve it over the greens. And should you toss
the sublime pot likker left over in the bottom of the pot?
Don't be crazy. It's for dunking cornbread. Use this same
recipe for boiled mustard greens or collards.

4 pounds turnip greens

1 medium smoked ham hock, skin removed

1 tablespoon sugar

2 teaspoons salt

2 medium onions, coarsely chopped

1 cup cider vinegar

Freshly ground black pepper to taste

Remove and discard the stems and ribs of the greens,
place the leaves in a sink or large pot of cold water, and
swish around to remove all the dirt and grit, repeating
the procedure with more fresh water if necessary. Tear
the leaves into several pieces each and set aside.

Place the ham hock in a large pot and add enough
water to cover. Bring to a boil, reduce the heat to low,
simmer for 15 minutes, and add the sugar and salt.
Return to a boil and gradually add the torn leaves.
Reduce the heat to low, cover, and simmer the greens
till very soft and tender, about 1 hour.

In a medium mixing bowl, combine the onions, vinegar,
and pepper and stir till well blended.

Drain the greens well in a colander, transfer to a large
serving bowl, top with the onions and vinegar, and toss
well. Pour any likker from the pot into a bowl and serve
for dunking cornbread.

Virginia Turnip and Red Onion Soufflé

Makes 8 servings

INTRODUCED TO AMERICA IN THE SEVENTEENTH century by French and English settlers, white turnips were almost immediately cultivated in Virginia (by colonists and Indians alike) and eventually became a favorite vegetable throughout the South. While today turnips are still primarily boiled and mashed with butter, sliced and fried, or incorporated in various casseroles, they can also serve as a foundation for much more sophisticated dishes, such as this beguiling soufflé, which a friend's sister included on a stylish dinner buffet at her home in Roanoke, Virginia. My mother prepares a very similar turnip soufflé, using only sweet Vidalia onions, but since red onions do produce a more colorful dish, I still prefer them when entertaining guests.

8 medium white turnips (about 2½ pounds), peeled and diced

2 large red onions, diced

3 tablespoons bacon grease

4 tablespoons (½ stick) butter, softened and cut into pieces

2 teaspoons salt

2 teaspoons freshly ground black pepper

1½ teaspoons sugar

½ teaspoon dry mustard

3 large eggs

1 cup fresh bread crumbs

1 teaspoon fresh lemon juice

Preheat the oven to 375°F.

In a large stainless-steel or enameled pot, combine the turnips, onions, and bacon grease and add enough water to cover. Bring to a boil, reduce the heat to moderate, cover, and boil till the turnips are soft, about 30 minutes. Drain the turnips and onions in a colander, then transfer to a large mixing bowl. Add the butter, salt, pepper, sugar, and dry mustard and beat with an electric mixer till smooth. Add the eggs one at a time, beating till well blended. Add the bread crumbs and lemon juice, stir till well blended, pour into a medium-size, well-buttered glass or ceramic casserole, and bake till a knife inserted into the center comes out clean but the soufflé is still moist, about 50 minutes. (Do not overbake.) Serve piping hot.

The Southern expression "a mess of greens" probably originated in Kentucky where, in the eighteenth century, frontier women would follow cows into the fields and, to assure that the bounty of wild greens were not poisonous, pick only those the cows ate, then boil them with some form of pork.

261

STEWED OKRA AND TOMATOES

Makes 4 to 6 servings

MARY RANDOLPH MAY HAVE GIVEN THE FIRST PRINTED recipe for okra and tomatoes in her early-nineteenth-century *The Virginia House-Wife*, but evidence shows that the dish was no doubt popular in a number of Southern states years before—despite a lingering fear with some that tomatoes might be poisonous and should be cooked "with great care" and "eaten sparingly." That tomatoes from Central America and okra from Africa were eventually paired has to be one of the most unlikely marriages in Southern cookery; it's also one of the most sensible combinations, with the smooth texture of the okra neutralizing the acidity of the tomatoes. Although this is the ultimate dish for true okra lovers, I'm well aware that there are thousands of timid eaters (Southerners and outsiders alike) who have a horror of okra's slimy texture; and when I see the way okra and tomatoes are so often overcooked almost to a mush, I can't much blame them. Here the two vegetables are stewed just till soft, yielding a dish that's not just succulent but worthy of the most sophisticated tables. If you still feel the vegetables could use a little "tightening," just stir in a few dry bread crumbs. Many recipes call for adding sugar to okra and tomatoes, but I find this a ludicrous sacrilege.

4 slices bacon

2 small onions, chopped

1 large garlic clove, minced

1½ pounds small, firm, fresh okra, stems removed, washed well, and cut into ¾-inch rounds

4 ripe but firm large tomatoes, peeled and chopped

1 small hot red pepper, seeded and finely chopped

2 teaspoons salt

Freshly ground black pepper to taste

Pinch of dried thyme

Pinch of dried basil

Cooked white rice

In a large, heavy, nonreactive skillet (not cast-iron or aluminum), fry the bacon over moderate heat till crisp, drain on paper towels, crumble, and set aside.

Pour off all but about 2 tablespoons of fat from the skillet, add the onions and garlic, and cook, stirring, about 5 minutes. Add the okra, tomatoes, red pepper, salt, pepper, thyme, and basil, reduce the heat to low, cover, and simmer till the okra and tomatoes are just soft but not mushy, about 15 minutes, stirring once or twice.

Serve the okra and tomatoes over mounds of rice and top each serving with crumbled bacon.

262

BATTER-FRIED OKRA

Makes 4 to 5 servings

WHILE YANKEES ALMOST GAG AT THE SIGHT OF THE slimy boiled or braised okra beloved by so many Rebels, I've yet to meet one who didn't take to dry, crisp fried okra almost from the first bite. And, Lord, there really is nothing more delicious or addictive than a basket of batter-fried okra nibbled with cocktails or served as a side dish to numerous Southern specialties. Only fresh okra should be fried, and use nothing but small, green pods that have no blemishes or dark spots (signs that the okra is tough and way over the hill). Some Southern cooks like to parboil okra briefly, refresh it under cold running water, and dry it to cut the frying time in half. Others believe that soaking the okra in ice water about 15 minutes makes it much crisper when fried. Whatever the method used, the two cardinal rules for frying okra are never to crowd the pan and never try to keep okra warm in the oven, which only makes it soggy.

1½ pounds small, firm fresh okra

1 cup white cornmeal or fine cracker crumbs

1 teaspoon salt

Freshly ground black pepper to taste

1 cup regular buttermilk

1 large egg, beaten

Tabasco sauce to taste

Lard or vegetable shortening, for deep frying

Rinse the okra well, remove the stems, and either leave the pods whole or cut them into ½-inch rounds. Bring a large pot of water to a boil, add the okra, and parboil 2 minutes. Drain in a colander, refresh under cold running water, and pat dry with paper towels.

In a shallow bowl, combine the cornmeal, salt, pepper, buttermilk, egg, and Tabasco and beat till the batter is smooth.

In a large, heavy iron skillet, heat enough lard or shortening to reach about ½ inch up the sides till very hot, about 375°F on a deep-frying thermometer. In batches, dip the okra into the batter till well coated, allowing excess batter to drain off, then carefully drop the battered okra into the fat, without overcrowding the pan, and fry till golden brown and crisp, 3 to 4 minutes. With a slotted spoon, transfer the okra to a large cookie sheet covered with paper towels and, if you like, sprinkle with a little extra salt. Serve hot with cocktails or as a side dish.

BAKED VIDALIA ONIONS STUFFED
WITH COUNTRY HAM AND CHANTERELLES

Makes 6 servings

VIDALIA ONIONS, LIKE WALLA WALLAS FROM
Washington State or Mauis from Hawaii, are some of the
sweetest onions on earth and one of the most treasured
vegetables of Southern cookery. Grown exclusively in or
around Vidalia, Georgia, the onions derive their delicacy
from soil with a low sulfur content (sulfur being the
culprit that makes most onions so strong). So protective
is the region of its valuable asset that each onion (or
string sack of onions) must be certified (and tagged) as
authentic by the Vidalia Chamber of Commerce. While
just ten years ago genuine Vidalias outside the South
were generally available only at specialty food markets
from about May to July, today the onions can be found
in most supermarkets during the growing season.
Southerners eat them fried, sautéed, roasted, even raw,
but never are the onions so loved as when stuffed with
all sorts of ingredients, slowly baked, and served as a
light luncheon dish or sophisticated side vegetable.

6 large Vidalia onions (about 4 pounds)

8 tablespoons (1 stick) butter

*4 medium scallions, trimmed of all but 2 inches
of green tops and finely chopped*

1 garlic clove, minced

4 dashes Tabasco sauce

*3 cups finely chopped fresh chanterelle
mushrooms*

2 cups finely chopped country cooked ham

½ cup finely chopped fresh parsley leaves

Pinch of powdered dried sage

Pinch of ground cinnamon

½ cup heavy cream

1 tablespoon dry sherry

Salt and freshly ground black pepper to taste

1 cup dry red wine

1 cup beef broth

4 tablespoons minced fresh chives

Preheat the oven to 350°F.

Peel each onion and cut off and discard a thick slice from the stem end. Scoop out the centers of each with a melon baller or sturdy spoon, leaving a ¼-inch shell. Finely chop enough of the centers to measure 1 cup and set aside.

Bring a large pot of salted water to a boil, add the onion shells, and cook 5 minutes. Invert the onions on paper towels and drain.

In a large skillet, melt 4 tablespoons of the butter over moderate heat, add the reserved chopped onions, the scallions, garlic, and Tabasco, and cook, stirring, till the vegetables are softened, about 3 minutes. Add the remaining 4 tablespoons of butter, the mushrooms, ham, parsley, sage, and cinnamon and continue stirring till the mushrooms are soft, about 5 minutes. Add the cream, sherry, and salt and pepper, stir well, and let cook about 5 minutes longer. Remove the stuffing from the heat.

Sprinkle the onion shells with salt and pepper to taste, arrange them open side up in a casserole or baking dish just large enough to hold them, and divide the stuffing among them, mounding it. In a bowl, combine the wine and beef broth, pour enough around the onions to reach 1 inch up the sides, cover with foil, and bake for 1 hour, basting once or twice.

To serve, transfer the onions with a slotted spoon to a heated serving platter and sprinkle the tops with chives.

VIDALIA ONION AND RICE CASSEROLE

Makes 4 to 6 servings

THIS IS THE SORT OF CASSEROLE A SOUTHERN COOK will whip up when sweet Vidalia onions are in season or when a simple but unusual side dish is needed to complement a baked ham, roasted leg of lamb, or barbecued chicken. Just remember not to cook the onions and rice too long before baking them with the other ingredients, and do check after about 50 minutes to make sure the casserole is still moist and not in the least dried out.

4 tablespoons (½ stick) butter

7 Vidalia onions, sliced

5 cups water

1 teaspoon salt

½ cup uncooked long-grain rice

1 cup grated genuine Swiss cheese (Emmenthaler)

⅔ cup half-and-half

Freshly ground black pepper to taste

Preheat the oven to 325°F.

In a large, heavy skillet, melt the butter over moderate heat, add the onions, and cook, stirring, till softened, about 10 minutes. Remove from the heat.

In a saucepan, combine the water and salt and bring to a boil. Add the rice, stir, cook for 5 minutes, and drain well.

In a large bowl, combine the onions, rice, cheese, half-and-half, and pepper, stir till well blended, scrape into a buttered 1½-quart casserole, and bake till golden, about 1 hour. Serve hot.

Fried Green Tomatoes

Makes 8 servings

ALTHOUGH THE EVER-ADVENTURESOME THOMAS Jefferson was growing tomatoes in 1782, it was not till well into the nineteenth century that the general public fully overcame the universal fear of tomatoes as poisonous and the vegetable (actually a fruit) developed the same popularity it enjoys today. Southern fried green tomatoes evolved simply as a breakfast or supper dish to be made with the season's last fresh tomatoes that refused to ripen before being hit by frost. I can still see my maternal grandmother coming back into the house on chilly fall mornings with her hands full of green tomatoes, which she'd proceed to slice and fry up in pure bacon grease. Today, like most sensible Southerners, I opt for peanut or vegetable oil for frying tomatoes, but rest assured that fried green tomatoes just wouldn't be the same without at least a tablespoon of bacon grease added to the oil for flavor. Personally, I've always loved the tomatoes primarily for breakfast (along with, of course, eggs, sausage, grits, and fresh biscuits), but after having them recently as an appetizer before attacking the copious Southern lunch buffet at the famous Lady & Sons restaurant in Savannah, Georgia, I could be about to change my mind.

5 medium green tomatoes

2 large eggs

½ cup whole milk

1½ cups white or yellow cornmeal

Salt and freshly ground black pepper to taste

Peanut oil for frying

1 to 2 tablespoons bacon grease

Cut out and discard the stems of the tomatoes, then cut the tomatoes into ¼-inch-thick slices.

In a shallow dish, beat the eggs with the milk. Combine the cornmeal and salt and pepper in another shallow dish. Dip the tomato slices in the egg mixture, dredge them lightly in the cornmeal, place the slices on a baking sheet, cover with plastic wrap, and chill about 30 minutes.

In a large cast-iron skillet, heat ½ inch of oil plus the bacon grease over moderately high heat till a little cornmeal flicked into the fat sputters. In batches, fry the tomatoes till golden, about 1 minute on each side, drain on paper towels, and keep warm on a platter till ready to serve.

CALABASH COLESLAW

Makes 6 to 8 servings

DERIVING FROM THE OLD ENGLISH WORD FOR CABBAGE (*cole*), "cole slaugh" was mentioned as early as 1839 in Lettice Bryan's *The Kentucky Housewife* and is, without question, the most popular form of salad in the South. It would be inconceivable to eat any style of pork barbecue without coleslaw; it is traditionally served at fish fries and oyster roasts; and crab cakes or barbecued ribs without a mound of fresh slaw on the side would be like hot blackberry cobbler without a scoop of vanilla ice cream on top. Coleslaw can be made with green or red cabbage, shredded or grated, enhanced with carrots, onions, sweet pickle, seeds, a little mustard or sugar, and even pineapple, and bound with mayonnaise, vinegar, sour cream, or a combination of all three. (In the old days, slaw in the South was always made with a boiled vinegar dressing, but you rarely find this today.) At the many fried fish houses that constitute the hamlet of Calabash, North Carolina, coleslaw is almost a religion, and the best, in my opinion, is served in almost unlimited quantities at a venerable place called Ella's. Like potato salad, coleslaw loses most of its character (and becomes soggy) after just a day, so I always make it fresh, and suggest you do the same. As for these more innovative creations today, which substitute various bell and chile peppers, exotic root vegetables, and strange leafy greens for the cabbage, they might taste good, but that ain't coleslaw.

1 medium head green cabbage (about 2 pounds)

1 large carrot, scraped

1 small onion, peeled

1½ tablespoons cider vinegar

½ teaspoon celery seeds

Salt and freshly ground black pepper to taste

¾ cup mayonnaise

Remove and discard the outer loose leaves of the cabbage, cut the head into quarters, cut out and discard the hard center core, and shred the quarters into a large glass bowl. Shred the carrots into the bowl, then the onion, and mix to blend.

In a small bowl, combine the remaining ingredients and mix till well blended and smooth. Pour the dressing over the cabbage mixture, toss till well blended, cover the bowl with plastic wrap, and chill 2 hours before serving.

268

Carolina Barbecue Coleslaw

Makes about 8 servings as a side dish

WHILE MEMPHIS-STYLE, ALABAMAN, AND EVEN MOIST western North Carolinian barbecue is almost always served with a creamy or mayonnaise-based coleslaw, in the self-proclaimed barbecue capital of the universe, namely eastern North Carolina (Goldsboro, Rocky Mount, Raleigh, Wilson, etc.), tangy-sweet vinegar coleslaw remains the law of the land. "Honey, if you want salad dressing, order a tossed salad," I was once told by an indignant waitress at Melton's Barbecue in Rocky Mount when I asked, simply out of curiosity, if the slaw contained any mayonnaise. With fried fish, crab cakes, and barbecued ribs, I definitely prefer a creamy coleslaw, but when it comes to a chopped dry pork barbecue sandwich, this is the coleslaw I spoon over the meat inside the bun. Since both styles can be easily tested with a single bowl of shredded cabbage, why not just experiment to determine your preference?

1 medium head green cabbage (about 2 pounds)

½ cup cider vinegar

¼ cup sugar

1 tablespoon butter, melted

¼ teaspoon celery seeds

¼ teaspoon dry mustard

¼ teaspoon red pepper flakes

¼ teaspoon salt

¼ teaspoon freshly ground black pepper

Remove and discard any blemished outer leaves of the cabbage, cut the head into quarters, cut out and discard the hard inner core, and shred the quarters into a large glass bowl.

In another bowl, whisk together all remaining ingredients till thoroughly blended, pour over the cabbage, and toss till the cabbage is well coated with the dressing. Cover the bowl with plastic wrap and chill 2 hours before serving with any barbecued meats or on a chopped pork barbecue sandwich.

269

Appalachian Cabbage and Bacon Pudding

Makes 4 to 6 servings

IT'S SAID THAT THE VAST CABBAGE FIELDS FOUND along the Appalachian borders of Virginia, North Carolina, and Tennessee were started by the region's original Scotch Irish settlers, but it took the modern-day culinary pioneer Bill Neal, owner/chef of Crook's Corner restaurant in Carrboro, North Carolina, to unearth this ancient pudding up in the Blue Ridge Mountains and transform it into a sublime, rather elegant custard that is served in slices. Bill used streak-o'-lean (lean salt pork) in his pudding, but craving a more smoky flavor, I've substituted slab bacon. Served with country ham biscuits, the pudding makes an unusual and delicious cold-weather luncheon dish, but since it's so attractive unmolded on a platter, it's also perfect for the more formal buffet table.

1 medium head of cabbage (about 2 pounds)

2½ quarts water

2 ounces slab bacon

1 dried red pepper pod

2 cups milk

3 large eggs

1 teaspoon salt

¼ teaspoon dry mustard

⅛ teaspoon cayenne pepper

Freshly ground black pepper to taste

1 cup small bread cubes

½ teaspoon dried thyme, crumbled

¼ cup fine white bread crumbs

2 tablespoons butter, melted

Preheat the oven to 350°F.

Remove and discard any outer blemished leaves of the cabbage, cut the head into quarters, and cut out the hard core. Pour the water into a large pot, add the bacon and the pepper pod, and bring to a boil. Add the cabbage quarters, boil 15 minutes, refresh under cold water, and drain, discarding the pepper pod and reserving the bacon. Chop the cabbage roughly, squeeze it with your hands to remove all excess moisture, and reserve in a large bowl.

In a bowl, combine the milk, eggs, salt, dry mustard, cayenne pepper, and black pepper, whisk till well blended, and pour over the cabbage. Dice the cooked bacon, combine in a small bowl with the bread cubes and thyme, and toss.

Sprinkle the bread crumbs evenly over the bottom and sides of a buttered 1½-quart soufflé dish or casserole, spread the cabbage mixture evenly over the dish, and top with the bacon-and–bread cube mixture. Drizzle the melted butter over the top and bake till the custard is set, about 50 minutes.

To serve, invert the pudding onto a platter and cut into rough slices. Serve hot.

Rice & Grits

Pecan Rice

Arkansas Dirty Rice

Mrs. Wilkes' Savannah Red Rice

Cajun Red Beans and Rice

Crawfish Jambalaya

Oak Alley Chicken and Ham Pilaf

Jefferson Perloo

St. Augustine Shrimp
and Oyster Pilau

Salmon and Rice Mold

Shrimp Bog

Brown Rice with
Shiitake Mushrooms

Grits with Red-Eye Gravy

Cheese Grits

Fried Grits

Paula's Tomato Grits

Grits, Ham, and Turnip Greens
Soufflé

Creole Grits and Grillades

Gullah Shrimp
and Grits Casserole

Captain Jules's Shrimp and Grits

Tennessee Shrimp and Grits

Baked Grits with Country Ham
and Oyster Mushrooms

Tarpon Springs Feta Grits Soufflé

Peabody Grits Pudding

PECAN RICE

Makes 4 to 6 servings

THIS IS THE TYPE OF SIMPLE RICE DISH A SOUTHERN cook might whip up at the last minute if he or she decided a starch was needed to complement a roast chicken or turkey, a meat stew, or a creamed seafood preparation. I've also made this rice with toasted pine nuts, poppy seeds, and even crushed peanuts, and in the Carolina Lowcountry, you might well find it with benne (sesame) seeds.

2 tablespoons butter

1 small onion, minced

3 tablespoons finely chopped fresh parsley leaves

2 tablespoons finely chopped pimentos

Salt and freshly ground black pepper to taste

1 cup raw long-grain rice

2 cups chicken broth

¼ cup crushed toasted pecans

In a saucepan, melt the butter over moderate heat, add the onion, and stir till golden brown, about 8 minutes. Add the parsley, pimentos, and salt and pepper and stir well. Add the rice and stir till just glistening, about 2 minutes. Add the chicken broth, bring to a boil, reduce the heat to low, cover, and simmer till all the liquid is absorbed and the rice is tender, 15 to 20 minutes. Remove from the heat and let stand, covered, about 10 minutes. Add the pecans, fluff well with a fork, and serve hot.

Arkansas Dirty Rice

Makes 6 to servings

BASICALLY A SPECIALTY OF THE LOUISIANA AND
Mississippi bayous, dirty rice, which derives its name
and color from the chicken livers and gizzards that
provide its rich, earthy, utterly compelling flavor, can be
found today in homes, cafés, and even some pretty
snazzy restaurants from West Virginia to Alabama to
Georgia. Generally, the meats in the rice are limited to
the chicken parts, but one of the most memorable
versions I've ever had, which also included a little pork
sausage, was at a delightful roadside café near Stuttgart,
Arkansas. (And people seem to forget not only that much
of the nation's rice is produced in the northwestern
lowlands of Arkansas, but also that Arkansas is the
home of the giant Tyson chicken empire.) Dirty rice is
usually served as a side dish, but it also makes a great
main course served with a salad and Scallion Cornsticks
(page 307).

½ pound bulk pork sausage

1 medium onion, finely chopped

2 ribs celery, finely chopped

*1 medium green bell pepper, seeded and finely
chopped*

1 garlic clove, minced

4 tablespoons (½ stick) butter

½ pound chicken livers, membrane removed

½ pound chicken gizzards, membrane removed

½ teaspoon dried thyme, crumbled

½ teaspoon dried oregano, crumbled

Salt and freshly ground black pepper to taste

2½ cups chicken broth

1½ cups long-grain rice

In a large, cast-iron skillet, break up the sausage, fry
over moderate heat till thoroughly cooked, about 10
minutes, drain on paper towels, and drain all but about
3 tablespoons of grease from the skillet. Add the onion,
celery, bell pepper, and garlic to the skillet and stir over
moderate heat about 3 minutes. Add the butter, livers,
gizzards, thyme, oregano, and salt and pepper, stir well,
and cook, stirring, till the meats are cooked through,
about 10 minutes. Add the chicken broth, return the
heat to moderate, stir, and continue cooking about 8
minutes. Add the sausage and rice, stir, reduce the heat
to low, cover, and cook till the rice has absorbed all the
liquid and is tender, 15 to 20 minutes. Serve hot.

Mrs. Wilkes' Savannah Red Rice

Makes 6 servings

SELMA WILKES FINALLY PASSED TO HER REWARD a couple of years ago at age ninety-five, after operating her legendary Mrs. Wilkes' Boarding House restaurant (today, Mrs. Wilkes' Dining Room) in Savannah for more than half a century. Many were the times I stood in the long lunch line out front to sit at a communal table, eat fried chicken, stewed okra and tomatoes, and squash casserole, and, of course, to chat with Mrs. Wilkes. The array of Southern dishes there was staggering, and none was so luscious as her version of this great Savannah rice specialty bursting with tomatoes. Today, Mrs. Wilkes' great-grandson continues most of the sacred tradition (minus breakfast), and, blessedly, the red rice is as glorious as ever. In Savannah, the rice is always served as a side dish, but if you want to transform it into a main course, as I've done on occasion, add about half a pound of small peeled and deveined shrimp or sliced link pork sausages that have been browned, along with a little chicken broth or water, before transferring the mixture to the casserole.

4 strips lean bacon

2 medium onions, chopped

2 medium green bell peppers, seeded and chopped

2 cups cooked long-grain rice

One 16-ounce can stewed tomatoes (juices included)

1 cup tomato juice

Salt and freshly ground black pepper to taste

Tabasco sauce to taste

Preheat the oven to 325°F.

In a large skillet, fry the bacon over moderate heat till almost crisp and drain on paper towels, reserving grease in the skillet. Crumble the bacon. Add the onions and bell peppers to the skillet and cook, stirring, till slightly browned, about 10 minutes. Add the rice, tomatoes plus their juices, tomato juice, salt and pepper, and Tabasco and cook, stirring, 5 minutes longer.

Scrape the mixture into a greased 2-quart casserole and bake, covered, till the rice is slightly dry, about 30 minutes.

Cajun Red Beans and Rice

Makes 6 servings

A BIG BOWL OF RED BEANS AND RICE, MAYBE A FEW links of spicy sausage, a small loaf of hot French bread, and bottles of ice-cold Dixie beer—such is the traditional menu on any given Monday in homes, cafés, and unpretentious restaurants throughout the Louisiana Delta and in New Orleans. No matter that the beans and rice can contain ham hocks, diced chicken, smoked sausage, salt pork, or a local packaged seasoning called "pickled pork"—depending on the self-appointed authority in the kitchen. So long as the beans and rice are tender and well-flavored and there's a bowl of chopped red onions to sprinkle over the top, everybody's happy. "Don't you ever eat a salad or some slaw to cut all that starch and fat?" I once asked a proudly stout local in Thibodaux. "Boy, if you gotta have stuff like that, you shouldn't be eatin' red beans and rice," he snapped indignantly.

1½ cups dried kidney beans, rinsed and picked over

3 tablespoons vegetable oil

1 medium onion, chopped

1 rib celery, chopped

½ small green bell pepper, seeded and chopped

1 garlic clove, minced

½ pound garlic or smoked sausage, thinly sliced

1 small hot red pepper, chopped

¼ teaspoon dried thyme, crumbled

¼ teaspoon dried oregano, crumbled

1 bay leaf

Salt and freshly ground black pepper to taste

1 tablespoon cider vinegar

1 cup uncooked long-grain rice

2 cups chicken broth

½ cup diced cooked ham

1 red onion, finely chopped

Place the kidney beans in a large, heavy pot with enough cold water to cover by 3 inches and let soak overnight. Drain the beans in a colander and dry the pot.

Heat the oil in the pot over moderate heat, add the onion, celery, bell pepper, and garlic, and stir till the vegetables soften, about 3 minutes. Return the soaked beans to the pot and add the sausage, red pepper, thyme, oregano, bay leaf, salt and pepper, vinegar, and enough water to cover by 1 inch. Bring to a low simmer, cover, and cook till the beans are tender and most of the liquid has been absorbed, 35 to 40 minutes.

Meanwhile, in a medium saucepan, combine the rice, chicken broth, ham, and salt to taste and bring to a boil. Reduce the heat to moderate, cover, and cook till all the liquid has been absorbed, about 15 minutes.

In a large serving bowl, combine the beans-and-rice mixture, stir well, and serve with chopped red onion sprinkled over each portion.

275

CRAWFISH JAMBALAYA

Makes 6 servings

POSSIBLY THE MOST FAMOUS OF ALL LOUISIANA Cajun-Creole creations, jambalaya has as many versions, and utilizes as wide a variety of ingredients, as any dish in all of American cookery. The name most likely derives from the French *jambon* (ham), the African *ya* (rice), with an *à la* tossed in to link the two primary ingredients, but as anyone who has visited New Orleans or Cajun country knows, everything from pork, sausage, chicken, crawfish, shrimp, and various vegetables and seasonings can show up in the dish. All Louisianans take their jambalaya very seriously, but none more so than the citizens of the Cajun town of Gonzales, where an official jambalaya cook-off takes place every year. My own romance with jambalaya began many years ago, when I was asked to judge an enormous buffet of dishes in New Orleans prepared by some two dozen unknown local chefs. When I pointed to a sublime jambalaya and said I'd like to meet the person responsible, over stalked an enormous man who quietly introduced himself as Paul Prudhomme. In this particular recipe, feel free to use small fresh shrimp if crawfish are not available, as well as a half a cup or so of cooked ham, spicy dried sausage, or even leftover cubed chicken.

8 tablespoons (1 stick) butter

1 large onion, finely chopped

3 garlic cloves, minced

2 ribs celery, chopped

½ green bell pepper, seeded and chopped

1 pound crawfish tails (fresh or frozen)

1½ cups chicken broth

1½ cups bottled clam juice

1 large ripe tomato, chopped

2 scallions (green tops included), chopped

¼ cup chopped fresh parsley leaves

¼ teaspoon dried thyme, crumbled

1 bay leaf

½ teaspoon salt

¼ teaspoon freshly ground black pepper

Tabasco sauce to taste

1½ cups regular long-grain rice

In a large pot, melt the butter over moderate heat, add the onion, garlic, celery, and bell pepper, and cook, stirring, till the vegetables are fully softened, about 10 minutes. Stir in all remaining ingredients except the rice, bring to a boil, reduce the heat to low, and simmer about 10 minutes. Return to a boil, add the rice, stir, reduce the heat again to low, and cook, covered, stirring occasionally from the bottom of the pot, till the rice has absorbed most of the liquid, 25 to 30 minutes. (If necessary, add a little more chicken broth to prevent the jambalaya from scorching or drying out too much.) Fluff the jambalaya with a fork and serve hot.

OAK ALLEY CHICKEN AND HAM PILAF

Makes 6 to 8 servings

EVERGREEN, NOTTOWAY, MADEWOOD, LAURA—THESE and other restored Mississippi River plantations dot the Louisiana landscape along "River Road" from Baton Rouge to New Orleans, and none is more regal than the two-story, white-columned, Greek Revival Oak Alley plantation at Vacherie, where I was once served a chicken and ham pilaf much like this one in the mansion's cypress-paneled dining room. Down in New Orleans, the dish would probably be called jambalaya, while over in the Carolinas and Georgia, it would be referred to as a "pilau" or "perloo". How *pullao* from India evolved in the American South as "pilaf", "pilau", "perloo", and even "purlow" in multiple guises remains, of course, one of the great culinary mysteries—the single unifying distinction being the importance of rice. Do remember that, like a jambalaya, this dish must be dry and fluffy.

5 strips bacon, cut into pieces

1 large onion, finely chopped

1½ cups raw long-grain rice

2 cups chicken broth

2 large ripe tomatoes, peeled, seeded, and chopped

2 tablespoons fresh lemon juice

2 teaspoons Worcestershire sauce

Salt and freshly ground black pepper to taste

Cayenne pepper to taste

2 cups diced cooked chicken

2 cups diced cooked ham

3 tablespoons chopped pimentos

¼ cup minced fresh parsley leaves

Preheat the oven to 350°F.

In a heavy skillet, fry the bacon over moderate heat till crisp, drain on paper towels, and crumble, reserving the grease.

Pour about 3 tablespoons of the bacon grease into a heavy, flameproof 2-quart casserole, add the onions, and cook, stirring, over moderate heat till softened, about 5 minutes. Add the rice and stir till well coated with the fat. Add the chicken broth, tomatoes, lemon juice, Worcestershire, salt and pepper, and cayenne pepper and bring the liquid to a boil. Place the casserole in the oven, cover, and bake 25 minutes.

Add the chicken, ham, pimentos, and bacon, stir till well blended, cover, and bake another 20 minutes. Remove from the oven and let stand 10 minutes. Sprinkle with the parsley, fluff with a fork, and serve hot.

JEFFERSON PERLOO

Makes 4 to 6 servings

SINCE RECORDS SHOW THAT THIS PERLOO WAS A
favorite of Thomas Jefferson, the dish must have been
almost as popular during Colonial days in Virginia as in
the rice-producing Carolinas. Both pistachios and
Mediterranean pine nuts were being cultivated in Italy
when Jefferson traveled there in the late eighteenth
century, and given his passion for importing and growing
exotic new foods in the vast Mount Vernon garden, most
likely he had a few of these tree varieties that would later
create such a large market in the American Southwest.
(Curiously, during Jefferson's time, pine nuts were also
referred to as "Indian nuts.") This is perloo in its
simplest form, a rice side dish that goes well with
virtually any meats, fowl, or creamed seafood.

1 cup chicken broth

1 cup water

4 tablespoons (½ stick) butter

1 teaspoon salt

1 cup raw long-grain rice

½ cup pine nuts

¼ cup shelled pistachio nuts

¼ teaspoon ground nutmeg

In a large saucepan, combine the chicken broth, water,
2 tablespoons of the butter, and salt and bring to a boil.
Add the rice, stir well, reduce the heat to low, cover,
and simmer till the rice has absorbed all the liquid and
is tender, about 20 minutes.

Meanwhile, melt the remaining butter in a medium
skillet over moderate heat, add the nuts, and cook,
stirring occasionally, till barely golden, about 10
minutes. Remove from the heat.

Transfer the rice to a serving bowl and fluff it with a
fork. Add the nuts and the nutmeg, toss till well
blended, and serve immediately.

278

St. Augustine Shrimp and Oyster Pilau

Makes 6 servings

IT'S EASY ENOUGH TO TRACE THE ORIGINS OF plantation culture in the Carolinas and Georgia back to the first shipments of rice (most probably from India) to the port of Charleston, South Carolina. It's another matter trying to explain the spellings and pronunciations of all the exotic "pilaus", "pilafs", "perloos", "pilloes", and "plaws" that evolved in kitchens all over the South and created a veritable genre of cooking. Pilaus, like Cajun jambalaya, were made with everything from chicken to ham to seafood to okra, and the more elaborate these rice preparations became, the more additional regions laid claim to them. Today, the citizens of St. Augustine, Florida, proudly tout their shrimp and oyster pilau as if it arrived with the city's founding fathers, reminding visitors that St. Augustine was settled some fifty years before the Virginia Jamestown colony. Just don't tell that to the perloo fans up in Charleston and Norfolk, Virginia, the pilaf enthusiasts of Kentucky, or the jambalaya experts in Louisiana.

6 slices bacon, cut into pieces

3 medium onions, chopped

2 cups uncooked rice

2 cups chicken broth

3 medium ripe tomatoes, chopped

One 4-ounce jar pimentos, drained and chopped

2 teaspoons Worcestershire sauce

1 teaspoon ground nutmeg

1 bay leaf

Salt and freshly ground black pepper to taste

½ teaspoon cayenne pepper

1 pound medium fresh shrimp, shelled and deveined

1 pint fresh oysters (liquor included)

In a large, heavy pot, fry the bacon over moderate heat till crisp, drain on paper towels, and set aside. Pour off all but about 3 tablespoons of fat from the pot, add the onions, and cook, stirring, till just softened, about 3 minutes. Add the rice and stir till the grains glisten with fat. Add the chicken broth, tomatoes, pimentos, Worcestershire, nutmeg, bay leaf, salt and pepper, and cayenne pepper and stir. Bring to a low simmer, cover, and cook for 30 minutes. Add the shrimp, oysters, and reserved bacon and toss well. Return to a simmer, cover, and cook till most of the liquid has been absorbed, the shrimp are pink, and the oysters curled, about 8 minutes. Fluff the pilau with a fork and serve hot.

SALMON AND RICE MOLD

Makes 10 to 12 servings

FOR GENERATIONS IN THE SOUTH, RICE HAS OFTEN been used instead of bread crumbs to bind all sorts of chopped, flaked, and minced savory concoctions, one reason being that the grain not only tightens a mixture better but contributes a good deal more to its texture than does innocuous bread. This particular dish is the type of elegant mold you find on large, elaborate spring or summer dinner buffets. It can be served either as is or with a chilled light tomato sauce or sour cream and dill mayonnaise on the side. You can also use this same recipe to produce a light, stylish luncheon "soufflé" by simply whisking the egg whites separately and folding them into the combined mixture before baking it in a soufflé dish.

Mild paprika

3 cups canned salmon, drained, picked over for skin and bones, and flaked

3 cups cooked rice of your choice

⅔ cup milk

4 large eggs, beaten

2 tablespoons butter, melted

1 small onion, finely chopped

¼ cup finely chopped green olives stuffed with pimentos

¼ cup finely chopped fresh parsley leaves

2 tablespoons finely chopped fresh dill

Juice of 1 lemon

Salt and freshly ground black pepper to taste

Thinly sliced cucumbers, for garnish

Preheat the oven to 475°F. Grease a large fish mold with butter, sprinkle the bottom and sides with paprika, and set aside.

In a large mixing bowl, combine the remaining ingredients except the cucumbers and, using your hands, mix till well blended. Scrape the mixture into the prepared mold and bake till firm, about 45 minutes. Transfer the mold to a wire rack, drain off any liquid, let cool completely, cover with plastic wrap, and chill for at least 2 hours.

To serve, invert the mold onto a large serving platter, sweep the paprika with a spoon to make fin designs, garnish the edges with cucumbers, and serve in thick slices.

SHRIMP BOG

Makes 6 servings

GENERALLY, A BOG IS A WETLAND, BUT IN THE Carolina and Georgia Lowcountry, the term more often refers to any dish that includes wet, soggy rice (unlike a dry, fluffy perloo or jambalaya). When I asked my old friend Bobby King, from Conway, South Carolina, to send me his recipe for chicken or shrimp bog, here's part of what he said: "Growing up in coastal South Carolina on a tobacco farm where they planted rice generations ago, we always had a live-in black housekeeper and cook— first Leila, then Kitsy, and finally Lizzie. Lizzie was the best cook, but she never used a cookbook or wrote anything down, so all we ever got in the way of recipes was a couple of fresh chickens or pounds of shrimp, a few big handfuls of rice, a stick of butter, onions and carrots, and some celery. Lord, Lizzie made the best bogs on earth, and the only time I didn't love her was when she'd poke a broomstick at me in the mornings to get me up to go to school." Bobby did manage to reconstruct Lizzie's chicken bog recipe, but, good as it is, for me there's nothing so sumptuous as this bog made with bacon, shrimp, and ripe tomatoes. Just remember that the rice must be almost soupy.

½ pound bacon, finely diced

2 medium onions, finely chopped

1½ cups uncooked rice

2¼ cups chicken broth

2 medium ripe tomatoes, peeled, finely chopped, with the juices retained

2 teaspoons fresh lemon juice

1½ teaspoons Worcestershire sauce

1 teaspoon salt

½ teaspoon freshly ground black pepper

¼ teaspoon cayenne pepper

¼ teaspoon ground nutmeg

2 pounds fresh, medium shrimp, shelled and deveined

¼ cup minced fresh parsley leaves

In a large, heavy pot, fry the bacon over moderate heat till crisp, drain on paper towels, and set aside. Pour off all but 3 tablespoons of the fat, add the onion to the pot, and cook, stirring, for 3 minutes. Add the rice and stir till it glistens with fat. Stir in the chicken broth, tomatoes with their juices, lemon juice, Worcestershire, salt, pepper, cayenne pepper, and nutmeg, bring to a low simmer, cover, and cook 20 minutes. Stir in the crumbled bacon and the shrimp and continue cooking, uncovered, for 10 minutes, adding a little more broth if the rice seems to be drying out. Stir the bog with a fork, taste for seasoning, sprinkle the parsley on top, and serve hot.

BROWN RICE WITH SHIITAKE MUSHROOMS

Makes 4 servings

BROWN RICE, WHICH IS THE ENTIRE UNPOLISHED grain containing the germ and outer layer of bran (hence the tan coloring), is much prized for its nutty flavor and chewy texture through much of the South, and is even used to make elaborate perloos and bogs in and around Charleston and Savannah. Because of the bran, however, brown rice needs more liquid and longer cooking than regular white long-grain (or Carolina) rice. Today, in better restaurants, you find more and more brown rice prepared with all sorts of earthy wild mushrooms, as in this recipe. To add even more flavor and textural contrast to the dish, some cooks are even adding ingredients such as toasted pine nuts or pecans. The rice should be fluffy but still quite moist. And be warned: once you're hooked on brown rice, the white can seem pretty bland.

1 medium onion, chopped

1 rib celery, chopped

2 tablespoons butter

Two 10½-ounce cans beef broth

1 cup uncooked brown rice

1 cup finely chopped fresh shiitake mushrooms

Salt and freshly ground black pepper to taste

In a large saucepan, combine the onion, celery, butter, and beef broth and bring to a boil. Gradually add the rice, stirring, reduce the heat to low, cover, and simmer for about 30 minutes. Add the mushrooms and salt and pepper, stir, cover, and simmer till all the liquid is absorbed by the rice, about 20 minutes longer. (The rice should be slightly moist but fluffy.) Serve hot.

282

GRITS WITH RED-EYE GRAVY

Makes 4 servings

CLASSIC SOUTHERN RED-EYE GRAVY IS TRADITIONALLY made by simply adding a little water or brewed coffee to a skillet in which slices of country ham have been fried and deglazing it by scraping the bottom with a spatula or spoon. When, however, grits are featured as the main item in a hearty breakfast, a deluxe version of the gravy, such as this one, is always in order. Typically, these grits would be served with eggs, maybe a few fried green tomatoes, biscuits, and some form of fresh fruit. I defy even the most uninitiated Yankee not to gobble up every morsel.

FOR THE GRAVY

2 strips bacon

8 ounces country ham, cut into bits

1 scallion (part of green top included), minced

1 teaspoon dried sage, crumbled

Freshly ground black pepper to taste

2 tablespoons all-purpose flour

½ cup brewed strong coffee

½ cup water

FOR THE GRITS

1 cup milk

1 cup water

½ teaspoon salt

½ cup regular grits

To make the gravy, fry the bacon in a skillet over moderate heat till crisp, drain on paper towels, and crumble. Add the ham to the skillet with the bacon grease and cook, stirring, till slightly browned, about 5 minutes. Add the scallion, sage, and pepper, and stir for about 1 minute. Sprinkle the flour over the top and cook, stirring, till nicely browned, about 2 minutes. Add the coffee and water, cook, stirring, till the gravy is thick, about 2 minutes. Keep warm.

To make the grits, combine the milk, water, and salt in a heavy saucepan and bring to a boil. Gradually add the grits, stirring, and cook, stirring constantly, till thick and creamy, 15 to 20 minutes.

283

To serve, spoon a mound of grits on each serving plate, spoon equal amounts of the gravy over the top, and sprinkle each serving with crumbled bacon.

Cheese Grits

Makes 6 servings

I'VE ALWAYS SAID THAT THE BEST WAY TO CONVERT non-Southerners to our sacred grits tradition is to serve them a casserole of cheese grits. And, to be honest, since grits by themselves can be pretty bland unless you're using the stone-ground variety, a little cheese does wonders to perk them up. To give the dish even more character, you can also add a clove of minced garlic to the mixture before baking, and I know at least one fellow Rebel who thinks nothing of stirring a few chopped herbs into his cheese grits. Do allow this casserole to "tighten up" for about 10 minutes outside the oven before serving.

3 cups water

1 teaspoon salt

1 cup quick-cooking grits

4 tablespoons (½ stick) butter, cut into pieces

½ cup whole sour cream

1 large egg, beaten

6 ounces Swiss cheese, shredded

¾ cup freshly grated Parmesan cheese

Freshly ground black pepper to taste

Paprika to taste

2 tablespoons butter, melted

Preheat the oven to 325°F.

In a large saucepan, combine the water and salt and bring to a boil. Add the grits, reduce the heat to moderately low, and cook, stirring, till the grits are thick and creamy, about 5 minutes.

Remove the pan from the heat, add the butter, and stir till the butter has melted. Add the sour cream, egg, Swiss cheese, ¼ cup of the Parmesan, pepper, and paprika and stir till the ingredients are well blended and the mixture is smooth. Scrape into a 1½-quart buttered baking dish or casserole, sprinkle the remaining ½ cup Parmesan over the top, drizzle the melted butter over the Parmesan, and bake till golden brown, 45 to 50 minutes. Let cool slightly before serving.

FRIED GRITS

Makes 4 servings

MUCH AS SOUTHERNERS LOVE GRITS, NOTHING IS MORE disgusting than cold, leftover grits that stick obstinately to the pan and make cleaning a maddening job. The solution, of course, is immediately to transfer all leftover grits to a bowl while they're still warm, beat in an egg or so, chill well, and later on make fried grits for another breakfast or to serve as a side dish for all types of meals. I have Yankee friends who balk at the sight of boiled grits but will devour fried grits as if they were the latest culinary discovery. Some Southerners even serve the squares at cocktail parties—and why not?

1 cup milk

1 cup water

½ teaspoon salt

½ cup regular or quick-cooking grits

2 large eggs

½ cup fine bread crumbs

2 tablespoons butter

1 tablespoon vegetable oil

In a heavy saucepan, combine the milk, water, and salt and bring to a boil. Gradually add the grits, stirring, and cook according to package directions till thick and creamy, stirring frequently to prevent sticking. Remove pan from the heat, lightly beat 1 egg, and, stirring constantly, add it to the grits. Scrape the mixture into an 8-inch-square pan or dish and chill till firm.

Cut the mixture into 1½-inch squares or wedges and spread the bread crumbs over a shallow plate. In a small bowl, beat the other egg, dip each square into it, and coat each with bread crumbs.

In a skillet, heat the butter and oil over moderate heat, fry the squares till golden brown and crisp, about 3 minutes on each side, and drain briefly on paper towels. Serve hot.

Paula's Tomato Grits

Makes 6 to 8 servings

NOBODY HAS DONE MORE TO PROMOTE THE CAUSE of authentic Southern cookery than Paula Deen, who, with her brother and two sons, owns and operates The Lady & Sons restaurant in Savannah, Georgia. The restaurant's groaning buffet features everything from fried chicken and barbecued ribs to collard greens with pot likker and Paula's legendary hoe cakes, but at least for me, the most sensational (and unusual) dish are these luscious tomato grits sparked with tiny green chiles. The grits should remain moist and creamy, so check them with a spoon after about 30 minutes to make sure they aren't drying out.

2 cups water

1½ cups milk

1 teaspoon salt

1 cup quick-cooking grits

9 tablespoons (1 stick plus 1 tablespoon) butter

2 scallions (white parts only), thinly sliced

¼ teaspoon garlic powder

2½ cups shredded sharp cheddar cheese

One 10-ounce can diced tomatoes and green chiles, drained

Preheat the oven to 350°F.

In a large saucepan, combine the water, milk, and salt and bring to a boil. Gradually add the grits and stir constantly for 1 minute. Reduce the heat to moderately low, cover, and cook 3 minutes. Add 8 tablespoons of the butter, stir till melted, cover, and cook till the grits are thick and creamy, about 4 minutes. Remove the pan from the heat.

In a small skillet, melt the remaining 1 tablespoon of butter over moderate heat, add the scallions, and stir till softened, about 1 minute. Add the scallions to the grits along with the garlic powder and 1½ cups of the cheese and stir till the cheese melts. Add the tomatoes and chiles, stir till well blended, scrape the mixture into a shallow buttered 2-quart baking dish, and bake for 30 minutes. Sprinkle the remaining cheese over the top and continue baking till golden, about 10 minutes. Serve piping hot.

286

GRITS, HAM, AND TURNIP GREENS SOUFFLÉ

Makes 4 servings

I CAN'T REMEMBER WHETHER THE GRITS SOUFFLÉ awarded a prize at a March of Dimes Gourmet Gala in Louisville, Kentucky, included country or regular smoked ham. Since then, I've made it with both types (as well as with various cheeses) and loved each and every rendition, so feel free to use whichever suits your taste. I do strongly advise, however, that you make the effort to acquire stone-ground grits for this particular recipe, since both the flavor and texture make all the difference. By no means try to prepare this soufflé with quick-cooking or instant grits.

1 cup bread crumbs

4 leaves of turnip greens, stems removed

2 cups water

½ teaspoon salt

½ cup stone-ground grits

½ cup freshly grated Parmesan cheese

2 tablespoons butter

Freshly ground black pepper to taste

Tabasco sauce to taste

½ cup chopped cooked ham

1 garlic clove, minced

4 large eggs, beaten

Preheat the oven to 350°F. Butter a 1½-quart soufflé dish or casserole, sprinkle the bread crumbs over the bottom and sides, and set aside.

In a pot of boiling water, blanch the turnip greens for 1 minute, drain, chop finely, and set aside.

In a heavy saucepan, combine the water and salt and bring to a boil. Gradually add the grits, stirring, reduce the heat to low, and cook 15 to 20 minutes or till thick and creamy, stirring constantly. Remove pan from the heat, add the turnip greens, cheese, butter, pepper, Tabasco, ham, and garlic and stir till well blended. Add the eggs and stir till well blended. Scrape the mixture into the prepared dish and bake till golden brown, 30 to 35 minutes. Serve hot.

287

CREOLE GRITS AND GRILLADES

Makes 4 servings

A BREAKFAST AND BRUNCH FAVORITE ON FLORIDA'S east coast and Keys is a combination of grits and small pan-fried fish called "grits and grunts," while over in Louisiana, the equivalent is a Creole mixture of grits and small pieces of beef or veal that are pounded thin and braised slowly with tomatoes and other vegetables. I've had grits and grillades in the shabbiest of country dives and cafés, but I've also seen them served very ceremoniously from a silver chafing dish at a christening brunch in New Orleans. If you really want to be authentic, sprinkle the portions with a few chopped scallions.

FOR THE GRILLADES

Two ½-inch-thick slices beef round (about 1½ pounds)

1 teaspoon salt

1 teaspoon freshly ground black pepper

⅛ teaspoon cayenne pepper

3 garlic cloves, minced

2 tablespoons all-purpose flour

2 tablespoons butter, melted

2 medium onions, chopped

2 ribs celery, chopped

½ green bell pepper, seeded and chopped

One 16-ounce can crushed tomatoes

1 cup water

FOR THE GRITS

3 cups milk

1 teaspoon salt

1 cup quick-cooking grits

1 tablespoon butter

With a mallet or rolling pin, pound the beef to a ¼-inch thickness and cut into 2-inch squares. In a bowl, combine the salt, pepper, cayenne pepper, and garlic, stir till well blended, rub the mixture into the beef, and sprinkle the beef with the flour.

In a large pot, melt the butter over moderate heat, add the floured beef, brown on both sides, and transfer to a plate. Add the onions, celery, and bell pepper to the pot and cook, stirring, till the vegetables are softened, about 5 minutes. Add the tomatoes and their juices plus the water, return the beef to the pot, reduce the heat to low, cover, and simmer till the grillades are tender, about 45 minutes.

Meanwhile, to make the grits, bring the milk and salt to a simmer in a heavy saucepan over moderate heat, taking care not to let it boil. Gradually add the grits, stirring, cover, and cook till the grits are thick and creamy, about 5 minutes. Remove from the heat, stir in the butter, and keep covered.

To serve, spoon a mound of grits on each serving plate and spoon equal amounts of the grillades over the grits.

288

GULLAH SHRIMP AND GRITS CASSEROLE

Makes 6 servings

SERVED AS A CASSEROLE AT THE GULLAH HOUSE Restaurant on St. Helena Island, South Carolina, this early version of shrimp and grits can be traced back to the descendants of plantation slaves (Gullahs) who, for generations, lived in isolation on South Carolina's Sea Islands, outside Beaufort. Today, Gullah culture (along with its distinctive language and style of cooking) has all but disappeared, preserved in part, fortunately, by a few local black cooks in the region determined to safeguard as many authentic recipes as possible. Although, no doubt, the original technique to produce a casserole such as this one was much more primitive, I like to think that the flavor and texture are nearly the same as they were over a century ago—and a far cry from the complex, sophisticated shrimp and grits you find most places these days.

1½ pounds fresh medium shrimp

3½ cups water

½ teaspoon salt

1 cup regular grits

¼ cup milk

2 large eggs

2 garlic cloves, minced

Salt and freshly ground black pepper to taste

1½ cups shredded sharp cheddar cheese

Preheat the oven to 350°F.

Place the shrimp in a large saucepan with enough water to cover, bring to a boil, remove from the heat, and let stand 3 minutes. When cool enough to handle, peel and devein the shrimp and set aside.

In another large saucepan, combine the water and salt and bring to a boil. Gradually add the grits, stirring, reduce the heat to low, cover, cook 10 minutes, and remove from the heat.

In a bowl, whisk together the milk and eggs and gradually stir them into the grits. Add the shrimp, garlic, salt and pepper, and 1 cup of the cheese and stir till well blended. Scrape the mixture into a buttered 2-quart casserole or baking dish, sprinkle the remaining cheese evenly over the top, and bake till golden, about 30 minutes. Let stand 5 minutes before serving.

Captain Jules's Shrimp and Grits

Makes 6 servings

SHRIMP AND GRITS ARE ARGUABLY THE MOST SUBLIME (and, today, famous) specialty of the Carolina and Georgia Lowcountry, and while I've praised the versions served at Louis's on Pawleys Island, at a friend's home on Tybee Island outside Savannah, and at maybe a half-dozen reputable restaurants in Charleston, I knew I'd finally found perfection when I recently attended a shrimp festival at Little River, South Carolina, and sampled (at an outdoor stand) the wondrous, creamy, spicy rendition prepared at a venerable waterfront restaurant called Captain Jules. Typically, the cooks told me they didn't have an exact recipe (ha!), but after gabbing with them for an hour about the dish, I left with enough information to concoct what I now deem to be the quintessential formula. My lifelong search for authentic shrimp and grits, therefore, is over—at least for the time being. Do make every effort to obtain stone-ground grits for this dish (if unavailable, use regular, not instant), and watch carefully to make sure the grits don't scorch while cooking, stirring periodically with a wooden spoon.

FOR THE SAUCE

1 tablespoon peanut oil

6 ounces andouille sausage (available in specialty food shops and many supermarkets), coarsely chopped

2 small onions, chopped

½ medium green bell pepper, chopped

½ medium red bell pepper, chopped

1 garlic clove, minced

1 teaspoon paprika

¼ teaspoon dried thyme

¼ teaspoon dried oregano

Salt and freshly ground black pepper to taste

1½ pounds fresh, medium shrimp, peeled, deveined, and cut in half

1½ cups chicken broth

¼ cup heavy cream

FOR THE GRITS

6 cups water

1½ teaspoons salt

1½ cups grits (preferably stone-ground, not instant)

3 cups half-and-half

6 tablespoons butter, cut into pieces

Freshly ground black pepper to taste

To make the sauce, heat the oil over moderate heat in a large, heavy skillet, add the sausage, and cook, stirring, for 3 minutes. Add the onions, both bell peppers, garlic, paprika, thyme, oregano, and salt and pepper and cook, stirring, until the vegetables are softened, about 3 minutes. Add the shrimp and cook, stirring, for 2 to 3 minutes. Add the chicken broth and cook, stirring, till slightly reduced, about 5 minutes. Add the cream, return to a simmer, and cook, stirring, till the sauce is slightly thickened, 5 to 7 minutes. Remove the sauce from the heat.

To make the grits, bring the water to a roaring boil in a large, heavy saucepan, add the salt, and gradually add the grits, stirring with a wooden spoon for about 5 minutes. Add the half-and-half and butter and bring to a simmer, stirring. Cover and cook the grits slowly till very smooth and creamy, stirring from time to time, for 50 to 60 minutes. Season with pepper and taste for salt.

To serve, reheat the sauce till hot, spoon mounds of grits on hot serving plates, and spoon sauce over the hot grits.

291

Tennessee Shrimp and Grits

Makes 4 servings

IT'S NOTHING LESS THAN HERESY EVEN TO SUGGEST that the folks in Tennessee might know as much about shrimp and grits as those in the Carolina and Georgia Lowcountry, where the specialty originated, but when my obsessed Mississippi cohort Julia Reed put me on to the cheesy, tomatoey creation served at Pearl's Foggy Mountain Café in the unlikely small town of Sewanee, Tennessee, I knew I'd encountered something altogether different, but special. Of course, this glorious dish is now becoming as fashionable in restaurants all over the country as blackened redfish once was, and God knows the abominable transformations it will suffer at the hands of cocky chefs. This, however, is one modification that gives the dish a truly exciting new dimension, without distorting its integrity.

FOR THE GRITS

4 cups water

½ teaspoon salt

1 cup regular grits

6 ounces sharp cheddar cheese, grated

3 tablespoons butter

FOR THE SHRIMP

1 pound fresh medium shrimp

2 cups water

4 tablespoons (½ stick) butter

1 large onion, chopped

½ green bell pepper, seeded and chopped

2 garlic cloves, minced

1 cup diced ripe fresh tomatoes

½ teaspoon dried thyme, crumbled

1 tablespoon all-purpose flour

1 tablespoon tomato paste

½ cup heavy cream

2 teaspoons Worcestershire sauce

Salt and freshly ground black pepper to taste

Tabasco sauce to taste

2 tablespoons chopped fresh parsley leaves

To make the grits, combine the water and salt in a heavy saucepan and bring to a boil. Gradually add the grits, stirring, reduce the heat to low, cover, and cook till the liquid has been absorbed, 15 to 25 minutes, stirring occasionally. Remove pan from the heat, add the cheese and butter, stir till melted. Keep warm.

Meanwhile, peel and devein the shrimp, combine the shells and water in a saucepan, and reserve the shrimp. Bring the water to a boil, reduce the heat slightly, cook till the liquid is reduced by half, and strain the stock into a bowl.

In a large skillet, melt the butter over moderate heat, add the onion, bell pepper and garlic and cook, stirring, till softened, about 3 minutes. Add the tomatoes and thyme and cook about 3 minutes longer. Sprinkle the flour over the top and stir well. Add the reserved shrimp and cook, stirring, till they turn pink, about 2 minutes. Add ½ cup of the stock, cook 3 minutes longer, add the tomato paste, and stir well. Add the cream, Worcestershire, salt and pepper, Tabasco, and, if necessary, a little more stock to make a sauce that easily coats the shrimp. Heat well.

To serve, spoon a mound of grits in the center of each serving plate, spoon shrimp around the grits, and sprinkle parsley over the top.

Baked Grits with Country Ham and Oyster Mushrooms

Makes 4 servings

IT'S DEBATABLE WHETHER FRANK STITT AT Highlands Bar & Grill in Birmingham, Alabama, is the most innovative chef in the South, but surely none of his creative dishes illustrates better the intelligent juxtaposition of Southern ingredients and French technique than these glorious grits ramekins topped with a mixture of pungent wild mushrooms and country ham and served with a spicy butter sauce. Yes, the dish takes a little time and effort to prepare, but it not only shows the sophisticated role grits can play in modern Southern cookery but also provides a truly elegant appetizer or luncheon dish that will have guests raving with joy.

FOR THE GRITS

4 cups water

1½ teaspoons salt

1 cup stone-ground grits

2 tablespoons butter

Freshly ground black pepper to taste

¼ cup freshly grated genuine Parmesan cheese

1 large egg, beaten

FOR THE SAUCE

½ cup dry white wine

¼ cup white wine vinegar

½ cup finely diced country ham

2 scallions (white parts only), finely chopped

1 sprig fresh thyme

1 bay leaf

1 dried red chile pepper

1 tablespoon heavy cream

½ pound (2 sticks) butter, cut into pieces

2 tablespoons freshly grated Parmesan cheese

Salt and freshly ground black pepper to taste

1 teaspoon fresh lemon juice

FOR THE TOPPING

1 tablespoon olive oil

2 thin slices country ham, cut into strips

½ pound fresh oyster mushrooms, cut into slices

1 garlic clove, minced

Sprigs of fresh thyme for garnish

Preheat the oven to 325°F. Grease four small ramekins with butter and set aside.

To make the grits, combine the water and salt in a heavy saucepan and bring to a boil. Gradually stir in the grits, reduce the heat to low, and cook, stirring constantly, till the grits are thick and creamy, 15 to 20 minutes. Scrape into a large bowl, add the butter, black pepper, and cheese, and stir till well blended. Add the egg and stir till well blended. Scrape equal amounts of the mixture into the prepared ramekins, place the ramekins in a baking pan, add enough water to come halfway up the outside of the ramekins, and bake till set, about 20 minutes. Remove the ramekins from the pan and let stand.

To make the sauce, combine the wine, vinegar, ham, scallions, thyme, bay leaf, and chile pepper in a heavy saucepan, bring to a boil, and cook till the liquid is reduced to 1 tablespoon. Reduce the heat to low and add the cream, stirring. Whisk in the pieces of butter till well blended, then strain into a bowl, discarding the solids. Add the cheese, salt and pepper, and lemon juice, stir well, and keep the sauce warm.

To make the topping, heat the oil in a skillet over moderate heat, add the ham, mushrooms, and garlic, and cook, stirring, till the mushrooms are softened, about 10 minutes.

To serve, invert the ramekins on serving plates, ladle sauce around each, and top each with equal amounts of the mushroom mixture. Garnish each plate with thyme sprigs and serve immediately.

295

TARPON SPRINGS FETA GRITS SOUFFLÉ

Makes 4 to 6 servings

TARPON SPRINGS, FLORIDA, HAS HAD ONE OF THE South's most active Greek communities ever since immigrants began developing the area's sponge industry decades ago, and as in my hometown of Charlotte, North Carolina, the Greek Americans were quick to adapt all sorts of Southern ingredients to the culinary traditions of their mother country. This combination of grits and feta cheese is stunning, a dish intended to be served as a main course, with maybe some sliced dried garlic sausage, a few marinated cucumbers, corn sticks, and a good chilled spicy white wine.

4 cups water

1 teaspoon salt

1 cup quick-cooking grits

3 cups whole milk

6 tablespoons (¾ stick) butter, at room temperature

4 large eggs, beaten

1 cup finely crumbled Greek or Romanian feta cheese

1 tablespoon Worcestershire sauce

Freshly ground black pepper to taste

Mild paprika to taste

In a large saucepan, combine the water and salt and bring to a boil. Gradually add the grits, reduce the heat to low, and stir till the grits are thick and creamy, 5 to 10 minutes. Add 2 cups of the milk, stir well, return the mixture to a boil, and continue cooking 5 minutes longer, stirring. Add the remaining 1 cup of milk, the butter, eggs, feta cheese, Worcestershire, and pepper and stir steadily till the butter and cheese are well incorporated. Scrape the mixture into a buttered 2-quart soufflé dish or casserole, cover with plastic wrap, and chill overnight.

Preheat the oven to 350°F, sprinkle top of the mixture with paprika, and bake till golden, about 45 minutes. Serve hot.

PEABODY GRITS PUDDING

Makes 6 servings

STEEPED IN SOUTHERN CHARM AND TRADITION
from its exquisite guest accommodations to its gracious
dining room to its twice-daily parade of ducks going
to and from their penthouse pond to the lavish lobby
fountain, the Peabody Hotel in Memphis is a slightly
eccentric but civilized landmark that no traveler in the
South should miss. At the Peabody, this unusual grits
pudding is normally served with peach slices sautéed in
honeyed orange butter. While that's always an option at
home, if you really want to dazzle guests, let the pudding
stand on its own; by itself, you can better appreciate both
the flavor and texture of the grits. Should you decide
to use the garnish, however, simply sauté a dozen fresh
peach slices in a tablespoon of butter over moderate heat
till barely browned, about 2 minutes, add ¼ cup of honey,
2 tablespoons of water, and a tablespoon of grated orange
rind, stir till the peaches are soft and the sauce slightly
thickened, and spoon over the pudding.

3 cups whole milk

1 stick cinnamon

Grated rind of ½ lemon

1 cup stone-ground or regular grits

3 large egg yolks

½ cup sugar

½ teaspoon pure vanilla extract

Preheat the oven to 375°F. Grease a 1½- to 2-quart
basking dish or casserole with butter and set aside.

In a heavy saucepan, combine the milk, cinnamon, and
lemon zest, bring to a boil, and reduce the heat to low.
Gradually add the grits and cook, stirring constantly,
till the grits are thick and creamy, 15 to 20 minutes.
Remove pan from the heat.

In a bowl, whisk together the egg yolks, sugar, and
vanilla till frothy, add to the grits mixture, and stir till
well blended. Scrape the mixture into the prepared
baking dish or casserole and bake till most of the liquid
has evaporated, about 15 minutes. Remove and discard
the cinnamon stick, spoon the pudding onto dessert
plates, and serve hot or warm.

Cornbread, Biscuits, Hush Puppies, & Other Breads

Skillet Cornbread

Hot-Water Cornbread

Harold's Cracklin' Cornbread

Buttermilk-Parmesan Cornbread

Ole Miss Black-Eyed Pea
and Sausage Cornbread

Awendaw

Nashville Corn Light Bread

Scallion Corn Sticks

Joseph's Hoecakes

Calabash Hush Puppies

Beer Hush Puppies

Perfect Buttermilk Biscuits

Maryland Beaten Biscuits

Mary Mac's Angel Biscuits

Cracklin' Biscuits

Ham and Grits Biscuits

Alabama Biscuit Muffins

Orange Tea Biscuits

Buttermilk Bread

Philpy Bread

Sally Lunn

Tennessee Monkey Bread

Peanut Butter Bread

Pecan Whole Wheat Bread

Memphis Casserole Cheese Bread

Sip 'n' See Lemon Tea Bread

Dinner Yeast Rolls

Pocketbook Rolls

Carolina Rice Muffins

Carrot-Pecan Muffins

Mystery Raisin Bran Muffins

Hootie's Blueberry Muffins with
Streusel Topping

Cheddar-Walnut Shortbread

Mother's Pecan Waffles
with Orange Syrup

SKILLET CORNBREAD

Makes 8 servings

SLATHERED WITH BUTTER AND EATEN WITH BARBECUE, fried fish, or any style of slow-simmered vegetable; crumbled into bowls of pot likker left over from boiled peas or greens; used to make all types of stuffings—skillet cornbread is one of the backbones of Southern cookery, from the mountains of West Virginia to the bayous of Louisiana. I can recall a time when no dinner was considered respectable without a big skillet of soft cornbread, and even today it's still a staple at church suppers, at home-style cafés and restaurants, and in even the most elegant dining rooms. I've eaten skillet cornbread from one end of the Confederacy to the other, but none (including my own mother's) can equal this miraculous version using water-ground yellow cornmeal (and no flour!), prepared almost daily by a close friend and transplanted Mississippi native now living in North Carolina. "The secret," says Ann, "is not just the cornmeal but the quantity of bacon grease and the blazing hot cast-iron skillet." Of course, finding water-ground cornmeal these days is a challenge, but I must say that batches of this cornbread made with regular yellow cornmeal are nothing to sneeze at.

2 cups yellow cornmeal (preferably water-ground)

1 teaspoon baking soda

1 teaspoon salt

2 large eggs, beaten

1 cup regular buttermilk

¼ cup bacon grease

Preheat the oven to 450°F.

In a large mixing bowl, combine the cornmeal, baking soda, and salt and stir till well blended. Add the eggs and buttermilk and stir with a wooden spoon till well blended and smooth. In a 9- to 10-inch cast-iron skillet, heat the bacon grease, add it to the cornmeal mixture, and stir till well blended. Scrape the batter into the hot skillet, place the skillet in the oven, and bake till the cornbread is golden brown, 20 to 25 minutes. Turn the cornbread out onto a serving plate or serve directly from the skillet, cutting it into small wedges.

HOT-WATER CORNBREAD

Makes about 1 dozen cornbread cakes

ESSENTIALLY, HOT-WATER CORNBREAD IS THE SAME AS hoecakes, a cornpone that can be traced back to Indian societies in the South and to our Colonial ancestors. Eventually the bread became more complex, as leavening, milk, and flavorful fats were added to the batter and better cooking equipment was made available. Today, nothing is loved more in Southern farmhouses or rural cafés than hot water cornbread served with sorghum or molasses. To produce the right dense crust and tender interior, it's almost obligatory to cook the bread in very hot oil, in a heavy cast-iron skillet that maintains even heat.

Grinding corn into meal is one of North Carolina's oldest industries, and it was here that the expression "strike the toll" originated. Early millers were paid with one-eighth bushel of corn instead of cash by using a stick to level dried corn in a toll dish. A miller would first strike the toll, then grind the corn.

---

2 cups white cornmeal

1 teaspoon salt

1 teaspoon sugar

½ teaspoon baking powder

¼ cup whole or 2 percent milk

1 tablespoon bacon grease

1½ cups boiling water

Vegetable oil for frying

In a large mixing bowl, combine the cornmeal, salt, sugar, and baking powder and stir till well blended. Add the milk and bacon grease and stir just till the mixture is moistened but still a little lumpy. With a wooden spoon, gradually add the boiling water, stirring constantly till the batter is the consistency of boiled grits.

In a large cast-iron skillet, heat about ½ inch of oil till very hot but not smoking, and drop the batter into the oil in batches, by ¼-cupfuls. Fry till the cakes are golden, about 3 minutes on each side, and drain on paper towels. Serve hot.

HAROLD'S CRACKLIN' CORNBREAD

Makes 6 to 8 servings

FOR AGES, FANS (BLUEBLOODS AND COMMONERS alike) have been going to Harold's Barbecue in Atlanta as much for the cracklin' cornbread and Brunswick stew as for the chopped pork barbecue—despite the restaurant's tacky decor and no-booze policy. And yes, the cornbread, made with buttermilk, lard, and bits of salt pork cracklin', is truly exceptional. No careful separate blending of the dry and wet ingredients at Harold's: they just dump all the ingredients in a big tub, stir away till well blended, scrape the batter into large pans, and bake till the cornbread is feather soft with a slightly crusty top. Sublime.

1 cup finely diced salt pork

3 cups yellow cornmeal

½ cup all-purpose flour

1 teaspoon salt

1 teaspoon baking powder

½ teaspoon baking soda

2½ cups regular buttermilk

¼ cup water

⅓ cup lard, melted

2 large eggs, beaten

Preheat the oven to 400°F. Grease a large baking pan or dish with butter and set aside.

In a skillet, fry the salt pork over moderate heat till well browned and crisp, about 10 minutes, then drain the cracklin's on paper towels.

In a large mixing bowl, combine all remaining ingredients and stir till thoroughly blended. Scrape the mixture into the prepared baking pan or dish, and bake till golden brown, 25 to 30 minutes. Serve hot.

Buttermilk-Parmesan Cornbread

Makes 1 large loaf

IN THE SOUTH, FLAVORED CORNBREADS ARE USUALLY intended more for stylish dinners and elaborate buffets than for earthy barbecues and fish fries. Various cheeses are often incorporated in the batter, but I've also seen chopped sautéed scallions, minced bell pepper, and even a few fresh herbs. Cooks up in Mayland, Delaware, and parts of Virginia would most likely add a little sugar to this particular recipe, a practice deemed nothing less than sacrilege in the Deep South. I do recommend that you use genuine Parmesan cheese (or a well-aged extra-sharp cheddar) for this cornbread.

2 cups yellow cornmeal

1 cup all-purpose flour

1 tablespoon baking powder

1 teaspoon baking soda

1 teaspoon salt

½ teaspoon freshly ground black pepper

1 cup freshly grated Parmesan cheese

1½ cups regular buttermilk

2 large eggs

Preheat the oven to 350°F. Grease a large baking pan with butter and set aside.

In a large mixing bowl, whisk together the cornmeal, flour, baking powder, baking soda, salt, and pepper, add the cheese, and stir till well blended. In another bowl, whisk together the buttermilk and eggs, add to the dry mixture, and stir till just blended (Do not over mix; the batter should be slightly lumpy.) Scrape the batter into the prepared baking pan and bake till a knife inserted in the center of the loaf comes out clean, 20 to 25 minutes. Serve hot.

OLE MISS BLACK-EYED PEA
AND SAUSAGE CORNBREAD

Makes 6 to 8 servings

I HAVEN'T BEEN A FOOTBALL FAN EVER SINCE I HUNG up my own helmet after playing guard for three years on the high school team, but when I heard about the veritable tailgate feasts thrown by students and alumni every season on the Ole Miss campus, in Oxford, my interest was revived. Groaning buffet tables of barbecue, roasts, casseroles, fried chicken, hot dips, pimento cheese sandwiches and sausage biscuits, rich layer cakes and elaborate pecan pies—the array of Southern dishes is staggering, not the least this sumptuous cornbread, the pride of one alumna. The unusual bread is almost like a firm spoonbread, so much so that you may choose to serve it (using a big spoon) as a casserole with no more than some fried okra, coleslaw, or a green salad.

½ pound bulk pork sausage

1 small onion, chopped

2 cups white cornmeal

1 cup all-purpose flour

1 teaspoon salt

½ teaspoon freshly ground black pepper

½ teaspoon baking soda

1 cup regular or 2 percent buttermilk

½ cup vegetable oil

2 large eggs

1 cup grated sharp cheddar cheese

One 15-ounce can black-eyed peas, drained

½ cup canned chopped green chiles

Preheat the oven to 375°F. Grease a large baking dish or pan with butter and set aside.

In a skillet, break up the sausage, add the onion, and cook over moderate heat, stirring, till the meat is browned, about 10 minutes. Drain the sausage and onion on paper towels.

In a large mixing bowl, whisk together the cornmeal, flour, salt, pepper, and baking soda. In another bowl, whisk together the buttermilk, oil, and eggs, add to the dry mixture, and stir just till the dry mixture is moistened. (Do not overmix; the batter should be slightly lumpy.) Add the cheese, black-eyed peas, and chiles and stir till the mixture is well blended. Scrape the batter into the prepared dish, and bake till golden brown, 40 to 50 minutes. Allow to cool about 10 minutes before serving.

304

Awendaw

Makes 1 loaf

IN *THE CAROLINA HOUSEWIFE* OF 1847, SARAH Rutledge's "Owendaw Corn Bread" is more like a pudding or custard than a bread, making me wonder if she ever really visited the old Indian town of Awendaw, which is still off Highway 17 just north of Charleston, South Carolina, or if the dish underwent a radical transformation over the centuries. (Today, I always stop at Awendaw on my way from Myrtle Beach to Charleston to buy not only a couple of loaves of this distinctive bread but also a few sweetgrass baskets and mats woven by the few remaining black natives of the area who still practice the rare craft.) I was originally introduced to the bread by Bill Neal, up in North Carolina (incredibly, not even the classic *Charleston Receipts* cookbook has ever included a recipe for Awendaw), and while I've since come across a couple of other versions, Bill's remains the most delicious. This is still another example of a fascinating Southern regional specialty that has tottered at the edge of extinction due to neglect and the modern mania for culinary novelty.

2 cups water

1 teaspoon salt

7 tablespoons regular grits

4 tablespoons (½ stick) butter

1½ cups milk

1 cup yellow cornmeal

3 large eggs

Preheat the oven to 350°F. Grease the bottom and sides of a 1½-quart loaf pan, dust the interior with a little cornmeal, and set aside.

In a saucepan, combine the water and salt and bring to a rapid boil. Gradually add the grits, reduce the heat to moderately low, and cook, stirring frequently to prevent sticking, for 25 minutes. Add the butter, remove pan from the heat, and stir till the butter has melted. Meanwhile, combine the milk and cornmeal in a mixing bowl, stir well, and let stand 15 minutes.

Stir the grits into the cornmeal mixture, then, one by one, beat in the eggs. Scrape the batter into the prepared loaf pan and bake till the bread is golden, about 50 minutes. Serve hot with plenty of butter or, if left over, lightly toasted and buttered.

Nashville Corn Light Bread

Makes 2 loaves

"YOU DO MEAN LIGHT CORN BREAD, DON'T YOU?" I ASK Anne Byrn ("The Cake Mix Doctor") as we share a platter of country ham, fried chicken, and biscuits with peach preserves at the eclectic Loveless Motel and Café just outside Nashville, Tennessee.

"No, honey, I mean just what I say: corn light bread. You're not the first person to act surprised, but you haven't lived till you've eaten it."

It ends up that corn light bread is a floury, sweet loaf that can be traced back to the early nineteenth century in Appalachia and is today almost an exclusive specialty of central Tennessee and particularly Nashville. Anne thinks it may be called "light" since it's a cross between ordinary cornbread and white bread, and because there is some evidence that it was once made with yeast. Some folks in Nashville told me the bread just wouldn't work without water-ground cornmeal (very difficult to find outside the area), but I think even Anne would approve of the loaves I've made with regular yellow cornmeal. Do slather this bread with lots of butter.

3 cups yellow cornmeal (preferably water-ground)

1 cup all-purpose flour

1 cup sugar

1½ teaspoons salt

½ teaspoon baking soda

3 cups regular buttermilk

¼ cup vegetable shortening, melted

Preheat the oven to 350°F. Grease two 1½-quart loaf pans with butter and set aside.

Sift together the cornmeal, flour, sugar, salt, and baking soda into a large mixing bowl. Gradually add the buttermilk and melted shortening and stir till the batter is well blended and smooth. Scrape equal amounts of batter into the 2 prepared loaf pans and bake till the bread pulls away from the sides of the pans and is golden, about 45 minutes. Transfer the loaves to a rack and let cool before slicing.

Scallion Corn Sticks

Makes about sixteen 5-inch-long corn sticks

THE IDEAL BREAD FOR BARBECUES, FANCY SUPPERS, and virtually any meal that features soup or stew, corn sticks are revered in the South almost as much as ordinary corn bread. Right there alongside different-size cast-iron skillets in the Southern kitchen are two or three cast-iron molds for corn sticks, which can be found in most hardware stores and supermarkets. There literally is no substitute for these heavy, inexpensive molds that distribute heat so evenly and steadily. Just remember that, for the corn sticks to be properly soft inside with a crispy exterior, the molds must be scorching hot before the batter is spooned in. Most Southerners consider it a sacrilege and outrage to add sugar to any cornmeal bread, but I must confess that lately I've been sneaking about a teaspoon into my corn stick batter, and I still can't decide which I like better.

2 cups yellow cornmeal

1 cup all-purpose flour

1 tablespoon baking powder

1 teaspoon baking soda

1 teaspoon salt

2 large eggs

1 cup regular buttermilk

¼ cup vegetable shortening, heated slightly

4 scallions, minced (white parts only)

In a large mixing bowl, combine the cornmeal, flour, baking powder, baking soda, and salt and stir till well blended. Add the eggs one at a time, beating the mixture well after each addition. Add the buttermilk and stir till well blended, then add the shortening and scallions and stir till smooth. Cover the bowl with plastic wrap and refrigerate for 1 hour.

Preheat the oven to 500°F.

Grease two or three cast-iron corn-stick molds and set in the oven till the molds are scorching hot. Spoon the batter into the molds and bake till the tops are golden and crisp, 10 to 12 minutes. Serve piping hot.

JOSEPH'S HOECAKES

Makes 16 to 18 hoecakes

HOECAKES, JOHNNYCAKES, ASHCAKES, GRIDDLE
cakes, Shawnee cakes—all are styles of cornpone that
can be traced back to the original Indians, Colonial
settlers, and black slaves, who cooked these primitive
breads on iron sheets, flat rocks, and the metal ends of
hoes over open fires. This particular recipe was obtained
years ago from my family's loyal black waiter, Joseph, in
the gracious dining room of The Patricia Inn at Myrtle
Beach, South Carolina (today a sad shadow of its former
self)—the same waiter who taught me how to surf-fish
for spots and bluefish and who introduced us to any
number of local rice breads. These are the simplest
hoecakes imaginable, but slathered with butter, the hot
patties are utterly addictive at any meal.

2 cups white cornmeal

1 teaspoon salt

1 cup boiling water

2 to 3 tablespoons bacon grease

In a large mixing bowl, combine the cornmeal and salt,
then pour on the boiling water in a slow, steady stream,
beating constantly with a wooden spoon till the batter
is smooth. For each hoecake, pat in your hands about 2
tablespoons of the batter into a flat round 3 to 4 inches
in diameter, and continue patting till all the batter is
used up, flouring your hands if necessary.

Heat about 1 tablespoon of the bacon grease in a large,
cast-iron skillet over high heat, reduce the heat to low,
add a few of the hoecakes, and fry till golden brown
and crisp, about 2 minutes on each side. Repeat with
the remaining grease and hoecakes, transferring them
to a platter and keeping them as hot as possible till
served.

CALABASH HUSH PUPPIES

Makes about 40 hush puppies

LEGEND HAS IT THAT NOT LONG AFTER THE WAR Between the States, Southern cooks would quiet yapping dogs at fish fries by tossing them scraps of batter and yelling, "Hush, puppies!" Whatever the origin of the term, it's for sure that fried hush puppies are one of the great breads of the South and that no fish fry, barbecue, seafood boil, or Brunswick stew party would be right without them. It's also true that I've spent my entire life not only looking for the perfect hush puppy but also trying to produce an ideal batch myself. At one point, I thought a catfish restaurant in Natchez, Mississippi, called Cock of the Walk had the quintessential formula and technique—until, that is, I swooned over the small dodgers at the Center Pier restaurant in Carolina Beach, North Carolina, then those at a church barbecue in Brunswick, Georgia, and, most recently, at Ella's seafood restaurant in Calabash, North Carolina. The quest for great hush puppies often seems part of the Southern soul itself, and once you sink your teeth into a crusty, greaseless, well-flavored, piping hot pup, you'll understand why. Be warned that nothing is worse than a cold hush puppy, and also be warned that guests gobble down good pups as fast as you fill the basket. And, yes, the best hush puppies do contain a little sugar.

2 cups all-purpose flour

1½ cups yellow cornmeal

2 tablespoons sugar

1 teaspoon baking powder

1 teaspoon salt

¼ cup finely minced onions

2⅓ cups whole milk

⅓ cup vegetable oil

1 large egg, beaten

Corn or vegetable oil for deep frying

Into a large mixing bowl, sift together the flour, cornmeal, sugar, baking powder, and salt and mix to blend thoroughly. Add the onions, milk, vegetable oil, and egg and stir with a wooden spoon long enough just to blend well.

In a deep-fat fryer or deep cast-iron skillet, heat about 3 inches of oil to 375°F on a thermometer, then drop the batter in batches by tablespoon into the fat and fry till the hush puppies are golden brown and crisp, about 3 minutes. Drain on paper towels briefly and serve immediately in a covered bread basket.

BEER HUSH PUPPIES

Makes about 1½ dozen hush puppies

SINCE FRIED CATFISH AND HUSH PUPPIES ARE ONE OF those sacred Southern culinary marriages, what more likely place to boast a recipe for perfect pups than The Catfish Institute in Belzoni, Mississippi? Of course, the addition of bell pepper to the batter would never be tolerated at fish fries or barbecues up in Georgia and the Carolinas, but even those purists would have to admit that the beer in this recipe produces one of the lightest hush puppies imaginable.

1 cup yellow cornmeal

½ cup all-purpose flour

2 teaspoons baking powder

2 teaspoons sugar

1 teaspoon salt

½ teaspoon freshly ground black pepper

½ cup lager beer

1 large egg

¼ cup finely chopped onion

3 tablespoons finely chopped green bell pepper

Peanut oil for deep frying

In a large bowl, combine the cornmeal, flour, baking powder, sugar, salt, and pepper and stir till well blended. In another bowl, whisk together the beer, onion, and bell pepper, add to the dry ingredients, and stir till the batter is well blended.

In a large skillet or saucepan, heat about 3 inches of oil over moderate heat till a morsel of batter tossed in sputters. Drop the batter by rounded tablespoons into the oil and fry in batches till golden brown and crisp, about 2 minutes on each side. Drain the hush puppies on paper towels and serve piping hot.

Perfect Buttermilk Biscuits

Makes about 16 biscuits

THIS IS THE QUEEN OF ALL SOUTHERN BISCUITS, THE one that cooks have been baking for ordinary home meals, formal buffets, church suppers, political rallies, and virtually any other occasion for as long as anybody can remember. They're the light, fluffy, tangy biscuits I make on the average of three times a week, and am never without. Ideally, the biscuits should be made with soft, low-gluten Southern winter flour, such as White Lily, Red Band, or Martha White, but given the difficulty in obtaining these premium flours outside the South, an acceptable substitute can be made by combining two parts of regular all-purpose flour with one part cake flour. Here are the basic rules for biscuit perfection: Never premix all the ingredients and allow the dough to stand even a short amount of time before baking. Do not roll the dough out, but rather pat it out with your fingers. Stir and handle the dough as little as possible to prevent toughness. Cut out the biscuits only with a sturdy, sharp, metal biscuit cutter to allow air to escape from the dough. And for even baking and no burnt bottoms, always use a heavy baking sheet (preferably one with no lips except on one side). There are about a hundred secondary rules that should be observed, but these you'll learn gradually after making maybe ten dozen batches of biscuits.

2 cups all-purpose flour (see headnote)

1 tablespoon baking powder

½ teaspoon baking soda

½ teaspoon salt

¼ cup chilled vegetable shortening

1 cup regular buttermilk

Preheat the oven to 450°F.

In a large mixing bowl, whisk together the flour, baking powder, baking soda, and salt. Add the shortening and cut it in with a pastry cutter or rub with your fingertips till the mixture is mealy. Gradually add the buttermilk, stirring with a wooden spoon just till the dough is soft and slightly sticky. (Do not overmix.)

Transfer the dough to a lightly floured surface and, using a light touch, turn the edges toward the middle, pressing with your hands. Press the dough out ½ inch thick and cut straight down into even rounds with a 2-inch biscuit cutter. Pat the scraps together and cut out more rounds. Arrange the rounds on a baking sheet no more than ½ inch apart and bake in the upper third of the oven till lightly browned on top, 12 to 15 minutes. Serve piping hot.

MARYLAND BEATEN BISCUITS

Makes about 50 biscuits

MARYLAND, VIRGINIA, AND KENTUCKY ALL LAY CLAIM
to these small, dry, crisp biscuits, but I must say that
Marylanders do seem to have the knack of making them
like nobody else. Conceived long before the introduction
of baking powder and baking soda (in the nineteenth
century) when the only means of leavening was to beat
the dough hard and repeatedly with a rolling pin,
hammer, or side of an axe till it blistered and turned
incredibly smooth, beaten biscuits still must be whacked
for at least 15 or 20 minutes and baked slowly to yield
the right soft interior and crackly crust. Enthusiasts
believe there simply is no other biscuit, and when a
batch comes out perfect for a tea party, for a crowd of
two dozen or so guests, or just for daily nibbling, you'll
understand why. The biscuits keep for up to a month in
an airtight container—and, yes, they're loads of fun to
make, especially for children.

4 cups all-purpose flour

1½ teaspoons salt

5 tablespoons chilled vegetable shortening

1 to 1½ cups water, as needed

Preheat the oven to 350°F.

In a large mixing bowl, combine the flour and salt and
stir well. Add the shortening and rub it into the flour
with your fingertips till the mixture is mealy. Gradually
add enough of the water to form a soft dough, stirring
with a wooden spoon.

Transfer the dough to a lightly floured surface and
begin beating it all over with a floured rolling pin,
folding it back on itself as it flattens and beating
constantly till very smooth, at least 15 minutes.

Pinch off small pieces of dough about the size of a
large marble, roll between the palms of your hands,
and place on a baking sheet about ½ inch apart.
Flatten the balls with a fork, then press again to form a
crisscross pattern. Bake in the upper third of the oven
till the biscuits are lightly golden and quite crisp, about
30 minutes. Let cool, then store in an airtight
container.

312

Mary Mac's Angel Biscuits

Makes about 20 biscuits

ALSO CALLED "BRIDE'S BISCUITS" IN CERTAIN AREAS of the South, angel biscuits are made feathery light with not only yeast but lard. At one time I thought the finest angel biscuits on earth were baked by a Greek lady at a restaurant in Charlotte, North Carolina, called The Epicurean. Then I tasted the billowy wonders brushed with butter at the legendary Mary Mac's Tea Room, in Atlanta (now more of a sprawling restaurant than a tearoom) and concluded that there was no further competition. "Honey," I was told by an elderly waitress, "the secret is to keep the lard a little bit flaky when you work it into the flour." And why are these sometimes called "bride's biscuits?" For the simple reason that all the leavening guarantees a fluffy, light biscuit for even the most inexperienced, awkward cook starting out in the kitchen.

1 envelope active dry yeast

¼ cup warm water

2½ cups all-purpose flour

2 tablespoons sugar

1½ teaspoons baking powder

½ teaspoon baking soda

½ teaspoon salt

½ cup chilled lard

1 cup regular buttermilk

In a small bowl, combine the yeast and water and let proof till bubbly, about 5 minutes.

In a large mixing bowl, whisk together the flour, sugar, baking powder, baking soda, and salt. Add the lard in pieces and cut it in with a pastry cutter till mealy but still slightly flaky. Add the yeast mixture and buttermilk and stir with a fork just till a soft, sticky dough forms.

Transfer the dough to a lightly floured surface, form into a ball, roll out ½ inch thick, and cut out rounds with a 2-inch biscuit cutter. Roll the scraps together and cut out more rounds. Arrange the rounds close together on a baking sheet, cover with a clean towel, and let rise in a warm area about 1 hour.

Preheat the oven to 400°F.

Bake the biscuits in the center of the oven till golden brown, 12 to 15 minutes.

CRACKLIN' BISCUITS

Makes about 1 dozen biscuits

CRACKLINGS (OR, IN SOUTHERN LINGO, "CRACKLIN'S"), which are crispy, delicious morsels of pork fat after it has been rendered in a skillet or during the roasting or barbecue process, have been an important component of Southern cooking ever since lard was first rendered after fall hog killings hundreds of years ago. Today, cracklin's (or "grattons," in Cajun Louisiana) are still used in homes all over the South to enhance vegetables, beans, chopped pork barbecue, and all sorts of cornbreads (or "cracklin' bread"), but never do I love the crunchy bits more than when they're scattered through hot biscuits. In the South, cracklin's are often sold packaged in supermarkets, but you can make your own very easily, simply by rendering finely diced salt pork in a heavy iron skillet. (When I barbecue a couple of pork shoulders in a pit or on a grill, I wouldn't dream of tossing out any extra cracklin's that haven't been added to the chopped meat.) Think seriously about doubling this recipe.

> ½ envelope active dry yeast
>
> 2 tablespoons warm water
>
> ¼ cup finely diced salt pork
>
> 2¼ cups unbleached all-purpose flour
>
> 1 teaspoon baking powder
>
> ¼ cup chilled vegetable shortening
>
> 1 cup whole milk or regular buttermilk

In a small bowl, sprinkle the yeast over the water and let proof till bubbly, about 5 minutes.

In a small, heavy skillet, fry the salt pork over moderate heat till well browned and crisp, about 10 minutes, then drain the cracklin's on paper towels.

In a large mixing bowl, whisk together the flour and baking powder. Add the shortening and rub it into the flour with your fingertips till the mixture is mealy. Add the cracklin's and stir till well blended. Make a well in the dry ingredients, pour the yeast mixture and buttermilk into the well, and stir gently just till the dry ingredients are moistened and the dough is soft. Cover with plastic wrap or a clean towel and let rise in a warm area about 1 hour.

Preheat the oven to 425°F.

Transfer the dough to a lightly floured surface and knead about 8 times. Roll out about ½ inch thick and cut out rounds with a 2½-inch biscuit cutter. Roll the scraps together and cut out more rounds. Arrange the rounds on a baking sheet about 1 inch apart and bake in the upper third of the oven till golden brown, about 15 minutes.

Ham and Grits Biscuits

Makes about 20 biscuits

SOME OF THE BEST BISCUITS I'VE PUT IN MY MOUTH have been found at humble diners, and none is more memorable than these husky ones served one morning with soft scrambled eggs at a sleek, chrome-trimmed beanery on the road from Covington, Virginia, to Charleston, West Virginia. No doubt this style of biscuit originally came about as a way to use up a mess of leftover grits and fried country ham, a tricky proposition unless you know to use enough baking powder and lard to lighten the dough. (Do not use butter.) Unlike conventional baking powder biscuits, these don't have to be pampered too much, meaning you're free to knead the dough till it's nicely pliable.

½ cup regular grits (not instant)

2 cups all-purpose flour

4 teaspoons baking powder

½ teaspoon salt

3 tablespoons chilled lard

½ cup whole or 2 percent milk, or as needed

¼ cup finely diced cured country ham

Preheat the oven to 400°F.

Cook the grits according to the package directions and let cool.

In a large mixing bowl, whisk together the flour, baking powder, and salt. Add the lard and rub it in with your fingertips till the mixture is mealy. Stir in the milk, then beat in the grits and the ham with a wooden spoon till well blended, adding more milk if necessary for a smooth dough.

Transfer the dough to a slightly floured work surface and knead 3 to 4 times or till pliable. Pat out ½ inch thick and cut out rounds with a 2-inch biscuit butter. Pat the scraps together and cut out more rounds.

Arrange the rounds on a baking sheet about 1 inch apart and bake in the upper third of the oven till golden brown, about 12 minutes. Serve hot.

ALABAMA BISCUIT MUFFINS

Makes 1 dozen muffins

CRAIG CLAIBORNE, WHO WAS BORN AND RAISED IN
Sunflower, Mississippi, used to tell me that the biscuit
muffins I so raved about were a specialty of his home
state—and that his mother's muffins were well known
throughout the land. No doubt Craig meant what he
said, the only problem being that I personally have never
encountered biscuit muffins in Mississippi. ("That's
because you haven't been to the right places in
Mississippi," snapped my friend Julia Reed, who's from
Greenville.) I have, on the other hand, had the muffins
on a number of occasions over in Alabama, most notably
at a fancy country club brunch in Montgomery and at a
college friend's mother's home in Tuscaloosa. No matter.
Let's just say that biscuit muffins are a very distinctive
bread of the Deep South and that the slightly sweet little
dodgers are even more sumptuous when spread with
homemade preserves at breakfast.

2½ cups all-purpose flour

2 tablespoons sugar

2 teaspoons baking powder

1 teaspoon salt

¼ teaspoon baking soda

*10 tablespoons (1¼ sticks) chilled butter,
    cut into bits*

1 cup regular buttermilk

Preheat the oven to 350°F. Grease a 12-cup muffin tin
with butter and set aside.

In a large mixing bowl, whisk together the flour, sugar,
baking powder, salt, and baking soda. Add the butter
and rub it into the flour with your fingertips till the
mixture is mealy. Add the buttermilk and stir till the
dough is slightly firm. Spoon the mixture into the
prepared muffin tin and bake in the center of the oven
till brown and crusty, 40 to 45 minutes.

ORANGE TEA BISCUITS

Makes at least 20 biscuits

IF ANY BREAD EVOKES A MORE GENTEEL ERA IN THE South, when afternoon tea on porches and verandas was almost a ritual in finer homes, it's these delicate rolled biscuits enhanced with orange rind and a sugary orange glaze. Just take care not to saturate the dough with the juice mixture; likewise, spread only enough of the mixture over the tops of the slices to give them a light glaze. The biscuits are equally delectable made with fresh lemon. They keep well in an airtight container up to about a week.

   2½ cups all-purpose flour

   4 teaspoons baking powder

   1 teaspoon salt

   ¼ cup sugar

   4 tablespoons (½ stick) chilled butter, cut into bits

   1 cup whole or 2 percent milk

   2 tablespoons butter, melted

   ⅓ cup orange juice

   1 tablespoon grated orange zest

Preheat the oven to 450°F. Grease a large baking sheet with butter and set aside.

In a large mixing bowl, whisk together the flour, baking powder, salt, and 1 tablespoon of the sugar. Add the chilled butter and rub it in with your fingertips till the mixture is mealy. Add the milk and stir till the dough is soft.

Transfer the dough to a lightly floured work surface and knead 3 or 4 times. Pat out the dough into a rectangle ¼ inch thick and brush the melted butter evenly over the top. In a small bowl, combine the remaining 3 tablespoons sugar and the orange juice, stir well, and spread about 2 tablespoons of the mixture evenly over the dough. Sprinkle the orange zest evenly over the top. Roll up the dough lengthwise jelly-roll style, securing the seam, then cut into slices about ½ inch thick.

Arrange the slices cut side down on the prepared baking sheet about 1 inch apart, spread the remaining sugar-and–orange juice mixture over the tops, let stand for 10 minutes, and bake in center of the oven till golden, 12 to 15 minutes. Let cool and serve at room temperature.

BUTTERMILK BREAD

Makes 1 large loaf

THE LEFTOVER LIQUID DERIVED FROM BEATING OR churning cream into butter, genuine buttermilk has been prized by Southerners for centuries, not only as a delicious drink but also as a key ingredient in certain biscuits, cornbreads, loaf breads, cakes, and pies. Today, most buttermilk you find in markets is cultured skim milk, and while it's not as thick or as rich as the beverage I drank as a child, I think it's still far superior to regular whole milk when it comes to baking virtually all Southern breads. This yeasty, tangy loaf, for example, is ideal for sandwiches and makes a mockery of commercial sliced bread at the breakfast table. Just never forget that when baking anything with buttermilk, you must neutralize the high acidity with an alkali such as baking soda—a cardinal rule that many cooks (and cookbook authors) fail to observe.

> 1 envelope active dry yeast
>
> ½ cup lukewarm water
>
> 1 teaspoon sugar
>
> 1 cup regular buttermilk
>
> ½ cup whole milk
>
> 3 teaspoons salt
>
> 4 cups all-purpose flour
>
> ½ teaspoon baking soda
>
> 1 egg white beaten with 1 tablespoon cold water

In a small bowl, combine the yeast, water, and sugar, stir, and let proof till bubbly, about 5 minutes.

In a large mixing bowl, combine the buttermilk and whole milk and add the yeast mixture and salt. Add 1 cup of the flour plus the baking soda and mix well. Continue adding the flour 1 cup at a time, mixing steadily with a wooden spoon and, if necessary, adding a little more flour till the dough is smooth and not sticky. Turn the dough out onto a lightly floured surface and knead about 5 minutes. Place in a well-greased bowl, turn to coat all sides, cover with plastic wrap, and let rise in a warm area till fully doubled in bulk, at least 2 hours.

Transfer the dough back to the working surface, punch down, and knead about 5 minutes. Grease a 9 by 5 by 3–inch loaf pan with butter. Place the dough in the loaf pan, cover again, and let rise till doubled in bulk, 1½ to 2 hours.

Preheat the oven to 400°F.

Slash three lines along the top of the dough with a razor blade, brush the top with the egg wash, and bake till the bread sounds hollow when thumped, about 45 minutes. Transfer the bread to a rack and let cool.

318

PHILPY BREAD

Makes 2 loaves

PHILPY, A RICE BREAD UNIQUE TO THE SOUTH CAROLINA
and Georgia Lowcountry, can be traced back to
eighteenth-century plantation culture and is a first
cousin to cornbread and johnnycakes. I know nothing
about the origins of the name. Recipes today are found in
only the most obscure regional cookbooks, and I became
familiar with the bread only when my friend "Hoppin'"
John Taylor (the major spokesman for Lowcountry
cookery) introduced it to my mother and me about fifteen
years ago, when we were visiting him in Charleston. John
makes his philpy the old-fashioned way, in a cast-iron
skillet, but the more I tinkered with and modernized the
bread, the more inclined I was to bake it in loaves that
could be sliced more easily. Either way, the bread is
delicious slathered with plenty of butter.

Bacon grease

2 cups long-grain rice, cooked till soft

1 cup regular buttermilk

2 large eggs, beaten

1¼ cups all-purpose flour

1 teaspoon baking powder

1 teaspoon baking soda

1 teaspoon salt

Preheat the oven to 425°F. Grease two 9 by 5 by 3–inch
loaf pans with bacon grease and set aside.

In a large mixing bowl, combine the cooked rice,
buttermilk, and eggs and mash the mixture with a
potato masher till well blended and smooth. In a small
mixing bowl, combine the flour, baking powder, baking
soda, and salt and stir till well blended. Add the dry
mixture to the rice mixture, stir till well blended, and
scrape equal amounts of batter into the prepared pans.
Bake till almost golden brown, about 30 minutes. Serve
hot or warm.

319

Cornbread, Biscuits, Hush Puppies, and Other Breads

Sally Lunn

Makes 1 loaf

NO SOUTHERN BREAD HAS A MORE OBSCURE OR colorful history than the yeast-leavened, rich tea bread known as Sally Lunn. Claimed by Virginia as its own and supposedly named after an English lass who sold buns on the streets of Bath in the eighteenth century, the original bread baked in shallow pans by the Virginia colonists most likely resembled a French brioche in flavor and texture. Legend has it that the stiff dough had to be beaten exactly one hundred times for the bread to come out exactly right. Sally Lunn seems to have evolved over the centuries from a sweet bun to a cake to a savory dinner bread back to a sweet dessert loaf, and on the rare occasions you find it today (mainly in historic Williamsburg, Virginia, and at a few quaint Southern country inns), chances are it will be served as a tea or dessert bread. Personally, I love the bread unsweetened, as in this recipe, and toasted for breakfast. If, however, you want an unusual sweet bread to serve with fresh fruit or ice cream, add about a quarter cup of sugar to the dough.

320

The state of Virginia can lay legitimate claim to the South's first peanuts, country-cured hams, crab cakes, corn pudding, Brunswick stew, Sally Lunn, cornbread, pound cake, apple pie, fruit cobblers, and bourbon whiskey. Much of the credit goes directly or indirectly to Thomas Jefferson, America's first true gastronome.

---

1 envelope active dry yeast

1 tablespoon sugar

¼ cup lukewarm water

1 cup lukewarm whole milk

2 large eggs, beaten

3½ cups all-purpose flour

8 tablespoons (1 stick) butter, melted

1 teaspoon salt

In a large bowl, combine the yeast, sugar, and water, stir, and let proof till bubbly, about 5 minutes. Add the milk and eggs and beat with a wooden spoon till well blended. Gradually add half the flour and continue beating. Add the butter and salt and beat till well blended, then beat in the remaining flour till a soft dough forms. Cover with plastic wrap and let the dough rise in a warm area till doubled in bulk, about 1 hour.

Punch the dough down, cover again, and let stand 15 minutes. Grease a 10-inch tube pan with butter. Scrape the dough into the tube pan, cover, and let rise again till doubled in bulk, about 45 minutes.

Shortly before the dough has finished rising, preheat the oven to 350°F, then bake till the loaf is lightly browned, about 1 hour. Serve immediately, or transfer to a rack, let cool, and serve at room temperature.

TENNESSEE MONKEY BREAD

Makes 1 loaf

FOR YEARS, I THOUGHT THE BEST MONKEY BREAD
I'd ever eaten was at the celebrated Fearrington House, outside Chapel Hill, North Carolina. Then, a member of the Junior League in Memphis exposed me to this Tennessee cheese version at a gracious luncheon, and I was instantly converted. The origins of this strange bread couldn't be more obscure but can most likely be linked to the African bakers on plantations. Some say the bread is so named because the layered balls of dough look like a pack of monkeys; others say it's because you have to "monkey around" so much to put it together. In the South, monkey bread can be either savory or sweet (flavored with raisins, nuts, and spices), but no matter the style, it has to be one of the most distinctive breads ever conceived. Note that you never slice monkey bread; simply tear if off with your fingers.

½ cup warm water

1 envelope active dry yeast

1 cup whole milk

⅓ cup sugar

⅔ cup vegetable shortening

1 cup cooled mashed potatoes

½ cup freshly grated Parmesan cheese

2 large eggs, beaten

2 teaspoons salt

5 cups all-purpose flour

4 tablespoons (½ stick) melted butter

The day before you plan to serve the bread, combine the water and yeast in a large mixing bowl and let proof till bubbly, about 5 minutes. In a saucepan, scald the milk, add the sugar and shortening, and stir till the sugar is dissolved and the shortening melted. Pour the milk into the yeast mixture, stirring. Add the mashed potatoes, cheese, eggs, and salt and stir till well blended. Gradually add the flour and stir till a soft dough forms. Cover with plastic wrap and let rise in a warm area 2 hours. Punch down the dough, cover, and refrigerate overnight.

Turn out the dough onto a floured surface and knead about 10 minutes or till the dough is elastic and pliable. Grease a Bundt pan with butter. Pinch off small amounts of dough, shape into balls the size of a walnut, dip in the melted butter, and layer the balls in the prepared pan about two-thirds full. Cover with a clean towel and let rise 2 hours longer.

Preheat the oven to 350°F, then bake the bread till the balls of dough have combined and the top is golden, about 45 minutes. Unmold and, when serving, tear the bread off instead of slicing it. Serve immediately, or let cool and serve at room temperature.

PEANUT BUTTER BREAD

Makes 1 loaf

I'VE HEARD TALES THAT MORE PEANUT BUTTER IS consumed in Alaska and Hawaii than in Southern states, but I don't believe a word of it. After all, virtually all peanut butter is made from roasted runner goobers grown in Virginia, Georgia, and Tennessee, and in what other regions is the delectable goo used to make velvety soups, gravies, pound cakes, ice creams, and, indeed, a large variety of breads? I know one lady in Richmond, Virginia, who eats peanut butter bread smeared with honey or topped with thinly sliced bananas for breakfast every morning of the week, and sometimes I'll even forego biscuits if there are a couple of toasted slices of this bread on which to spread homemade strawberry or peach preserves. For some years, I was a certified member of The Peanut Butter Lovers Club, headquartered in Atlanta. Overnight, this august organization mysteriously and sadly ceased to exist, but not before I sent them this recipe for their biannual bulletin.

2 cups all-purpose flour

¼ cup sugar

¼ cup firmly packed light brown sugar

1 teaspoon baking powder

½ teaspoon salt

1 cup whole milk

1 large egg

1 cup smooth peanut butter

Preheat the oven to 350°F.

In a large mixing bowl, combine the flour, two sugars, baking powder, and salt and stir till well blended. In another bowl, whisk together the milk and egg, add to the dry mixture, and stir till just moistened. Gradually stir in the peanut butter till well blended, scrape the mixture into a 9 by 5 by 3–inch loaf pan, and bake till a knife inserted in the center of the loaf comes out clean, about 1 hour. Transfer the loaf to a rack and let cool.

PECAN WHOLE WHEAT BREAD

Makes 2 loaves

IF MEMORY SERVES, THIS IS THE AMAZING NUT BREAD
I raved about at the Nu-Wray Inn, in Burnsville, North
Carolina, after visiting my country ham man (Clayton
Long) over in Glendale Springs, high in the Blue Ridge
Mountains. (All I have are the recipe ingredients
scribbled on a piece of oily paper.) Despite the yeast and
white flour, it's a sturdy, fairly heavy loaf, but the flavor
is incredible. To lighten it more, I once tried using lard
instead of butter. That was a mistake. This is about the
only whole wheat bread I bake these days, mainly
because I love it sliced thin and toasted for breakfast—
usually with a fried egg on top.

3 cups all-purpose flour

3 cups whole wheat flour

1 cup finely chopped pecans

⅓ cup sugar

4 teaspoons salt

2 envelopes active dry yeast

4 tablespoons (½ stick) butter

1½ cups water

¾ cup whole or 2 percent milk

In a large mixing bowl, combine the flours, pecans,
sugar, salt, and yeast and blend well. In a saucepan,
heat the butter, water, and milk till hot. Stir into the
dry ingredients, let stand 5 minutes, then stir with a
wooden spoon to form a smooth ball of dough. Turn out
the dough onto a lightly floured surface and knead 8 to
10 minutes. Place the dough in a well-greased bowl,
turn to coat all surfaces, cover with plastic wrap, and let
rise in a warm area till doubled in bulk, at least 1 hour.

Grease two 9 by 5 by 3–inch loaf pans with butter and set
aside. Punch the dough down, transfer back to the work
surface, cut in half, and shape each half into a loaf. Fit
the loaves snugly into the prepared loaf pans, cover
again, and let rise till doubled in bulk, about 45 minutes.

Preheat the oven to 400°F, then bake the loaves till
hollow-sounding when thumped, about 30 minutes.
Transfer to a rack and let cool.

MEMPHIS CASSEROLE CHEESE BREAD

Makes 8 servings

WHY I'VE BEEN INTRODUCED TO SO MANY UNUSUAL breads in the state of Tennessee I can't explain. This yeasty, herbal cheese bread a hostess served in Memphis is one example. Dating back at least to the nineteenth century, this beguiling bread can be made strictly by hand with a wooden spoon for a coarse texture or, for a refined and somewhat lightened texture, an electric mixer can be used. Either way, the bread is traditionally baked in a casserole, must be flavored with oregano—why, nobody knows—and is never cooked less than 1 hour. Once I tried baking the bread without the oregano, and even with the two cheeses it was almost bland. Prepared exactly as directed, the bread is memorable.

2 envelopes active dry yeast

2 cups warm water

4½ cups all-purpose flour

2 tablespoons salt

2 tablespoons finely chopped fresh oregano leaves (or 1½ teaspoons dried)

1 tablespoon sugar

½ cup finely shredded extra-sharp cheddar cheese

½ cup freshly grated Parmesan cheese

2 tablespoons butter, softened

In a large mixing bowl, combine the yeast and water and let proof till bubbly, about 5 minutes. Add 3 cups of the flour, the salt, oregano, sugar, both cheeses, and the butter and beat with an electric mixer at low speed till well blended. Increase the speed to medium and beat till smooth, about 2 minutes. Scrape the batter off the beaters and back into the bowl and, using a wooden spoon, beat in the remaining 1½ cups flour till the batter is smooth. Cover with plastic wrap and let rise in a warm area till doubled in bulk, about 1 hour.

Preheat the oven to 375°F. Grease a 2½-quart casserole or baking dish with butter and set aside.

With a wooden spoon, beat the batter in the bowl vigorously for 30 seconds, scrape it into the prepared casserole or baking dish, and bake till lightly browned, about 1 hour. Transfer the bread to a rack to cool completely, then serve in wedges.

SIP 'N' SEE LEMON TEA BREAD

Makes 1 loaf

REFINED SOUTHERN HOSTESSES DON'T MERELY INVITE friends to tea. The event must have a theme, a notion, a concept. There's an April tea to welcome springtime. There's a pink tea, where the tablecloth, napkins, tiny cakes, butter mints, and even the tea itself are pink. There's a pageant tea to honor a town's beauty queens. And there's a sip 'n' see tea, where a new bride's friends sip tea from dainty porcelain cups and view wedding presents. (I understand there's also an intimate trousseau tea to display everything a bride plans to wear on her honeymoon, including bras and panties.) At a typical sip 'n' see, the tea cups are antique, the silver by Towle or Reed and Barton, the finger sandwiches perfectly trimmed of their crusts, and the delicate tea bread flavored with lemon or orange and lightly glazed. Most civilized. This is also the sort of loaf that might be kept at the ready for those who simply drop by the house just "to visit."

8 tablespoons (1 stick) butter, at room temperature

1 cup sugar

2 large eggs

1½ cups all-purpose flour

1½ teaspoons baking powder

¼ teaspoon salt

½ cup whole or 2 percent milk

Grated zest of 1 lemon

1 cup confectioners' sugar

2 tablespoons fresh lemon juice

½ teaspoon pure vanilla extract

Preheat the oven to 350°F.

In a large mixing bowl, cream the butter and sugar together with an electric mixer, then add the eggs and beat till well blended. In another bowl, combine the flour, baking powder, and salt and stir. Add the flour mixture alternately with the milk to the creamed mixture and mix till well blended. Stir in the lemon rind.

Scrape the batter into a 9 by 5 by 3–inch loaf pan and bake till a straw inserted into the center comes out clean, about 50 minutes. Transfer the bread to a rack and let cool completely before slicing.

In a bowl, combine the confectioners' sugar, lemon juice, and vanilla, stir till smooth, and pour the glaze over the cake.

DINNER YEAST ROLLS

Makes 3 to 3½ dozen rolls

NO SERIOUS SOUTHERN COOK WOULD BE CAUGHT
dead without a dozen or so yeast rolls in the freezer
ready to be popped into the oven for both casual and
formal dinners. To freeze these rolls up to 3 months,
bake as directed about 10 minutes, let them cool, freeze
on baking sheets just till firm, then transfer to airtight
containers or resealable plastic bags and place in the
freezer. When ready to serve, bake in a preheated 350°F
oven about 10 minutes or till golden. (I always brush
mine with a little extra melted butter before baking.)

1½ cups warm water

1 envelope active dry yeast

8 tablespoons (1 stick) butter, melted

2 large eggs, beaten

¼ cup sugar

1 teaspoon salt

5 cups all-purpose flour

*4 tablespoons (½ stick) cup melted butter for
     brushing*

The day before you plan to serve the rolls, combine the
water and yeast in a large mixing bowl and let proof till
bubbly, about 5 minutes. Add the butter, eggs, sugar,
and salt and mix till thoroughly blended. Gradually add
the flour, stirring constantly till a soft dough forms.
Cover with plastic wrap and refrigerate overnight.

Grease 2 baking sheets with butter and set aside. Turn
out the dough onto a floured surface and knead for
about 15 seconds. Roll the dough out about ½ inch
thick, cut into rounds with a biscuit cutter, arrange the
rounds on the prepared baking sheets about 1 inch
apart, cover with clean towels, and let rise in a warm
area about 45 minutes or till doubled in bulk.

Preheat the oven to 350°F.

Brush the rolls with melted butter then bake till golden
brown, about 15 minutes. Serve hot.

326

Pocketbook Rolls

Makes about 2 dozen rolls

DON'T TELL ANY PROUD SOUTHERNER THAT OUR delicate, beloved pocketbook rolls (so named because the folded dough resembles small purses or pocketbooks) bears an uncanny likeness to the famous Parker House rolls created in Boston. Do notice that, unlike less complex yeast rolls, these need to rise at least 2 hours to attain the right feathery texture when baked. The rolls freeze well, and if this is your intent they should be baked no longer than 5 minutes, cooled, frozen in an airtight container, and, when ready to be served, baked in a preheated 400°F oven about 5 minutes or till golden.

1 envelope active dry yeast

½ cup lukewarm whole milk

¼ cup vegetable shortening, at room temperature

4 tablespoons (½ stick) butter, at room temperature

¼ cup sugar

½ cup boiling water

1 large egg, beaten

3 cups all-purpose flour

1½ teaspoons salt

8 tablespoons (1 stick) butter, melted

In a small bowl, combine the yeast and milk and let proof till bubbly, about 5 minutes.

In a large mixing bowl, cream the shortening, the room-temperature butter, and the sugar with an electric mixer, then gradually beat in the boiling water. Add the yeast mixture and stir till well blended. Add the egg and stir till well blended. Sift in the flour, add the salt, and mix well. (The mixture will keep up to 1 week in the refrigerator covered tightly with plastic wrap.)

Three hours before ready to use, roll out the dough on a floured surface to ½-inch thickness and cut into rounds with a 2- to 2½-inch biscuit cutter. Fold each round in half and place on a large greased baking sheet. Brush each roll generously with the melted butter, cover with a towel, and let rise in a warm area about 2½ hours.

Preheat the oven to 400°F.

Bake the rolls till golden brown, 5 to 7 minutes. (If you're planning to freeze part of the rolls, remove those from the oven after 5 minutes, let cool, and store wrapped tightly in aluminum foil.) Serve hot.

CAROLINA RICE MUFFINS

Makes 1 dozen muffins

SARAH RUTLEDGE INCLUDES A NUMBER OF RECIPES for rice bread in *The Carolina Housewife* of 1847, as does the Georgian Annabella Hill in *Mrs. Hill's New Cook Book* a few years later. And when the grain was king all along the Lowcountry during the eighteenth and early nineteenth centuries, there was no better way to use up leftover rice than in all types of loaf breads, muffins, fritters, and even biscuits. Today's authority on the cooking in this area, Damon Lee Fowler, notes, however, that cheap, plentiful rice was more than just an economical filler in expensive white breads; it also contributed a rich moistness to the crumbs and could even transform a quick breakfast bread into a starchy side dish for other meals. Unlike so many other batter breads, alas, these muffins do not freeze well and always need to be made from scratch.

2 cups all-purpose flour

1 cup cooked, cooled, long-grain rice

3 tablespoons sugar

2 teaspoons baking powder

¼ teaspoon salt

¼ teaspoon ground nutmeg

1 cup whole or 2 percent milk

½ cup vegetable oil

1 large egg

Preheat the oven to 400°F. Grease the cups of a 12-cup muffin pan with butter and set aside.

In a large mixing bowl, combine the flour, rice, sugar, baking powder, salt, and nutmeg and mix till well blended. In another bowl, whisk together the milk, oil, and egg, add to the dry mixture, and stir just till the dry mixture is moistened but still slightly lumpy. Spoon equal amounts of the batter into the prepared muffin pans, filling each cup about two-thirds full, and bake till golden brown, 20 to 25 minutes. Transfer to a rack and serve hot or at room temperature.

CARROT-PECAN MUFFINS

Makes about 2 dozen muffins

CARROT BREADS, MUFFINS, AND CAKES ARE FOUND all over the South (still another example of the Southern penchant for any sweet ingredient), but the most amazing carrot muffins I ever tasted were these spicy ones with pecans, prepared by a contestant at a March of Dimes Gourmet Gala cook-off in Birmingham, Alabama. Typically, the muffins would be served at a stylish bridge luncheon or informal coffee get-together. Since the batter freezes well, it's wise to make enough to fill at least two standard muffins pans. As with most muffins, the batter for these should be slightly lumpy and never overmixed, to prevent toughness.

2½ cups all-purpose flour

1 cup sugar

2 teaspoons baking powder

½ teaspoon ground cinnamon

½ teaspoon ground nutmeg

½ teaspoon salt

1 cup whole or 2 percent milk

4 tablespoons (½ stick) butter, melted

2 large eggs

4 medium carrots, scraped and shredded (about 2 cups)

½ cup chopped pecans

329

Preheat the oven to 400°F. Grease the cups of two 12-cup muffin pans with butter and set aside.

In a large mixing bowl, sift together the flour, sugar, baking powder, cinnamon, nutmeg, and salt. In another bowl, whisk together the milk, butter, and eggs till well blended, add to the dry mixture, and stir till well blended. Add the carrots and pecans and mix just till well blended but still slightly lumpy.

Spoon equal amounts of the batter into the prepared muffin pans, filling each cup about two-thirds full, and bake till golden brown, 20 to 25 minutes. Transfer to a rack and serve at room temperature.

Mystery Raisin Bran Muffins

Makes about 2 dozen muffins

I CALL THESE "MYSTERY" MUFFINS NOT BECAUSE THEY contain some secret ingredient but because, frankly, I've never remembered or figured out who the "Ann" is/was on the handwritten recipe in my file. Lord knows there must be a dozen or so Anns around the South whom I've begged for recipes over the years, but none whom I've asked turns out to be the mystery lady behind this formula. No matter. These have been my standard breakfast bran muffins for years, and they are unfailingly sublime. Best of all, the batter freezes beautifully, so make plenty of it for future use.

2½ cups all-purpose flour

1½ cups sugar

2½ teaspoons baking soda

½ teaspoon ground cinnamon

½ teaspoon salt

2 cups regular buttermilk

½ cup vegetable oil

2 large eggs

2 cups raisin bran cereal

½ cup seedless dark or golden raisins

Sift together the flour, sugar, baking soda, cinnamon, and salt into a large mixing bowl. In another bowl, beat together the buttermilk, oil, and eggs with an electric mixer till well blended, add to the dry mixture, and beat till well blended and smooth. Stir in the cereal and raisins till just mixed and the batter is still slightly lumpy (do not beat), cover the bowl with plastic wrap, and refrigerate till thickened, about 2 hours.

Preheat the oven to 400°F. Grease the cups of two 12-cup muffin pans with butter and set aside.

Spoon equal amounts of batter into the prepared muffin pans, filling each cup about two-thirds full, and bake till golden brown, 20 to 25 minutes. Transfer to a rack and serve warm or at room temperature.

Hootie's Blueberry Muffins with Streusel Topping

Makes 1 dozen muffins

WHEN AND HOW THE GERMAN WORD *STREUSEL* ("a sprinkling" or "crumbs") evolved in the South to denote a crumbly, sweet, spicy topping sprinkled on breads, muffins, cakes, and coffee cakes is a real mystery, but I don't think I know a serious cook who doesn't boast his or her special streusel topping. I first tasted my sister's blueberry muffins at a big Sunday brunch she threw at her home in Wilmington, North Carolina. Over the years, she modified the topping from time to time with different nuts and spices, as most Southern housewives tend to do. I still prefer her original formula and use it when blueberries are in season and I decide to make these blueberry muffins for any number of occasions. Do note that, in the South, these muffins would just as likely be served as a dinner bread as at a brunch or breakfast—just as Southerners think nothing of nibbling sugared nuts and sweet pastries with cocktails.

FOR THE TOPPING

2 tablespoons butter

2 tablespoons firmly packed light brown sugar

¼ teaspoon ground cinnamon

¼ cup finely chopped nuts

FOR THE MUFFINS

1½ cups all-purpose flour

2 teaspoons baking powder

½ teaspoon salt

4 tablespoons (½ stick) butter, at room temperature

½ cup sugar

1 large egg

1 teaspoon pure vanilla extract

½ cup whole milk

1½ cups fresh blueberries, picked over and rinsed

Preheat the oven to 400°F. Grease the cups of a 12-cup muffin pan with butter and set aside.

To prepare the topping, melt the butter in a small saucepan, add the brown sugar, and stir over low heat till it dissolves. Add the cinnamon and nuts, mix well, and set aside.

To make the muffins, sift together the flour, baking powder, and salt into a bowl. In a large mixing bowl, cream together the butter and sugar with an electric mixer till fluffy. Add the egg and vanilla and continue beating till well blended. Alternately, stir in the flour mixture and milk, mix well, then fold in the blueberries.

Fill each cup of the prepared muffin pan two-thirds full with batter, spoon a little streusel topping on each, and bake till golden, about 20 minutes. Serve hot or at room temperature.

CHEDDAR-WALNUT SHORTBREAD

Makes about 42 shortbreads

SHORTBREAD, SHORTNIN' BREAD, SHO' BREAD—THE spelling and pronunciation change from area to area, the cooking techniques differ, and the taste can be savory or sweet, but however it's prepared, Southern shortbread (usually made with either butter or lard) is one of the most fascinating descendants of the original Scottish bread baked by the first colonists. I was served this particular version at a very elaborate cocktail reception in Louisville, Kentucky (and I would not have been one bit surprised if it had been sweet instead of savory), but the small shortbreads are also remarkably compatible with either fresh fruit or ice cream. And of course, they're great to keep around just for snacks or last-minute drop-ins.

1¼ cups all-purpose flour

½ teaspoon paprika to taste

¼ teaspoon ground nutmeg

8 tablespoons (1 stick) butter, softened

2 cups grated sharp cheddar cheese, at room temperature

½ cup finely chopped walnuts

Preheat the oven to 400°F. Grease a large baking sheet with butter and set aside.

In a small bowl, combine the flour, paprika, and nutmeg and blend well. In a large mixing bowl, cream the butter with an electric mixer, add the cheese gradually, and beat till well blended. Gradually add the dry ingredients, beating steadily.

Transfer the dough to the prepared baking sheet, roll into a rectangle 12 by 7 inches, cut into pieces 1 by 2 inches, and sprinkle walnuts over the tops. Bake till golden, 12 to 15 minutes, separate the pieces carefully, and let cool on racks.

MOTHER'S PECAN WAFFLES WITH ORANGE SYRUP

Makes 12 to 14 waffles

PREDICTABLY, IT WAS THE EVER-CURIOUS THOMAS Jefferson who returned from France to Virginia with the first long-handled, patterned waffle iron at the end of the eighteenth century, inspiring a culinary tradition that is as popular today in the South as it was two centuries ago. I've heard about but have yet to taste a Baltimore Sunday specialty called kidney stew on waffles, but I have eaten gritty rice waffles in Georgetown, South Carolina, and cornmeal waffles (or "Virginia waffles") with sorghum in Roanoke, Virginia. As for standard breakfast waffles, none can hold a candle to these pecan-studded wonders with a tangy orange syrup that my mother created years ago and still serves at weekend brunches. Remember never to cover cooked waffles while keeping them warm in the oven; it makes them soggy.

FOR THE BATTER

> *2 large eggs*
>
> *1½ cups half-and-half*
>
> *4 tablespoons (½ stick) butter, melted*
>
> *1½ cups all-purpose flour*
>
> *2 teaspoons baking powder*
>
> *1 teaspoon salt*
>
> *½ cup finely chopped pecans*

FOR THE SYRUP

> *2 cups sugar*
>
> *1 cup fresh orange juice*
>
> *¼ cup light corn syrup*
>
> *Grated zest of 1 orange*

To make the batter, combine the eggs, half-and-half, and melted butter in a large mixing bowl and beat with an electric mixer till smooth. Into a small mixing bowl, sift together the flour, baking powder, and salt, add this to the egg mixture, and beat at medium speed till well blended. Add the pecans, beat till well blended and smooth, and set aside.

To make the syrup, combine the sugar, orange juice, and corn syrup in a medium saucepan, bring to a boil over moderate heat, and stir till the sugar is completely dissolved and the mixture syrupy. Remove the pan from the heat, add the orange zest, stir till well blended, and keep warm.

To make each waffle, ladle a small mound of the batter onto the middle of a greased electric waffle iron set at high heat (the amount of batter depends on the size of the iron) and cook according to the manufacturer's instructions till golden brown. Stack the waffles on a plate and keep warm till ready to serve with the syrup.

333

Desserts

Basic Pie Shell

Southern Pecan Pie

Lemon-Buttermilk Chess Pie

Jefferson Davis Pie

Joe's Key Lime Pie

Bourbon—Sweet Potato Pie

Chocolate-Butterscotch Pie

Blackberry-Lemon Icebox Pie

Orange Ice-Cream Pie

Caramel Pound Cake

Cold Oven Pound Cake

Lane Cake

Millionaire Pound Cake

Hummingbird Cake

Lady Baltimore Cake

Missy's White Fruitcake

Real Southern Strawberry Shortcake

Huguenot Torte

Pecan-Cinnamon Coffee Cake

Mrs. Smith's Southern Peach Cobbler

Lattice Blackberry Cobbler

Mixed Berry Cobbler

Florida Papaya Cobbler

Persimmon Pudding with Hard Sauce

Peach Crumble

Creole Bread Pudding
with Whiskey Sauce

Lemon-Date Pudding

The Original Bananas Foster

Ambrosia

Kentucky Fried Peaches

New Orleans Beignets

New Orleans Calas

Chocolate Chip—Peanut Drop Cookies

Nutty Fingers

Old Salem Moravian Cookies

Dibby's Mississippi Pralines

Divinity Fudge

Nancy's Old-Fashioned Peanut Brittle

Fresh Peach Ice Cream

Georgia Corn Custard Ice Cream

BASIC PIE SHELL

Makes one 9- to 10-inch pie shell

THIS BASIC PIE SHELL CAN BE MADE WITH LARD, butter, or margarine as well as with vegetable shortening. As all serious Southern cooks know, nothing produces a flakier pastry (or biscuit) than lard, and if the quality of the lard is good, it can give desserts a unique nutty flavor. Vegetable shortening also yields a flaky texture but lacks the distinctive flavor of lard. Butter and margarine are both richer in flavor than lard or shortening, but since they are only 80 percent fat, they have less shortening power than lard or vegetable shortening, and thus yield a heavier texture (especially butter, because of its milk solids). When I do use shortening, I use only Crisco.

1½ cups all-purpose flour

½ teaspoon salt

½ cup vegetable shortening, lard, butter, or margarine

4 to 5 tablespoons ice water, as needed

In a large mixing bowl, combine the flour and salt, then cut in the shortening with a pastry cutter or two knives till the mixture resembles coarse meal. Mixing with a wooden spoon, gradually add enough of the water so that a ball of dough is formed. Wrap the dough in plastic wrap and chill for 1 hour (or up to 1 day). Grease a 9- or 10-inch pie plate and set aside.

Place the chilled dough on a lightly floured surface and roll it out from the center with a lightly floured rolling pin to a ⅛-inch thickness. Carefully fold the pastry in half, lay the fold across the center of the prepared pie plate, unfold it, and press it loosely into the bottom and sides of the plate. Prick the bottom and sides with a fork, trim and crimp the edges, and place on a heavy baking sheet.

To partially bake the shell, preheat the oven to 425°F and bake till the shell is just firm and slightly golden, 6 to 8 minutes.

Southern Pecan Pie

Makes 6 servings

AT THE RISK OF ALIENATING A FEW HUNDRED Southern friends, family members, and culinary historians, I'm not about to proclaim what does and does not constitute genuine Southern pecan pie. Should the pecans be throughout the filling or just on top of the pie? Can both sugar and corn syrup be used as sweeteners. And what about substituting molasses or sorghum for the corn syrup? Must the batter be mixed only with a wooden spoon for the right texture, or does an electric mixer suffice? Like most Southerners, I firmly believe that pecan pie should be made only with fresh in-season pecans (not those half-rancid nuts sold in cans and cellophane packages), and I'm pretty adamant about my pecan pie not being cloyingly sweet, the way so many are. Furthermore, I always give guests the option of plopping dollops of whipped cream on their wedges, but I'm personally convinced that's only gilding one very beautiful lily that needs no adornment.

The pecan-producing states of Georgia, Alabama, Mississippi, and Louisiana all lay claim to the creation of Southern pecan pie, but Louisiana is considered the most likely contender: cane syrup was produced there in the late eighteenth century. (Has anybody ever proposed Virginia, where Thomas Jefferson grew pecan trees and molasses was readily available?) Curiously, no recipes for pecan pie as we know it today existed till the 1940s.

---

4 large eggs

1½ cups light corn syrup

1½ teaspoons all-purpose flour

1 teaspoon pure vanilla extract

¼ teaspoon salt

4 tablespoons (½ stick) butter, melted

2 cups pecan halves

One unbaked 9-inch Basic Pie Shell (page 336)

Whipped cream, for garnish

Preheat the oven to 350°F.

In a large bowl, beat the eggs with an electric mixer till frothy. Add the corn syrup, flour, vanilla, and salt, and beat till well blended. Stir in the butter and pecans and mix well. Turn the mixture into the pie shell and bake till the filling is cooked but still soft in the center when the pie is gently shaken, 50 to 60 minutes. Cool the pie completely on a rack, chill slightly, and serve with dollops of whipped cream on top.

337

Lemon-Buttermilk Chess Pie

Makes 6 to 8 servings

THE DINER IN QUESTION WAS IN ALABAMA, OR Kentucky, or Arkansas (depending on who's telling the story), but wherever the locale, this classic Southern pie supposedly got its name from a waitress who, when asked by a customer about the rich pie, responded, "Oh, honey, it's jes' pie." Another anecdote traces chess pie back to an eighteenth-century English "cheese pie," and still another links it with a chest in a Southern kitchen where confections were once stored. Whatever the origins of the name, I've eaten chess pie in every Southern state (and nowhere else), sometimes made with plain granulated sugar and flour instead of cornmeal, enriched even more with heavy cream instead of milk or buttermilk, and flavored with everything from coconut to cider vinegar to multiple spices (in which case the pie almost becomes a Jefferson Davis pie, page 339). Feel free to experiment in any way you choose.

4 large eggs, beaten

4 tablespoons (½ stick) butter, melted

¼ cup regular buttermilk

3 tablespoons fresh lemon juice

1 teaspoon pure vanilla extract

1½ cups firmly packed light brown sugar

2 teaspoons yellow cornmeal

¼ teaspoon salt

2 teaspoons grated lemon zest

One unbaked 9-inch Basic Pie Shell (page 336)

Preheat the oven to 350°F.

In a large mixing bowl, combine the eggs, butter, buttermilk, lemon juice, vanilla, brown sugar, cornmeal, and salt and beat with an electric mixer till well blended and smooth. Add the lemon zest and stir till well blended. Scrape the mixture into the pie shell and bake till a straw inserted in the center comes out clean, about 30 minutes. Cool the pie completely on a rack.

Jefferson Davis Pie

Makes at least 8 servings

NAMED AFTER THE PRESIDENT OF THE CONFEDERACY and most likely created during The War Between the States, this pie is basically a spicy version of chess pie and has as many versions throughout the South as pecan pie and sweet potato pie. I've eaten it in Mississippi with chopped dates, in Tennessee with dried apricots, and at home in North Carolina with crystallized fruits, but I still say the best Jeff Davis pie is one not gussied up with anything but a few golden raisins. This, by the way, is a great pie to serve at a gumbo or Brunswick stew party.

8 tablespoons (1 stick) butter, softened

1 cup granulated sugar

½ cup firmly packed dark brown sugar

1 tablespoon all-purpose flour

2 large eggs, beaten

1 cup half-and-half

1 tablespoon bourbon

½ teaspoon ground cinnamon

½ teaspoon ground allspice

½ teaspoon pure vanilla extract

½ cup seedless golden raisins

One unbaked 9- or 10-inch Basic Pie Shell (page 336)

Preheat the oven to 425°F.

In a large mixing bowl, cream together the butter and two sugars with an electric mixer till fluffy. Add the flour and eggs, and beat till well blended. Add the half-and-half, bourbon, cinnamon, allspice, and vanilla and continue to beat till well blended and smooth. Stir in the raisins, scrape the mixture into the pie shell, and bake for 10 minutes. Reduce the oven temperature to 350°F and continue baking till a knife inserted in the center comes out clean, about 30 minutes. Cool the pie completely on a rack. Serve in wedges at room temperature or chilled.

JOE'S KEY LIME PIE

Makes 6 to 8 servings

ORIGINALLY MADE WITH STANDARD PASTRY CRUST, Key lime pie has presumably been a prized specialty of southern Florida and the Keys ever since the distinctive yellowish limes were first cultivated there in the early nineteenth century. Over the years, a richer graham-cracker crust became the norm for this pie, providing the perfect counterpoint to the highly acidic limes; and cooks now gild the lily by topping the pie with either whipped cream or meringue. Until just recently, genuine Key limes (similar to pale Mexican limes) were next to impossible to find outside southern Florida except in specialty food shops, but during the spring months, I am noticing more and more netted bags of tiny green "Key limes" in finer supermarkets. (The green color baffles me, but they do *taste* like Key limes.) The much larger and more common green Persian (or Tahiti) limes can be substituted, but there is a definite difference in flavor. Without question, the best Key lime pie I've ever tasted is the one served for decades at Joe's in Miami Beach, Florida, the same legendary Joe's where locals and tourists alike flock to eat sumptuous stone crabs. Of course, the folks at the restaurant insist that the recipe is a closely guarded secret, but rest assured that my rendition produces the exact same results.

FOR THE CRUST

6 ounces graham crackers, pulverized in a blender or food processor

1 cup sugar

6 tablespoons (¾ stick) butter, melted

FOR THE FILLING

4 large egg yolks

1 tablespoon grated lime zest

One 14-ounce can sweetened condensed milk

1 cup fresh Key lime juice (or Persian lime juice)

FOR THE TOPPING

1 cup heavy cream, chilled

2 tablespoons confectioners' sugar

Thin slices of lime, for garnish

Preheat the oven to 350°F.

To make the crust, combine the graham cracker crumbs, sugar, and butter in a 9-inch pie plate and rub the mixture with your fingertips till the crumbs are fully moistened. Press the mixture firmly on the bottom and sides of the plate, bake till the crust is golden, about 8 minutes, and set aside on a rack to cool.

To make the filling, place the egg yolks and lime zest in a mixing bowl and beat with an electric mixer till fluffy, about 5 minutes. Gradually add the condensed milk and lime juice and continue beating till just blended. Pour the mixture into the pie crust. Bake just till the filling has set, about 10 minutes, let cool completely on a rack, and place in the freezer for about 20 minutes before serving.

To make the topping, combine the cream and confectioners' sugar in a bowl, beat with an electric mixer till stiff peaks form, and spread evenly over the cold pie, swirling and peaking the cream with a spoon in a decorative manner. Cut the pie into wedges, garnish the top of each wedge with a curled lime slice, and serve immediately. If not serving immediately, store in the refrigerator and then place in the freezer for about 20 minutes before serving.

341

BOURBON SWEET POTATO PIE

Makes 6 to 8 servings

AT MAGNOLIA GRILL IN DURHAM, NORTH CAROLINA, Ben Barker has become one of the most innovative chefs in the entire nation, while his wife, Karen, has probably done more to add new dimension to Southern desserts than any other pastry expert. Her lemon-coconut tart was what impressed me first. Then, when I tasted this light, silky, beautifully balanced sweet potato pie spiked with bourbon, I realized that the more standard pie I'd always baked at Thanksgiving was utterly bland by comparison. This is an example of modern Southern cooking at its most intelligent and blissful.

3 sweet potatoes (about 1½ pounds)

1 cup half-and-half

5 tablespoons light brown sugar

5 tablespoons maple syrup

4 tablespoons (½ stick) butter, melted

3 large eggs

¼ cup bourbon

1 teaspoon pure vanilla extract

¼ teaspoon ground cinnamon

¼ teaspoon ground nutmeg

¼ teaspoon salt

⅛ teaspoon ground cloves

Freshly ground black pepper to taste

One unbaked 9-inch Basic Pie Shell (page 336)

Preheat the oven to 425°F.

Place the potatoes in the oven and roast till easily pierced with a fork, about 1 hour. When cool enough to handle, peel the potatoes, place the flesh in a large mixing bowl, and mash with a potato masher to a smooth purée.

Reduce the oven to 350°F.

Add all remaining ingredients to the potato purée and whisk steadily till thoroughly blended. Scrape the mixture into the pie shell and bake till a knife inserted in the center comes out clean, about 50 minutes. Transfer the pie to a rack to cool completely.

342

Chocolate-Butterscotch Pie

Makes 6 to 8 servings

SOUTHERNERS HAVE HAD A PASSION FOR BUTTER-scotch for as long as there's been a codified style of cooking in the South, and the array of butterscotch pies, cookies, icings, toppings, and candies is truly staggering. Basically no more than a blend of butter and brown sugar, butterscotch can be enriched even more with egg yolks and cream or milk; flavored with lemon, chocolate, vanilla, and spices; and transformed into various textures. What's most amazing about this particular pie is the way it separates into layers of butterscotch and chocolate as it bakes. The pie is so delicious that I could eat it just by itself, with no meringue to dress it up. The pie is almost as good chilled as at room temperature, despite the change in the meringue's texture.

2 ounces (2 squares) unsweetened chocolate

6 tablespoons (¾ stick) butter, softened

1½ cups firmly packed light brown sugar

3 large eggs, separated

One 13-ounce can evaporated milk

1 teaspoon pure vanilla extract

One unbaked 9-inch Basic Pie Shell (page 336)

6 tablespoons sugar

Preheat the oven to 325°F.

In a small, heavy saucepan, melt the chocolate over low heat and set aside to cool.

In a mixing bowl, cream the butter and brown sugar with an electric mixer till fluffy, add the egg yolks, and beat till well incorporated. Add the melted chocolate, evaporated milk, and vanilla and stir till the batter is well blended and light. Scrape the batter into the pie shell and bake till set, about 50 minutes. Cool the pie completely on a rack.

In a bowl, beat the egg whites with an electric mixer till firm peaks form, then gradually add 5 tablespoons of the sugar, beating steadily till the whites stiffen. Spread the meringue over the pie to seal the edges completely, sprinkle the remaining sugar over the top, and bake just till the meringue is slightly browned, about 10 minutes. Cool the pie on a rack and serve at room temperature.

BLACKBERRY-LEMON ICEBOX PIE

Makes 6 to 8 servings

GRASSHOPPER PIE, BLACK-BOTTOM PIE, BUTTERSCOTCH pie—all are basically what used to be commonly called "icebox" pies, meaning those that require no rolling of pastry dough, no exotic fillings, and no final baking. I'm not saying that icebox pies are exclusively Southern today, only that I haven't encountered a single one (not even in roadside diners) outside the South for decades. And, I declare, these clever pies deserve renewed attention, not only because they're so delicious but because they lend themselves to endless experimentation with multiple ingredients. And talk about quick and easy to prepare: you simply come up with a good crumb crust and tasty filling and refrigerate the pie till it's set.

FOR THE CRUST

1½ cups finely ground graham crackers

5 tablespoons butter, melted

1 tablespoon sugar

¼ teaspoon salt

FOR THE FILLING

¼ cup cornstarch

¼ cup water

5 cups fresh blackberries, rinsed

2 teaspoons fresh lemon juice

1 cup sugar

½ teaspoon ground cinnamon

1 tablespoon butter

Preheat the oven to 350°F.

To make the crust, combine the graham crackers, butter, sugar, and salt in a mixing bowl and stir till the crumbs are moistened. Press the mixture tightly onto the bottom and sides of a 9-inch pie plate, bake till crisp, about 8 minutes, and cool the crust on a rack.

To make the filling, combine the cornstarch and water in a small bowl and stir till smooth. In a saucepan, combine 3 cups of the berries, the lemon juice, sugar, and cinnamon and bring to a boil, stirring. Reduce the heat to moderate, add the cornstarch mixture, and stir constantly till the mixture thickens. Continue cooking 2 minutes longer, then remove the pan from the heat, add the butter and remaining blackberries, and stir till the filling is well blended.

Scrape the filling into the cooled pie crust, cover with plastic wrap, and refrigerate for 5 to 6 hours or till the filling is completely set. Serve chilled.

ORANGE ICE-CREAM PIE

Makes 6 to 8 servings

IN THE SOUTH, ICE-CREAM PIES ARE A FIRST COUSIN TO icebox pies, and a particular favorite both at children's birthday parties and at ice-cream socials held in the summertime. The variations are limitless (different-flavored ice creams, different secondary flavorings, etc.), and it's truly amazing how the ice cream maintains its firm texture even when the pie is briefly baked to brown the meringue. Obviously, however, this is a pie that should be served the second it comes out of the oven.

1 cup graham cracker crumbs

8 tablespoons (1 stick) butter, cut into bits and softened

1 quart vanilla ice cream, softened slightly

4 large egg whites

⅛ teaspoon cream of tartar

1 teaspoon pure vanilla extract

1 cup confectioners' sugar, sifted

3 tablespoons grated orange zest

In a bowl, combine the cracker crumbs and butter and rub the mixture with your fingertips till well blended. Press the mixture onto the bottom and sides of a 9-inch pie plate and chill for 2 hours. Fill the shell with the ice cream, spread evenly with a rubber spatula, cover with plastic wrap, and freeze till the ice cream is hard, about 2 hours.

Preheat the oven to 450°F.

In a large mixing bowl, combine the egg whites and cream of tartar and beat with an electric mixer till soft peaks form. Add the vanilla plus the sugar a tablespoon at a time, beating constantly till the meringue holds stiff peaks. Sprinkle the orange zest evenly over the ice cream, spread the meringue evenly over the top, and bake just till the meringue is golden brown, about 2 minutes. Serve immediately.

345

Caramel Pound Cake

Makes at least 10 servings

QUEEN OF SOUTHERN
..., sensuous masterpiece that
...any sighs of ecstasy on a
birthday or... ...t as at the family dinner table.
Caramel is by far the ... ost popular icing in the South,
but the cake is equally sensational when glazed with an
orange or raspberry icing. Just be sure to allow time for
the cake to stand at least 2 hours before serving, so that
the icing sets properly. Wrapped tightly in foil, the cake
keeps for weeks in the refrigerator without losing too
much of its moisture or savor.

FOR THE CAKE

3½ cups all-purpose flour

1 teaspoon baking powder

½ teaspoon salt

2 cups firmly packed light brown sugar

1½ cups granulated sugar

3 sticks butter, softened

6 large eggs

1½ cups milk

FOR THE ICING

8 tablespoons (1 stick) butter

1 cup firmly packed dark brown sugar

½ cup whole milk

½ teaspoon pure vanilla extract

4 cups confectioners' sugar, sifted

Preheat the oven to 325°F. Grease a 10-inch tube or
Bundt pan with butter and set aside.

To make the cake, sift together the flour, baking
powder, and salt into a mixing bowl and set aside. In
another large mixing bowl, cream together the two
sugars and butter with an electric mixer, then add the
eggs one at a time, beating after each addition till well
blended. Alternately, add the flour mixture and milk to
the creamed mixture and beat till well blended and
smooth. Scrape the batter into the prepared pan and
bake till a knife inserted in the center comes out
almost clean, about 1 hour. (Do not overbake.) Cool
the cake on a rack for 10 minutes, then turn it out
onto the rack to cool completely.

To make the icing, melt the butter in a large, heavy
saucepan over low heat, then add the brown sugar and
milk and, stirring, bring the mixture almost to a boil.
Remove from the heat and let cool. Stir in the vanilla,
then gradually add the confectioners' sugar and stir till
well blended and smooth.

Transfer the cake to a cake plate and ice the top and
sides using a heavy knife or rubber spatula. Let the
cake stand at least 2 hours before serving.

Cold Oven Pound Cake

Makes 10 to 12 servings

WHEN I HEARD ABOUT AN ELDERLY LADY IN JOHNSON City, Tennessee, who used both butter and shortening in her pound cake and started the cake in a cold oven, I couldn't get the recipe from her fast enough—out of sheer curiosity. "Well, son, this cake's been in my family for generations," she began, "and I have no earthly idea why it has to start out in a cold oven. It just does, and if you do it any other way, it won't turn out real moist and light and good." No doubt the shortening explains why the cake (which has no baking powder) is indeed lighter than most pound cakes, but the only possible explanation for the cold oven (and I've consulted any number of cake experts, including my mother) is that in the old days some vessels used to bake cakes (most likely a form of pottery) risked cracking if exposed to a sudden blast of heat from a preheated oven. Who knows? Except for adding a little almond extract for additional flavor, I baked the cake just as directed, and, for whatever reasons, it turned out beautifully. I do like to think that this is what a Southern pound cake tasted like a century or more ago.

3 cups sugar

2 sticks butter, softened

8 tablespoons vegetable shortening

5 large eggs

3 cups all-purpose flour

1 cup whole milk

1 teaspoon pure vanilla extract

1 teaspoon almond extract

1 teaspoon fresh lemon juice

Grease a 10-inch tube pan with butter and set aside. In a large mixing bowl, cream together the sugar, butter, and shortening with an electric mixer, then add the eggs one at a time, beating till well blended. Alternately, add the flour and milk and beat till the batter is smooth. Add the two extracts and the lemon juice and mix till well blended.

Scrape the batter into the prepared pan and place in the center of the oven. Heat the oven to 325°F and bake till a cake tester or knife blade inserted in the center comes out clean, about 1½ hours. Turn the cake out onto a rack and let cool completely.

LANE CAKE

Makes 10 to 12 servings

IF EVER THERE WAS A TRUE SOUTHERN CEREMONIAL layer cake, this is it. Created in Clayton, Alabama, by Emma Rylander Lane and called simply "Prize Cake" in her hometown cookbook of 1898, *Some Good Things to Eat,* the cake quickly assumed her name, and its fame spread far and wide. There were no pecans or coconut in the original recipe, only raisins and "one wine glass of good whiskey or brandy," but as the cake evolved in the twentieth century, these two extra ingredients became standard. I know some cooks in the Deep South who, to this day, refer to the masterpiece as Prize Cake, and it is indeed a winning cake for special occasions, worth every bit of the effort it takes to make.

FOR THE CAKE

½ pound (2 sticks) butter

2 cups sugar

1 teaspoon pure vanilla extract

3½ cups all-purpose flour

3 teaspoons baking powder

1 teaspoon salt

1½ cups whole milk

8 large egg whites, beaten till stiff

FOR THE FILLING

10 large egg yolks

1½ cups sugar

1 teaspoon grated orange zest

½ cup bourbon

1 teaspoon pure vanilla extract

½ teaspoon ground nutmeg

1 cup seedless golden raisins

1 cup chopped pecans

1 cup shredded unsweetened coconut (fresh or frozen)

FOR THE ICING

2 large egg whites

1 cup sugar

½ cup water

½ teaspoon salt

⅛ teaspoon cream of tartar

1 teaspoon pure vanilla extract

Preheat the oven to 350°F. Grease three 9-inch round cake pans with butter and set aside.

To make the cake, cream the butter, sugar, and vanilla in a large mixing bowl with an electric mixer till fluffy. In another bowl, sift together the flour, baking powder, and salt, then add it alternately with the milk to the creamed mixture, stirring. Beat in half the egg whites, then fold in the remaining whites. Spoon equal amounts of batter into each of the three prepared pans, bake 20 to 25 minutes, and turn out the cake layers on racks to cool.

To make the filling, combine the egg yolks, sugar, and orange zest in the top of a double boiler over simmering water and cook gently, stirring constantly, till the mixture thickens enough to coat a wooden spoon. Remove the pan from the heat, add the bourbon, vanilla, nutmeg, raisins, pecans, and coconut, and stir till well blended. Allow the filling to cool, then spread it evenly between the cake layers.

To make the icing, beat the egg whites in a bowl with an electric mixer till stiff, and set aside. In a saucepan, combine the sugar, water, salt, and cream of tartar, bring to a boil, reduce the heat to moderate, and cook, stirring, for 5 minutes. Add the vanilla, stir, then pour the mixture slowly over the egg whites, beating constantly with a wooden spoon.

Spread the icing evenly over the top and sides of the cake and let stand for at least 2 hours before serving.

Millionaire Pound Cake

Makes at least 10 servings

THROUGHOUT THE SOUTH, THERE ARE "MILLIONAIRE" (or "million-dollar") pies, cakes, puddings, trifles, and Lord knows what else—the implication being that the dessert is super rich. Like a traditional Southern pound cake, this sumptuous beauty, the pride of an elderly belle I once knew in Jackson, Mississippi, contains neither baking powder nor baking soda. Yes, the cake is rich and sturdy, as any respectable pound cake should be, and it almost begs to be served with dishes of home-churned ice cream or fresh fruit. If you like a slightly undercooked, sweet, moist "sad streak" in pound cake, as I do, reduce the baking time about 15 minutes or till the cake tester or knife blade comes out almost clean.

1 pound (4 sticks) butter, softened

4 cups sugar

6 large eggs

4 cups all-purpose flour

1 cup whole milk

1 teaspoon pure vanilla extract

1 teaspoon almond extract

Preheat the oven to 300°F. Grease a 10-inch tube pan with butter, dust the bottom and sides with flour, and set aside.

In a large mixing bowl, cream the butter and sugar with an electric mixer and add the eggs one at a time, beating after each addition. Alternately, add the flour and milk, stirring with a wooden spoon till the batter is smooth. Add the two extracts and stir till well blended.

Scrape the batter into the prepared pan and bake till a cake tester or knife blade inserted in the center comes out clean, about 1½ hours. (Do not bake till the cake is dry.) Cool the cake in the pan on a rack for 5 minutes, then turn it out on the rack to cool completely.

Hummingbird Cake

SOUTHERNERS' PASSION FOR BIG, RICH, COMPLEX cakes is perhaps best exemplified by this spicy masterpiece, which has won blue ribbons at county fairs all over the South and is served at any occasion, from birthday parties to weddings to bereavements. Of course nobody knows for sure how the cake got its name, but the most logical explanation so far comes from my own mother: "You see, the cake is sweet as molasses, and everybody knows how hummingbirds love red sugar water and the sweet nectar of flowers, so the reasoning makes lots of sense." Right.

FOR THE CAKE

3 cups all-purpose flour

2 cups sugar

1 teaspoon baking soda

1 teaspoon ground cinnamon

1 teaspoon salt

3 large eggs, beaten

1½ cups vegetable oil

One 8-ounce can crushed pineapple, undrained

2 cups chopped nuts (pecans, walnuts, or hazelnuts)

2 cups chopped bananas

1½ teaspoons pure vanilla extract

FOR THE ICING

Two 8-ounce packages cream cheese, at room temperature

½ pound (2 sticks) butter, at room temperature

Two 16-ounce boxes confectioners' sugar, sifted

2 teaspoons pure vanilla extract

Preheat the oven to 350°F. Grease three 9-inch round cake pans with butter, dust the bottom and sides with flour, and set aside.

To make the cake, combine the flour, sugar, baking soda, cinnamon, and salt in a large bowl and stir till well blended. Add the eggs and oil and stir till the dry ingredients are moistened, taking care not to beat them. Stir in the pineapple, 1 cup of the nuts, the bananas, and vanilla.

Divide the batter evenly among the prepared pans. Bake till a straw inserted into the center of the cakes comes out clean, 25 to 30 minutes. Let the cakes cool in the pans for 10 minutes, then turn them out onto racks to cool completely.

To make the icing, combine the cream cheese and butter in a large bowl and cream with an electric mixer till smooth. Add the confectioners' sugar, beat till light and fluffy, and stir in the vanilla. Spread the icing between the cakes stacked on a cake plate, ice the top and sides of the cake, and sprinkle the remaining nuts over the top.

LADY BALTIMORE CAKE

Makes 10 to 12 servings

IT'S DEBATABLE WHICH OF THE SOUTH'S ELABORATE
cakes is more ceremonial: Lane cake or Lady Baltimore
cake. What is for sure is that the latter is in no way
connected with the city of Baltimore but, rather, with
Owen Wister's 1906 romantic novel entitled *Lady
Baltimore,* in which the cake is described. In reality, the
luscious cake was most probably created in Charleston,
South Carolina, by Alicia Rhett Mayberry around the turn
of the twentieth century and not named till after Wister's
novel was published. Some, on the other hand, believe it
could have originated in a Charleston tearoom of the time
called Lady Baltimore. Whatever its origins, the cake's
fame spread quickly throughout the South, and today the
versions are multiple. Notice that to make this complex
cake, you'll need both a standing electric mixer and a
hand mixer. Lady Baltimore cake is always prepared for a
very special occasion—which seems appropriate.

FOR THE CAKE

1½ sticks butter, softened

1½ cups sugar

1 teaspoon pure vanilla extract

1 teaspoon almond extract

3 cups cake flour

3 teaspoons baking powder

1½ cups whole milk

4 large egg whites

FOR THE ICING

2 large egg whites

⅓ cup cold water

1½ cups sugar

¼ teaspoon cream of tartar

1 teaspoon pure vanilla extract

¾ cup coarsely chopped pecans

½ cup seedless golden raisins

¼ cup diced seedless figs

½ teaspoon almond extract

Preheat the oven to 350°F. Generously grease two 9-inch cake pans with butter and set aside.

To make the cake, cream the butter in the bowl of a standing electric mixer on high speed while gradually adding 1 cup of the sugar. Add the two extracts and continue beating till the mixture is light. Sift together the flour and baking powder into the butter mixture, adding it alternately with the milk and beating till the batter is smooth.

In a bowl, beat the egg whites with an electric mixer till firm peaks form, add the remaining ½ cup of sugar, and beat till the meringue is fairly stiff and glossy. Gently fold the egg whites into the batter, then scrape equal amounts of batter into the prepared cake pans, tapping the bottoms to remove any air bubbles. Bake the cakes till a cake tester or knife blade comes out clean, 35 to 40 minutes, then turn them out onto racks to cool.

Meanwhile, make the icing by combining the egg whites, water, sugar, and cream of tartar in the top of a double boiler over simmering water and beating them with an electric mixer till stiff peaks form. Off the heat, stir in the vanilla. Scrape about one third of the icing into a bowl, add the remaining ingredients, and mix till well blended.

To assemble the cake, place 1 cake layer on a large plate and cover with the fruit icing, smoothing it with a rubber spatula. Cover with the second layer and then ice the top and sides with the remaining icing. Let the cake stand about 1 hour before serving.

353

MISSY'S WHITE FRUITCAKE

Makes 1 large 5- to 6-pound cake and two 2½-pound cakes

FOR THOUSANDS OF SOUTHERN COOKS, MAKING fruitcakes between Thanksgiving and Christmas is an age-old ritual that's as alive today in home kitchens as it was two hundred years ago. Some make dark fruitcakes (with all sorts of dark fruits, spices, and macerated citrus peels), others only white ones (with only crystallized fruits). My mother makes both, usually with friends at a "spend-the-day" fruitcake party. If you're still under the illusion that all fruitcakes are by nature heavy, this simply means that you've sadly never tasted a light, moist, boozy Southern masterpiece like this white one, which Mother serves at every holiday occasion imaginable and often gives away as gifts (baked in small individual pans). There are Southern heirloom fruitcakes that have been periodically doused with bourbon or brandy, carefully stored and aged, and literally passed down from one generation to the next. I know, for I've been nursing one of Mother's in the bottom of my refrigerator since 1971—and it just gets richer and more complex every time I pinch off a morsel.

1 pound (4 sticks) butter, softened

3 cups sugar

14 large eggs

5 cups all-purpose flour

2 teaspoons baking powder

1½ cups light rum or bourbon, plus more for soaking

2 teaspoons pure vanilla extract

2 teaspoons pure almond extract

2 teaspoons pure lemon extract

2½ pounds crystallized pineapple, coarsely chopped

2½ pounds crystallized cherries, coarsely chopped, with about 8 whole cherries

2¼ pounds pecans, chopped

Preheat the oven to 250°F and place a small pan of water on the bottom rack of the oven to provide moisture. Grease one 10 by 4–inch tube pan and two 8 by 4½ by 2½–inch loaf pans and set aside.

In a large mixing bowl, cream together the butter and sugar with an electric mixer till light and fluffy, then add the eggs one at a time, beating constantly. Sift together 3 cups of the flour and the baking powder into the mixture and blend thoroughly with a wooden spoon. Add 1 cup of the rum or bourbon and the 3 extracts and blend thoroughly. Mix the chopped fruit and pecans with the remaining 2 cups of flour in another large mixing bowl and fold them into the creamed mixture.

Scrape the batter evenly into the prepared pans, arrange the reserved cherries in a decorative manner over the tops, and bake till a cake tester or knife blade inserted in the centers comes out clean, about 3 hours. Pour the remaining ½ cup rum or bourbon over the tops of the cakes and let them cool completely in the pans. Wrap each cake securely in cheesecloth soaked in rum or bourbon and store them in airtight containers at least 3 weeks before cutting.

Real Southern Strawberry Shortcake

Makes 6 servings

I SUPPOSE THERE ARE SOUTHERNERS WHO STOOP TO using those small commercial sponge cakes to make strawberry shortcake, the way most people in the country foolishly do, but I don't know any. Genuine Southern strawberry shortcake is and always has been made with only one style of bread: split and buttered baking powder biscuits. Nor do I know any respectable Southern cook who would destroy a strawberry shortcake with something so atrocious as Cool Whip instead of fresh whipped cream. And, finally, shortcake prepared with anything but fresh, ripe, sweet strawberries (no white cores) defeats the whole idea of strawberry shortcake, meaning that serious folks make strawberry shortcake only when summer berries are at their peak. In short, Southerners are unapologetic elitists when it comes to the ritual of strawberry shortcake—always served warm, of course.

2 cups all-purpose flour

3 tablespoons sugar

1 tablespoon baking powder

¼ teaspoon salt

8 tablespoons (1 stick) butter, softened

1 large egg, beaten

⅔ cup half-and-half

Butter for spreading

4 cups fresh, ripe strawberries, rinsed, hulled, sliced in half, and sugared to taste

1 cup heavy cream, whipped to stiff peaks

Preheat the oven to 450°F.

In a large mixing bowl, combine the flour, sugar, baking powder, and salt and mix well. Add the butter and, using a pastry cutter or two knives, cut the butter into the mixture till crumbly. In a small bowl, combine the egg and half-and-half and beat till well blended, then add to the flour mixture and stir till thoroughly moist. Turn the dough out onto a floured surface and knead very briefly. With your hands, pat out the dough to about a ½-inch thickness, then, using a floured 3-inch biscuit cutter, cut out 6 biscuits. Place the biscuits on an ungreased baking sheet and bake on the upper rack of the oven till slightly brown on top, about 12 minutes.

While they're still hot, split open the biscuits, spread lightly with butter, and arrange close together on a crystal cake plate. Spoon the berries and cream onto the biscuits and serve while still warm. (For attractive individual servings, prop one biscuit half at an angle on the other on small dessert plates and spoon berries and cream over the tops.)

355

Huguenot Torte

Makes 6 servings

FOR A LONG TIME, IT WAS TAKEN FOR GRANTED THAT this glorious specialty of the South Carolina Lowcountry originated with the persecuted French Protestants who fled to the area in the late seventeenth century. Then some killjoy discovered that the dessert is neither French nor old and was probably named after Charleston's Huguenot Tavern, where, during the 1940s, it was adapted from a Mississippi River delta recipe and served to great acclaim. No matter, for whatever its origins and age, the fluffy dessert (which is not really a torte) is one of the most delicious creations in the Southern repertory—and one of the easiest to make. I like to serve it at Thanksgiving, for a nice change.

1½ cups all-purpose flour

2½ teaspoons baking powder

¼ teaspoon salt

2 large eggs

1½ cups sugar

½ teaspoon pure vanilla extract

1 cup finely chopped pecans

1 cup apples, cored, peeled, and finely chopped

1 cup heavy cream

1 tablespoon sweet sherry

Preheat the oven to 350°F. Grease a 2-quart baking dish with butter and set aside.

Sift together the flour, baking powder, and salt into a large mixing bowl. In a medium mixing bowl, whisk together the eggs, sugar, and vanilla together till frothy, add to the dry mixture, and stir till well blended. Gently fold the pecans and apples into the batter. Scrape the batter into the prepared baking dish and bake till a cake tester or knife blade inserted in the center comes out clean, about 35 minutes. Let the torte cool completely.

In a small mixing bowl, beat the cream and sherry together with an electric mixer till stiff peaks form, spread the cream mixture evenly over the top of the torte, and serve in squares.

PECAN-CINNAMON COFFEE CAKE

Makes 8 to 10 servings

SOUTHERNERS DON'T EAT "DANISH" WITH THEIR coffee for breakfast the way Yankees do—much less (heaven forbid!) gummy bagels. They eat coffee cake— homemade coffee cake like this spicy pecan classic that might well be smeared with fruit preserves and consumed *after* all the eggs and sausage and biscuits. Rich coffee cakes are also served at teas, taken to shut-ins and bereavements, or given as housewarming, birthday, or wedding gifts in the South. Since they freeze so beautifully, I know some home cooks who make two or three at a time for future needs. If you do freeze coffee cake, first make sure it's wrapped tightly in foil and stored in an airtight plastic bag—whole or cut into individual wedges.

2½ cups all-purpose flour

1½ cups sugar

1 tablespoon baking powder

1 teaspoon salt

1 cup whole milk

½ cup vegetable shortening

1½ teaspoons pure vanilla extract

2 large eggs

1½ cups coarsely chopped pecans

1 teaspoon ground cinnamon

2 tablespoons butter, cut into pieces

Preheat the oven to 350°F. Grease a 9- or 10-inch round baking pan with butter and set aside.

In a large mixing bowl, sift together 2 cups of the flour, 1 cup of the sugar, the baking powder, and salt. Add the milk, shortening, and vanilla and beat for 3 minutes with an electric mixer. Add the eggs, beat for 2 minutes longer, and scrape the batter into the prepared baking pan. Distribute the chopped pecans evenly over the top.

In a bowl, combine the remaining ½ cup of flour, ½ cup of sugar, and the cinnamon, add the butter, and work with your fingertips till the mixture becomes mealy. Distribute the mixture evenly over the pecans and bake the cake till a knife inserted in the center comes out clean, about 45 minutes. Let the cake cool completely on a rack, transfer to a round serving dish, and cut into wedges.

Mrs. Smith's Southern Peach Cobbler

Makes 10 to 12 servings

FORGET MOST OF WHAT YOU'VE HEARD ABOUT
Georgia peaches. Yes, Georgia peaches are certainly far
superior to the pulpy, bitter peaches they grow in
California, but where I go for sweet peach perfection is
to the South Carolina Piedmont region, intersected by
Interstate 77, and, more specifically, to The Peach Tree
and other orchards in and around Filbert. Peach fanatics
from as far away as Pennsylvania and Kentucky flock to
The Peach Tree every summer to see and smell and taste
the luscious Early Belles, White Ladies, Lorings, and
Indian Red clings, and owner Ben Smith and his wife,
Merwyn, actually mail out periodic picking schedules to
regular customers. Who better to ask how to make the
best Southern peach cobbler than Mrs. Smith herself,
who seems to have a new version each year? When I told
her about my most recent idea of adding a couple of ripe
mangoes and some almond extract to the peaches in my
cobbler, her candid reaction was, "Then, of course, it's
no longer a real peach cobbler—but why not?" If you
would like to try my sublime variation, simply substitute
two peeled and cut-up ripe mangoes for a pound of the
peaches and add ½ teaspoon almond extract to the
sugared mixture.

- *6 pounds ripe Southern peaches, peeled, pitted, and cut into ½-inch-thick slices*
- *1½ cups plus 2 tablespoons sugar*
- *4 tablespoons (½ stick) butter, cut into small pieces*

- *2 cups all-purpose flour*
- *1 tablespoon baking powder*
- *2 teaspoons salt*
- *¼ cup vegetable shortening*
- *1 cup heavy cream*
- *Vanilla ice cream*

Preheat the oven to 400°F. Grease a 3- to 3½-quart
baking dish with butter and set aide.

In a large mixing bowl, combine the peaches and 1½
cups of the sugar and toss well. Spoon the fruit into the
prepared baking dish and dot the top with the butter.

Into a large mixing bowl, sift together the flour, baking
powder, salt, and remaining 2 tablespoons of sugar,
then cut in the shortening with a pastry cutter or two
knives till the mixture resembles coarse meal. Add the
cream and stir till the dough forms a ball. Turn the
dough out onto a lightly floured work surface, roll out ¼
inch thick, and trim as necessary to fit the baking dish.
Place the dough over the fruit, crimp the edges, and
bake till the pastry is golden brown and the peaches are
still slightly juicy, about 30 minutes. Transfer the dish
to a rack and let the cobbler cool for about 10 minutes,
then serve warm topped with ice cream.

LATTICE BLACKBERRY COBBLER

Makes at least 8 servings

SOUTHERN LATTICE COBBLERS ARE LEGENDARY, THE most famous being hot blackberry cobbler topped with scoops of vanilla ice cream or freshly whipped cream. Every rural Southerner has lurid tales of being eaten alive by chiggers while picking blackberries as a child, with their only consolation being the prospect of eating as many cobblers as the buckets of fat berries would produce. Some cobblers are made with both a bottom crust and the lattice pastry strips woven on top. This one incorporates crunchy pieces of baked pastry in the filling itself for a more balanced texture. Although this same recipe could be used for any fresh berries, nothing evokes the true soul of the South like an authentic blackberry cobbler.

FOR THE FILLING

6 cups fresh blackberries, stemmed and rinsed

1½ cups sugar

3 tablespoons all-purpose flour

1 teaspoon fresh lemon juice

3 tablespoons butter, cut into pieces

FOR THE DOUGH

2 cups all-purpose flour

1½ teaspoons baking powder

½ teaspoon salt

¼ cup vegetable shortening

½ cup whole milk

Preheat the oven to 375°F. Grease a baking sheet and a 3-quart rectangular baking dish with butter and set aside.

To make the filling, combine the blackberries, sugar, flour, and lemon juice in a large bowl, toss well, and let stand.

To make the dough, combine the flour, baking powder, and salt in a mixing bowl and whisk till well blended. Add the shortening and cut with a pastry cutter or two knives till the mixture is mealy. Add the milk and stir till a soft ball of dough forms. Transfer to a floured surface, roll out half the dough ¼ inch thick, and cut into 1-inch-wide strips. Place the strips on the prepared baking sheet, bake till lightly browned, about 10 minutes, and let cool. Break the strips into small pieces. Roll out the remaining dough ¼ inch thick, cut into 1-inch-wide strips, and set aside.

To assemble the cobbler, spoon half the blackberries into the prepared baking dish and scatter the browned pastry pieces over the top. Add the remaining berries, dot with the butter pieces, and weave the unbaked pastry strips in a lattice design over the top. Place the dish on a heavy baking sheet and bake till the berries are bubbly and the pastry browned, about 40 minutes. Serve hot or warm.

MIXED BERRY COBBLER

Makes 6 to 8 servings

QUITE OFTEN THE FRUITS AND BERRIES USED FOR classic Southern cobblers are preboiled slightly to produce maximum juice and flavor when baked. The concept behind this mixed berry cobbler is different, in that the berries are softened naturally with sugar and almost macerated in their own juices while the pastry is being made. The one major stipulation is that the berries be perfectly ripe, meaning that this is strictly a seasonal summer cobbler. Unlike many cobblers, which are made with a lattice crust, this one is covered completely and snugly with dough to contain as much of the moisture and flavor as possible. This same recipe can also be used for single or mixed fresh fruit cobblers.

FOR THE FILLING

2 cups fresh, ripe, medium strawberries, stemmed and rinsed

2 cups fresh, ripe raspberries, stemmed and rinsed

2 cups fresh, ripe blueberries, stemmed and rinsed

½ cup sugar

FOR THE DOUGH

1 cup all-purpose flour

½ cup yellow cornmeal

3 tablespoons sugar

2 teaspoons baking powder

¼ teaspoon salt

6 tablespoons (¾ stick) butter, cut into pieces

¼ cup whole milk

Preheat the oven to 375°F. Grease a 2- to 2½-quart baking dish with butter and set aside.

In a large bowl, combine the three berries and sugar, toss well, arrange evenly in the baking dish, and set aside.

To make the dough, combine the flour, cornmeal, 2 tablespoons of the sugar, the baking powder, and salt in a mixing bowl and whisk till well blended. Add the butter and cut it in with a pastry cutter or two knives till the mixture is crumbly. Gradually add the milk, mixing lightly with a fork till a loose dough forms, adding a little more milk if necessary. Transfer the dough to a lightly floured surface and knead about 10 times or till smooth. Roll out the dough just wide enough to fit the baking dish, place it snugly on top of the filling, and cut a few vent holes in the top.

Bake the cobbler till golden brown and the juices bubble in the center, 30 to 35 minutes. Transfer the dish to a rack and let the cobbler cool for about 10 minutes before serving.

Florida Papaya Cobbler

Makes 6 to 8 servings

I'VE LOVED PAPAYAS EVER SINCE MY FIRST VISIT TO
Florida's Daytona Beach and St. Augustine as a child,
and now that this silky, juicy, tart-sweet fruit indigenous
to that state seems more and more available in
supermarkets everywhere, perhaps home and
professional cooks alike will begin to exploit its many
culinary possibilities. Ripe, soft, golden papayas are
best eaten raw (the shiny dark seeds, by the way, are
delicious in salad dressings), but what you want for
dishes like this luscious cobbler is fruit that is still
greenish yellow and slightly firm. Papayas do ripen
very quickly at room temperature, so beware, or you
might end up with a soupy cobbler.

> 3 slightly green papayas (about 1½ pounds
>   each), peeled, seeded, and cut into ¼-inch
>   slices
>
> ½ cup firmly packed light brown sugar
>
> ¼ teaspoon ground cinnamon
>
> ¼ teaspoon ground nutmeg
>
> 2 cups all-purpose flour
>
> 1 tablespoon baking powder
>
> 1 tablespoon sugar
>
> 1 teaspoon salt
>
> 8 tablespoons (1 stick) cold butter, cut into pieces
>
> 1 cup half-and-half
>
> Juice and grated zest of 1 lime

Preheat the oven to 400°F. Grease a shallow 2½-quart
baking dish with butter and set aside.

In a bowl, combine the papaya, brown sugar,
cinnamon, and nutmeg, toss well, and set aside.

In another bowl, combine the flour, baking powder,
sugar, and salt and stir till well blended. Add half the
butter and quickly work it into the dry ingredients with
your fingertips till the mixture is mealy. Gradually add
the half-and-half, stirring with a wooden spoon just till
a ball of dough forms. (Do not overmix.) Place the
dough on a lightly floured surface, roll it out about
¼ inch thick or till slightly smaller than the prepared
baking dish. Trim the edges and crimp the dough to
make an attractive border.

Spoon the papaya mixture into the prepared dish,
drizzle the lime juice and sprinkle the grated zest over
the top, and dot with the remaining butter pieces. Lay
the rolled-out dough over the top so the edges do not
quite touch the sides of the dish, cut several steam
vents in the dough, and bake till nicely browned, 30 to
35 minutes. Transfer the dish to a rack and let the
cobbler cool for about 10 minutes before serving.

Persimmon Pudding With Hard Sauce

Makes 10 to 12 servings

"ONE OF THE MOST PALATABLE FRUITS OF THIS LAND," proclaimed John Smith in Virginia at the beginning of the seventeenth century, referring, no doubt, not to disagreeably astringent, unripe summer persimmons but to the succulent ripe ones that fall off the trees in late fall. Today, Indiana may grow more Japanese persimmons than any state in the nation, but only in the South do you still find the more flavorful, fat, reddish-orange, native American persimmons that so impressed our ancestors. Southerners use these persimmons to make cakes, pies, and preserves (some even grind the seeds to be used as a coffee substitute), but without question, the most popular and glorious dessert (especially at Thanksgiving) is persimmon pudding with either whipped cream or a buttery hard sauce. The pudding is perfect for a large holiday buffet.

FOR THE PUDDING

2 cups boiling water

4 large, ripe persimmons, stemmed and rinsed well

1¼ cups firmly packed light brown sugar

3 large eggs

1¼ cups all-purpose flour

1 teaspoon baking powder

1 teaspoon baking soda

½ teaspoon salt

2 teaspoons ground cinnamon

1 teaspoon ground nutmeg

1 teaspoon ground ginger

2½ cups half-and-half

4 tablespoons (½ stick) butter, melted

FOR THE SAUCE

8 tablespoons (1 stick) butter, softened

2 cups confectioners' sugar, sifted

¼ teaspoon salt

1 teaspoon pure vanilla extract

¼ cup heavy cream

Preheat the oven to 325°F. Grease a 3-quart baking dish with butter and set aside.

To make the pudding, pour the boiling water over the persimmons in a large mixing bowl, stir for about 2 minutes, then drain in a colander. Run the persimmons through a food mill (do not use a food processor) to produce 2 cups of pulp, then, in a large mixing bowl, combine the pulp, brown sugar, and eggs and beat with a fork till well blended. In a small mixing bowl, combine the flour, baking powder, baking soda, salt, and spices and stir this mixture alternately with the half-and-half into the persimmon mixture. Add the melted butter and stir till well blended and smooth. Scrape the mixture into the prepared baking dish and bake till firm, about 1½ hours.

To make the sauce, combine the softened butter and sugar in a mixing bowl and beat with an electric mixer till light and fluffy. Add the salt and vanilla and beat well, then add the cream and beat till the sauce is smooth. (Do not chill this sauce for any length of time, which would alter the texture.)

Serve the pudding warm topped with the hard sauce.

363

PEACH CRUMBLE

Makes 6 to 8 servings

CRUMBLES, CRISPS, BUCKLES, GRUNTS, PANDOWDIES, *cobblers*—the number of names used in the South to designate various styles of batter desserts made with fruits and berries is truly amazing, and most likely all derive from our British heritage. One may be crunchy, another mushy, and others more like cake than short pastry, but all are basically simple to make and provide delicious alternatives to more ordinary pies and puddings. This particular peach crumble, textured with oats, almost demands to be served with scoops of vanilla ice cream on top.

4 cups peeled, sliced fresh peaches (about 1½ pounds)

1 tablespoon fresh lemon juice

1 cup firmly packed dark brown sugar

½ cup all-purpose flour

½ cup quick oats (not instant)

½ teaspoon ground cinnamon

¼ teaspoon salt

¼ cup vegetable shortening

2 tablespoons butter

1 tablespoon whole milk

1 teaspoon pure vanilla extract

Preheat the oven to 375°F. Grease a 2- to 2½-quart baking dish with butter and set aside.

In a large bowl, combine the peaches and lemon juice, toss, spoon into the prepared baking dish, and set aside.

In another large bowl, combine the brown sugar, flour, oats, cinnamon, and salt and stir till well blended. Add the shortening and butter and cut them in with a pastry cutter till the mixture is crumbly. In a small bowl, stir together the milk and vanilla and drizzle over the dry mixture, tossing with a fork.

Spread the mixture evenly over the peaches and bake till the crumbs are browned and the peaches bubbly. Transfer the dish to a rack and let the crumble cool slightly before serving.

Georgia's most famous and glorious peach, the Elberta, was developed by accident near Marshallville in 1857 when, for fun, Samuel Rumph planted a few old dried-out seeds his grandmother was in the habit of dropping into her sewing basket. When the seeds budded and the plants were cross-pollinated by bees with other trees in the orchard, a wondrous new golden peach was born, and Rumph named it after his grandmother, Elberta.

CREOLE BREAD PUDDING WITH WHISKEY SAUCE

Makes 8 servings

BREAD PUDDING HAS BEEN SYNONYMOUS WITH New Orleans for at least two centuries, and I still consider the classic one with whiskey sauce served at the Bon Ton Café to be the finest in the city. At one point, chopped dried fruits were also added to the pudding, suggesting that the dessert's origins were not French Creole but, somehow, English. The pudding can certainly be made with day-old commercial white bread, but it does make all the difference in texture if you use a homemade, crusty country bread.

FOR THE PUDDING

1 quart whole milk

10 slices day-old white bread, torn into pieces

1 cup heavy cream

4 large eggs, beaten

1 cup sugar

1 teaspoon pure vanilla extract

1 teaspoon ground cinnamon

½ teaspoon ground nutmeg

8 tablespoons (1 stick) butter, melted

½ cup seedless dark raisins

½ cup broken pecans

FOR THE SAUCE

3 large egg yolks

1 cup sugar

1 pint heavy cream

1 tablespoon pure vanilla extract

3 tablespoons bourbon or blended whiskey

Preheat the oven to 350°F. Grease a 2- to 2½-quart baking dish with butter and set aside.

To make the pudding, heat the milk in a medium saucepan over moderate heat until bubbles just begin to form around the edges of the pan. Combine the scalded milk, bread, and cream in a large mixing bowl and stir till well blended. In a medium mixing bowl, mix the eggs and sugar together till well blended, then stir into the bread mixture. Add the vanilla, cinnamon, and nutmeg and mix till well blended. Stir in the melted butter, raisins, and pecans. Scrape the mixture into the prepared baking dish, set the dish in a larger baking pan filled with warm water about 1 inch deep, and bake till a cake tester or knife blade inserted in the center comes out clean, about 1 hour. Remove the dish from the pan of water, transfer the dish to a rack, and let the pudding cool.

To make the sauce, place the egg yolks in a medium-size heavy saucepan and beat slightly. Add the sugar, cream, and vanilla, mix till well blended, and cook over moderate heat, stirring constantly, till the mixture comes to a low boil. Immediately remove the pan from the heat and stir in the bourbon. Let the sauce cool slightly before spooning it over the pudding, served in deep bowls.

LEMON-DATE PUDDING

Makes 6 servings

IN SOUTHERN COOKING, DATES SHOW UP IN ALL SORTS of breads, pies, puddings, and, of course, dark fruitcakes, and one of the most popular canapés found at snazzy cocktail parties is dates stuffed with cream cheese. I was served this particular pudding at a stately home in Charlottesville, Virginia, prepared, no less, by the family's private chef for an elaborate Christmas buffet. Suffice it to say that it's nothing less than sumptuous. Like bread-and-butter pudding, this one almost has to be baked in a water bath for the right delicate texture. The pudding is just as delicious served at room temperature as warm.

4 tablespoons vegetable shortening

4 tablespoons (½ stick) butter, softened

½ cup sugar

2 large eggs

½ cup fresh lemon juice

1 tablespoon grated lemon zest

1½ cups all-purpose flour

2 teaspoons baking powder

¾ cup whole milk

½ cup pitted and finely chopped dates

Preheat the oven to 350°F. Grease a 2-quart baking dish with butter and set aside.

In a large mixing bowl, cream the shortening, butter, and sugar with an electric mixer till light, then add the eggs one at a time, beating till well blended. Add the lemon juice and zest and beat till well blended. Sift the flour and baking powder directly into the mixture, stir well, then gradually add the milk, beating steadily as it is added. Add the dates and stir till well blended.

Scrape the mixture into the prepared baking dish. Place the dish in a large baking pan, pour enough boiling water into the pan to come 1 inch up the sides of the dish, and bake till firm and slightly browned, 50 to 55 minutes. Remove the dish from the pan of water, transfer the dish to a rack, and serve warm or at room temperature.

The Original Bananas Foster

Makes 2 servings

FOR YEARS, THERE'S BEEN LOTS OF BANTER ABOUT THE origin and correct preparation of Bananas Foster, without question one of the South's (indeed, America's) most famous desserts. Well, I happen to own a letter from Ella Brennan (today one of the owners of Commander's Palace, in New Orleans) describing all the colorful details, and suffice it to say that around 1950, when she and her family were involved in Brennan's Restaurant in New Orleans, her brother, Owen, asked her to create a special dessert for a dinner in honor of the chairman of the city's vice commission, Richard Foster. Bananas were a major import in New Orleans, and Ella's mother always served sautéed bananas with scrambled eggs, so after a little experimentation and embellishment, Bananas Foster was introduced to the world with plenty of flair. The rest is history. This is the original recipe; any other is bogus.

4 tablespoons (½ stick) unsalted butter

½ cup firmly packed dark brown sugar

2 ripe bananas, peeled and sliced fairly thin lengthwise

½ teaspoon ground cinnamon

2 tablespoons banana liqueur

3 ounces light or dark rum

1½ cups French vanilla ice cream

In a flat chafing dish or skillet, melt the butter over moderately low heat, add the brown sugar, and stir till the sugar has melted. Add the bananas and sauté gently till tender, about 3 minutes on each side. Sprinkle the cinnamon over the bananas. Pour the banana liqueur and rum over the bananas, shake the pan to distribute the liquid, ignite the liquid, and baste the bananas with the flaming sauce till the flames die out. Immediately serve the bananas and sauce over the ice cream.

367

Ambrosia

Makes 6 servings

FRANKLY, I'VE NEVER ONCE SEEN AMBROSIA OUTSIDE the South, served either as a salad or a dessert. Likewise, I've never seen ambrosia served in the South as a salad as it originally was in the nineteenth century. And to add to the confusion, I've seen everything from grapefruit to bananas to grapes to liqueurs added to what is traditionally only a subtle combination of fresh orange, coconut, and sugar. Personally, I like a few crushed pecans in my ambrosia, for textural contrast, and I know of no other dessert that is a more perfect foil to rich pies and fruitcakes during the winter holidays. Fresh coconut and orange juice are almost obligatory in this dessert.

4 large oranges

1 large grapefruit

2 cups grated fresh coconut

½ cup crushed pecans

½ cup fresh orange juice

½ cup confectioners' sugar

Peel the oranges and grapefruit, cutting away all the white pith, then carefully remove the sections from the membranes that surround them and discard any seeds. Arrange a layer of the mixed sections in the bottom of a large crystal bowl and sprinkle a little of the coconut and pecans over the top. Repeat the layers till the ingredients are used up, ending with a layer of coconut and pecans. Drizzle the orange juice over the top, cover the bowl with plastic wrap, and chill well. Serve the ambrosia in crystal compote dishes and sprinkle the top of each portion with confectioners' sugar.

KENTUCKY FRIED PEACHES

Makes 2 to 4 servings

IN MY EXPERIENCE, COUNTRY-STYLE RESTAURANTS (particularly barbecue pits) in both Georgia and Arkansas seem to pride themselves on small fried peach pies and turnovers, but it's only in Kentucky where I've come across these spicy fried peaches served almost without exception atop large scoops of vanilla ice cream. One restaurant in Louisville even went so far as to have waiters very ceremoniously flame the peaches tableside in chafing dishes, perhaps just another indication of how our noble peaches are revered no matter where or how they're prepared. Served with slices of homemade pound cake, these fried peaches couldn't be easier to produce, provided you pay careful attention to the flaming and don't singe every hair off your head.

The small, delicate, half-moon Southern fried pie most likely originated in Alabama, where today the sugared hot pies are traditionally filled with fresh peaches or peach butter.

2 large firm ripe peaches

3 tablespoons butter

2 tablespoons sugar

2 tablespoons light brown sugar

⅛ teaspoon ground cinnamon

1 ounce bourbon

Vanilla ice cream

Peel the peaches with a sharp paring knife, cut them in half, remove the seeds, and pat the halves dry with paper towels.

In a large enameled or stainless-steel skillet, combine the butter, two sugars, and cinnamon over moderate heat and stir well till the butter melts. Add the peaches cut side down and cook till the bottoms are nicely glazed, about 2 minutes. Turn them over, baste with the liquid, and cook 2 minutes longer.

Meanwhile, warm the bourbon in a tiny pot, ignite it carefully, and, when the flames die, pour over the peaches. Slide the pan back and forth till the flames die, and serve immediately over scoops of ice cream.

369

New Orleans Beignets

Makes about 6 servings

PART OF THE UNIQUE NEW ORLEANS EXPERIENCE IS perching at the legendary (and usually rambunctious) Café du Monde (open twenty-four hours a day), ordering cups of strong chicory coffee, and popping into your mouth the small, deep-fried, doughnutlike fritters known as beignets. Covered with confectioners' sugar, they're also delectable with crushed fresh fruit, berries, or any fruit sauce spooned over the top. When frying the beignets, make sure not to crowd the vessel and to maintain the heat at exactly 325°F. Otherwise, they could be greasy and soggy.

3 cups all-purpose flour

2½ tablespoons baking powder

½ cup sugar

1 teaspoon salt

1 cup whole milk

1 cup water

1 large egg, beaten

Vegetable oil for deep frying

½ cup confectioners' sugar

Sift together the flour, baking powder, sugar, and salt into a large bowl. In a small bowl, combine the milk, water, and egg and whisk till well blended. Add the wet ingredients to the dry ingredients and stir till the batter is well blended and smooth.

In a deep-fat fryer or deep, heavy skillet, heat about 2 inches of oil over moderately high heat till it reaches 325°F on a deep-fat thermometer. Drop the batter by heaping teaspoons into the fat about 10 at a time (never crowding the vessel), fry till golden brown, 6 to 7 minutes, and drain on paper towels. Place the confectioners' sugar in a fine sieve and sprinkle generously over the beignets.

New Orleans Calas

Makes about 2 dozen

"BELLES CALAS, BELLES CALAS," THE STREET VENDORS of New Orleans used to hawk in the nineteenth century, selling the hot, spongy rice balls from colorful stands in the French Quarter. Today, anyone who visits the Crescent City stops by the Café du Monde for chicory coffee and the sugared squares of fried dough known as beignets, but just about the only place you might find the equally delectable calas is in African American homes on the first day of Mardi Gras and at special weekend breakfasts. Although nobody knows whether the soft balls can be traced back to African or French traditions, calas are one of the most distinctive of all Creole creations. They're particularly delectable for breakfast, and I love them served with plenty of honey.

2 cups boiled and cooled long-grain white rice

3 large eggs, beaten

¼ teaspoon pure vanilla extract

¼ teaspoon grated nutmeg

¼ teaspoon ground cinnamon

¼ teaspoon grated lemon zest

1 cup all-purpose flour

½ cup sugar

3 teaspoons baking powder

½ teaspoon salt

1 quart vegetable or peanut oil

Confectioners' sugar, for dusting

In a large mixing bowl, combine the rice, eggs, vanilla, nutmeg, cinnamon, and lemon zest and stir till well blended. Into another bowl, sift together the flour, sugar, baking powder, and salt, add to the rice mixture, and stir till well blended, adding a little more flour if necessary to make a batter that is thick but loose enough to be dropped easily from a spoon.

Pour the oil into a large pot and heat to about 350°F on a deep-fry thermometer. Drop the batter by heaping tablespoons into the oil, fry till nicely browned, about 2 minutes, and drain on paper towels. Dust the calas with confectioners' sugar and serve hot.

371

Chocolate Chip–Peanut Drop Cookies

Makes about 30 cookies

THE ONLY COOKIE SOUTHERNERS LOVE MORE THAN ultrachewy chocolate chip cookies are ultrachewy chocolate chip cookies that have the added crunch of peanuts. Just as we like an undercooked "sad streak" running through our pound cakes, we've learned that the softest cookies are drop cookies baked just till they begin to brown slightly—an explanation for why these should not be cooked a second longer than 10 minutes, if that. I know one lady in Virginia who is so particular about these cookies that she refuses to make them with anything but genuine extra-large Virginia peanuts, which she orders in the mail and roasts herself (as I now do).

8 tablespoons (1 stick) butter, softened

½ cup smooth peanut butter

½ cup firmly packed light brown sugar

½ cup granulated sugar

2 large eggs

1½ cups all-purpose flour

1 teaspoon baking powder

½ teaspoon salt

1 cup semisweet chocolate chips

¾ cup finely chopped roasted peanuts

1 teaspoon pure vanilla extract

Preheat the oven to 350°F.

In a large mixing bowl, cream the butter and peanut butter together with an electric mixer till well blended. Add the two sugars and the eggs and continue beating till the mixture is well blended and smooth. Into a small mixing bowl, sift together the flour, baking powder, and salt and gradually beat this into the creamed mixture. Add the chocolate chips, peanuts, and vanilla and stir till well blended. Drop the batter by tablespoons 2 inches apart onto ungreased baking sheets and bake just till the cookies begin to brown slightly, about 10 minutes. Let the cookies cool for 10 minutes, then transfer them to a rack to cool completely.

Nutty Fingers

Makes about 35 fingers

These feathery light, fragile, addictive cookies covered with confectioners' sugar are still further testimony to the monumental role that pecans play in all Southern cookery. They are ideal for holiday entertaining, but since they tend to fall apart at the least touch, they shouldn't be included in confection gift boxes or tins. Also, since pecans can turn rancid after a few weeks, even in airtight containers, the cookies should be used up as soon as possible or given away. Believe it or not, cookies like these are devoured at Southern cocktail parties with great relish.

2 sticks butter, at room temperature

¼ cup plus 1 tablespoon sifted confectioners' sugar

2½ cups all-purpose flour

1 cup finely chopped pecans

1 teaspoon pure vanilla extract

½ teaspoon almond extract

Dash of salt

Sifted confectioners' sugar, for rolling

Preheat the oven to 350°F.

In a large mixing bowl, cream together the butter and sugar with an electric mixer, then gradually blend in the flour with a wooden spoon. Add the nuts, the two extracts, and salt and mix till well blended.

Take small pieces of dough, form into finger shapes, and place on an ungreased baking sheet about ½ inch apart. Bake till lightly browned, about 30 minutes, let the fingers cool, then roll them generously in confectioners' sugar. Store in an airtight container up to 2 weeks.

373

OLD SALEM MORAVIAN COOKIES

Makes 3 to 4 dozen

CLOSELY LINKED HISTORICALLY WITH THE Pennsylvania Dutch, the pious sect of German Protestants known as Moravians, who settled in the piedmont sections of Maryland, Virginia, and North Carolina during the eighteenth century, were renowned for the spicy cakes and cookies baked at Christmas and Easter. The most famous settlement of all was around Winston-Salem, North Carolina, and today, Old Salem boasts not only some of the most exquisite restored houses and buildings in the entire country but a few authentic bakeries that still turn out these delectable cookies. Their number, sadly, seems to diminish more each year, meaning that those like me who can remember the thrill of ordering a batch of Moravian cookies every Christmas have had to learn to make their own. Fortunately, they couldn't be easier or more fun to produce.

4 tablespoons (½ stick) butter, softened

¼ cup vegetable shortening

½ cup firmly packed light brown sugar

1 cup cane syrup (available in specialty food or Latino shops and often labeled Golden Syrup) or molasses

2 tablespoons brandy

4 cups all-purpose flour

1 teaspoon baking soda

1 teaspoon salt

1 tablespoon ground cinnamon

1 teaspoon ground ginger

1 teaspoon ground cloves

½ teaspoon ground allspice

In a large mixing bowl, cream the butter, shortening, and brown sugar with an electric mixer till creamy, add the syrup (or molasses) and brandy, and stir till well blended. In another bowl, sift together the flour, baking soda, salt, and spices, add to the butter mixture, and mix the dough with your hands till well blended and stiff. Cover with plastic wrap and chill the dough at least 3 hours and preferably overnight.

Preheat the oven to 375°F. Grease two baking sheets with butter and set aside.

On a lightly floured surface, roll out about one third of the dough ⅛ inch thick, cut out the cookies with various cookie cutters in the shape of stars, animals, crescents, circles, etc., and arrange them on one of the two prepared baking sheets about 1 inch apart. Repeat with another third of the dough, then the final third, and bake till the cookies are lightly browned, 7 to 8 minutes. (Do not overbake, which makes the spices bitter.) Transfer to a rack to cool till crisp, then store in airtight containers.

374

Dibby's Mississippi Pralines

Makes about 3½ dozen pralines

NAMED AFTER A SEVENTEENTH-CENTURY DIPLOMAT, César du Plessis-Praslin, and one of the great delicacies of Louisiana Creole cuisine for more than three hundred years, pralines today come in every flavor and texture imaginable. (Ultrasoft ones with orange rind are a favorite at Mardi Gras, and in New Orleans at Christmas, you even find some dyed pink.) Sinfully rich, pralines couldn't be easier to make, the one requirement being a candy thermometer to indicate the exact instant the caramelized mixture reaches the soft ball stage. (You can drop a small amount of the hot mixture into ½ cup of cold water and roll the glob between your thumb and index finger to see if a soft ball forms, but this technique is very chancy.) This particular recipe (one of the best I know) comes from an old-fashioned Mississippi belle who had no use for classic Louisiana pralines. "Those folks have still never learned that praline batter must be beaten for the candy to have the right texture," Dibby would rave indignantly. And I think she made a good point, since these are indeed lighter and more delicate than New Orleans pralines. Do take note that all pralines lose much of their subtle flavor and soft delicacy (even in airtight containers) after about 2 weeks. And take special pride in your pralines with the knowledge that the ones you find in quaint shops of New Orleans, Savannah, and Charleston now cost an exorbitant buck *apiece!*

2 cups firmly packed dark brown sugar

2 cups granulated sugar

4 tablespoons (½ stick) butter

1 cup evaporated milk

1 cup whole milk

¼ teaspoon salt

1½ teaspoons pure vanilla or maple extract (or a combination of both)

3 tablespoons light corn syrup

2 cups broken-up pecans

In a large, heavy saucepan, combine all the ingredients except the pecans and mix till well blended. Cook, stirring, over moderate heat till the mixture registers 240°F on a candy thermometer. Cool the mixture slightly, then beat with a wooden spoon till creamy. Add the pecans and stir till well blended and smooth. Drop the batter by heaping teaspoons onto waxed paper and let the pralines cool completely before serving or storing in airtight containers.

DIVINITY FUDGE

Makes at least 3 dozen morsels

FLUFFY, CREAMY, AND RICH AS SIN, DIVINITY FUDGE (or simply "divinity" in some states) is one of the South's most distinctive candies and a staple at formal Christmas dinner buffets and cocktail parties. The basic recipe rarely varies from state to state, though I have had divinity fudge that included chocolate, coconut, and any number of flavorings. Traditionally, it is made with only granulated sugar, but I personally prefer a blend of granulated and light brown sugar for added depth and flavor. It's said that one test of a good Southern cook is his or her ability to turn out perfect divinity, and, yes, the technique can be a bit tricky till you get the hang of it.

3 large egg whites

1½ cups granulated sugar

1½ cups firmly packed light brown sugar

1 cup water

1 cup light corn syrup

½ teaspoon salt

1 teaspoon pure vanilla extract

Pecan halves for garnish

In a mixing bowl, beat the egg whites with an electric mixer till stiff peaks form. Set aside.

In a heavy saucepan, combine the two sugars, water, corn syrup, and salt and bring to a boil, stirring till the sugar dissolves. Reduce the heat to moderately low and continue cooking till the syrup reaches 255°F on a candy thermometer, or till it spins a long thread when dribbled from a fork or spoon. Remove immediately from the heat and pour in a slow stream over the egg whites, beating constantly with an electric mixer on high speed. Add the vanilla and continue beating till the fudge begins to thicken and hold its shape.

Using 2 teaspoons, shape the fudge into bite-size morsels (adding a few drops of hot water if it becomes too stiff to handle), place on two large baking sheets covered with wax paper, and press a pecan half into each top. When cooled, store in an airtight container.

376

NANCY'S OLD-FASHIONED PEANUT BRITTLE

Makes about 1½ pounds

THE CANDY CALLED BRITTLE HAS BEEN A SPECIALTY IN various areas of the South for well over a century, and while pecans, hazelnuts, and even almonds are often used to make brittles in the Deep South and Appalachia, by far the most popular types in Georgia, the Carolinas, and Virginia involve the region's superior peanuts. (President Jimmy Carter always loved nothing more than his mother's peanut brittle.) To this day, the best peanut brittle I've ever tasted was that made by a paraplegic lady in Charlotte, North Carolina, who never allowed her affliction to curtail her passion for cooking. I can still see Nancy in her wheelchair pushing and pulling her sheet of brittle on a marble slab till it was almost as thin as paper. Once I asked her to write down the exact recipe and technique, part of which I include here in her own words. Take note that, as with pralines, to make peanut brittle correctly, you must use a candy thermometer.

Legend has it that peanut brittle was created by a West Virginian logger named Tony Beaver. Tossing a handful of peanuts into a vat of maple syrup and emptying the remains on a log, he and his fellow lumberjacks tasted—and liked—the cooled mixture, and called it peanut brittle.

---

2 cups sugar

½ cup light corn syrup

½ cup water

4 tablespoons (½ stick) butter

1 teaspoon baking soda

1 teaspoon pure vanilla extract

2 cups roasted, unsalted peanuts

In a large saucepan, combine the sugar, syrup, and water, bring to a simmer, and stir till the sugar dissolves. Continue cooking over low heat till 300°F is reached on a candy thermometer, then remove the pan from the heat. Add the butter, baking soda, and vanilla and stir till well blended. Add the peanuts and mix well.

"Pour the mixture onto a greased slab of marble or cookie sheet and, using a metal spatula, spread as thin as possible, with peanuts distributed clear to the ends. The sheet of candy should be pulled as thin as possible as soon as it's cool enough to handle. But be careful! You can get a bad burn if you go too fast. A good way is to run the spatula under the poured candy as soon as it's workable, letting air between candy and slab. Helps prevent sticking. As soon as the batch is firm enough to handle (don't wait too long), turn the edges back a little on the far side and take hold to see if the candy holds together. If so, turn the sheet of candy and stretch it in all directions as thin as possible, pushing and pulling. The thinner the better. When thoroughly cold, break the brittle into pieces and store in airtight jars."

FRESH PEACH ICE CREAM

Makes ¾ gallon; 12 to 15 servings

SOUTHERNERS CAN BE PRETTY PARTICULAR ABOUT lots of regional dishes, but when it comes to fresh peach ice cream (or peach cobbler or peach preserves), the debates can become brutal. Which is the more ideal peach: a Georgia Belle or South Carolina Elberta? Are June cling peaches juicy enough for ice cream, or will only freestones do? Can cornstarch be used to thicken the custard, or will only extra egg yolks and plenty of heavy cream produce the right texture? How long should the ice cream be allowed to "mellow" before being served? Does an electric freezer make as good ice cream as an old-fashioned, hand-cranked one? All I know is that I've never, ever eaten perfect peach ice cream except in the South (and only during the summer), and, all modesty aside, there's no better basic recipe than this one, prepared in a wooden-bucket electric ice cream freezer. I will confess that lately I've been adding a fresh mango or a little freshly grated ginger to my peach ice cream, and either makes it even more sublime. "Heresy!" I can hear certain friends in Georgia and Kentucky and Mississippi bellow.

6 large fresh, ripe peaches

1½ cups sugar

3 large eggs

2 cups half-and-half

2 tablespoons cornstarch

Dash of salt

1 pint heavy cream

2 tablespoons pure vanilla extract

Peel and pit the peaches, cut them into small pieces, and place half the pieces in a medium mixing bowl. Add 1 cup of the sugar and stir till the sugar is dissolved. Cover the peaches tightly with plastic wrap and let stand in the refrigerator at least 2 hours. In another bowl, mash the remaining peaches with a heavy fork and refrigerate.

Meanwhile, in a large, heavy saucepan, whisk the eggs till frothy, add the half-and-half, and whisk till well blended. In a small bowl, combine the cornstarch, the remaining ½ cup sugar, and the salt, mix till well blended, and gradually whisk this into the egg mixture. Cook the mixture over low heat, stirring constantly, till the custard thickens slightly. Remove the pan from the heat, let cool, cover, and chill for 2 hours.

In a bowl, combine the mashed peaches, heavy cream, and vanilla, add this to the cold custard, and stir till well blended. Pour the mixture into the container of a wooden-bucket electric ice cream freezer and freeze according to the manufacturer's directions. When the ice cream is frozen (it will still be slightly soft), remove the dasher and stir the peach pieces and any juice into the ice cream. Cover the container, pack more ice and ice cream salt around the container if necessary, and allow the ice cream to mellow for 2 to 3 hours before serving. Freeze any leftover ice cream in airtight containers.

GEORGIA CORN CUSTARD ICE CREAM

Makes 1 quart

CORN, LIKE PECANS, RICE, BUTTERMILK, AND BOURBON, seems to find its way into virtually every facet of Southern cooking, and this honeyed ice cream, which is the pride of a faculty wife in the university town of Athens, Georgia, has to be one of the most amazing examples in the dessert category. Do be careful to temper the egg yolks very slowly with the hot honey to prevent curdling. It's a good idea also to allow this ice cream to mellow about an hour before serving or storing in the freezer.

4 cups fresh or defrosted frozen corn kernels

1 cup half-and-half

⅓ cup honey

2 tablespoons water

3 large egg yolks

1 teaspoon fresh lemon juice

1 cup heavy cream

1 teaspoon pure vanilla extract

1 teaspoon grated nutmeg

Place the corn in a saucepan with enough water to cover, and bring to a boil. Reduce the heat to moderate, cover, cook 3 to 4 minutes, and drain well. In a blender or food processor, combine the corn and half-and-half, reduce to a fine puree, and set aside.

In a small saucepan, combine the honey and water, bring to a boil, remove from the heat, and let cool slightly. In a mixing bowl, beat the egg yolks with an electric mixer till thick and creamy, then, while beating constantly, very slowly add the honey. Still beating, add the lemon juice, heavy cream, corn mixture, vanilla, and nutmeg and beat till thoroughly blended and smooth.

Scrape the mixture into the container of an electric ice cream freezer and freeze according to the manufacturer's directions.

Pickles, Relishes, & Preserves

Watermelon Rind Pickles

Bread-and-Butter Pickles

Green Tomato Pickle

Pickled Peaches

Pickled Okra

Corn Relish

Vidalia Onion and
Bell Pepper Relish

Chow Chow

Key West Mango Chutney

Strawberry Preserves

Damson Plum Preserves

Blackberry Jam

Ozark Blueberry Jam

Hot Pepper Jelly

Blue Ridge Apple-Mint Jelly

Three-Fruit Marmalade

Peach, Apricot,
and Citrus Conserve

Lemon Curd

Appalachian Apple Butter

Brandied Figs

How to Sterilize and Seal Jars for Canning

There are two schools of thought on the proper way to preserve foods in sterilized, sealed jars. One method is to fill washed jars with food, seal the jars with lids, and process the filled jars on a rack fitted into a large pot of boiling water for 10 to 15 minutes. What I (and many other Southerners) object to with this method is the fact that cooked foods such as fruits, pickles, and certain relishes risk being overcooked and becoming mushy from the extra boiling. Preferable and easier is the fail-proof method described below, so long, that is, as you take care not to touch the insides of the sterilized jars, wipe the rims clean, make sure the food is boiling hot, and screw the lids on tightly. This is the method I've used for decades, and I've never once "lost" a jar of pickles or preserves.

Unscrew the ring bands from the canning jars, remove the lids, and wash both thoroughly with soap and hot water. Arrange the jars open ends down in a large baking pan and cover with water. Bring the water to a boil, cover, and sterilize the jars for 10 minutes.

Remove the jars from the water with tongs and pack them with the food to be canned, taking care not to touch the insides of the jars once they have been sterilized. Wipe the rims very clean with moist paper towels, then use tongs to dip the sealing lids into the water used for sterilizing the jars. Fit the lids on top of the jars and screw the ring bands on tightly.

Place the filled jars in a draft-free area till the lids ping and remain down when pushed with a finger (signs they are sealed). Store in the refrigerator any jars whose lids remain convex and use these first.

The first cookbook printed in America was Eliza Smith's *The Compleat Housewife*, produced by a public printer in Williamsburg, Virginia, in 1742. The book included several cornmeal dishes, plus recipes for "pompkin" pie, cranberry tart, and "watermelon-on-rind" pickles.

WATERMELON RIND PICKL[

Makes seven 1-pint jars

"STOP THE CAR!" MONNIE ALMOST SCREAMED
somewhere on the road between Montgomery and
Tuscaloosa, Alabama, fixing her eyes on a wagon of
dark green watermelons in front of a farm stand. "Those
look right for pickling." "Right," of course, meant melons
with thick rinds, and, like my mother and me, Monnie
wouldn't even consider buying one till the man had
"plugged" it to check the rind. Without question, elegant
watermelon rind pickles represent the pinnacle of the
art of Southern canning, and I value the jars ageing on
my basement shelves as highly as I do certain bottles
of fine wine. Yes, the process is time-consuming (if
basically easy), but I promise you'll never begrudge the
effort once you've tasted the pickles. The only cardinal
rule is that every trace of pink flesh must be removed
from the rind, so be patient. I have jars of watermelon
rind pickles that are almost amber, and like pickled
peaches, they only improve with age. The one eternal
problem is finding a good-hearted vendor willing to
either plug the melon or cut it while you're looking on.
These are pickles to put up in quantity.

6 pounds thick watermelon rind

*2 cups pickling lime (available in Southern
    supermarkets and by special order from Ball)*

*1 tablespoon alum (available in spice section of
    supermarkets)*

*½ pound fresh ginger, peeled and cut into
    quarters*

6 cups sugar

6 cups white vinegar

3 cups water

1 tablespoon wh[

1 tablespoon clo[

Two 3-inch-long cinnamon sticks

Remove all the dark green outer rind and all pink flesh
from the watermelon rind, discard, and cut the
trimmed pale rind into 2-inch fingers. Place the fingers
in a large glass or enameled container. Dissolve the
lime in 2 gallons of cold water, pour over the rind,
cover with plastic wrap, and let soak overnight.

In a large container, combine the alum with 1 gallon of
cold water, transfer the drained rind fingers to the
solution, and let soak for 5 minutes. Drain the rind.

In a large enameled pot, combine the ginger with 1
gallon of cold water, add the rind, bring to a boil,
reduce the heat to moderately low, and simmer for 30
minutes. Drain, remove the ginger, and rinse the rind
thoroughly under cold running water for exactly 5
minutes. Rinse out the pot.

In the pot, combine the sugar, vinegar, 3 cups of water,
allspice, cloves, and cinnamon, bring to a boil, and add
the rind. Return to a boil, reduce the heat to low, and
simmer slowly, uncovered, 3 hours.

Pack the fingers and syrup into seven 1-pint sterilized
jars (see page 382) to within ¼ inch of the tops, seal,
and store for at least 4 months at room temperature
before serving.

BREAD-AND-BUTTER PICKLES

Makes eight 1-pint jars

THESE ARE THE SAME EVERYDAY BREAD-AND-BUTTER pickles I helped my mother put up when I was a child in North Carolina, and that I still can in large quantities when the first small, firm summer Kirbys ripen in the garden—or sell for less than forty-nine cents a pound in the market. All modesty aside, they are the finest bread-and-butter pickles in the South—and a far cry from those bland, limp, overpriced commercial ones found in supermarkets. Fail to allow the salted cucumber rounds to crisp a full 3 hours in ice, or allow them cook a minute more than indicated, and you'll end up with soggy pickles. And why so many onions? Because I love plenty of pickled onions. Guests eat these pickles like peanuts, so be sure to make them in quantity, as I do. For maximum flavor, I think the pickles need to be stored at least 2 months before serving, but not so long that they oversoften.

6 pounds pickling cucumbers (Kirbys), scrubbed and sliced into ¼-inch rounds

6 medium onions, thinly sliced

⅓ cup salt

4½ cups sugar

1½ teaspoons turmeric

1½ teaspoons celery seeds

2 tablespoons mustard seeds

3 cups cider vinegar

In a large mixing bowl or baking pan, arrange alternate layers of cucumber rounds and sliced onions, sprinkling each layer with the salt. Cover the top of the mixture with ice cubes or crushed ice, mix the ice thoroughly with the cucumbers and onions, and let stand 3 hours. Drain thoroughly.

In a large stainless-steel or enameled pot, combine the sugar, turmeric, celery seeds, and vinegar and bring to a boil. Add the cucumbers and onions and return to a boil. Remove from the heat.

Pack the cucumbers, onions, and hot liquid into eight 1-pint sterilized jars (see page 382) to within ¼ inch of the tops, seal, and store for at least 2 months at room temperature before serving.

Green Tomato Pickle

Makes three 1-pint jars

FRIED GREEN TOMATOES HAVE BEEN A PRIZED breakfast item in the South for centuries, but equally important are the green tomatoes picked in late summer and early fall, pickled with brown sugar and lots of spices, and served throughout the year with hamburgers, meat hashes and croquettes, fish cakes, and any number of other dishes. The ideal tomato for this pickle is one that is slightly pink but still firm.

15 medium green tomatoes (about 4 pounds), stemmed and thinly sliced

3 medium onions, thinly sliced

½ cup salt

3 cups white vinegar

1 cup firmly packed light brown sugar

1 teaspoon ground allspice

1 teaspoon ground ginger

1 teaspoon ground cloves

1 teaspoon mustard seeds

1 teaspoon celery seeds

Salt and freshly ground black pepper to taste

1 large red bell pepper, seeded and thinly sliced

1 garlic clove, minced

In a large baking dish or casserole, combine the tomatoes and onions, sprinkle salt over the top, toss well, cover with plastic wrap, and let stand overnight. Transfer the vegetables to a large colander, rinse under cold running water, and set aside.

In a large stainless-steel or enameled pot, combine all remaining ingredients and add the tomatoes and onions, stirring. Bring to a boil, reduce the heat to low, and simmer, stirring often, till the tomatoes are transparent, about 1 hour.

Pack the pickle and liquid into three 1-pint sterilized jars (see page 382) to within ¼ inch of the tops, seal, and store for at least 1 month at room temperature before serving.

PICKLED PEACHES

Makes two 1-quart jars

AS FAR AS I'M CONCERNED, PICKLED PEACHES WERE created (probably in Colonial times) to serve primarily with pork barbecue and country ham. Like many Southerners, I keep an eager eye open for June's first firm clingstones, with the express intention of canning them as quickly as possible in quart jars. (Freestone peaches can also be used, but since they tend to be softer than clings, they can become mushy much more quickly.) Some cooks like to simmer the peaches 5 or 10 minutes in the hot syrup before canning them, while others prefer to crush the cinnamon sticks and add bits and pieces to the jars. Whatever you do, just make sure the peaches are not too ripe, and for a truly special dish, be sure to make the Congealed Pickled Peach and Pecan Salad on page 78.

12 firm ripe peaches (about 3 pounds)

24 whole cloves

3 cups white vinegar

4½ cups sugar

Three 2-inch-long cinnamon sticks

Bring a large pot of water to a boil, drop the peaches into the water 3 or 4 at a time, and let cook 2 to 3 minutes. With a slotted spoon, transfer the peaches to a colander, douse with cold water, then remove their skins with a knife. Stud each peach with 2 cloves.

In a large stainless-steel or enameled saucepan, combine the vinegar, sugar, and cinnamon, bring to a boil, stirring, reduce the heat slightly, and cook till a medium-thick syrup forms, 15 to 20 minutes.

Pack the peaches into two 1-quart sterilized jars (see page 382), ladle the hot syrup over the peaches to within ¼ inch of the tops, seal, and store for at least 2 months at room temperature before serving.

PICKLED OKRA

Makes four 1-pint jars

OKRA WAS NO DOUBT BROUGHT TO THE SOUTH SOME three hundred years ago by Ethiopian slaves, who alone knew how to cultivate it. Since non-Southerners generally have an aversion to (if not a horror of) the pods when they're boiled to a viscous (okay, slimy) consistency, I've always said that the best indoctrination for these timid souls is either fried or pickled okra. Throughout the South (and especially in the Deep South), pickled okra is almost routine at cocktail parties, picnics, genteel bridge or charity lunches, and some bars, and more than once in Louisiana I've seen small pickled okra substituted for olives in martinis. Never try to pickle any okra that is not impeccably fresh. When shopping, look for young pods that are no longer than about 2 inches, bright green, firm, and not in the least blemished. If the pods bend, walk away. Fresh okra maintains its color and texture for about 3 days when stored in plastic bags in the refrigerator.

In the early nineteenth century, many Savannah gentlemen carried small silver boxes of minced bird's-eye hot peppers to enhance various foods, and today it's still not unusual to see pots of these local tiny red peppers growing on front porches and windowsills, ready to be added to all sorts of soups, stews, sauces, pastes, and breads.

3½ pounds small, firm, fresh okra

4 teaspoons dill seeds

4 small red chile peppers

4 small green chile peppers

8 garlic cloves, peeled

4 cups white vinegar

1 cup water

6 tablespoons salt

Trim the stems off the okra. Rinse the pods well and pat dry.

Add ½ teaspoon dill seeds to the bottom of each of four 1-pint sterilized canning jars (see page 382). Pack the okra into the jars, taking care not to bruise the pods. Add another ½ teaspoon dill seeds and 1 of each color chile pepper and 2 garlic cloves to each jar.

In a large stainless-steel or enameled saucepan, combine the vinegar, water, and salt, bring to a boil, and pour equal amounts of the liquid over the okra to within ¼ inch of the top. Seal and store at least 1 month at room temperature before serving. Serve the okra at room temperature or chilled.

CORN RELISH

Makes six 1-pint jars

AFTER HOT CORN-ON-THE-COB SLATHERED WITH plenty of butter, and maybe succotash, and surely corn pudding and spoonbread . . . well, suffice it to say that corn relish is high on any Southerner's list of ways to use our many superior varieties of fresh summer corn. Of course, the arguments over whether white or yellow corn is ideal for relish will never end—white is supposedly sweeter, yellow has better texture, speckled is too pulpy, and on and on. The point on which there's absolutely no debate, however, is that corn relish must be made only with fresh corn—preferably right out of the field—and that the milk scraped from the cobs is just as important as the plump kernels. And what do we serve corn relish with or on? Virtually anything and everything. I'm just waiting for someone to come up with a corn relish ice cream.

12 medium ears fresh white corn

3 medium onions, finely chopped

1 medium green bell pepper, seeded and finely chopped

1 medium red bell pepper, seeded and finely chopped

1 cup sugar

2 tablespoons dry mustard

2 teaspoons ground turmeric

1 teaspoon celery seeds

1 small red chile pepper, seeded and chopped

2 cups white vinegar

Cut the kernels from the corn cobs into a large stainless-steel or enameled pot, then scrape as much of the corn milk as possible from the cobs into the pot. Add all remaining ingredients and stir till well blended. Bring to a boil, reduce the heat to low, and simmer, stirring often, till most of the liquid has evaporated, about 45 minutes.

Pack the relish into six 1-pint sterilized jars (see page 382) to within ¼ inch of the tops, seal, and store for about 1 month at room temperature before serving.

VIDALIA ONION AND BELL PEPPER RELISH

Makes four 1-pint jars

PAIRED WITH TANGY GREEN BELL PEPPERS AND SPICES, sweet, juicy Vidalia onions have been turned into a delectable relish throughout Georgia and the neighboring states ever since the distinctive onion was cultivated in and around Vidalia, Georgia, some sixty-five years ago. (It's believed that the low percentage of sulfur in the area's soil is what makes the onion so sweet.) Recipes for the relish vary enormously, but this one from a lady in Macon is the best I've tried. Spoon a little on your next hot dog and you'll see what I mean. Be sure to extract as much liquid from the onions and peppers as possible; if not, the relish could be too runny.

5 pounds Vidalia onions

1 small green bell pepper, seeded

2 tablespoons salt

2 cups cider vinegar

2 cups sugar

½ teaspoon ground turmeric

¼ teaspoon ground cinnamon

¼ teaspoon ground allspice

¼ teaspoon ground cloves

Cayenne pepper to taste

Grate the onions and bell pepper coarsely into a large mixing bowl, add the salt, stir well, and let stand for about 30 minutes. Using paper towels, squeeze the onions and bell pepper till they're almost dry and place in a large stainless-steel or enameled pot. Add the remaining ingredients, stir well, and bring the mixture to a boil. Reduce the heat to low and simmer, stirring often, till most of the liquid has evaporated and the relish is thickened, about 30 minutes.

Pack the relish into four 1-pint sterilized jars (see page 382) to within ¼ inch of the tops, seal, and store for at least 1 month before serving.

CHOW CHOW

Makes eight 1-pint jars

ALSO CALLED INDIAN PICKLE IN CERTAIN AREAS of the South, chow chow supposedly originated in California with Chinese immigrant laborers in the nineteenth century. John Egerton, however, in his authoritative *Southern Food,* traces the complex relish as far back as a late-eighteenth-century recipe in South Carolina. In any case, today chow chow is as Southern as watermelon rind pickles, and every home cook has his or her special combination of ingredients and seasonings. Typically, the relish is served on elaborate buffets or, at the family table, with roasted meats, fried chicken, and, as one lady I know in Kentucky says, "everything but ice cream." And chow chow is always made in large quantities.

3 cups chopped green cabbage

3 cups chopped green tomatoes

½ cup salt

3 cups seeded and chopped green bell peppers

3 cups seeded and chopped red bell peppers

3 cups chopped onions

1 large head celery, chopped

½ medium head cauliflower, chopped

3 cups white vinegar

One 16-ounce box light brown sugar

¼ cup all-purpose flour

1½ tablespoons dry mustard

2 teaspoons turmeric

4½ teaspoons water

In a large bowl, combine the cabbage, tomatoes, and salt, add enough cold water to cover, and let soak overnight.

Drain the mixture thoroughly and transfer to a large stainless-steel or enameled pot. Add the two peppers, the onions, celery, cauliflower, vinegar, and brown sugar and bring almost to a boil. In a small bowl, combine the flour, dry mustard, and turmeric, add the water, mix well to make a paste, and add the paste to the pot. Gradually bring the liquid to a roaring boil, stirring constantly. Remove the pot from the heat, spoon the chow chow into eight 1-pint sterilized jars (see page 382) to within ¼ inch of the tops, seal, and store for at least 1 month at room temperature before serving.

KEY WEST MANGO CHUTNEY

MAKES *four 1-pint jars*

IT ALWAYS AMUSES ME THAT THE NATIVES OF KEY WEST (and most other Floridians) rave about their mango chutneys as if the condiment had been created in their locale and had not existed in India for centuries. No matter, for, as far as I'm concerned, it is indeed the queen of chutneys, whether served with ham, pork, or roast duck or spread on rice muffins, buttermilk bread, or even pecan waffles. One hint: the chutney is even better if the ingredients are mixed and allowed to stand overnight before cooking.

4 slightly firm mangoes (about 4 pounds), peeled, seeded, and cut into 1-inch chunks

3 cups cider vinegar

1½ cups firmly packed dark brown sugar

2 medium onions, finely chopped

2 cups seedless golden raisins

1 small red chile pepper, seeded and finely chopped

1 teaspoon grated fresh ginger

1 teaspoon ground cloves

½ teaspoon ground nutmeg

In a large stainless-steel or enameled pot, combine all the ingredients and bring to a boil, stirring. Reduce the heat to low and simmer till the mango chunks are tender but not mushy, about 30 minutes.

Ladle equal amounts of the chutney into four 1-pint sterilized jars (see page 382) to within ¼ inch of the tops, seal, and store for at least 1 month at room temperature before serving.

STRAWBERRY PRESERVES

Makes four ½-pint jars

I DON'T KNOW WHAT IS LOVED MORE SPOONED ON hot buttery biscuits at breakfast in the South: peach, blackberry, or strawberry preserves. Every Southern home cook has his or her special recipe for strawberry preserves, and this is the one I've been using for decades, every year beginning with the day in June when I see the first local berries in the field or the market. The berries must certainly be ripe (with no white cores), but make sure they're also firm enough to withstand the necessary boiling process. Allowing the berries to stand overnight before canning causes them to plump up beautifully. Afterwards, you can either put them up cold and seal them with hot paraffin (tilting the jars slowly back and forth till the paraffin begins to set all over the tops) or reheat them enough so that they seal themselves in hot sterilized jars. For optimum flavor, store at least 4 months before serving.

1 quart slightly firm fresh strawberries, hulled and washed

4 cups sugar

2 teaspoons fresh lemon juice

2 tablespoons liquid pectin (Certo)

If the strawberries are large, cut them in half. In a large saucepan, combine the strawberries and 2 cups of the sugar, bring slowly to a boil, and cook rapidly at a boil, stirring constantly, for 5 minutes. Add the remaining sugar, return to the boil, and cook for 8 minutes longer, stirring in the lemon juice 2 minutes before removing the pan from the heat. Add the pectin and stir well. Skim off any foam from the surface, cover, and let the strawberries stand overnight, stirring when possible.

Stirring constantly, return the strawberries to a boil and remove immediately from the heat. Ladle into four ½-pint sterilized jars (see page 382) to within ¼ inch of the tops, seal, and store for at least 4 months at room temperature before serving.

Damson Plum Preserves

Makes six ½-pint jars

SMALL, OVAL, BLUISH, EXTREMELY TART DAMSON plums (not to be confused with sweet purple plums) make the most sublime preserves on earth, the only problem being that they've become as rare as hen's teeth since I was a youngster helping my mother can the ones some farmer used to sell her by the bucket. Today, fashionable markets proudly boast sapotes, loquats, cherimoyas, cactus pears, and a score of other trendy fruits, while all the time something like our Southern damson plums are allowed to virtually disappear. Go figure. Fortunately, a few damsons can still be found in late summer, at truly reputable markets, and all I can say is grab them when you can for these preserves, which are so exquisite spread on hot biscuits or any toasted homemade bread.

3 cups sugar

½ cup water

1½ pounds damson plums, seeded and coarsely chopped (about 6 cups)

In a large stainless-steel or enameled saucepan, combine the sugar and water and stir till the sugar dissolves. Bring to a boil, add the plums, and return to the boil. Reduce the heat to moderately low and simmer the plums gently, uncovered, till the fruit is clear and the syrup thick, 30 to 40 minutes. Ladle into six ½-pint sterilized jars (see page 382) to within ¼ inch of the tops, seal, and store for at least 2 months at room temperature before serving.

BLACKBERRY JAM

Makes four to five ½-pint jars

BLACKBERRY JAM AND PRESERVES ARE TWO OF THE South's most ubiquitous condiments, each used not only to spread on breakfast breads but also to make all sorts of pastry fillings, glazes, icings, and sauces. Since the natural pectin in blackberries is what allows the jam to jell, do not discard any berries just because they're underripe; these contain the most pectin. You can try to check the jam for consistency the old-fashioned way, by testing a teaspoon of it on an ice-cold plate to see if it jells, but to avoid mishaps I recommend using a candy thermometer. Lots of people refuse to eat blackberry jam with seeds, so if you object to them too, the hot jam can be strained through a fine-meshed wire sieve or squeezed tightly in cheesecloth. Personally, I find this a big to-do about nothing, and, besides, the yield can be reduced considerably by straining.

6 cups fresh ripe to semiripe blackberries

½ cup water

2 tablespoons fresh lemon juice

4 cups sugar

Rinse and pick over the berries, removing the stems and caps and discarding any that show signs of mold, then wash them thoroughly in a large colander under running water. Place in a large stainless-steel or enameled pot, add the water, lemon juice, and sugar, and bring to a boil, stirring. Reduce the heat to moderate and cook, stirring often, till the jam reaches a temperature of 220°F on a candy thermometer. Remove the pot from the heat and skim any foam off the surface.

Ladle the jam into four or five ½-pint sterilized jars (see page 382) to within ¼ inch of the tops, seal, and store for at least 1 month at room temperature before serving.

Ozark Blueberry Jam

Makes four to five ½-pint jars

BOTH WILD LOW-BUSH BLUEBERRIES (AND strawberries) and wild honey can still be found in the hill country of Arkansas's Ozarks, and when these two ingredients are simmered together with water and a little lemon juice, the result is one of the most blissful jams ever conceived. (Look for the small jars in the food and tourist shops of both Little Rock and the Ozark resort towns.) The fat, cultivated high-bush blueberries of North Carolina, which are legendary in the South, also make delicious jams, preserves, and chutneys, but the intense Ozark jam is truly like none other you'll ever taste. The yield in this recipe using cultivated blueberries can vary, depending on the size and ripeness of the berries and how thick you like your jam. The larger and riper berries, the closer you'll come to replicating the Ozark jam.

6 cups fresh ripe blueberries

1½ cups honey

1 cup water

1 teaspoon fresh lemon juice

Rinse, pick over, and stem the blueberries, discarding any that are moldy or shriveled, and place in a stainless-steel or enameled saucepan. Add the honey, water, and lemon juice and bring to a boil, stirring. Reduce the heat to low and simmer till the mixture has thickened, 1 to 1¼ hours, stirring often to prevent sticking. Remove the pan from the heat and skim any foam off the surface.

Pack the jam into four or five ½-pint sterilized jars (see page 382) to within ¼ inch of the tops, seal, and store for at least 1 month at room temperature before serving.

Hot Pepper Jelly

Makes six ½-pint jars

GO TO ANY LARGE SOUTHERN COCKTAIL PARTY AND there's a good likelihood that among the toasted pecans and crab dip and celery stuffed with pimento cheese on side tables will be a slab of cream cheese topped with hot pepper jelly, to be spread on crackers. Exactly when and how this spicy-sweet condiment originated is something of a mystery (some authorities say it didn't exist before the 1940s), but it's for sure that its popularity today has only been heightened by the availability of so many exotic chile peppers now on the market. The jelly also does lots to enhance cold ham and pork dishes, but never have I seen it served at breakfast. Remember that it's always a good idea to wear rubber gloves when handling chile peppers.

2 medium red bell peppers, seeded and chopped

3 small hot green chile peppers, seeded and finely chopped

1½ cups cider vinegar

6½ cups sugar

One 6-ounce bottle liquid pectin (Certo)

In a blender or food processor, combine the two types of peppers and 1 cup of the vinegar and blend till the peppers are finely minced. Transfer the mixture to a stainless-steel or enameled saucepan, add the sugar and remaining vinegar, and bring to a boil. Stir, remove the pan from the heat, and skim any foam off the surface. Stir in the pectin, return the pan to the heat, and boil hard for exactly 1 minute. Remove the pan from the heat and skim any foam off the surface again.

Pour the jelly into six ½-pint sterilized jars (see page 382) to within ¼ inch of the tops, seal, and store for about 1 month at room temperature before serving.

BLUE RIDGE APPLE-MINT JELLY

Makes four ½-pint jars

DESPITE THE SOUTH'S FAMOUS MINT JULEPS, MINT jelly has never enjoyed the popularity here that it does elsewhere in the country (possibly because lamb has never been a major meat in the South). One exception, I've discovered, is the unusual apple jelly flavored with mint leaves found in those areas of the Blue Ridge Mountains of Virginia and West Virginia where tart, red-skinned Stayman and Winesap apple trees are cultivated and where wild mint grows in profusion along every river and stream. Since most of the natural pectin needed to jell the liquid is in the apple skins, be sure not to peel the fruit, and by no means squeeze the cheesecloth to speed up the dripping process, unless you want cloudy jelly.

10 firm, unpeeled cooking apples (3 to 3½ pounds), cored and chopped

3 cups hot water

4 cups sugar

3 tablespoons chopped fresh mint leaves

In a large stainless-steel or enameled pot, combine the apples and water and bring to a boil. Reduce the heat to low, cover, and cook till the apples are very tender, about 30 minutes.

Line a large sieve with a double thickness of cheesecloth and place over a large stainless-steel or enameled saucepan. Pour the apples and water into the sieve and allow the juice to drip into the pan for about 4 hours, never squeezing the cloth.

Discard the cheesecloth and apple pulp, add the sugar to the juice in the pan, bring to a boil, and stir till the sugar dissolves. Reduce the heat to moderate and continue cooking till the juice reaches 200°F on a candy thermometer. Add the mint, stir, and continue cooking till the thermometer reaches 220°F. Remove the pan from the heat and skim any foam from the surface of the jelly. Ladle into four ½-pint sterilized jars (see page 382) to within ¼ inch of the tops, seal, and store for about 1 month at room temperature before serving.

THREE-FRUIT MARMALADE

Makes seven ½-pint jars

I LEARNED TO MAKE THIS LUSCIOUS MARMALADE from a transplanted English lady living in Palm Beach, Florida, who never stopped complaining about not being able to find the ideal thick-skinned Seville oranges in the States and who, consequently, always referred to the confection as "my Southern marmalade." Temple oranges will suffice, however, and what I usually do is add an extra half teaspoon of blanched, coarse-cut orange rind to each ½-pint jar.

> *3 medium Temple oranges, washed thoroughly*
>
> *1 medium grapefruit, washed thoroughly*
>
> *1 lemon, washed thoroughly*
>
> *1 cup water*
>
> *¼ teaspoon baking soda*
>
> *6 cups sugar*
>
> *3 ounces liquid pectin (Certo)*

Remove the rind from the oranges, grapefruit, and lemon with a sharp knife, then cut off and discard all the outer white pith. Place half of the rind and half the water in a blender or food processor, chop coarsely, and transfer to a large stainless-steel or enameled saucepan. Repeat the process with the remaining rind and water and add to the saucepan. Add the baking soda, bring to a boil, reduce the heat to moderate, cover, and cook for 10 minutes.

Meanwhile, quarter the fruit and remove all the seeds. Place the fruit in a blender or food processor, cover, and reduce to a purée. Add the purée to the saucepan, cover, and simmer over low heat for 20 minutes.

Transfer the mixture to a large kettle or Dutch oven (not cast-iron), add the sugar, bring to a full rolling boil, and boil hard for 4 minutes, stirring. Remove from the heat, add the pectin, skim any foam from the surface, and stir 5 minutes. Ladle the marmalade into seven ½-pint sterilized jars (see page 382) to within ¼ inch of the tops, seal, and store for at least 2 months at room temperature before serving.

Peach, Apricot, and Citrus Conserve

Makes two 1-pint jars (or more)

THIS CONSERVE IS UTTERLY DELICIOUS SERVED WITH any type of ham or pork dish, and one of its most welcome features is that, for once, you don't have to bother cutting away the pith from the oranges and lemon. Since the citrus peel is essential to the flavor and texture, however, it must be allowed to temper and soften a little overnight along with the firm peaches and apricots.

8 to 9 medium firm, ripe peaches (about 2 pounds)

½ pound fresh, firm, ripe apricots

2 unpeeled oranges, rinsed

1 unpeeled lemon, rinsed

3 cups sugar

1 cup seedless golden raisins

1 cup cracked pecans

½ cup bourbon

Bring a large pot of water to a boil, drop the peaches and apricots into the water, and cook for about 2 minutes. Drain in a colander and, when cool enough to handle, remove the skins with a knife, cut the fruits in half, discard the seeds, chop the flesh coarsely, and combine in another stainless-steel or enameled pot.

Slice the oranges and lemon into ¼-inch-thick slices, pick out the seeds, chop the slices coarsely in a food processor or with a knife, and add to the peaches and apricots. Add the sugar, stir well, cover with plastic wrap, and let stand overnight.

Bring the fruit to a boil, stirring constantly, reduce the heat to low, and simmer till the mixture thickens and coats a spoon, about 1 to 1¼ hours, stirring often to prevent sticking. Add the raisins, pecans, and bourbon and continue to simmer for about 15 minutes, stirring.

Ladle the conserve into two 1-pint sterilized jars (see page 382) to within ¼ inch of the tops (using also a half-pint jar for any extra), seal, and store at least 1 month at room temperature before serving.

Lemon Curd

Makes four ½-pint jars

I DON'T RECALL EVER SEEING LEMON CURD OUTSIDE the South except in the most upscale food shops and in highly innovative restaurant desserts. Spread on biscuits or toast, spooned over ice cream, or used to make rich tarts, this silky, zesty, sweet condiment (introduced, no doubt, by our English ancestors) couldn't be more distinctive. I've watched guests go through an entire half-pint jar at a single brunch for four. Since the curd lasts for weeks tightly capped in the refrigerator, I don't even bother to can it unless I make large quantities.

4 lemons, thoroughly washed

2 sticks butter, softened

2½ cups superfine sugar

4 large eggs, beaten

Grate the zest of the lemons onto a plate and set aside. Cut the lemons in half, squeeze the juice through a sieve into a small bowl, and set aside.

In a saucepan, cream together the butter and sugar with an electric mixer and cook over low heat till the consistency of honey, about 10 minutes, stirring. Add the grated lemon zest and the reserved juice, stir well, remove the pan from the heat, and let cool 10 minutes. Add the eggs, stir well, and cook over low heat till the mixture is custardlike, about 10 minutes, stirring.

Spoon the curd into four ½-pint sterilized jars (see page 382) to within ¼ inch of the tops, seal, and store at room temperature till ready to use.

Appalachian Apple Butter

Makes about six ½-pint jars

FROM WEST VIRGINIA DOWN TO KENTUCKY, THE
mountain tradition of making apple butter in the fall
dates back at least to the late eighteenth century, when
the condiment was prepared out of doors in large black
iron kettles. Today, the Pennsylvania Dutch lay claim to
apple butter as a commercial specialty, but I've yet to
sample a jar of theirs that can compare with the silky
smooth, perfectly spiced, homemade examples I've had
deep in the Southern Appalachians. And, by the way, the
folks in Mississippi, for some reason, also seem to know
a thing or two about what constitutes superior apple
butter. One secret to their success is long, slow
simmering over very low heat. Apple butter is good
spread on any breads—including pancakes, waffles, and
even coffee cake.

*6 pounds unpeeled Granny Smith apples, cored
and cut into eighths*

3 cups apple cider

3 cups firmly packed light brown sugar

1 teaspoon ground cinnamon

½ teaspoon ground cloves

½ teaspoon allspice

¼ teaspoon salt

In a large stainless-steel or enameled pot, combine the
apples and cider. Bring to a boil, reduce the heat to
low, cover, and simmer till the apples are mushy, about
45 minutes, stirring occasionally to prevent sticking.

Drain the apples, then either reduce them to a purée in
a food processor or mash them with a potato masher
till very smooth. Place the soft pulp in another
stainless-steel or enameled pot, add the brown sugar,
spices, and salt, stir well, and simmer slowly over very
low heat, uncovered, till quite thick, 1 to 1½ hours,
stirring often.

Remove from the heat, ladle into sterilized ½-pint jars
(see page 382) to within ¼ inch of the tops, seal, and
store for about 1 month at room temperature before
serving.

401

BRANDIED FIGS

Makes about 3 cups

SOUTHERNERS LOVE TO BRANDY PEACHES, PEARS, strawberries, and Lord knows what other fruits, but never have I been so impressed as I was by the brandied figs that Louis Osteen serves on slices of corn cake with buttermilk ice cream at his restaurant on Pawleys Island, South Carolina. The most popular fig in the South is the pear-shaped Celeste (or "sugar fig"), with purple skin and pink flesh, but the more widely available Black Missions and Kadotas (available from June to September) work just as well in this recipe. I don't like to can these figs, since they become too soft and mushy with age.

2 cups water

1 cup brandy

4 cups sugar

One vanilla pod, split lengthwise

One 2-inch cinnamon stick

1 whole clove

1 pound fresh figs

In a large saucepan, combine the water, brandy, and sugar and bring to a simmer. Scrape the seeds out of the vanilla pod and add both the pod and the seeds to the saucepan. Add the cinnamon stick and clove, stir well, and simmer till the mixture has reduced to a thin syrup, about 45 minutes. Remove and discard the vanilla pod, cinnamon stick, and clove. Add the figs to the syrup, remove the pan from the heat, and let cool to room temperature. Tightly covered, the figs keep about a week in the refrigerator.

Beverages

Ice' Tea

Sun Tea

Fizzy Strawberry Lemonade

Palm Beach Cobbler

Kentucky Eggnog

Hot Bourbon Nog

Milk Punch

Syllabub

Spiced Holiday Shrub

Sazerac

Ramos Gin Fizz

Mint Julep

River Road Planter's Punch

Graduation Fruit Punch

Wedding Champagne Punch

Chatham Artillery Punch

St. Cecilia's Punch

ICE' TEA

Makes 2 quarts

MOST AMERICANS MAY HAVE A GLASS OF ICED TEA from time to time during the summer, but so beloved and sacred is "ice' tea" below the Mason-Dixon Line that Southerners couldn't survive without the brew on a daily basis twelve months of the year—at brunches, picnics, church suppers, cookouts, and formal dinners; at beach parties, pig pickin's, football games, and bereavement buffets; and as much at fancy restaurants as at barbecue joints and diners. (Little wonder that the only tea leaves grown in the United States are on Wadmalaw Island off the coast of South Carolina.) The varieties are endless (sugar tea, mint tea, spice tea, Russian tea, lemon tea, sun tea), and so engrained is ice' tea in Southern culture that such legendary concoctions as St. Cecilia's Punch, Chatham Artillery Punch, goalpost punch, and all sorts of cotillion and wedding punches are based on the brewing of tea leaves. Generally, Southerners have no use for exotic or weirdly flavored teas, and we pay little attention to the trendy practice of making ice' tea only with bottled water. We are careful to brew our tea in a nonreactive pot to prevent a bitter metallic taste, and we also know that ice' tea is almost as good brewed in a drip coffee maker as in a pot. Never would we dilute tea by using crushed ice, and if tea happens to cloud when stored in the refrigerator, we know to clear it by simply adding a little hot water before serving it. And never forget that when somebody in the South says, "How 'bout a glass of tea?" the implication is ice' tea.

4 tablespoons loose orange pekoe tea or 12 tea bags

2 quarts cold water

Sugar to taste

Lemon wedges, for garnish

Place the loose tea or tea bags in a large nonreactive pot. In another large pot, bring the water to a rolling boil, pour the water over the tea, and let steep 10 minutes or to desired strength. Let cool to room temperature, then either strain the tea through a fine wire-mesh strainer into a large pitcher or squeeze and discard the tea bags and pour the tea into the pitcher. Sweeten the tea with sugar to taste, if desired, and pour over ice cubes (not crushed ice) in tall glasses garnished with lemon wedges.

Sun Tea

Makes 2 quarts

NEVER, I CAN ASSURE YOU, WILL YOU ENCOUNTER sun tea outside the South, and even in the northernmost states of the region, this method of making ice' tea is virtually unknown. But from North Carolina over to Kentucky down to Mississippi, sun tea is almost a ritual for those who're convinced there's simply no better way to prepare ice' tea, and it's never unusual to see a big jug steeping in the sun on back porches, patios, and window sills. Is sun tea really better than ordinary tea made with boiling water? Personally, I love it, but I'm not about to argue the point.

4 tablespoons loose orange pekoe tea

2 quarts water

½ lemon, seeded

Sugar to taste

Place the tea in a large jug or jar with a screw top and add the water. Squeeze the lemon into the water and then drop it in, cover tightly, place the container in full sunlight, and let the tea steep from 1 to 3 hours, depending on the intensity of the sun and how strong you like your tea. Strain the tea through a fine wire-mesh strainer into a pitcher, sweeten with sugar to taste, if desired, and pour over ice cubes (not crushed ice) in tall glasses.

405

Fizzy Strawberry Lemonade

Makes about 2 quarts

HOMEMADE LEMONADE IS STILL AS LOVED IN THE South during summertime as ice' tea, and the variations folks come up with are amazing. No matter that other ingredients might detract from the lemonade itself—as in this fizzy version a friend in Huntsville, Alabama, takes great pride in serving at bridge parties. What's most important about this or any other lemonade (plain or flavored) is that the lemon juice be fresh squeezed.

1½ cups water

1 cup sugar

1½ cups fresh lemon juice (about 8 large lemons)

1 cup fresh ripe strawberries, stemmed and cut in half

1 liter club soda, chilled

In a saucepan, combine the water and sugar, bring to a boil, stir till the sugar dissolves, about 2 minutes, and let cool.

In a blender or food processor, combine the cooled syrup with the lemon juice and strawberries, blend till smooth, transfer to a large pitcher, and chill several hours.

When ready to serve, stir in the club soda and serve immediately over ice cubes in tall glasses.

Palm Beach Cobbler

Makes about 8 drinks

YES, COBBLER IS INDEED AS MUCH A BEVERAGE IN THE South as a baked, deep-dish fruit dessert topped with a biscuit crust, referring, no doubt, to an old English punch made with wine or liquor, fruit juice, and sugar. I've had cobblers made with rum and pineapple juice, and with gin and cranberry juice, but one of the most refreshing was this simple concoction served at a smart beach party in Palm Beach, Florida.

One 750-ml bottle white wine

½ cup fresh orange juice

½ cup fresh lemon juice

½ cup sugar

1 lemon, thinly sliced and seeded

Fresh mint sprigs, for garnish

In a large pitcher, combine all the ingredients except the mint, stir till the sugar is dissolved, and let stand at least 1 hour before serving.

When ready to serve, pour into tall glasses filled with ice and garnish each with a sprig of mint.

407

KENTUCKY EGGNOG

Makes about 8 drinks

ALTHOUGH *NOG* IS AN OLD ENGLISH TERM FOR ALE, most early references to what we know as eggnog mention red wine as a main ingredient. By the mid-eighteenth century in America, it seems the creamy drink was made primarily with rum, followed in the South by the substitution of bourbon, which, henceforth, became the standard spirit for the rich beverage served everywhere at Christmastime. Throughout most of the South, eggnog is made exclusively with heavy cream and bourbon, the salient exception being this less cloying version (often found, ironically, in the bourbon-producing state of Kentucky), which includes not only both bourbon and brandy but either half-and-half or a mixture of milk and heavy cream. It is, quite simply, the best eggnog I've ever tasted.

8 large pasteurized eggs (Davidson's brand, available in many specialty food shops and some supermarkets), separated

1 cup sugar

½ cup bourbon

½ cup brandy

½ cup half-and-half

Ground nutmeg for sprinkling

In a large bowl, combine the egg yolks and sugar and beat with an electric mixer till light and frothy. Beating, add the bourbon and brandy till well blended. In another bowl, beat the half-and-half till very thick and fold into the egg yolk mixture. In another bowl, beat the egg whites till stiff and fold them into the mixture.

Serve the eggnog in punch glasses or glass mugs and sprinkle each with a little nutmeg.

Hot Bourbon Nog

Makes about 1½ quarts

SOUTHERNERS LOVE A GOOD HOT TODDY AS MUCH AS anybody when the temperature drops, and this nog I was once served in a stately Virginia home near Danville, while on the farm to inspect a new litter of beagles (my canine of choice for the past forty years), left a glowing impression. All I kept wondering was what the drink's English ancestor must have tasted like made with ale (*nog*) and probably some form of brandy. To reap the full flavor benefits of this drink, don't serve the nog too hot.

2 cups whole milk

2 cups half-and-half

1 cup apple cider

2 large eggs

½ cup sugar

¼ teaspoon ground nutmeg

⅛ teaspoon ground allspice

½ cup bourbon

Ground cinnamon for garnish

In a large enameled pot, whisk together the milk, half-and-half, cider, eggs, sugar, nutmeg, and allspice over moderate heat till well blended. Reduce the heat to low and cook till the mixture thickens, about 15 minutes, whisking from time to time. Add the bourbon, whisk 1 minute longer, and serve the nog in punch cups or heavy Old-Fashioned glasses sprinkled with cinnamon.

MILK PUNCH

Makes 8 drinks

A CLOSE RELATIVE OF EGGNOG, MILK PUNCH (OR MILKY Way) is typically served in the South both at elegant winter brunches and as a festive Christmas drink. (The ritual in my own family has always been to sip milk punches while opening Christmas presents, and no doubt this was my initial—and harmless—introduction to alcoholic beverages as a child.) The drink is also made with rum or brandy, but whichever spirit you choose, shake the punch as quickly as possible to prevent excess dilution. And don't overdo the nutmeg.

8 ounces bourbon

3 cups whole milk

5 teaspoons confectioners' sugar

5 drops pure vanilla extract

Cracked ice

Ground nutmeg to taste

In a tall cocktail shaker, combine all the ingredients except the nutmeg and shake till icy cold and frothy. Pour the punch into Old-Fashioned glasses and sprinkle each drink lightly with nutmeg.

410

Syllabub

Makes 6 to 8 drinks

TRACED BACK TO A THICK, FROTHY CONCOCTION served in Elizabethan England, the term *syllabub* derives from *sille* (a French wine) and *bub* (a bubbling drink) and describes one of the South's most distinctive beverages/desserts (depending on its consistency). I remember watching my Georgian grandmother beat liquidy syllabub with a whisk for one of her afternoon "cake socials," but I also recall eating it with a spoon when my parents visited friends in Louisiana and we kids were served syllabub and cookies. (I've also seen thick syllabub used as a topping for cakes and fresh fruit.) These days, you don't see much syllabub, but when you do, it's usually a spicy drink served with tea cakes or cookies at late-afternoon social get-togethers. I still love it and am convinced that syllabub not only does wonders for a sour stomach but is a sensible way to introduce children to alcoholic beverages.

¼ cup fresh lemon juice, strained

2 cups sweet white wine, Madeira, or sherry

½ cup superfine sugar

2 teaspoons finely grated lemon zest

3 cups half-and-half

Ground nutmeg, for sprinkling

In a large stainless-steel bowl, combine the lemon juice, wine, and sugar and stir till the sugar is completely dissolved. Add the lemon zest and stir till well blended. Add the half-and-half and beat with an electric mixer till the mixture thickens slightly.

Cover the syllabub with plastic wrap, chill for 30 minutes, pour into a glass bowl, and ladle into punch cups.

411

SPICED HOLIDAY SHRUB

Makes about 2 quarts

GROGS, NOGS, JULEPS, SHRUBS, BLUSHES, SOURS,
coolers—nothing betrays the South's rich and diverse
ethnic heritage like the array of intriguing names
applied to many of our alcoholic and nonalcoholic
beverages. A shrub is always made with some form of
berry or berry juice and can be hot or cold, plain or
spiced, sweet or slightly tart. During the winter holidays,
this particular shrub would be served with shortbread or
pound cake at an informal afternoon social.

2 cinnamon sticks, cracked in pieces

5 whole cloves

½ lemon, sliced

1 quart apple cider

1 quart cranberry juice

2 tablespoons light brown sugar

Cinnamon sticks for garnish

Wrap the cracked cinnamon sticks, cloves, and lemon
in cheesecloth and tie securely. In a large enameled
pot, combine the cider, cranberry juice, brown sugar,
and the prepared spice packet, bring to a boil, reduce
the heat to low, and simmer slowly for about 15
minutes. Remove and discard the packet and serve the
shrub in mugs or heavy Old-Fashioned glasses
garnished with a cinnamon stick.

412

SAZERAC

Makes 1 drink

OF ALL THE EXOTIC COCKTAILS ASSOCIATED WITH THE city of New Orleans, none has a more colorful history or enjoys greater popularity than the glorious Sazerac, made with whiskey, bar syrup, bitters, and an anise-flavored liqueur. Originally made with a French brandy called Sazerac-du-Forge, the drink was probably created around 1850 at the Sazerac Coffee House (later called simply the Sazerac House) in the city's French Quarter, but by the end of the century, the recipe had been changed to include not only a dash of local Peychaud's bitters but also American rye whiskey and a little absinthe. When absinthe was banned in 1912 for its putative lethal elements, Louisiana Herbsaint was substituted (only to be replaced later by Pernod), and when the city's famous Roosevelt Hotel (today the Fairmont Hotel) bought the Sazerac House in 1949, rights to the cocktail recipe were included in the deal, resulting in the creation of the hotel's Sazerac Bar (where, as a frequent visiting college student, I drank my fair share of the potent libation). Peychaud's bitters do have a very distinctive flavor and can now be found in both specialty food shops and finer supermarkets. Take note that a proper Sazerac is never served on the rocks, and that each drink should be made separately.

FOR THE BAR SYRUP

1 cup water

2 cups sugar

FOR EACH COCKTAIL

1 ounce Pernod or other anise-flavored liqueur

⅓ ounce bar syrup

1½ ounces rye whiskey or bourbon

4 dashes Peychaud's bitters

2 dashes Angostura bitters

Crushed ice

1 lemon twist

413

To make the bar syrup, combine the water and sugar in a small saucepan and stir well. Bring to a boil, reduce the heat to low, and simmer for 5 minutes. Let the mixture cool and pour into a jar. Store the syrup in the refrigerator till ready to use. (It keeps indefinitely.)

To make 1 cocktail, pour the Pernod into a chilled Old-Fashioned glass, roll the glass around till the sides are well coated with the liqueur, and pour off any excess. In a cocktail shaker, combine the bar syrup, whiskey, both bitters, and plenty of ice, stir quickly till very cold, and strain into the prepared glass. Garnish the drink with the lemon twist.

Ramos Gin Fizz

Makes 4 drinks

SECOND ONLY TO THE SAZERAC AS NEW ORLEANS'S most famous and unusual cocktail, the Ramos gin fizz was created by a bar owner named Henry C. Ramos in the late nineteenth century and eventually became a trademark drink at the city's famous Roosevelt Hotel Bar. Religiously made with gin (never vodka, blessedly), some form of cream, lemon juice, orange flower water, and egg whites, the Ramos gin fizz is a suave, relatively tame drink traditionally sipped in New Orleans before a genteel sit-down lunch—preferably in a shaded garden or on an elegant patio. Personally, I can't imagine drinking a Ramos in a bar. Experts do agree that the cocktail needs a rigorous, lengthy shaking to achieve the perfect texture.

6 ounces gin

2 cups half-and-half

4 large pasteurized egg whites (Davidson's brand, available in many specialty food shops and some supermarkets)

Juice of 2 lemons

4 teaspoons superfine sugar

4 teaspoons orange flower water (available in specialty food shops)

Crushed ice

In a large cocktail shaker, combine all the ingredients plus plenty of crushed ice, shake very well, and strain into highball glasses.

MINT JULEP

Makes 1 drink

THE CLASSIC COCKTAIL OF KENTUCKY, TRADITIONALLY served virtually all over the state on the first Saturday in May at the running of the Kentucky Derby in Louisville, the mint julep actually predates the creation of its now prime ingredient, namely bourbon, which was not distilled until the late eighteenth century—not in Kentucky but in what was then Bourbon County, Virginia. Today, debate still rages in Kentucky over whether a mint julep must be served in a special frosted silver julep cup to maintain its icy integrity (I own six monogrammed such cups.) But the arguments really heat up when it comes to the question of whether the mint leaves should be crushed with sugar in the cups before the bourbon is added. All Southerners do agree that each drink must be made separately, that the ice must be shaved and never in chunks, and that the sides of the cups or glasses should never be touched once they've been frosted. Does the mint julep really live up to its reputation as the world's most refreshing cocktail on a hot summer day? You bet it does.

5 fresh mint leaves, plus 1 sprig fresh mint

2 teaspoons superfine sugar

1 tablespoon cold water

Finely shaved ice

4 ounces bourbon

In a silver julep cup or heavy Old Fashioned glass, place the mint leaves, sugar, and water, crush the leaves well with a pestle or heavy spoon, and stir till the sugar dissolves. Fill the glass with shaved ice, packing it down firmly, then add the bourbon and carefully mix the ice and whiskey together, cutting through the ice instead of stirring it. Wipe the outside of the glass with a clean towel and place in the freezer till it is frosted, about 15 minutes. Carefully remove the glass from the freezer to keep from wiping off the frost, garnish the drink with the mint sprig, and serve at once with a party straw.

415

River Road Planter's Punch

Makes 4 drinks

IT'S MY GUESS THAT MOST OF THE ELABORATE alcoholic punches that played such an important role at lavish social gatherings on the eighteenth-century rice plantations of the Carolina Lowcountry and on sugarcane and cotton plantations along the Mississippi River in Louisiana were imported from West Indian sugar plantations. Whatever their origin, the drink that evolved as planter's punch may not be as popular today in and around Charleston and Georgetown, South Carolina, as it was two hundred years ago, but in New Orleans and along the stretch of old plantations called River Road from the Crescent City to Baton Rouge, you can still encounter every version of this potent libation imaginable. Typically, a cook or hostess will keep a large pitcher of fruit mixture in the refrigerator (as I often do during the summer months), ready to be spiked with rum when drinks are called for. Ideally, a planter's punch should be made with three different styles of rum for optimal flavor (and buzz), but this is not absolutely necessary. What is obligatory (for sweetness and color) is the grenadine.

4 ounces light rum

4 ounces amber rum

4 ounces dark rum

Ice cubes

8 ounces pineapple juice

8 ounces orange juice

6 ounces fresh or bottled lime juice

¼ cup grenadine

Pour 1 ounce of each type of rum into each of four tall, narrow highball glasses and fill each glass with ice cubes. In a large pitcher, combine the three fruit juices, add the grenadine, stir well, fill each glass to the top with the fruit juice mixture, and stir well.

GRADUATION FRUIT PUNCH

Makes about 3 quarts

HIGH SCHOOL AND COLLEGE GRADUATIONS IN THE South still warrant almost as much social attention as weddings and christenings, and no celebration is right without a bowl or big pitcher of fruit punch (alcoholic or nonalcoholic) when the time comes to make toasts. Gin, run, or vodka can be added to give this punch a kick, and if you're entertaining a large crowd, double the portions and serve the punch in a punch bowl with a block of ice or an ice ring made in a Bundt pan.

1½ cups water

1½ cups sugar

¼ cup grated lemon zest

1 quart pineapple juice

2 cups orange juice (not from concentrate)

1 cup fresh lemon juice

One 1-liter bottle club soda, chilled

In a saucepan, combine the water, sugar, and lemon zest, bring to a boil, reduce the heat to moderate, and stir for 5 minutes. Remove from the heat and let cool completely.

Pour the mixture into a large pitcher, add the pineapple juice, orange juice, and lemon juice, stir till well blended, and chill for at least 4 hours.

When ready to serve, stir in the club soda and serve immediately in punch cups.

WEDDING CHAMPAGNE PUNCH

Makes about 3 quarts

A WEDDING PUNCH IN THE SOUTH ALMOST automatically implies plenty of champagne in a large crystal punch bowl. As for the other ingredients, the sky's the limit, including highly colorful ice rings made with fruit juices, crushed fruits, and even colas, as well as citrus rinds, mint leaves, whole berries, and maraschino cherries floating around in the liquid. Some punches can be pretty outrageous. This particular punch is discreetly tame compared with others I've seen, and my only suggestion is that you try to use genuine French champagne.

2 cups orange juice (not from concentrate)

2 cups cranberry juice

1 cup fresh lemon juice

1 cup sugar

Two 750-ml bottles champagne, chilled

In a large pitcher, combine the orange juice, cranberry juice, lemon juice, and sugar and stir till the sugar dissolves. Pour the mixture into a punch bowl, add the champagne, and stir gently till well blended. Add a block of ice or an ice ring made in a Bundt pan and ladle the punch into punch cups.

Chatham Artillery Punch

Makes about 1 gallon

REGIMENTAL PUNCHES HAVE BEEN CONCOCTED IN THE South for ceremonial events ever since The War Between the States, and none is more famous (or infamous) than Savannah's superpotent Chatham Artillery Punch, which locals make a week in advance of any big social shindig. According to the city's resident epicure and a good friend, Damon Lee Fowler, the original punch base was devised just before the Civil War to honor a military group called the Republican Blues and was probably mixed in horse-watering buckets and left to steep in large tubs several days before ice and prodigious quantities of champagne were added. Today, serving methods are a bit more civilized, and all I can say is that the one time I made this punch for a small pork barbecue event held on my outdoor deck, there wasn't a drop left in the punch bowl—or a sober soul in sight.

2 ounces green tea leaves

6 cups water

1 quart dry white wine

1½ cups bourbon

1½ cups dark rum

1½ cups gin

1½ cups brandy

1 cup orange juice

1 cup fresh lemon juice

½ cup firmly packed light brown sugar

1 quart champagne

Eight days before you plan to serve the punch, combine the tea leaves and water in a stainless-steel or enameled pot, cover with plastic wrap, and let steep overnight.

Strain the tea through a fine wire-mesh strainer into a large bowl and add all remaining ingredients except the champagne. Stir till the sugar dissolves, cover with plastic wrap, and let stand at room temperature for at least 1 week.

When ready to serve, pour the punch over a block of ice in a large punch bowl, add the champagne, stir briefly, and serve in punch cups.

St. Cecilia's Punch

Makes about 1½ gallons

REFLECTIVE OF THE ENGLISH (TEA), FRENCH (champagne and cognac), and West Indian (rum) influences on Carolina Lowcountry culture, St. Cecilia's Punch was introduced at the St. Cecilia Musical Society in Charleston in the early eighteenth century and is still as popular today at elaborate weddings and social occasions as it was three hundred years ago. Certain locals insist that the punch be made with only green tea leaves, dark Myer's rum, and genuine French champagne, and that nothing will do but to serve it over a huge block of ice in a silver punch bowl. All I can say is that the delicious punch deals such a wallop that, after a few cups, nobody really cares about the variety of tea leaves, the brand of rum or champagne, or the pedigree of the serving vessel. Since using simple ice cubes will only dilute the punch's flavor and strength, however, I do try to find room in the freezer to freeze blocks of ice in large plastic tubs. Of course, if you own a deep freeze, so much the better.

4 lemons, thinly sliced and seeded

1 pint brandy

2 cups water

2 cups sugar

¼ cup green tea leaves

½ fresh pineapple, peeled, cored, and thinly sliced

1 pint dark rum

Three 750-ml bottles dry champagne

Two 1-liter bottles club soda

Place the lemon slices in a large glass bowl, pour the brandy over them, cover with plastic wrap, and let marinate overnight.

In a large saucepan, combine the water and sugar and bring to a boil over moderate heat, stirring. Place the tea leaves in a large bowl, pour the sugar water over them, and let cool. Add the pineapple to the lemon-and-brandy mixture and strain the cooled tea into the mixture.

Pour the fruit-and-brandy mixture into a large silver or glass punch bowl, add the rum, and mix well. When ready to serve, place a large block of ice in the mixture, add the champagne and club soda, stir to blend well, and ladle the punch into silver or glass punch cups.

ACKNOWLEDGMENTS

THIS COOKBOOK COULD NOT HAVE SEEN THE light of day without the generous help, encouragement, and friendship of numerous fellow Southerners who, over the years, have shared my passion for our beloved style of cookery. Many are mentioned throughout the book, but to those nameless waiters and waitresses in restaurants, diners, coffee shops, and sundry shacks and joints who've patiently explained dishes to me and jotted down recipes; to fishermen, country ham producers, barbecue pit masters, and pecan farmers who've allowed me to intrude in their special lives; and to countless gracious hosts and hostesses who've invited me into their homes to sample their proud fare, I offer a blanket but heart-felt "Thank you."

Particularly helpful to me—and always there in moments of panic—have been two of the most respected (and obsessed) experts on Southern cooking, Jean Anderson and Damon Lee Fowler. John Edge, John Egerton, and the other good folks keenly involved in the Southern Foodways Alliance in Oxford, Mississippi have served as major inspirations, and how can I not thank such eponymous Southern cooks as Louis Osteen, Paul Prudhomme, "Hoppin" John Taylor, Frank Stitt, Ben and Karen Barker, Emeril Lagasse, and the late Craig Claiborne, Bill Neal, and Edna Lewis for introducing me to unfamiliar regional traditions, dishes, and cooking techniques?

Julia Reed set me straight once and for all on the one and only way to prepare shrimp remoulade, frozen tomato, and other such delicate matters; Ella Brennan finally unveiled for me the truth about the origin of bananas Foster; Gail Killian Kennedy showed me how to produce the ideal "sad streak" in pound cake; and to prove that perfect grits require both superhuman patience and stamina, my friend Adam Lewis forced me to sit on a stool at his stove for one hour stirring the pot.

Once again and forever, I peck the bourbon-flushed cheek of my irrepressible mother, Martha Pearl Villas, who originally taught me how to work with sticky biscuit dough, gut and scale freshly-caught fish, reject okra and peaches without fuzz, and skim every trace of foam off the top of hot strawberry preserves. When I tamper with certain sacred dishes, she still says I've lived up north too long and don't know much about real Southern cooking.

My former editor at John Wiley & Sons, Susan Wyler, was the one who insisted that I take on this book, but it has been Justin Schwartz who, with insatiable curiosity and great professional style, has shepherded the project from beginning to end, made invaluable suggestions and beneficial changes, and even gradually grasped the monumental importance of "streak-o'-lean" in Southern cooking. No matter that both of them happen to be Yankees.

INDEX

423

424

427

430

431